For my father.

Acknowledgments

While I have been working with HyperCard since Bill Atkinson and John Sculley first previewed WildCard for me in March of 1986, I still fondly recall those who helped me bring the first edition of the *Handbook* to the world in 1987. In a chronology that is still vivid in my mind, I haven't forgotten the valuable assistance on the Apple side of things from Jane Anderson, Chris Espinosa, Dan Winkler, Olivier Bouley, and Ted Kaehler. On the publishing side, Kenzi Sugihara and Jono Hardjowirogo gave me the leeway to work on a book about some new software that no one could tell anybody about.

Interim editions, particularly the major overhaul for version 2.0, had the benefit of help from many members of the HyperCard team at both Apple and Claris. They included Mike Holm, David Leffler, Robertson Reed Smith, Robin Shank, and Stacey Chaney.

And just when I thought the HyperCard team would be tired of hearing from me, their cooperation for this fourth edition was the most helpful of any project I've worked on. In alphabetical order, Kevin Calhoun, Tom Hammer, Param Singh, and Clark Warner made themselves available and responded to questions faster than if they had been my own staff. I've never felt closer to a product team that wasn't in Bill Atkinson's basement.

Also for this edition, I thank Kenzi Sugihara, Steve Guty, and Mike Roney at Random House for their continued support, and to Carol Barth, Greg Reynolds, and the crew of Modern Design, whose superhuman effort kept to an impossibly tight production schedule.

Without a doubt, this edition would not have been possible without the support of the hundreds of thousands of readers of earlier editions around the world. I have read the many letters and e-mail messages with care, always looking for ways to make this book better for you. You are the inspiration for this edition.

CONTENTS

Volume I

PART III HyperCard's Programming Environment 371

Read Me First

HyperCard was first unveiled to the world on August 11, 1987. The product was the result of Bill Atkinson's genius, plus help from many talented programmers, artists, and writers. At first, HyperCard was very difficult to define. Part of the problem, I believe, was that some influential folks at Apple were afraid to associate anything that came bundled in the Macintosh box—as HyperCard did at the time—with a seeemingly frightful word: programming. Programming has long been considered the realm of supertechnical people whose caricature portraits emphasize pocket protectors and propellered beanie hats.

Yet that was just the point about packaging HyperCard with every Mac: It was a self-contained programming environment for non-propellerheads. HyperCard was meant to lower the barrier between your idea of what the Macintosh should do (over and above off-the-shelf applications, such as desktop publishing and spreadsheets) and having the computer really do it. That was a noble ambition, but one from which literally hundreds of thousands of Macintosh users have benefited.

As HyperCard progressed through various upgrades and improvements, the climate and business at Apple changed, as is likely in any dynamic company in a fast-moving industry. For a time, HyperCard was shifted to Apple's Claris division. When this decision was made, a few other system software-related products were also supposed to go to Claris, so HyperCard's transfer made sense within that context. Unfortunately, HyperCard was the only product to make the trip.

During its life at Claris, HyperCard underwent a number of significant changes at Apple. For one, the complete product was removed from the Macintosh box. For awhile, a version with only a couple of stacks and a thin manual was packaged with Macs. Later, only a HyperCard Player was included. Those of us who watched HyperCard's impact on the Macintosh community were dismayed at these decisions, because we believed that HyperCard provided a competitive advantage for the Macintosh that no Intel-based computer could. Still, the focus on the bottom line said that only enough to play HyperCard stacks would be included with Macs (outside the United States, each Apple division made its own policy decisions about bundling or unbundling HyperCard and the Player).

For a long time after Claris' release of version 2.1 as the HyperCard Development Kit, the HyperCard team was hard at work on feature enhancements to the product. To those of us on the outside, the delays in producing new versions and what seemed to be a lack of concern about HyperCard's future on the part of Claris' management were cause for significant alarm.

The good news, however, is that in late 1993, Apple resumed responsibility for HyperCard, and put the core team to work on a new release: the version 2.2 covered in this book. Many of the improvements to the product are based on the fact that a wide range of Macintosh users—neophytes to professional programmers—use HyperCard as a development tool. It is still far easier than the other environments out there. And the dreamers among the HyperCard faithful dream of a programmable version of HyperCard one day returning to inside the Macintosh box.

Enjoy your tour through HyperCard 2.2.

Preface to the Fourth Edition

This volume incorporates changes from new features of two HyperCard releases since the last edition. Versions 2.1 and 2.2 each brought their own brand of added power to HyperCard users. Because so many readers have purchased new editions as HyperCard improves, I believe it is important to retain the same organization and presentation styles for the HyperTalk parts of the book that have apparently worked well for these many years. I have also retained the major improvements from the last edition, which included much more information about each command, such as the most common problems and what other HyperTalk items are related.

Part IV, dedicated to authoring techniques, has been expanded with new chapters covering Apple events, AppleScript, color, creating standalone HyperCard applications, plus some insights to advanced report printing. All other discussions have been painstakingly updated to reflect the state of the art in multimedia presentations, third-party tools, and the latest Macintosh hardware. Many of the applications in Part V have been updated to take advantage of the latest user interface and HyperTalk programming abilities of version 2.2. A new application demonstrates linking HyperCard to FileMaker Pro with AppleScript.

2.1

2.2

As special pointers for readers of previous editions, I have included symbols in the margins wherever the discussion turns to a new or improved feature for both HyperCard 2.1 and 2.2. In case you haven't had a chance to work with 2.1, these should help you more quickly locate what's new and different with each version since 2.0.

INTRODUCTION

COPING WITH THE INFORMATION REVOLUTION

Long before my hands touched a computer keyboard or my eyes peered into a computer monitor, I saw television advertising for worldwide computer companies that talked about "moving information." The screen showed colorful, mystical interconnections linking New York with New Delhi, via dozens of stops in Europe, Asia, and everywhere. When I watched these commercials, I had great difficulty visualizing "information" and why anyone would want to "move" it.

The problem was my failure to understand how all-encompassing the term "information" can be, and how many forms information can assume. Nor, I think, was I the only one unsure about what "information" truly means.

Our inability to grasp the concept is largely the result of information's intangible nature. It can be printed, spoken, drawn, and projected but these forms are mere representations of information. The marks on a page or screen, the sounds of speech and music—none of this is information unless it conveys meaning to someone. Yet human history demonstrates a long-standing need for information and the skills to manipulate it.

The Historical Chain of Information

The earliest surviving evidence of information recording (other than the artistic expressions of cave painting) comes from the ancient Sumerian civilization in the Middle East, dating back to 3000 B.C. Clay tablets bearing pictographic impressions of a wedge-shaped stylus record the movement of commodities through the marketplace. Unlike the oral tradition, which was responsible for great epic poetry like the stories of Gilgamesh and Odysseus, writing provided a medium for accurate and lasting information. Even 5000 years ago, civilization and its commerce placed information burdens on its participants greater than their ability to manage solely by memory and word of mouth.

Eventually, pictographic Indo-European languages evolved into phonetic languages, in which combinations of alphabet letters spelled out sounds. Written information spread to include not only business transactions but also literature and personal correspondence. We have much archaeological evidence from the ancient Egyptian, Greek, Roman, and Oriental cultures to demonstrate the growing diversity of information through the millennia.

Information's Early Speed Limits

The movement of information from person to person, however, remained at the mercy of the transportation systems available. For centuries after Gutenberg's printing press, goods and information traveled no faster than animal- and natural-powered transport. The speed at which information flowed, even well into the nineteenth century, is considered intolerably slow today. American farmers in rural sections of Atlantic seaboard states had no direct way of knowing what the prevailing market prices were for their goods, especially if those products were purchased by overseas buyers and their agents in the port cities. Information that made the journey back to the farm was hopelessly out of date.

To offset this information bottleneck, levels of sales agents, brokers, jobbers, wholesalers, and credit systems intervened. Control over information was essentially handed to others who worked closer to where the information changed hands. Cumbersome though it was, this form of distributed information handling worked adequately in its time, especially since goods themselves moved slowly, drawn overland by horse or across oceans by wind-powered sailing ships.

The Early Information Age

In the 1830s, applications of two powerful technologies—steam power (for transportation and manufacturing energy) and the telegraph—signaled radical changes in information quantity and distribution. According to contemporary reports of comparative travel times between major cities, steam-powered locomotives increased the throughput of goods three to ten times during the first quarter-century of steam railroads. For example, the trip from New York to Chicago shrank from a horse-drawn three weeks to a railroaded two days.

Railroad companies adopted the telegraph as a means of controlling their spreading empires (indeed, most telegraph lines ran along railroad rights-of-way). But telegraphy quickly became a major information pipeline for commercial, as well as personal, data, as goods and people moved through the steam-powered rail and water transportation systems at great speeds and with predictability.

With the spread of these transportation and communications systems—infrastructures, they're called—came an increased need for controlling the systems themselves. Timetables, fee schedules, collecting of ticket fees from passengers, monitoring the location of rolling stock, and similar controls became more important as the infrastructures became larger than one person could manage. The word *control* implies that information proceeded outward, from a "central office" to the extremities of the infrastructure. In truth, however, control requires a two-way movement of information: control going out and *feedback* returning home as a means of measuring the effectiveness of the outgoing control. This was the beginning of a class of workers whose sole job was gathering and manipulating information, rather than processing energy or materials.

As the decades passed into the twentieth century, the spiraling codevelopment of technologies (energy utilization and communication, in particular) increased the speed at which goods, services, and people moved throughout the world. With each increment of the transportation speedometer came an increased need for control.

The controlling mechanisms themselves required additional information gathering and processing for adequate feedback. For example, consumer advertising was an established method of controlling the buying patterns of consumers even in the late nineteenth century. By 1910, advertising agencies widely employed information workers whose jobs were to compile statistics on the effects of advertising—feedback on the control, if you will. Later, as advertisers discovered radio, they sought information about their audiences with the help of feedback innovations such as Archibald Crossley's telephone surveys of radio audiences (1929) and A. C. Nielsen's audimeter, which recorded a radio listener's station preferences throughout the day (1935). (A detailed history of these spiraling developments is chronicled in *The Control Revolution* by James R. Beniger, published by the Harvard University Press in 1986.)

Information Today

The process of harnessing energy and devising ways of controlling it continues today, except that the energy most often singled out is that of the microprocessor, rather than steam or electricity. This difference is not insignificant, because in harnessing earlier powers, the effects were first applied to goods, services, and people; the informational backdrop developed slightly later. But with the application of the microprocessor and related integrated circuit chips, the power under harness immediately affects the informational part of our lives. A chip doesn't move goods or people from one town to another; it manipulates information. The result is a speedup in the quantity of information passing before our eyes and around us. With today's discussions about a data superhighway crisscrossing the globe, the ability to exchange information will extend to virtually any spot on the globe, whether there is a wire or not.

From Batch Processing to Real Time

Not many years ago, it was commonplace for a small business equipped with a centralized computer system to print reports in "batches." Every Tuesday at 3 P.M., the Computer Department would distribute printouts of the previous week's sales activity and finished goods inventory. That, of course, was a vast improvement over the gathering of quarterly inventory counts and seat-of-the-pants tallying of sales. But today a weekly printout is often insufficient. We virtually demand instantaneous access to the information. Instead of batch processing, the computer is now responsible for tracking numerous parts of the business in "real time," with video terminals on the desks where tons of printouts had once dropped regularly.

Personal computers contribute to the increasing need for up-to-the-second information. If you are active in the stock market, for example, you can retrieve real-time stock exchange data with the computer and a modem, then perform calculations on that data with the help of a spreadsheet or other analysis program. Similarly, you can maintain a database of information that is particularly useful to you, even if the corporate computer department doesn't have time to think about your application.

Personal computer software, in general, encourages the creation of "new" information, even if "new" means a different way of viewing existing data. For instance, you may have always had to prepare a quarterly budget forecast for your division or department. Without a computer, the budget was probably prepared on a columnar pad (with many erasure marks) and then transferred to a typewritten spreadsheet. With a personal computer and spreadsheet software, you have the chance to analyze the budget from different perspectives in less time than it took to create a draft of the manual budget. You might even chart the results as bars or pie wedges for the forecast meeting—perhaps to get a competitive leg up over your colleagues in nearby office cubicles.

Information Overload

The rapid increase in information throughput is not without its problems. All it takes is a casual look through virtually any business computer magazine to see that a primary concern today is passing personal computer information from machine to machine. Even within the confines of a particular computer brand and model, it is often difficult (if not impossible, at times) to pass information between two software programs. For example, if the maker of a particular Macintosh word processing program doesn't make a concerted effort to allow transfer of files between its program and others already on the market, you, as a purchaser of that product, won't be able to share your nicely formatted word processing files with colleagues, except in printed form. Worse yet, if you have information files stored on floppy disks and attempt to read or modify those files on someone else's Macintosh, that other machine must have the identical software you used to create the files in the first place.

The Macintosh, with its propensity to mix text and graphics into the same document, actually complicates matters of file compatibility among programs and between Macintoshes and other computer makes. While users of Macintosh technology benefit from this convergence of text and graphics modes, the complexity of storing, sharing, and distributing such information for everyone to use demonstrates the absence of what I call an information infrastructure.

Just as transportation spread across the United States first with an infrastructure of rail lines, then with highways, and most recently with flight paths linking airports, so will computer information become prevalent around the world when an information infrastructure is established. It will entail many computer companies reaching agreements on storage standards, file formats, graphics layouts, and several other technical aspects of personal computing. While this issue may not seem important to the lone personal computer user, it is critical for most large organizations. Finding a solution is a top priority for most computer hardware companies today.

We have seen progress in this arena. The "cross platform" buzz phrase has prompted many software companies to produce the same or compatible programs on multiple hardware and operating systems. Many different kinds of personal computers can connect to the same local area network to exchange files and electronic mail. Driven by practical needs of customers, the computer industry is driving toward an information infrastructure, with much work still to be done.

Information Threads and Links

If you've performed any kind of research, like preparing a term paper, you may have recognized that hardly any fact exists in a vacuum. For example,

Julius Caesar was assassinated on March 15th in 44 B.C., yet it's difficult to consider that bit of information entirely on its own. You probably have other questions relating to the incident that require additional information: Who were the assassins; what was their motivation; on what literature is the actual date based; what was the political and social climate of the time; what happened after the assassination?

The trouble is, if you find an information source for the event, that source likely won't have all of the additional information you require. You need to branch away from a strictly date-based collection of facts to other collections, such as information bases centered around literature of the time or historical observations made many centuries later. What this points to is that information very often consists of threads emanating in many directions from a single fact. At the end of each thread is a fact that itself, has additional threads running in yet other directions, and so on.

(The idea of linking the world's information threads for desktop video terminal retrieval was popularized in the mid-1960s by Ted Nelson. The term he coined for this concept, *hypertext*, is still popular today, and is at the core of several research and commercial projects. A common mistake is to view HyperCard as strictly a hypertext environment. While you can perform hypertext-like links in HyperCard, this is only one of many HyperCard features. The HyperCard name was attached to the product very late in development, after Apple's legal department discovered the desired name, WildCard, was not clear in a trademark search.)

You may have found yourself making such threaded connections in a research project. Visualize a large bulletin board filled with index cards. Each card contains a fact or quotation extracted from a research source. No matter how you label the cards by subject, a card may relate to more than the card positioned next to it. To help you visualize the relationships from a distance, you link two distant cards by a strand of colored string, thumbtacked to the board. After a while, you may have many different colors crisscrossing the board.

Everyday Links

Even in our personal lives, we are surrounded by interrelated facts. For example, if you buy a major appliance, the transaction has many implications on your personal information management. You have to make sure you have the money to pay for the item or have an amount set aside from a monthly budget to make payments. You have to adapt your schedule to accommodate delivery, making sure someone will be home to meet the truck. The value of the new appliance may affect your insurance coverage. Record of the sale must also be maintained for possible tax deductions when you next file your income tax. And on it goes.

If all this is for a relatively simple transaction, consider all the information generated and managed by each individual in a lifetime. This phenomenon is best summed up in an excerpt from Alexander Solzhenitsyn's *Cancer Ward*:

> As every man goes through life, he fills in a number of forms for the records, each containing a number of questions. . . . There are thus hundreds of little threads radiating from every man, millions of threads in all. If these threads were suddenly to become visible, the whole sky would look like a spider's web. . . .

Research Links

As those webs grow, whether they contain threads of personal or business information, it becomes increasingly difficult to locate a particular item. For example, if you are researching a topic, you might start the search in the *Reader's Guide to Periodical Literature*, an index to articles that have appeared in 200 popular consumer magazines. But if the subject might also be covered in technical journals, you will have to check reference works similar to the *Reader's Guide* that cover the subject. If you're not familiar with those reference works, you must take an additional step away from the material you seek and look into something like The *New York Times Guide to Reference Materials*. In other words, even the number of information cross-references is so large that we need a "guide to the guides."

Each information level we are forced to transcend in search of a fact lessens the desire to perform the search in an inverse square proportion. If a related fact is two levels away, we're one-fourth as likely to make the effort to track it down; for three levels, it's one-ninth as likely.

It's one thing to be thwarted in a search for "external" information, such as that found in libraries and electronic information services, because of intervening information levels. It's quite another to experience that same difficulty with the information you work with daily on the computer.

Program Information

Any applications program you use that saves files on the disk is an information handler. A word processing program, for example, is often the tool for turning ideas into something a bit more tangible for printing or communicating over the telephone. A spreadsheet program, on the other hand, might be more often used as a transitional information tool, transforming existing figures into presentation graphics or extrapolated forecasts. Even a graphics program, like MacPaint or MacDraw, is an information handler. Any picture you save on the disk (whether created with the program or captured by way of a video digitizer) is information.

Owing to the way we've been brought up on computers and their programs, we too often consider each document as a stand-alone hunk of data. And unless we're working in an integrated applications environment, we probably look at a particular kind of document as having no implications beyond the current program.

It's important to recognize, however, that very few saved documents exist in their private vacuums. More often, a document is only one piece of information within a larger context. A business letter, for instance, may be one point along a communications continuum comprising a much larger project. Part of the letter, such as the addressee's name, address, and greeting, may be merged from a database; another part may contain an excerpt from a job-costing spreadsheet. Even among your own documents, then, invisible colored yarns stretch from file to file.

As more mainstream applications take advantage of Interapplication Communication (IAC) of Macintosh System 7 and beyond, these "strings" will become more concrete. An address may remain in the database, while the business letter has a hole in it that "knows" to retrieve that database information whenever the letter is displayed or printed.

The Database Software Heritage

One type of information management software you may already know about is a category called database management software (DBMS). For decades, DBMS has been the cornerstone of information management on large computers. It has also been adapted for use with today's personal computers. Within the personal computer category, there are two broad types of database management: file management and relational database management.

File Managers

File management software is the simplest kind of database software. The file part of its name does not refer to the kinds of files your applications generate. Rather, the file is like a finite collection of information, usually replicating a drawerful of filled-out forms. For example, one database file may consist of a collection of names, addresses, and telephone numbers for your business contacts. Before you can use the database, you essentially create an on-screen form to be filled out each time you add a new contact to the file. The form probably has blanks for the person's name, title, company, street address, city, state, ZIP code, and phone number, and perhaps a blank for additional notes.

Once you have designed the empty form, you can begin entering information. As with its paper counterpart, you fill in the blanks on a given form with information for one contact. You wouldn't type in Sarah's phone number on Tom's form, of course. In other words, all the information you deem important about that contact will be viewable on a single form.

It is the additional duty of the file management software to offer you ways of sorting the forms so that you can "thumb through" forms in any order you see fit. Therefore, while you might keep a paper version of this file in alphabetical order by the contact's last name, the file management software allows you to sort the forms by ZIP code. The information on the forms hasn't changed, just the order in which the forms are stored.

An important function of file management software is the search. If you wish to look at only those contacts located in Chicago, you can instruct the software to display only those forms whose "city" blank is filled in with the word "Chicago."

From there, you should be able to have the file management program print out a report that lists information on the forms of all contacts you selected with the search criteria. Good file management software will give you multiple search criteria, with which you could select all contacts whose "city" blank says Chicago, and whose "notes" blank contains the word "prospect." You can then use the printed report as a way of following up on leads.

Relational Databases

A much more sophisticated type of database management is called "relational," because it extends links between individual files. For instance, if your name and address database also has a blank for a consecutive serial number for each form you filled out, a relational database will let you use that number to link the name and address database to a different database.

Let's say you wish to keep a record of orders placed by companies whose names are stored in the name and address database. When designing the order form, you would set up a blank into which you will eventually type the serial number of the customer. You would then establish links between name and address blanks in the order form and the database that actually holds that information. As soon as you type a serial number into an order form, the relational database program looks up the name and address information from the name and address database, and displays the relevant data in the blanks. In other words, you establish threads between forms.

Relational database programs also have the same kind of sorting, searching, and reporting features that file managers do. But with the ability to retrieve information from multiple databases, the job of filling in potentially redundant blanks is greatly simplified.

Both types of database management programs are valuable applications for their intended jobs. By and large, current database management programs for the Macintosh are text-oriented, despite their abilities to incorporate graphics elements in places. Moreover, until more programs take advantage of System 7's Apple event mechanism and Open Scripting Architecture (with which programs can interact with each other), database programs generally work by themselves: There is little interactivity between a database and the rest of your Macintosh work.

HyperCard and the Databases

The above introduction to database management software is a helpful prerequisite to talking about HyperCard because the HyperCard and databases may appear to do the same kinds of things. In some respects that's true, but HyperCard is not intended to replace database management software as we know it today. In fact, there will likely be many cases in which a Macintosh owner will use a database management program and HyperCard together. We'll see exactly how that works much later in the book.

Let's look at HyperCard in comparison with database management software.

You can use HyperCard to perform a number of operations found in file management software. For example, you use HyperCard to design information input forms on the screen, insert information into the forms, sort the filled-out forms, and search for a particular form. But in this context, you should notice some significant differences. First, you have total control over the appearance of your forms with HyperCard. In fact, you are encouraged to design on-screen forms that resemble noncomputerized objects as much as possible. And by "form," we mean a much wider range than something you fill out like an application form. A HyperCard "form" can be virtually anything that you can recreate on the Macintosh screen: a Rolodex-type file card, a weekly appointment book, a product specification sheet, and so on. In other words, you can use HyperCard to recreate computerized versions of real-life objects. If that sounds boring to you, then also be aware that you can create environments that are impossible in the physical world of paper and ink. Imagine a form that plays digitized sound, displays a color video clip, or retrieves up-to-the-minute information from another computer.

HyperCard also has what a database management devotee would call "relational capabilities." That's because information stored in one stack of HyperCard forms can be retrieved by forms in other stacks (although this is not an inherently speedy function of HyperCard). HyperCard takes quite a large additional step, however. Unlike a relational database, HyperCard actually lets you zip over to other stacks to view the full context of related information. Thus, while a relational database generally restricts its relational capabilities to simply retrieving information from elsewhere, HyperCard lets you hop around as your information needs require. You can also use HyperCard to establish generic links between forms to speed the search for related information. For example, if a generic link exists between a monthly calendar and a daily appointment book, you can click on a day in the calendar to have HyperCard pick out and display the card in the appointment book file for that day.

Nor are the links you establish finite or rigid. You can adjust the links as you please or create new ones as additional files of related information are added to your collection. The threads, in other words, can keep growing and weaving, like an ever-expanding spider web.

A major distinction between HyperCard and DBMS software is in the way retrieved information is displayed and printed. A raison d'etre for DBMS programs is the ability to generate reports. A report usually consists of columnar data that lists some or all elements of a form. The reporting software then usually performs various math functions, such as providing a total count of items in the report or creating subtotals and totals of numeric information in the report. Such reports can appear on the screen or be sent to the printer.

HyperCard, on the other hand, is not designed for generating reports of that nature (although it is capable of simpler report printing, and third-party add-on products offer full report printing). Instead, it is optimized for quickly looking through existing cards—browsing—in search of desired information. Therefore, while a DBMS program might produce a screen report listing based on desired selection criteria (presuming you have already set up the report format), HyperCard very quickly finds cards matching your criteria. While HyperCard's report printing abilities have improved in recent versions, true databases are much more powerful in this department, as they should be.

Programming for Poets

A major barrier between potential computer users and the machines has been the lack of software tailored to narrow applications. Most commercial software tries to appeal to as broad a user spectrum as possible. Specialists —users who could truly benefit from a computer like the Macintosh— simply haven't had the tools to use a machine profitably.

In the past, educators and business people dedicated to putting computers to work for them studied to become nearly professional programmers. They wrote the custom software that no publisher or commercial developer would bother with. That was difficult, but not impossible, on simple computers like the Apple II and the early IBM PC. But today, as computers like the Macintosh become easier to use, they become extremely difficult to program. It can take an experienced programmer a year or more to begin writing quality programs based on visual desktop environments such as the Macintosh.

HyperCard significantly narrows the gap between the nonprogramming specialist and the sophisticated program he or she needs. As you'll learn in later stages of this book, HyperCard handles the hard parts of programming for the Macintosh. You'll spend more time on applying your ideas than on technical issues. Or, as HyperCard's creator, Bill Atkinson, says, "It's programming for 'the rest of us.'"

What to Do with HyperCard

If you are still unclear about what HyperCard might mean to your computing experience, it will be beneficial to learn what others have done with HyperCard. Much of the best work came from the hands of Macintosh owners who had little or no prior programming experience. It was HyperCard that opened the doors to their imaginations.

Because a majority of HyperCard applications are special-purpose (or *vertical market*) programs, only a small percentage of the tens of thousands of HyperCard stacks have broad enough appeal for retail distribution. While such products garner the attention of reviewers and the computer press, their paucity belies a heavy HyperCard following by consultants, in-house corporate developers, and academia.

During the 1988 presidential campaign, ABC Television News created a HyperCard application that assisted news anchor Peter Jennings in retrieving facts about the candidates. In previous campaigns, the data had been meticulously written on file cards and kept in boxes near the anchor desk. With the HyperCard version, however, the on-camera announcers could view instant data about a candidate's views on specific issues, outcomes of primaries, and personal data. A touch screen replaced the mouse, as pressing on-screen buttons linked related cards to each other in that web of data.

ABC News has gone even further. With a huge archive of video material gathered over the years, a new division, ABC News Interactive, is placing material on specific subjects onto laser videodiscs. With a HyperCard stack on the Mac, a serial cable between the Mac and disc player, and the videodisc, an educator or student has a personal learning laboratory on the desk covering such important topics as the Arab-Israeli conflict and Dr. Martin Luther King. The HyperCard stack (displayed on the Macintosh screen) is the guide to the video material (displayed on a separate video monitor). The stack also lets students create their own personal documentaries from the videodisc material.

Personal information management is another popular use for HyperCard. Many users modify the address book and appointment stacks that come with HyperCard—user modifiability is a distinct advantage to most HyperCard applications. Personal information includes many other kinds of data, such as hobby collection databases and other tools for which commercial software does not exist. World-renowned author Douglas Adams, in researching a book and television program on disappearing species, used HyperCard on a portable Mac to design a stack that calculated the total volume of the predominantly undergound nest of a rare ground-nesting bird.

Using HyperCard's ability to replay prerecorded sound, HyperGlot Software has created foreign language training stacks. Unlike using sequential audio tapes or records, the HyperCard language trainers let students click on buttons at their own pace to hear words and phrases spoken by native speakers. And in the case of non-Roman languages, the graphical Macintosh can even train students in Chinese symbols, for example, as one program (designed by a New Hampshire businessman) does.

Linking HyperCard text and graphics to digital sound and video is all part of what is known as multimedia—multiple media working together. While such concepts have obvious application in education—ranging from talking flashcards for preschoolers to college-level film editing—multimedia is also finding its way into business-oriented HyperCard applications.

HyperCard makes an ideal base on which to build computerized presentations for group display via a projection device. It is very easy to create "slides" with text and graphics to liven up a dog and pony show. Numerous animation techniques (described in Chapter 54) can make your presentation more meaningful and memorable. Add some digitized audio or a video clip right on the computer screen, and the presentation can literally speak for itself.

That's not to say that HyperCard stacks must be all razzle dazzle. Huge volumes of information—reference works, product catalogs, procedure manuals, or frequently updated printed material—can be published as a HyperCard file. Whether distributed via one or more floppy disks, on a CD-ROM (with a capacity of 550 megabytes), or as a read-only file on a network server, this type of HyperCard application has wide appeal.

Increasingly, HyperCard is also becoming the software "glue" between Macintoshes and mainframe computers. Easy-to-use HyperCard-based applications can provide friendly access to otherwise complex databases, electronic mail systems, and group software running on IBM, DEC, Tandem and other mainframes. Such *front ends* are not the easiest of applications to write, but connectivity tools for HyperCard authors are making the job simpler all the time. In any event, the HyperCard version can be up and running much faster than similar applications developed in other programming environments. The same goes for gluing together data and functions from disparate in multiple Macintosh programs. HyperCard's access to system-level scripting languages, such as AppleScript, lets you design control panels for an unlimited number of processes and productivity tasks.

The key to HyperCard's success has been that it empowers people with expertise who might otherwise not have been able to express themselves on the Macintosh. Whether that expertise be in mainframe electronic mail, a department's personnel policies, the Cyrillic alphabet, or a compact disc library organization, HyperCard lets you put that expertise on the Mac—to offer tools to others in your same field, to share information, and to be more productive every day.

How to Learn HyperCard

The HyperCard package may seem intimidating at first—so many manuals and disks. But as you'll see, the HyperCard structure lends itself to learning in stages.

If you've started HyperCard and have clicked on an icon or two, you have participated in only one of its three stages of complexity, the *Browsing/Typing* level. Its second stage, which is hardly obvious (and purposely so), is its *Painting/Authoring* level, which is followed closely by its third stage, the *Programming* level. Let's use an automotive analogy to distinguish the three levels.

For the majority of us, an automobile is a convenient, if not necessary, method of transportation. We buy an auto because we have a desire to get from point A to point B. Through driver training classes, we've learned how to start, stop, and maneuver the vehicle in traffic. When the fuel needle nears E, we head for a gas station to refill the tank. And when things don't sound right or, as with tires, appear to be worn, most of us take the car into a service shop for the appropriate repairs. Our main concern, in other words, is using the vehicle as a reliable means of transportation. Our choice of model is usually dependent upon budgetary and aesthetic considerations.

But many of us also see more to an automobile than just its utility or its aesthetic appeal. Curiosity about what lies under the hood leads many of us to take a peek. After overcoming trepidations about opening the hood, we might check a fluid level or tug on a belt to make sure everything is secure. We may then progress to doing minor maintenance jobs like adding a quart of oil. Suddenly we're concerned with grades of oil, trying to determine which is best for the type of engine and climate. Even at this relatively simple level of auto maintenance, we're getting our hands dirty while influencing the performance and longevity of the vehicle.

At the far end of the scale are dedicated weekend mechanics—"hackers" of the grease pits, if you will. They are likely to spend more energy on improving a vehicle's performance or rebuilding carburetors than thinking about its utilitarian function. They see an automobile in terms of what makes it run rather than where it's going.

Using HyperCard's Browsing/Typing level is analogous to driving the auto as a driver only. You use HyperCard to find or enter information. You need not know anything else about the program. In fact, you may see HyperCard set up in browsing and typing applications that virtually disguise the fact that they are running inside HyperCard. The applications are there to help you get from point A (needing information) to point B (having information).

In contrast, HyperCard's Painting/Authoring level gives you the power to peek and tinker "under the hood" to design simple, though useful, applications. HyperCard comes with a remarkably powerful set of design tools, which you can use to modify existing applications or develop your own.

Lastly, the Programming level allows you to modify the performance and operation of HyperCard applications, or design entirely new applications from scratch. This level is built around an English-like language called HyperTalk. While it's true that you can be a HyperCard author without programming in HyperTalk, I believe that anyone with a desire to write an application won't be satisfied, ultimately, unless he or she investigates HyperTalk's possibilities.

Use Part I of this book first to learn how to drive HyperCard. Then in Part II take a peek under the hood to perform simple maintenance and repairs. Graduate to Part III, in which you'll don overalls and learn how to dismantle, rebuild, and create HyperCard applications with HyperTalk. In Part IV you'll learn techniques that make your vehicles run with high performance—tips that help add pizazz to your information. Finally, in Part V you start working on real vehicles, applying your newly found knowledge to real information-handling problems. You'll then know HyperCard well enough to mold it into the master of *your* Macintosh World.

CHAPTER

36

HYPERCARD PROPERTIES

In Chapter 31, we introduced the concept of properties, which can be retrieved and set by the Get and Set commands, respectively. Now you'll see precisely what these properties are all about and how useful they can be when you try to automate processes for nonprogramming HyperCard browsers. Virtually every setting you can make in an object dialog box or in the HyperCard Preferences card can be made from a HyperTalk script.

Properties define the details of an object, just as, say, a driver's license defines your details: name, address, height, weight, and so on. If you had a list of every property about a field, you could recreate that field exactly.

The importance of being able to "get" a property is that you can read what it currently is from within a script. If the setting is different from what you want it to be (something the script can determine with an *if-then-else* control structure), the script can make the desired setting. You should also endeavor to reset properties to their original settings after you've modified them for the purposes of a single message handler.

When you use the Get command to retrieve a property, HyperCard places the current reading into It. From there, your handler may make whatever decisions or conversions are necessary inside that variable.

HyperCard properties come in nine varieties, although some varieties have many more properties than others:

global	menu
window	paint
stack	background
card	field
button	

We'll follow this classification system, working our way from the most "global" to the narrowest property settings, those having to do with fields and buttons.

The syntax for referring to properties is simple:

```
get [the] <property> [of <object>]
set [the] <property> [of <object>] to <new setting>
```

The word "the" is optional, but often makes the statement sound more complete when reading the script aloud. Therefore, the following property setting commands are allowed:

```
get the location of field 1
get location of field 1
set the cursor to watch
set cursor to watch
```

It helps to be consistent within your own code, but there is no penalty for using *the* in some commands and not in others.

Next to the property names in the listings below, we indicate the nature of the setting each property works with. The properties for each of the object types are listed in alphabetical order.

Global Properties

In the global properties categories are those that can have a major effect on the operation of HyperCard at any given instant. You might think of these properties as properties of the HyperCard object in the hierarchy of objects.

blindTyping <true or false>

Purpose: Controls the ability to type into a hidden Message Box.

When to Use It: When you check the Blind Typing checkbox in the Home Stack Preferences card, the blindTyping property is set to true, meaning that you can type into the Message Box even if it is not showing on the screen. Beginners should probably keep this property set to false, because it may be disconcerting to type and not get any visual feedback that the Message Box is actually accepting the text. But more experienced HyperCard users may prefer to be able to type blindly to enter quick commands without having to show the Message Box.

When typing blind, however, you had better be an accurate typist. Since you can't see any mistakes you make, all you'll get is a beep and an alert box from HyperCard if you make a slip of the digit. Fortunately, because whatever you type into a hidden Message Box stays in the box, you can see it by typing Command-M or choosing Message from the Go menu.

Examples:

```
get the blindTyping
set the blindTyping to false
```

You Try It: Use a blank Addresses stack card for this experiment. Make the Message Box visible, and type the following messages into it:

```
get the blindTyping
set the blindTyping to true
hide msg
put "howdy" into field 1
show msg
set blindTyping to false
hide msg
uh oh
(Command-M)
set the blindTyping to it
```

cursor <id number or name>

Purpose: Controls which preset cursor displays on the screen during handler execution.

When to Use It: You may change the shape of the cursor during the execution of a script by setting the cursor property to an existing cursor. HyperCard has seven predefined cursors that you can call up by their names. They are shown in Figure 36–1.

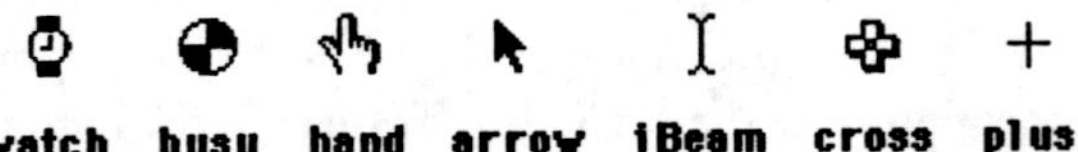

Figure 36–1. The seven cursors built into HyperCard and their names.

By setting the cursor to None, the cursor disappears while a handler is running. This is desirable when the other actions in the handler affect the screen (as in showing or hiding a picture). In these cases, the cursor may flicker and be distracting to the visual effect you're trying to achieve. Turning off the cursor eliminates this distraction.

It is frequently helpful to set the cursor to the watch. If you have designed an extensive script that causes the user to have to wait more than about one second, it would be a good idea to set the cursor to watch prior to undertaking the rest of the lengthy script. Macintosh users are accustomed to waiting relatively patiently when the watch cursor is on the screen. If the hand or arrow is showing while a script is silently churning away, the user may feel that the program has "hung up" or is unnecessarily slow in its execution. Surprisingly, the watch cursor eliminates many of those negative feelings.

You may recreate the effect of the spinning beachball cursor, which HyperCard does during stack sorting and finding. By setting the cursor to Busy, the cursor changes to the beachball. Each time the cursor is set to busy in the same handler, the beachball "rotates" one-eighth of a turn. Therefore, to achieve the effect of a spinning beachball, your handler must set the cursor to Busy several times. As a result, this effect is best achieved inside repeat loop constructions, which advances the beachball one-eighth turn each time through the loop. In long handlers without a repeat loop, the spinning beachball effect will be achieved only by liberal sprinkling of the `set cursor to busy` statement throughout.

2.2 The cursor property always reverts to HyperCard's normal cursor settings when a script ends, that is, when HyperCard starts sending idle messages (see Chapter 52 about changing the normal cursor). This property is settable only. The Get command does not work with the cursor property.

You may also add custom cursors to your stack. With tools such as ResEdit, you can create resources of type CURS and move them to your stack. Setting the cursor to that resource name displays your cursor (see also Chapter 54 about animating with cursors).

Examples:

```
set cursor to none
set cursor to busy
set cursor to iBeam
```

You Try It: Because the cursor reverts to the current tool at idle time, you'll have to experiment with this property in a handler. Create a card button in any stack, and enter the following script into the button.

```
on mouseUp
   put "watch,busy,hand,arrow,iBeam,cross,plus,none" into cursorList
   repeat with x = 1 to the number of items of cursorList
      put "This is the" && item x of cursorList && "cursor."
      set cursor to item x of cursorList
      wait 5 seconds -- time to see it
   end repeat
   put "Now spinning..."
   repeat 100
      set cursor to busy
   end repeat
   put empty
end mouseUp
```

Click on the button, and bring the cursor into the Message Box so you can read the type of cursor and see it at the same time. You'll also see how quickly the Busy cursor spins, even if you are using a Macintosh Classic.

debugger <name of current debugger>

Purpose: Controls the debugging program to use (the one started at a script checkpoint).

When to Use It: The standard HyperTalk debugger is called ScriptEditor. If you install a third party debugger, either it or you will have to set the Debugger property to alert HyperTalk to start that external debugger at a checkpoint.

Examples:

```
get the debugger
set the debugger to "ScriptEditor"
```

You Try It: Type the following messages into the Message Box in any stack:

```
the debugger -- see the current debugger
```

dialingTime <ticks>

2.1

Purpose: Controls how long HyperCard keeps the serial port open after a Dial command (default is 180 ticks—3 seconds).

When to Use It: Before the Dial command sends a string to the modem port, it must "open" the port; after it sends the string, it "closes" the port. Some modems react to the closing of the port, while others merely carry on with their dialing tasks no matter what. If your modem needs to keep the modem port open while it dials, then you can lengthen the dialingTime property value as needed. The value remains in effect until you quit HyperCard.

Importantly, this property rarely affects the length of time the modem stays off-hook (i.e., connected to the phone line). That behavior belongs to the S7 register in most modems. See the Dial command discussion (Chapter 26) for more information.

Example:

```
set the dialingTime to 300 -- 5 seconds
```

You Try It: This is one of those unobvious properties that don't affect the way things look or sound. Your modem may not even need the adjustment.

dialingVolume <level 0 through 7>

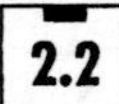

Purpose: Controls the volume of the Dial command's tones when played through the speaker.

When to Use It: By distinguishing dialing volume from regular sound volume, it is possible to let HyperCard play sound resources at the Sound control panel setting, while maintaining a dialing volume commensurate with the amount of sound your phone requires. The default value of 7 is quite loud, especially on Macs with large built-in speakers or external amplified speakers. A value of 0 may not completely quiet the sound on some machines, especially if played in quiet surroundings. This property reverts to its default value upon quitting HyperCard.

Examples:

```
get the dialingVolume
set dialingVolume to 3
```

You Try It: Type the following messages into the Message Box in any stack:

```
set dialingVolume to 7
dial "555"
set dialingVolume to 2
dial "555"
```

dragSpeed <number>

Purpose: Controls the speed, in pixels per second, at which the Drag command operates.

When to Use It: If your script uses the Drag command, principally to draw shapes on the screen with any of the painting tools, you can control the speed at which the drawing occurs with the dragSpeed property. If you set the number to zero, the tool will drag at the fastest speed of which your Macintosh is capable. Other settings, however, control the number of pixels per second at which the tool will traverse the screen.

In certain instructional stacks, you may want to slow down dragging so the user can see exactly how a drawing is made. A comfortable speed to watch drawing is at around 150. At idle time, the dragSpeed property returns to zero.

Examples:

```
get the dragSpeed
set the dragSpeed to 185
```

You Try It: Since the dragSpeed property returns to zero at idle time, you'll have to place a script in a button to see how various settings affect the drag speed of a painting tool. Go to a blank card in the Addresses stack and create a new button. Enter the following script into the button, and watch what happens when you click that button.

```
on mouseUp
    choose line tool
    set the lineSize to 2
    set the dragSpeed to 25
    drag from 120,175 to 120,75
    set the dragSpeed to 100
    drag from 140,175 to 140,75
    set the dragSpeed to 200
    drag from 160,175 to 160,75
    set the dragSpeed to 0
    drag from 180,175 to 180,75
    choose browse tool
end mouseUp
```

editBkgnd <true or false>

Purpose: Controls the edit domain.

When to Use It: If your scripts perform any actions in a background—painting pictures, pasting buttons or fields—use the editBkgnd property to go to and from the background domain. Setting this property to true places you in the background editing mode, complete with hash marks on the menubar.

As in the nonscripted world of HyperCard, if your script chooses the Browse tool, the editBkgnd property is set to false and the background editing mode is cancelled.

Examples:

```
get the editBkgnd
set the editBkgnd to true
```

You Try It: Type the following messages into the Message Box in any stack:

```
get the editBkgnd
it
set the editBkgnd to true
choose pencil tool
choose button tool
choose browse tool
```

environment <development or player>

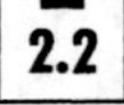

Purpose: Reveals whether the stack is being run with the HyperCard Player (or as a stand-alone stack) or with the full scriptable version of HyperCard.

When to Use It: In most cases, your stacks shouldn't care whether they are running with the development version of HyperCard or in some more restrictive environment. But if that distinction is important, this property can tell you. When the stack is opened with the development version, the value of this property is "development." For the HyperCard Player or a stack that has been saved as a standalone application, the value is "player." This property is read-only.

Example:

```
get the environment
```

You Try It: Create a small test stack, with one background field. Add the following openStack handler to the stack script:

```
on openStack
    put "Thank you for using this stack with the" && the environment ¬
    && "version of HyperCard." into field 1
end openStack
```

Close the stack and reopen it. Next, save the stack as a stand-alone stack, and open it from the Finder.

id <application signature>

2.2

Purpose: Reveals the four-character signature of the application running the stack.

When to Use It: Saving a stack as a custom application allows the author to assign a four-character signature that is different from HyperCard's WILD signature. These signatures are used by the Finder to help document files locate their applications and for applications to display their unique icons. Your scripts may verify that the application running them is HyperCard or the custom application. This property is read-only. See Chapter 57 for more information about standalone stacks and signatures.

Example:

```
get the id
```

You Try It: Type the following message into the Message Box in any stack:

```
the id -- HyperCard's signature
```

itemDelimiter <character>

Purpose: Sets the character HyperCard recognizes as separators between HyperTalk items.

When to Use It: HyperCard's default behavior is to treat text between commas as an item. For example, item 1 of "win, place, show" is "win." But sometimes a string comes your way that has other delimiters, which you'd like to treat as item delimiters. Colon-delimited Macintosh file pathnames are good examples. To obtain the file name from a pathname, you would set the itemDelimiter property to colon (colon is a constant you can use as a more readable alternative to the colon symbol), and then get the last item of that string.

Whenever you append items to a string, the value of the itemDelimiter property rules as well. HyperTalk inserts the delimiter into the string where necessary.

Like many global properties, itemDelimiter returns to its default value (comma) at idle time. But if you change the property within a script, it's usually a good idea to restore it to comma (also a constant) in case a statement later in the handler expects comma-delimited items.

Examples:

```
set the itemDelimiter to colon
set itemDelimiter to comma
```

You Try It: In a card of the Home stack, create a temporary card button with the following handler in it:

```
on mouseUp
    set itemDelimiter to colon
    answer file "Choose any file:"
    put item 1 of it into theVolume
    set itemDelimiter to comma
    answer "The file comes from the volume" && theVolume
end mouseUp
```

language <language name>

Purpose: Controls which language translator is in use.

When to Use It: HyperCard includes an internal mechanism that allows language translators to be added. Such a translator would convert the English scripts stored on disk to the user's native language for display and editing in the Script Editor. The default value is English.

Examples:

```
get the language
set the language to German
```

You Try It: Since your edition of HyperCard most likely does not have any language translators in it (the potential for this feature was never fully realized), you won't be able to try this property, other than to get the alert box that tells you no translator is installed for that language. You can try it anyway. Type the following messages into the Message Box in any stack:

```
get the language
it
set the language to Japanese
set the language to it
```

lockErrorDialogs <true or false>

2.1

Purpose: Controls whether script execution errors produce error message dialogs (the default behavior) or suppress the dialogs (property set to true).

When to Use It: Script errors that occur while a script runs (i.e., after compilation is successful) generate error dialogs in HyperCard. These messages may not be helpful to users of a published stack. By setting the lockErrorDialogs property to true, you can suppress these error dialogs.

As with any script error, script execution halts, whether or not the dialogs are locked. Therefore it is incumbent on the stack designer to provide some kind of feedback or hidden corrective action as the result of an error. When error dialogs are locked, HyperCard sends the message errorDialog <message text> to the current card. A handler to trap for this message can then examine the text of the error message (which is the same that appears in HyperCard's error dialogs), and process accordingly. Such a handler might look like this:

```
on errorDialog errMsg
    if errMsg is "Expected number here." then
        answer "The required information must be a number.  Please try again."
    else
        answer "Sorry, an error has occurred.  Contact " & ¬
        "Technical Support for assistance."
    end if
end errorDialog
```

Since you want to see errors during the authoring process, set this property to true only near the end of your development cycle. This property reverts to false at idle time. Also see the Lock Error Dialogs and Unlock Error Dialogs commands (Chapter 35) for simpler ways to adjust this property.

Examples:

```
set the lockErrorDialogs to true
set lockErrorDialogs to false
```

You Try It: In the Home stack, create a temporary card button with the following handler in it:

```
on mouseUp
    set lockErrorDialogs to true
    ask "Enter a button number:"
    if the result is "" then
        answer short name of card button it
    end if
end mouseUp
```

Temporarily add the following handler to the card script:

```
on errorDialog errMsg
    if errMsg is "There is no card button number 0." then
        answer "You did not enter a number.  Try again."
    else
        if errMsg contains "There is no card button number" then
            answer "There are only" && number of cd btns && "buttons available."
        end if
    end if
end errorDialog
```

Now click the temporary button and try different (or no) values to see how the error messages are trapped. Also comment out the lockErrorDialogs statement in the button to see HyperCard's typical way of handling errors. Which would you prefer to see as a user?

Be sure to delete the errorDialog handler and card button before moving on.

lockMessages <true or false>

Purpose: Controls whether open and close object system messages are sent while a handler executes.

When to Use It: While this global property is often confused with controlling the Message Box, it actually concerns itself with system messages. Frequently, when a handler retrieves information from another card or stack, it may be thrown off the track because an openCard, closeCard, openBackground, closeBackground, openStack, or closeStack handler has gotten in the way. For instance, let's say a stack's openStack handler automatically takes you to the last card of the stack to see the most recently added card. If another stack needs to fetch data from a named card in the stack, the openStack handler will leave you at the last card of the stack, rather than at the named card. Further action may be impossible if the two cards don't have the same field names. In any case, the correct data won't be where you expect it.

To obviate this hazard, your handler should set the LockMessages property to true before leaving the current card. Not only will this halt HyperCard's sending of open and close object system messages while the handler runs, but it also will probably speed up handler execution. Without those system messages and handlers running, only the current handler takes up clock time. This will also prevent the Message Box from flashing on and off if one or more of the system message handlers in the transaction normally shows or hides the Message Box. Locking the screen, on the other hand, does not prevent a Message Box from appearing if a handler shows it. Only the LockMessages property can prevent the Message Box from appearing mid-stream.

The LockMessages property returns to false at idle time, although you may set this property as often as necessary while a handler is running. See also the Lock Messages and Unlock Messages commands discussed in Chapter 35.

Examples:

```
set lockMessages to true
set lockMessages to false
```

You Try It: Since this property reverts to false at idle time, you'll need to test this inside a button. Shifting from the Home stack to the Addresses stack normally deletes the Home menu and adds the Utilities menu. In the Home stack, create a temporary card button with the following handler in it:

```
on mouseUp
    set lockMessages to true
    go to stack "Addresses"
end mouseUp
```

Try this button with the LockMessages setting and without. When closeStack and openStack messages are locked, no menus change as they should.

lockRecent <true or false>

Purpose: Controls whether the cards are being written to the Recent history for display in the Recent dialog box.

When to Use It: This global property differs from LockScreen or LockMessages in that the only action it inhibits is whether a card will be recorded in the Recent dialog box as being a card visited in the course of navigation. HyperCard normally writes to the Recent buffer any card you see on the screen. Thus, when you lock the screen, only cards you actually see are stored in Recent. The LockRecent property, however, lets you keep the screen unlocked, but prevents the visit to the card from being stored in Recent.

The LockRecent property returns to false at idle time.

Examples:

```
set LockRecent to true
set LockRecent to false
```

You Try It: Since this property reverts to false at idle time, you'll need to test this inside a button. From any stack, create a temporary card button and insert the following handler, substituting the name of a stack that you haven't gone to in the current HyperCard session.

```
on mouseUp
    set lockRecent to true
    go to stack "Your Stack"
    go back
end mouseUp
```

Click the button. Notice first that you can see the second stack when it opens. Upon your return to the first card, check the Recent dialog box. The miniature picture of that other stack's card will not be present.

lockScreen <true or false>

Purpose: Controls screen updating during script execution.

When to Use It: Some message handlers need to go to various cards on their way to retrieve information or find a specific card in another stack. All the screen activity associated with such motions may be distracting to the user and definitely slows execution speed, especially on slower Macintoshes. If you prefer to hide all the commotion from sight, you can set the lockScreen property to true, prior to shifting around the stacks. This action essentially freezes and disconnects the screen from HyperCard. In the meantime, HyperCard can go ahead and perform any activity it would do normally, including putting information into fields, cutting and pasting buttons, and drawing graphics in the background. HyperCard also records each card the script attends to in its card history (although not in Recent), even though you don't see the cards pass before your eyes.

By locking the screen, you also help speed execution of a script that would otherwise be drawing many cards on the screen each time a new card appeared. You might still wish to set the cursor property to watch, to indicate that something is happening, when there is no action on the screen.

Even though the screen is locked, Message Box showing and hiding is still active. That means, however, that if the Message Box is hidden in the middle of a locked screen script, the Macintosh won't fill in the blank space behind the box until the handler ends. Therefore, carefully orchestrate the showing and hiding of the Message Box to take place when the screen is not locked.

The lockScreen property reverts to false at idle time, so you needn't set the property to false at the end of a script. You may, however, wish to lock the screen during only part of a lengthy script. In that case, set lockScreen to false or use the more convenient Unlock Screen command when you're ready for the user to see some action and the script still has more to do. See also the Lock Screen command equivalent discussion (and its cumulative effects) in Chapter 30.

Examples:

```
get the lockScreen
set the lockScreen to true -- same as Lock Screen command
```

You Try It: Because the lockScreen property returns to false at idle time, you won't be able to test it from the Message Box. Go to the Addresses stack and create a card button on a blank card with the following script. Then click on the button and watch what happens and what doesn't happen.

```
on mouseUp
    set the cursor to watch
    set the lockScreen to true
    go next
    go next
    go "Home"
    go card "Stacks"
end mouseUp
```

longWindowTitles <true or false>

Purpose: Controls whether the entire pathname or just the stack name appears in card window titlebars.

When to Use It: If the window to a stack displays the titlebar (it may be hidden or shown with the Hide Titlebar and Show Titlebar commands), you have the choice as to how much information about the stack name should appear in the titlebar. Because pathnames are not a common sight in other Macintosh application windows, the sight of the long string with all the colons could be confusing to someone using your stack. For them, the stack name by itself would be appropriate.

For stack authors, however, it can be very beneficial to display the entire pathname in the titlebar. This is especially true when you have more than one copy or generation of a stack under development on your hard disk. Having the full pathname can help you make sure you are using the desired version or copy.

HyperCard truncates long pathnames in such a manner that it tries to display at least the volume name and the stack name. If there is insufficient width in the titlebar to display the entire pathname, then HyperCard places an ellipsis where it removes folder names to squeeze as many clues to the pathname as it can.

Because this is a global property, if you set it in your stack, that setting affects all open HyperCard windows at the time. If you must set the property to true (the default setting is false), consider setting back to false in suspendStack and closeStack handlers.

Examples:

```
get the longWindowTitles
set the longWindowTitles to true
```

You Try It: If you have a sufficient HyperCard memory partition, open multiple stacks, and type the following commands into the Message Box, watching the titlebars of all open windows after each command:

```
set longWindowTitles to true
set longWindowTitles to false
```

messageWatcher <message watcher XCMD name>

Purpose: Controls which message watcher debugging XCMD is in force.

When to Use It: HyperCard comes with an XCMD, called messageWatcher, which is a debugging tool for scripters. It displays a palette style window and a list of all messages being sent in real time. You can see how messages are being sent as you move the mouse, click on buttons, navigate, and so on. If you use this feature often, use the shortcut handler built into the Home stack by typing mw into the Message Box.

The Message Watcher also has three special window properties associated with it: Visible, hideUnused, and hideIdle (see "Window Properties," below).

Additional, third-party message watcher XCMDs may become available for you to plug into your own Home or other stack. You choose which message watcher XCMD you wish to open by setting the messageWatcher property. The one supplied by Apple is called, simply enough, MessageWatcher.

See Chapter 48 on using HyperCard's built-in debugging tools.

Examples:

```
get the messageWatcher
set the messageWatcher to "Ultra Msg Watcher"
```

You Try It: Other than retrieving the standard local watcher name, there isn't much you can try.

name <name of current HyperCard>

2.1

Purpose: Contains the name (and pathname) of the HyperCard program that executes the command.

When to Use It: HyperCard presents two options for its name property. The plain property returns the name of the HyperCard application that executes the request for the name property. Some users rename their HyperCard programs (or append version numbers) to distinguish one copy from another on the hard disk. By checking this property, a script can discriminate among copies. Perhaps more valuable is the Long Name version of this property, which returns the pathname to the HyperCard copy. While HyperCard accepts other versions (Short Name and Abbreviated Name), they return the same information as the plain version.

Examples:

```
get the name of HyperCard
get long name of HyperCard
```

You Try It: Type the following messages into the Message Box in any stack:

```
name of HyperCard
long name of HyperCard
```

numberFormat <format string>

Purpose: Controls the format of the displayed result of a math calculation.

When to Use It: Scripts often perform calculations on numbers. Currency or metric conversions, for instance, often require that highly disparate magnitudes of values be multiplied or divided. When such calculations are performed, their accuracy is heavily influenced by the number of digits to the right of the decimal point to which the calculations are carried out. The greater the number of digits, the higher the accuracy. In math circles, this type of accuracy is called *precision.*

Unlike a spreadsheet program, HyperCard stores numbers in its fields as straight text. If a number is stored as 3.96, that's all that HyperCard knows about the number, even if it was the result of a much more precise calculation that had several digits further to the right of the decimal. When the number was stored in the HyperCard field with two decimal digits, any further precision was lost.

The numberFormat property establishes the precision (that is, the number of digits to the right of the decimal point) to which the result of any calculations in a script will be displayed or stored in a container. After the script, at idle time, the numberFormat returns to the default setting of six digits to the right of the decimal. This also means, however, that a change of format in a subroutine handler remains in effect even after execution returns to the main handler. It may be wise to reset the property to its default value after a special format is used.

The parameter to the numberFormat property is a string with a sample of what the format should be, using three special characters: the zero, the decimal, and the crosshatch. When you specify a zero in a location on either side of the decimal point, you tell HyperCard to display a zero in that location if no other number fills it. For example, the format "0.00" is the one you would use for displaying dollars and cents, because you always want the one cent column to have a digit there. A calculated result of 7.6 would display as 7.60.

Use the crosshatch character when you are not concerned about displaying zeros but want displayed precision to a certain number of digits to the right of the decimal. Therefore, the format "0.######" displays the result with up to six digits to the right of the decimal and always shows a zero in the ones column of a result that is less than 1.

Since the format change takes effect only after the next arithmetic operation, the script may have to perform a "dummy" operation, like adding a zero, to apply the format to the number. If the new format is shorter than the previous one, HyperCard rounds the digits cut off by the new format.

Examples:

```
get the numberFormat
set the numberFormat to "0.00"
set the numberFormat to "0.############"
set the numberFormat to "00.00"
```

You Try It: The numberFormat property returns to the default setting (0.######) at idle time, so you'll have to experiment with the help of a button script in a blank card of the Practice stack. Enter the following script in a card button:

```
on mouseUp
    set the numberFormat to "0.00"
    put 1/8 into line 1 of field 3
    set the numberFormat to "0.000"
    put 1/8 into line 2 of field 3
    set the numberFormat to "0.00"
    put "$" && 1/8 into line 3 of field 3
end mouseUp
```

powerKeys <true or false>

Purpose: Controls Power Keys setting.

When to Use It: Power Keys are the keyboard shortcuts available when you use the Painting tools and Icon Editor. The powerKeys global property is the one that turns them on for you when you set the Preference card to do so. It is unlikely you'll need to adjust this setting in a script, but the stack script in the HyperCard Home stack sets it each time you start HyperCard.

Examples:

```
get the powerKeys
set the powerKeys to true
```

You Try It: You may send a set powerKeys to false message from the Message Box if you like, just to verify that this property does work. Then choose a painting tool, select a graphic element, and try one of the Paint menu items normally controlled by a Power Key. It won't work from the keyboard. We suggest you keep Power Keys turned on to help speed your painting work.

printMargins <left | top | right | bottom>

printTextAlign <left | center | right>

printTextFont <font name>

printTextHeight <line height>

printTextSize <font size>

printTextStyle <plain | bold | italic | underline | outline | shadow>

Purpose: Controls characteristics of text printed with the Print <expression> command and the default printing properties for report printing.

When to Use Them: These properties affect the printed results of the Print <expression> command, the one that prints any expression that doesn't evaluate to a field name (Chapter 34). You may also set the default text properties of items printed in reports with these settings. Usually, the latter won't be necessary if you've specified anything other than default fonts for report format items (see Chapter 4).

All the printText- style properties should be self-explanatory, since the possibilities are identical to the kinds of text properties set in a font dialog box. The printMargins setting, however, needs a bit of explanation.

The four parameters represent the number of pixels from the edges of the printable area of a page. Pixels, in this case, are the same 72 dot-per-inch pixels of the Macintosh screen, even if you are printing on a laser printer or other device with much higher resolution. The default setting is 0,0,0,0, which means that the margins on all sides are zero—printing will be to the maximum printable area on the page (default margins on laser printers are usually wider than the ImageWriter). If you wished to specify a left margin of one inch, then the printMargin property would be set to 72,0,0,0. Both a one inch left margin and a one-half inch right margin would be specified as 72,0,36,0.

Examples:

```
set printMargins to 72,36,36,36
set printTextFont to Palatino
set printTextSize to 12
set printTextHeight to printTextSize + 2
```

You Try It: The easiest way to experiment with the command is to print and expression with several different settings. Use an expression that contains a few lines of text, including at least one line that will wrap on a full width printed line. To pick up such an expression, type a bunch of text into a field of any card. Then put that that field into a variable by way of the Message Box command. That variable will be a global variable. Issuing the Print command with the variable name as the parameter is the Print <expression> command. Start with a sample in the default properties. Then experiment with different margin settings and other text properties. Afterward, set the properties to their default settings with the Reset Printing command.

scriptEditor <editor name>

Purpose: To choose a specific Script Editor application.

When to Use It: Because HyperCard allows the connection of script editors other than the one delivered with it, you may wish to change over to an external script editor. To change script editors, you would set the ScriptEditor property to the name of that editor.

HyperCard's standard script editor is called *ScriptEditor*, which is the text returned when getting this property for the first time. Other editors, written as XCMDs, may contain features not found in the standard HyperCard editor. Unless you have another editor installed in your message hierarchy, you won't be able to take advantage of interchangeable editors.

Examples:

```
get the scriptEditor
set the scriptEditor to "Joe's Editor"
```

You Try It: Other than retrieving the standard editor name, there isn't much you can try unless you have access to a third-party editor.

scriptTextFont <font name>

scriptTextSize <font size>

Purpose: Controls the text attributes of the script editor window.

When to Use Them: You may change the font attributes of the script editor window. Set any of these properties to change the appearance of all text in the next script window you open (i.e., does not change windows already open). The parameters are the same you use for field font characteristics.

Examples:

```
get the scriptTextFont
set the scriptTextSize to 12
```

You Try It: Position a small card window and a script editor window so that you can see both. Close the window. Type the following messages into the Message Box in any stack and open the script window to see the changes take effect:

```
set the scriptTextFont to Chicago
set the scriptTextSize to 12
set the scriptTextFont to Monaco
set the scriptTextSize to 10
```

stacksInUse <extra stacks in hierarchy>

Purpose: Reveals a return-delimited list of all stacks added to the hierarchy via the Start Using command. This property is read only.

When to Use It: Use this property to obtain a readout of complete pathnames to stacks added to the message hierarchy. Once you add or delete extra stacks to the hierarchy, it is easy to lose track of what's there and in what order. The data supplied by the StacksInUse property provides a list of all stacks, except the current stack and Home stack, that are in the hierarchy (the Stacks function lists all open stacks).

Examples:

```
put the stacksInUse into stackList
get the stacksInUse
```

You Try It: Type the following messages into the Message Box in any stack:

```
get last line of the stacksInUse
it -- last line of (empty if none added)
```

suspended <true or false>

Purpose: Reveals whether HyperCard is running in the background (under MultiFinder or System 7).

When to Use It: If execution of parts of your scripts need to behave differently while running in the background, this property lets you determine which state you're in. For example, you may elect to bypass an Ask or Answer dialog box while running in the background. This avoids the Macintosh Notification Manager from flashing the HyperCard icon over the Apple menu, requesting user interaction.

textArrows <true or false>

Purpose: Controls whether text arrow keys work as cursor navigation keys within text fields.

When to Use It: The TextArrows setting in the Home stack's Preferences card is usually the setting a user prefers, and should rarely, if ever, be changed unless a particular setting is essential to the operation of your stack. When TextArrows is set to true, the user may navigate through a text field with the arrow keys on the keyboard. When the text insertion pointer is no longer in a field, the arrow keys take on their card-to-card navigation powers. When the property is set to false, the arrow keys do card-to-card navigation, even if the text insertion pointer is in a field.

If a user expects arrow keys to work in a field because that's the Preferences card setting, your stack design should have a very good reason to set the property to the opposite. Removing the power of textArrows from someone who expects them may result in an unhappy user.

Examples:

```
get the textArrows
set the textArrows to true
```

You Try It: So you can see the difference in behavior of the two settings, go to the Addresses stack and set the property to each setting, trying the arrow keys while editing text in a field.

traceDelay <ticks>

Purpose: Controls the number of ticks (1/60ths of a second) between execution of each HyperTalk line when tracing with the debugger.

When to Use It: The Trace command in the debugger (Chapter 48) allows the scripts to execute, while you watch the debugger highlight each line. Unless adjusted otherwise, the default time delay between execution of each HyperTalk script line is 0 ticks—execution is as fast as possible with the debugger running. You may, however, wish to slow down the execution so you can more readily examine how parts of the script (e.g., repeat loops or if-then-else constructions) are flowing without single-stepping through the script.

While it is possible to set this property in scripts—perhaps to alter the tracing speed in various parts of a script—you are more likely to set this property as needed via the Message Box. A setting of 30 ticks makes it much easier to watch the flow across multiple handlers and object script windows.

Examples:

```
get the traceDelay
set the traceDelay to 30
```

You Try It: Once you are comfortable with the debugger, set a checkpoint in a handler, run the script, and initiate a trace through the handler. Then set the traceDelay property to 30 and repeat the process. Notice how much easier it is to follow what's going on as the script executes.

userLevel <1 through 5>

Purpose: Controls the User Level for an entire HyperCard session.

When to Use It: The five possible settings correspond to the levels listed in the Home Stack's Preferences card:

1 Browsing
2 Typing
3 Painting
4 Authoring
5 Scripting

As you recall, each of these levels provides a fixed amount of access to modifying information in a stack or the stack itself. If you are distributing a stack whose access you wish to restrict, your openStack script would set the userLevel property to the one that is most appropriate for that stack.

2.1 2.2

Of extreme importance is realizing that your stack may be used with the HyperCard Player or saved as an application, both of which have default user levels of 2 (and cannot be changed by the user within the Player). Therefore, if your scripts perform any operations that require higher user levels (e.g., painting, creating buttons, deleting fields), your script should set the userLevel property in its openStack handler to guarantee your scripts will work properly in all circumstances.

If you do change the userLevel in a stack, it is your responsibility to get the previous userLevel (or fetch it from the Preferences card) and restore the property to its original setting upon closing the stack. You might want to get the property at the open, place the numbered setting in a global variable, and use that variable to restore the setting in a closeStack script.

Examples:

```
get the userLevel
set the userLevel to 2
set the userLevel to priorLevel -- a global variable
```

You Try It: Type the following messages into the Message Box and check the menubar and menus after each to see how the setting changed the user access to the system.

```
get the userLevel
it
set the userLevel to 1
set the userLevel to 2
choose pencil tool -- not at this level!
set the userLevel to 3
choose pencil tool -- OK now
choose browse tool
set the userLevel to it -- restore level
```

userModify <true or false>

When to Use It: If a stack's cantModify property is set to true (either automatically because it's on a locked disk or manually by setting the property), a user will be prevented from making any changes to the stack. Even attempting to type a character in an unlocked field will result in an alert message that you cannot modify the stack. The UserModify property is a global property (i.e., it doesn't belong to any particular object), which allows the user to type into fields, move or resize buttons and fields, and edit pictures with the Painting tools.

Any changes made to a card whose CantModify and UserModify properties are set to true are discarded the instant the user closes the current card. Thus, if you wish to maintain a data entry card in its original, pristine form for each person who comes to it, you would set these properties to true. It is up to your handlers, however, to manipulate the information entered by each user before the card closes and loses the data. Perhaps that means posting information in other (unlocked) cards or stacks; perhaps you need to gather the information in global variables, which will survive the close of the card.

When the CantModify and UserModify properties are set to true, HyperCard does not write manual or HyperTalk script-based field entries to the disk, as it normally does.

The UserModify property comes into play only when the stack is locked. If the stack is not locked, the UserModify property is ignored. In other words, when a stack is unlocked, setting the UserModify property to false has no effect.

Examples:

```
set userModify to true
set userModify to cantModify of this stack
```

You Try It: The best way to see the difference this property makes is to go to a stack and lock it via the Protect Stack dialog. Do that in the Addresses stack, checking the Can't Modify checkbox of that dialog. The padlock icon should appear in the menubar. Try to type or edit an entry in a field. At the first character, you receive the alert that you cannot modify the stack. Now, type the following message into the Message Box

```
set userModify to true
```

and try to edit the field again. The field accepts your entry. Go to the next card and come back. Your previous entry or edit will have disappeared.

variableWatcher <variable watcher XCMD name>

Purpose: Controls which variable watcher debugging XCMD is in force.

When to Use It: HyperCard comes with an XCMD, called variableWatcher, which is a debugging tool for scripters. It displays a palette style window and a list of all local and global variables and their values as a handler executes. You can display this window to watch how execution of your scripts affects the values inside global and local variables.

Whenever your script encounters a checkpoint, the HyperTalk debugger switches on. If the Variable Watcher window is not showing, you can show it by choosing Variable Watcher from the Debug Menu.

Additional, third-party variable watcher XCMDs may become available for you to plug into your own Home or other stack. You choose which variable watcher XCMD you wish to open by setting the variableWatcher property. The one supplied by Apple is called, simply enough, VariableWatcher. A Home stack shortcut handler lets you show the Variable Watcher any time by typing VW into the Message Box.

You may control visual characteristics of the Variable Watcher via three special window properties: rect, hBarLoc, and vBarLoc.

See Chapter 48 on using HyperCard's built-in debugging tools.

Examples:

```
get the variableWatcher
set the variableWatcher to "Nancy'sVars"
```

You Try It: Other than retrieving the standard variable watcher name, there isn't much you can try unless you have access to a third-party variable watcher.

Menu Properties

HyperCard's standard and custom menus have properties that give you much control over their appearance once items are in the menus. With these settings, you may create menu attributes identical to those of other Macintosh programs. These properties affect individual menu items in a menu. Therefore, the syntax for getting or setting these items must include reference to the menu item and menu. No property adjustments are possible for the System Help or Application menus in System 7.

checkMark <true or false>

markChar <character>

Purpose: Controls whether a menu item is preceded by a symbol, and what that symbol is.

When to Use Them: If a menu choice turns on a particular mode or other action that affects the way the program functions, you should mark that menu item with a checkmark. Setting the CheckMark property of a menu item sets that mark; setting the property to false removes the check mark (Figure 36–2).

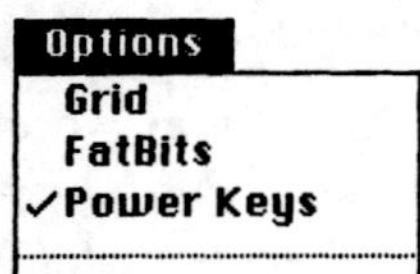

Figure 36–2. Setting the checkMark property of a menuItem to true leaves the mark in the menu's margin.

The checkmark allows a single menu item to serve double duty as an "On" and "Off" menu item for a setting or mode. A checkmark signifies the setting is in effect. You can see examples of this in HyperCard's Options menu when a painting tool is selected. When the Grid is turned on, it has a checkmark next to it. Choosing that menu item again turns off the Grid and removes the checkmark.

The default character is a checkmark symbol. If you make no changes to the markChar property for a particular menu item, then the checkmark symbol will appear whenever you set the checkMark property to true. If you change the symbol, and wish to restore the the checkmark symbol, you'll have to use the numToChar function to set this symbol (the checkmark is not part of the regular keyboard character set). To restore the checkmark symbol, use this syntax:

```
set markChar of <menuItemExpression> of <menuExpression> to numToChar(18)
```

Don't get too crazy setting many different mark characters—you probably haven't seen too many used in commercial programs. The diamond symbol used in the MultiFinder Apple menu when an application needs attention is created by Option-Shift-V.

All this action must be done from your HyperTalk scripts that handle the messages sent by the menu item. You can toggle the property quite simply, and then use the current setting as the trigger for what comes next, as in this fragment:

```
on customMenu
    -- set property to its opposite
    set the checkMark of menuItem "Custom Mode" of menu 3 ¬
    to not the checkMark of menuItem "Custom Mode" of menu 3
    if the checkMark of menuItem "Custom Mode" of menu 3
    then
        -- ... statements to turn on custom mode
    else
        -- ... statements to turn off custom mode
    end if
end customMenu
```

Examples:

```
get the checkMark of menuItem 3 of menu 2
set the checkMark of menuItem 5 of menu 4 to true
set markChar of menuItem 3 of menu 2 to numToChar(215)
```

You Try It: You may experiment with HyperCard's standard menus and setting checkmarks on its items. The settings won't necessarily mean much, because except for items like Background, there aren't many items that toggle. But the exercises will still give you practice. Type the following commands into the Message Box, and pull down the affected menu to see the results:

```
set checkMark of menuItem 1 of menu 2 to true
set checkMark of menuItem "Icon..." of menu "Edit" to true
set MarkChar of menuItem "Icon..." of menu "Edit" to "◊"
set checkMark of menuItem "Icon..." of menu "Edit" to false
reset menubar
```

commandChar <character>

cmdChar <character>

Purpose: Controls the Command-key keyboard equivalent of a menu item.

When to Use Them: Assign a keyboard equivalent to a menu command when the command is a frequently-used one. Experienced Macintosh users often look for keyboard shortcuts for commands they need often.

Valid characters include any letter, number, or punctuation mark available from the keyboard without pressing any modifier keys (Shift, Option, Command). If you set the commandChar as a lowercase letter, HyperCard automatically turns it into an uppercase letter in the menu.

You may reassign Command-key equivalents from their original HyperCard menu values. Be careful, however, to assign the same command character to only one menu item. A command character you set for a custom menu item overrides the same command character attached to a HyperCard menu item; and if you assign the same command character to two different menu items, the first one to which you assign the character is activated when the keyboard command is given.

A number of Command-key conventions have evolved since the early days of the Macintosh. A number of these are outlined in the *User Interface Guidelines.* To reassign such ever-popular keyboard commands as Command-O (for Open) and the editing foursome Command-Z, -X, -C, and -V (for Undo, Cut, Copy, and Paste) could upset your users.

Examples:

```
set the commandChar of menuItem 3 of menu File to Y
set cmdChar of menuItem "New" of menu "Action" to N
```

You Try It: Type the following commands into the Message Box and pull down the affected menu to see the results:

```
put the cmdChar of menuItem 3 of menu "Edit"
set the cmdChar of menuItem "Icon..." of menu "Edit" to 7
set the cmdChar of menuItem "Icon..." of menu "Edit" to ,
reset menubar
```

enabled <true or false>

Purpose: Controls whether a menu in the menubar (other than the Apple, System Help, or Application menus) or a single menu item is enabled or disabled (dimmed).

When to Use It: If a menu item should not be available to a user because of a certain setting or other conditions, you should disable the item. Disabling the item dims it in the menu (Figure 36–3), making it impossible for the user to choose the item.

Figure 36–3. The Enabled property lets you dim or activate a menu or menu item.

Entire menus may also be disabled by setting the enabled property of a menu to false. This dims the item in the menubar, and prevents the user from pulling down the menu. From a user interface point of view, the trend is to remove menus that don't apply to a given mode or background, rather than disabling them.

If you are modifying the HyperCard menus for your application, it is better to remove HyperCard's standard items that you don't use rather than dim them. A dimmed item should be available at some time within your program—it's just dimmed on certain cards, when certain settings are made, or some other circumstance under the user's control.

Examples:

```
set enabled of menu "Font" to false
set enabled of menuItem 5 of menu "Special" to false
set enabled of menuItem 3 of menu 2 to not enabled of menuItem 3 of menu 2
```

You Try It: Type the following commands into the Message Box and pull down the affected menu to see the results:

```
set enabled of menuItem 1 of menu "File" to false
set enabled of menuItem 1 of menu "File" to true
set enabled of menuItem "New Card" of menu "Edit" to false
set enabled of menu "Style" to false
reset menubar
```

menuMessage <message name>

menuMsg <message name>

Purpose: Designates the message to be sent whenever a custom menu item is chosen by the user.

When to Use Them: As described in Chapter 33, a custom menu item may send its own message in lieu of the more standard DoMenu message. The handler that traps a message you assign to a menu item must be in the current card, background, or stack script, Home stack script, or in a stack script of any stack added to the hierarchy.

The default value for a menu item is no message. Instead, HyperCard sends a DoMenu message with the text of the menu item as the parameter, just as it does with HyperCard's standard menus.

Messages must be a single word or a word followed by any number of comma separated parameters. A good technique is to assign a unique message name to a menu item and stick with it, no matter how you later decide to shift or rename the menu item. If the MenuMessage property is the same, you won't have to rework the handler.

Examples:

```
set menuMessage of menuItem 3 of menu 2 to "Backup"
set menuMsg of menuItem "Custom Mode" of menu "Special" to "special true"
```

You Try It: In a blank card of any stack, enter the following handler:

```
on myHandler fromMenu
   if fromMenu is empty
   then put false into fromMenu
   if fromMenu
   then answer "This came from the menu."
   else answer "This came from elsewhere."
end myHandler
```

Then type the following commands into the Message Box:

```
put "My Command" after menu "Objects"
set menuMsg of menuItem "My Command" of menu "Objects" to "myHandler true"
```

Now trigger the card script by both typing myHandler into the Message Box and choosing the new menu item.

name <menu or menu item text>

Purpose: Controls the name of a menu or single menu item. Also reveals the English name of HyperCard's menus and menuItems when they are localized to another language.

When to Use It: When you create a new custom menu, you normally use the Put command to assign new menu item names at the same time. If you are using an existing menu (e.g., File or Edit) but wish to name items differently from the ones supplied by HyperCard, you would then set the Name property of a menu item.

Some commercial programs you see occasionally change a menu item depending on conditions. Instead of using a checkmark to indicate that a feature is turned on, for instance, the menu item changes from something like "Tool On" to "Tool Off." Many user interface followers don't like the idea of a menu item changing its text midstream. It might make sense, however, to change menu items' name under a menu when going between very different parts of the program.

Also, try to keep your menu item name short. As you add menus to the right of the HyperCard menus, the screen real estate may get a bit crowded on a 9-inch Macintosh monitor.

2.2 Whenever HyperCard is localized to a language other than its native English, its menus send doMenu messages bearing the localized names of the menuItem and menu. A doMenu handler that traps for a specific menuItem in English won't automatically respond to the menuItem that arrives in a different language. You may, however, derive the English name of a menuItem at the top of a doMenu handler with a special modifier to the name property. Such a handler would begin as follows:

```
on doMenu theItem,theMenu
   put english name of menuItem theItem of menu theMenu into theItem
   if theItem is ...
   pass doMenu
end doMenu
```

Examples:

```
set name of menuItem 4 of menu "File" to "Backup"
set name of menuItem 6 of menu 5 to "-"
get name of last menu
```

You Try It: Type the following commands into the Message Box and pull down the affected menu to see the results:

```
put "-, Test Item" after menu "Objects"
set name of last menuItem of menu "Objects" to "Something Different"
set name of last menuItem of menu "Objects" to empty
reset menubar
```

rect <menubar coordinates>

2.2 **Purpose:** Reveals the screen (global) coordinates of the menubar.

When to Use It: When a user has multiple monitors connected to the Mac, it may be important to know the coordinates of the menubar within the overall screen area so that HyperCard windows or palettes may be placed in the same monitor as the menubar. By obtaining the four coordinates of the menubar, you can position windows relative to those coordinates. The coordinates appear as a four-item string (left, top, right, bottom). In a single, RGB monitor environment, the value is 0,0,640,20. This property is read-only.

Example:

```
get rect of menubar
```

You Try It: In any stack, type the following command into the Message Box:

```
rect of menubar
```

textStyle <font style>

Purpose: Controls the style of the Chicago font of a menu item

When to Use It: Few menu items should ever have a text style other than the default plain Chicago font. You may, however, adjust this property of any menu item if it applies to your user interface (perhaps a custom Style menu). Acceptible font styles are: plain, bold, italic, underline, outline, shadow, condense, and extend. Apply multiple styles with a comma-delimited list.

Examples:

```
get the textStyle of menuItem 3 of menu "Edit"
set textStyle of menuItem 2 of menu "Style" to bold
```

You Try It: In any stack, type the following message into the Message Box:

```
textStyle of menuItem 4 of menu "Style"
set textStyle of menuItem 2 of menu "Go" to outline, extend -- inspect the Go menu
reset menubar
```

visible <true or false>

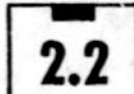

Purpose: Controls whether the menubar is visible or not.

When to Use It: The Visible property of the menubar is the property that is set in response to the Hide Menubar and Show Menubar commands. While you may change the visibility of the menubar by setting this property, it is more likely you'll check the value of this property at the deciding point of an if-then decision tree.

Examples:

```
get the visible of menubar
set visible of menubar to true
```

You Try It: In any stack, type the following message into the Message Box:

```
set visible of menubar to not visible of menubar
```

Press the Return or Enter key several times, and watch how this command sets the Visible property to whatever it is not.

Window Properties

In addition to the current card windows, HyperCard has five windows whose properties you may read and, in some cases, change from a script. The windows are known as *Message* (and its variants: *Message Window, Message Box*, or just *Msg*), *Tools, Patterns, Scroll*, and *FatBits*. With these properties, you may derive various location and size definitions for any HyperCard window. One additional property, for card windows, lets you find out if a window, sized smaller than the card, has been scrolled from the upper left corner. It is important to remember that there are two grids used to measure locations for the card window and all other windows. Measures of the card window are relative to the upper left corner of the screen (0,0); measures of other windows are relative to the upper left corner of the HyperCard card window (0,0).

External windows—those created by external commands, such as the Variable Watcher, Message Watcher, pictures, and palettes—also have a number of properties that may be set via HyperTalk. Some of these windows may include special properties that are unique to those windows. In this section, we also cover those unique properties for external windows included with HyperCard.

buttonCount <integer>

commands <return-delimited list>

hilitedButton <integer>

properties <comma-delimited list>

Purpose: Allows scripts to obtain information about a currently open palette window, as well as set the highlight of a button in a "state" type palette. These properties are unique to palette windows created with the Palette command.

When to Use Them: All of these properties except hilitedButton are read-only, so you can use them only to derive information about a particular palette window. Palettes are described more fully in Chapter 52 and in connection with the Palette command discussion in Chapter 30.

To call these properties, the palette must be open, created by the Palette command. The call must also reference a palette window by name. For instance, if you have created a palette called "Toolkit," then you could obtain the number of defined buttons with the following command:

```
get buttonCount of window "Toolkit"
```

As described in Chapter 51, a palette may have any number of buttons, each defined as a rectangular area in the window. Since the basic properties of palettes are defined by the PLTE resource, and are therefore not adjustable on the fly, you may use the buttonCount property to derive the number of buttons defined in the PLTE resource.

The commands property furnishes a return-delimited list of messages that each button in a palette sends. Again, these messages are defined in the resource, and may not be adjusted as a property.

A palette may be defined as an "action" or "state" palette. This terminology refers to the way a clicked button in a palette highlights. An action palette means that the button highlights while the mouse is down inside the button, and returns to normal upon releasing the mouse, or moving the cursor off the clicked button. A state palette, on the other hand, means that a clicked button stays highlighted either until another button is clicked or until it is turned off by script control. The latter type is especially useful when the buttons in a palette are used for selecting tools, like HyperCard's own Tools palette.

To adjust the highlighted button in a palette, set the hilitedButton property to whichever number the button is. The button number is entirely dependent upon the button definitions in the PLTE resource. If the palette is an action type, the button flashes with the highlight three times, and returns to normal; for a state palette, the button highlights once and stays that way.

The properties property of a palette window lets your scripts obtain a comma-delimited list of properties that the palette contains.

Examples:

```
get the commands of window "Navigator"
put buttonCount of window "Toolkit" into howManyButtons
set hilitedButton of window "Toolkit" to 4
```

You Try It: Type the following messages into the Message Box from any stack:

```
nav -- show navigator palette
buttonCount of window "Navigator"
number of lines of commands of window "Navigator"
line 1 of commands of window "Navigator"
hilitedButton of window "Navigator" -- action palette
set hilitedButton of window "Navigator" to 3
```

dithering <true or false>

globalLoc <point>

globalRect <rectangle>

scale <integer between -5 and 5>

zoom <in or out>

Purpose: Controls the properties unique to external windows created by the Picture command.

When to Use Them: In addition to several properties in common with other windows (rect, loc, visible, and scroll), picture windows have additional properties that only they enjoy. For example, when a picture window is created on a monitor larger than the card window, you may wish to adjust its rectangle or location in terms of the screen's coordinate system instead of the card window's coordinates. Use the globalRect and globalLoc properties to make those tweaks.

Picture windows may magnify or reduce the bitmapped contents based on scale factors ranging between -5 and 5. The normal size parameter is zero. Depending on the picture subject matter, you can get some interesting effects by sequencing through scale factors in a repeat loop. You can even program scale sequences as a way to transition between pictures.

Some of the window styles available for picture windows produce a zoom box in the window's upper right corner. Toggling between the "in" and "out" property settings is the equivalent of repeated clicking of the zoom box. You get only one level in and out of the window.

To learn more about picture windows and their properties, see the Picture command discussion in Chapter 30. Also see the discussion of the zoomed property of card windows at the end of this section.

Examples:

```
get the globalRect of window "Title Screen"
set the scale of window "Shrink Me" to -1
set zoom of window "Flamingo" to "out"
set dithering of window "Wow" to true
```

You Try It: See the examples to the Picture command in Chapter 30.

hBarLoc <integer>

vBarLoc <integer>

Purpose: Controls the location of the horizontal and vertical dividing bars inside the Variable Watcher window. This property is unique to the Variable Watcher window.

When to Use Them: The black dividing lines between various segments of the Variable Watcher are normally dragged by the user while debugging. Dragging the horizontal bar between the variable listings and the variable content viewing area may allow you to see more variables without scrolling. Similarly, dragging the vertical bar between the variable names and the brief display of the variable contents may allow you to see long variable names that are otherwise obscured.

If you find that in debugging a certain piece of code over multiple sessions you constantly rearrange the bar locations of the Variable Watcher window, you can set these properties in the script itself so that when the checkpoint comes up, the window is set as you like it. Once you've successfully debugged the script, you'd then probably remove these property settings.

The zero point for both of these properties is the edge of the active area of the window. For the horizontal bar, that means the area just below the titlebar of the Variable Watcher window. The reference point on the bar is the top edge of the horizontal bar and the left edge of the vertical bar.

Be careful not to set the value of the horizontal bar so high that you cannot see the grow box in the window. If that happens, you'll have to adjust the Rect property of the window or restart HyperCard to get the window back to its default size.

Examples:

```
get the hBarLoc of window "Variable Watcher"
set vBarLoc of window "Variable Watcher" to 200
```

You Try It: Type the following commands into the Message Box and watch the results:

```
show window "Variable Watcher"
put vBarLoc of window "Variable Watcher"
set vBarLoc of window "Variable Watcher" to 50
set vBarLoc of window "Variable Watcher" to 200
set hBarLoc of window "Variable Watcher" to 100
hide window "Variable Watcher"
```

hideIdle <true or false>

hideUnused <true or false>

Purpose: Controls the Hide Idle and Hide Unused checkboxes in the Message Watcher window. These properties are unique to the Message Watcher window.

When to Use Them: In the Message Watcher window are two checkboxes. One, called Hide Idle, prevents the typically endless stream of idle messages from registering in the Message Watcher window when no other action is taking place. The other checkbox, called Hide Unused, inhibits the display of unused messages—those messages sent that do not cause any action to take place or are not trapped by any handlers. For instance, if there is no openCard handler anywhere in the current message hierarchy, then the openCard message goes unused. With the Hide Unused checkbox checked, this message would not show up in the Message Watcher window.

It is unlikely that you'll set these properties from a script, but you may wish to let the Message Watcher grab the unused messages during a specific operation in a script just to make sure that the messages you think HyperCard should be sending are, in fact, sent. In that case, you would set hideUnused to true for a time in the handler, and then set it to false. Since the Message Watcher captures only the last 150 messages, an unbridled capture of unused messages may make the stream of messages that is important to you scroll off before you can halt the process to view the message history.

For more on these options and the Message Watcher window, see Chapter 48.

Examples:

```
set the hideUnused of window "Message Watcher" to false
set hideIdle of window "Message Watcher" to hideUnused ¬
    of window "Message Watcher"
```

You Try It: Type the following commands into the Message Box, and watch the results after each command:

```
show window "Message Watcher"
set hideUnused of window "Message Watcher" to false
set hideIdle of window "Message Watcher" to false
set hideIdle of window "Message Watcher" to true
hide window "Message Watcher"
```

id <integer>

name <window name>

number <integer>

2.1

Purpose: Read-only properties to help scripts control windows.

When to Use Them: All windows—palettes, picture windows, and card windows alike—have these three properties, which help your scripts make sure they address the desired window for commands (such as Hide and Show).

Of the three properties, the name property is the least reliable, because HyperCard allows more than one window at a time to have the same name. Even though they may not always be visible, the following palette domain windows are always open:

Message Watcher	Message
Variable Watcher	Tools
Scroll	Patterns
FatBits	

plus whatever stacks and non-windoid picture windows are also open (there is always at least one card window open). Card windows bear the name that appears in the card window's titlebar; picture windows bear the name of the file or resource containing the picture.

Windows also have numbers, based on the layered order. All palette-domain windows (e.g., Message, Tools, Variable Watcher, palette domain picture windows) are grouped together, while all card windows and non-windoid picture windows are grouped together. Within each group, the lowest numbered window is the frontmost window. To view the order of all open windows at any time, type the following command into the Message Box:

```
answer the windows
```

By far the most accurate way to refer to a window is via its ID, an integer unique to the set of windows open at any time. Unlike other HyperCard object IDs, however, the ID of any window may be different from session to session (the number comes from deep within HyperCard, and is generated by the Mac toolbox when the window is created in memory). But as you open each new card or non-windoid picture window (both are in the card layer), you can quickly get the ID of window number 8 (assuming that only HyperCard's palette windows are open) and assign the ID value to a variable for use elsewhere in the script.

Examples:

```
get the name of window 12
set id of window "Home"
```

You Try It: Open two or three stacks in separate windows, and display both the Message Box and Tools palette. Type the following command into the Message Box:

```
answer the windows
```

Notice how the Message Box is the first window in the list. Click on the Browse tool and press Return to issue the command again. Notice how the Tools window, which you clicked last, is not number 1.

Jot down the list of windows, and then type the following commands into the Message Box:

```
name of window 1
get id of window "Tools"
it -- internal id
hide window id it
show window id it
show window "Patterns"
set loc of window "Patterns" to 250,150
name of last window
name of window 8
```

left <integer>

top <integer>

right <integer>

bottom <integer>

topLeft <point>

bottomRight <point>

botRight <point>

width <integer>

height <integer>

Purpose: To retrieve or set specific coordinate dimensions of a button, field, or window.

When to Use Them: While the Rect property allows you to derive and set the coordinates of the top left and bottom right corners of an object's rectangular area (in item form, as in 45,100,250,300), extracting one coordinate takes extra programming. Similarly, finding the width or height of an object in pixels requires programming some calculations on those coordinates. The properties in this section provide shortcuts to obtaining or setting whatever elements of coordinates you need.

Changing any coordinate property (left, top, right, bottom, topLeft, bottomRight, botRight) does not affect the size of the object. In other words, if the Rect of a button is 100,100,200,200, and you change the topLeft to coordinate 0,0, then the bottomRight coordinate will also change to follow the topLeft. In this example, the new rect of the button would be 0,0,100,100. The size of the button didn't change, just its location on the screen.

Adjusting the width or height of a button or field is possible by setting the width and height properties of those objects. All adjustments are performed from the center of the object. Therefore, if you double the width of a button, its center point (its Loc) stays the same, but both sides extend in equal direction. Similarly, shrinking an object brings its sides closer to the unchanging center point.

2.1

The exception to this rule is setting the width and height of card windows. Any reduction to the width of a card window comes from the right side; reduction to the height comes from the bottom. Adjustments to the card window affect only the size of the view to the card (and all other cards in the stack). To adjust the size of the card, see the Rect property of cards.

Of all these properties, the only ones that will complain if you try to set these for fixed size windoids are the width and height properties. Since the Tool, Pattern, Message and Scroll windows are all of a fixed size, their width and height properties may only be retrieved, but not altered.

While you may set the arguments to these properties to negative numbers or to numbers greater than the number of pixels on your screen, be careful not to move a windoid out of view. You may not find it again until you restart HyperCard (or not at all for a card window, which remembers its properties). While there may be valid reasons to positioning an object off the screen, it is usually better to hide an object you don't wish to see.

Examples:

```
get topLeft of field "Name"
set width of bkgnd button "OK" to 100
set height of bg btn 2 to 2 * height of bg btn 2
set bottomRight of msg window to 512,342
set width of cd window to 250
```

You Try It: On a fresh card in the Practice stack, create a new card button. Also, show both the Tools and Scroll palettes. Then, type the following messages into the Message Box.

```
put topLeft of card button 1 into field 3
put bottomRight of card button 1 into line 2 of field 3
put rect of card button 1 into line 3 of field 3
set height of cd btn 1 to 3 * height of cd btn 1
set width of cd btn 1 to height of cd btn 1
set topLeft of cd btn 1 to 50,50
topLeft of tool window
set topLeft of tool window to 256,171
get topLeft of card window -- original spot
set topLeft of card window to 100,100 -- wild on 9" monitor
set topLeft of card window to it -- restore location
get width of card window
set width of card window to 100 -- check Scroll window
set width of card window to it
```

loc[ation] <point>

Purpose: Controls the top left corner point of a window' content region.

When to Use It: You may get and set the location of any window on the screen, using that window's coordinate system. When you get the location of a window, HyperCard returns (into It) the coordinates of the top left corner of the window's content region (just below the grey title bar). To place the window somewhere else on the screen, simply set the location to a different set of coordinates. Coordinate parameters, which list the horizontal measure first, must be separated by a comma.

Because the Message, Tools, Patterns, and Scroll window coordinates are relative to the card window, it is possible to specify coordinates outside the card window. For example, a Tools palette dragged above and to the left of the card window will have negative numbers for both figures of the window's location. You may set the location of any of these windows beyond what might be visible on the screen. On a 9-inch Macintosh screen containing a full-screen card window, for instance, if you set the location of the Message Box to 30,750, the Message Box won't be visible at all. It will be visible, however, on a much larger display, like the Apple two-page or portrait monitors.

Setting the location of a window does not influence whether the window is visible. Therefore, you may set the location of a window, like the Message Box, without showing it first on the screen.

Examples:

```
get the location of card window
get the location of Tool Window
set the loc of Pattern Window to 200,70
set the loc of Msg to 25,310
set the loc of card window to 0,0
```

You Try It: Type the following messages into the Message Box in any stack:

```
get the loc of msg
it
show tool window
get the loc of tool window
it
subtract 25 from item 1 of it
set the loc of tool window to it
hide tool window
the loc of card window
```

nextLine <expression>

Purpose: Appends text to a new line at the bottom of text in the Message Watcher window. This write-only property is unique to the Message Watcher.

When to Use It: The Message Watcher window, when visible, tracks the names of messages sent in the course of script execution. As an additional debugging tool, you may set the nextLine property of the Message Watcher window to place a user-defined string in the list of messages captured in the window. This helps in case you cannot tell from the list of messages where execution is going. Since the text you write to the Message Watcher can be any expression, you may write the results of any functions (HyperCard or user-defined) or the contents of any container to the Message Watcher as signals for you to trace in the window. For example, you can use the Ticks function to display timings of various segments of handlers.

The text is written to the Message Watcher window at the same indentation as the other messages in the same handler. If you wish the next message to appear on its own line, append a return character after the <expression> parameter.

See Chapter 48 for more information about the Message Watcher.

Examples:

```
set nextLine of "Message Watcher" to "Point A" & return
set nextLine of "Message Watcher" to the ticks & return
```

You Try It: An artificial way to watch the results of setting this property is to show the Message Watcher, and set the property from the Message Box. In doing this, you'll see a lot of messages (lots of keyDown messages), which you don't normally see in script executions. But the point is, you'll see the expression at the end of the list. Type the following messages into the Message Box:

```
mw -- Message Watcher shortcut
set nextLine of "Message Watcher" to "howdy"
```

owner <owning application or XCMD>

Purpose: Reveals the application or XCMD that created a window.

When to Use It: This read-only property comes in handy when a script needs to verify that a particular window is the one it expects. For example, if a card window and picture window have the same name (and you don't know their IDs), you could cycle through all open windows to find which one is owned by HyperCard and which one is owned by Picture (the XCMD):

```
put empty into windowId
repeat with x = number of windows down to 1
   if owner of window x = "Picture" then
      put id of window x into windowId
      exit repeat
   end if
end repeat
if windowId is not empty
then set loc of window id windowId to 10,10
```

In this example, we count from high to low, because non-windoid picture windows are among the higher-numbered document layer windows, so we don't have to repeat through all the palette windows.

Examples:

```
get owner of window "Home"
get the owner of last window
```

You Try It: Open the Home and Addresses stacks in separate windows. Then type the following messages into the Message Box:

```
picture "navigator",resource -- an XCMD
owner of window "Home"
owner of last window
owner of window "Tools"
owner of window "Message Watcher" -- an XCMD
owner of window "navigator"
```

Close the "navigator" window when you're finished.

rect[angle] <left>,<top>,<right>,<bottom>

Purpose: Reveals and controls the top left and bottom right coordinates of a window.

When to Use It: For all windows except the card window, the Rect property cannot be set, because the sizes of those four windows are fixed within HyperCard. You can, however, get their screen coordinates if it is important for you to make sure they don't overlap each other or some graphical element on your screen when the windows appear.

You may get and set the rectangle coordinates of a card window. Setting the card window rectangle is the same as resizing the window in the Stack Info dialog box.

The rectangle coordinates returned by the *get rect* command (the coordinates go into It), are in the form *left,top,right,bottom*—four numbers separated by commas. You are free to perform calculations on any item in the coordinates. For example, if you determine that the bottom right corner of a window will overlap a special graphics area on a card by 15 pixels in the horizontal plane, then you can subtract 15 from the first item in It, delete the last two items, and set the location of the window to It.

Examples:

```
get the rectangle of Message Box
get the rect of Tool Window
set the rect of card window to 0,0,512,342
set the rect of window "Variable Watcher" to 20, 20, 100, 200
```

You Try It: Since this is a read-only parameter for the four windoid style windows, the following experiment lets you find the current coordinates of the four windows. Type these messages into the Message Box in any stack:

```
get the rect of Message
it
get the rect of Tool Window
it
get the rect of Pattern Window
it
the rect of Scroll Window
```

Now we'll try the card window:

```
put the rect of card window into startRect
get startRect
it
subtract 100 from item 3 of it
set rect of card window to it
set rect of card window to 20,20,200,200
set rect of card window to startRect
```

scroll <left>,<top>

Purpose: Controls the scrolling of a card within a card window set smaller than the card's rectangle.

When to Use It: This property is useful only if the size of the card window (*Rect of the card window*) is smaller than the size of the card (*Rect of the card*). This means that you could scroll within the card window to see the rest of the card, either manually (Command-Shift-E-and-drag) or with the aid of the Scroll window.

The scroll point is the coordinate point (relative to the card) of the top left corner of the visible area. In other words, when you are viewing the upper left corner of a card through a window, the point is 0,0, because that's the upper left corner of the viewing area. If you scroll the window 20 pixels horizontally, the upper left corner of the viewing area is at point 20,0.

If you try to set the scroll to a value beyond the scrollable range of the current card and window setup, HyperCard sets the scroll to the maximum value.

An interesting use for this property is the idea of creating a very large card; then program navigation buttons to move the scroll of the window around the large card to bring different areas into view (this might be in lieu of flipping cards). Another possibility is for those cases in which you suspect your users may be using smaller monitors than the cards you create. If you want the user to start out at the upper left corner of the card, set the scroll of the card window to 0,0 in an openStack or openCard handler.

Examples:

```
get the scroll of card window
set the scroll of card window to 513,0
```

You Try It: Before working with the origin property, we'll adjust the window size of the Home stack. Type the following commands into the Message Box:

```
put rect of card window into startRect
set rect of card window to 0,0,200,200
scroll of cd window -- should be 0,0
set scroll of cd window to 30,0
set scroll of cd window to 0,0
set scroll of cd window to 0,30
set scroll of cd window to 0,0
set scroll of cd window to 30,30
set scroll of cd window to 300,300
scroll of cd window -- maximum values
set rect of cd window to startRect
```

visible <true or false>

Purpose: Controls the visibility of a window.

When to Use It: The Visible property is more likely to be used with the Get command than the Set command, because it is quicker to type the shorter Hide and Show commands into a script. In practice, it will be more efficient for your script to simply hide or show a window regardless of its current visibility state. To test for whether a window's visible property is true or false will be a waste of HyperTalk's time. There is no penalty for hiding a window that is already hidden.

Examples:

```
get the visible of msg
set the visible of tool window to true
set the visible of window "Message Watcher"
```

You Try It: Although it's a lot more typing than the Hide and Show commands, type the following Visible property messages into the Message Box in any stack:

```
get the visible of msg
it
set the visible of tool window to true
set the visible of tool window to false
set the visible of msg to false
set the visible of msg to true -- can you type blind?
```

zoomed <true or false>

Purpose: Controls whether a document layer window is centered and expanded to maximum viewable size in the current monitor.

When to Use It: When you click the zoom box in the upper right corner of a card window, HyperCard expands the window as far as it can, and centers the window on the primary screen. At that point, the card window's zoomed property is true. By setting this property of a card window to true, a script performs the same action as clicking the zoom box.

The zoom box is a toggle between that centered position and one other location to which the window was moved. Setting the property to false positions and sizes the window at that other setting.

Examples:

```
get the zoomed of card window
set zoomed of card window to true
```

You Try It: In any stack, use the Scroll palette to shrink the current card window. Also drag the window to a corner of the screen. Then type the following message into the Message Box:

```
set zoomed of cd window to not zoomed of cd window
```

Press the Return or Enter key several times to see the window toggle between its two zoomed states. Click the zoom box to see the same behavior.

Painting Properties

When your scripts invoke the painting tools to draw graphics on cards, you will probably need access to various painting properties. These are the settings largely contained in the Options menu, which applies to all tools, and in the font dialog box, which applies to the text tool only. Virtually everything you can set manually can also be set from a script, giving your scripts the ability to work as fully as a human operator could.

brush <brush number 1 to 32>

Purpose: Controls the brush shape for the Paintbrush tool.

When to Use It: Prior to dragging the brush from one point to another, you may wish to choose a brush shape other than the default round dot. Setting this property to one of the thirty-two possible brush shapes is the same as clicking on one of the shapes in the brush shape dialog box.

In that dialog box are graphic representations of all brush shapes in a 12 × 8 table. Each brush shape has a number assigned to it from 1 to 32. The numbering starts at the top left corner and works its way down the first column. The brush shape at the top of the second column from the left is number 5. Unless you change the brush shape, the default setting is shape number 8. Use the Set command to set the Brush property to the desired shape.

Examples:

```
get the brush
set the brush to 12
set the brush to 8
```

You Try It: To see the effect setting the Brush property has, you can leave the cursor anyplace on a card and type the following messages into the Message Box. Watch the cursor change with each command.

```
choose brush tool
set the brush to 1
set the brush to 32
set the brush to 9
set the brush to 8
choose browse tool
```

centered <true or false>

filled <true or false>

Purpose: Controls the Options menu settings Draw Centered and Draw Filled.

When to Use Them: Both the Draw Centered and Draw Filled commands apply to drawing shapes with the Rectangle, Round Rectangle, and Oval tools. Draw Filled also applies to the Curve, Regular Polygon, and Irregular Polygon tools. If your scripts are about to invoke any of these tools for drawing, consider whether you want the drawing to be from a centerpoint or filled with a pattern. Bear in mind that setting the Filled property to true causes HyperCard to paint with the currently selected pattern. If you prefer a different pattern, then adjust the Pattern property (see below).

Examples:

```
get the centered
set the centered to true
get the filled
set the filled to false
```

You Try It: The simplest way to watch these properties react to the Get and Set commands is to select any paint tool and pull down the Options menu after each command to see how the checkmark settings in the menu are affected. When the property is set to true, the item is checked in the menu, even though it was turned on by command rather than by menu selection. Type the following messages into the Message Box and inspect the Options menu after each command.

```
choose rect tool
get the centered
it
set the centered to true
get the centered
it
set the filled to true
```

grid <true or false>

Purpose: Controls the painting Grid.

When to Use It: Turning on the Grid from a script may make sense if you're not sure that the coordinates you assign to the drag commands are completely accurate. With the Grid in force, the shapes will be drawn to the nearest 8-pixel square, assuring that shapes will be aligned to the invisible grid.

When a script turns on the Grid, the Grid item in the Options menu is checked, just as if you had turned it on with a menu selection.

Examples:

```
get the grid
set the grid to false
```

You Try It: Pull down the Options menu after typing each of the following lines into the Message Box. Watch the check mark next to the Grid menu item.

```
choose pencil tool
set the grid to true
set the grid to false
set the grid to true
choose browse tool
```

lineSize <line thicknesses 1, 2, 3, 4, 6, or 8 pixels>

Purpose: Controls the thickness of lines painted by various tools.

When to Use It: Prior to dragging any tool that leaves a line (except the single-pixeled Pencil), consider adjusting the LineSize property. This is the same as selecting from the line size dialog box. If you don't adjust the LineSize property, the default setting is one pixel line thickness.

Examples:

```
get the lineSize
set the lineSize to 3
```

You Try It: Because the crosshair cursor for all tools that draw with lines of varying thicknesses adjusts itself to the thickness of the LineSize property, you may watch the cursor get fat and thin with the typing of the Message Box messages below.

```
choose rect tool
set the lineSize to 2
set the lineSize to 3
set the lineSize to 8
get the lineSize
```

```
it
set the lineSize to 1
choose browse tool
```

multiple <true or false>

multiSpace <1 to 9>

Purpose: Controls the Draw Multiple menu option and the number of pixels between multiple images.

When to Use Them: By setting the Multiple property to true, you turn on the Draw Multiple item in the Options menu. This setting applies to drawing shapes with tools like the Rectangle, Round Rectangle, Oval, and Regular Polygon tools. A script may also adjust the spacing between multiple drawings by setting the MultiSpace property to a number from 1 to 9. The number represents the number of pixels between each of the multiple shapes left in the wake of the tool.

Examples:

```
get the multiple
set the multiple to true
set the multiSpace to 5
```

You Try It: Create a new card in the Addresses stack in which you can experiment with drawing multiple shapes. After each Set MultiSpace command below, drag the chosen paint tool to see the effects.

```
choose round rect
set the multiple to true
set the multiSpace to 1
set the multiSpace to 4
set the multiSpace to 8
choose browse tool
```

pattern <pattern number 1 to 40>

Purpose: Controls the currently selected pattern.

When to Use It: Filling areas with patterns and drawing filled patterns are both possible from scripts. Before you can do either, however, you must set the desired pattern by way of the Pattern property.

Each of HyperCard's forty patterns has an identifying number based on its location in the Patterns palette. This palette displays samples of the patterns in four columns of ten patterns. Numbering starts with 1 at the upper left corner and works its way down the leftmost column. The pattern at the top of the second column from the left is pattern number 11.

To fill an existing enclosed region from a script, first set the pattern. Then choose the Bucket tool and issue the Click At command, specifying a pixel coordinate someplace inside the enclosed region.

Examples:

```
get the pattern
set the pattern to 12
```

You Try It: Type the following messages into the Message Box in any stack, and watch the pattern palette change with each setting of the pattern property.

```
show pattern window
get the pattern
it
set the pattern to 1
set the pattern to 25
set the pattern to 40
hide pattern window
```

polySides <number of polygon sides greater than two >

Purpose: Controls the number of sides drawn by the Polygon tool.

When to Use It: The Regular Polygon tool lets the HyperCard author select from a palette of six standard polygons with 3, 4, 5, 6, 8, and infinite sides. Whatever number of sides is selected is stored in the PolySides painting property. The minimum number of sides allowed is 3. You can set polySides to 12 to make a dodecagon. The problem with polygons with too many sides, however, is that the resolution of the Macintosh screen limits your ability to distinguish sides. After about fifteen sides, the objects look like circles.

Just as you set the number of polygon sides before dragging a regular polygon tool, so too do you set the PolySides property in a script before the Drag command.

Examples:

```
get the polySides
set the polySides to 8
```

You Try It: Type the following messages into the Message Box. After each Set polySides command, drag a polygon on a blank card to see how the number of sides looks.

```
choose reg polygon tool
get the polySides
it
set the polysides to 2 -- 3 is the minimum
```

```
set the polysides to 12
set the polysides to 20
set the polysides to 5
choose browse tool
```

textAlign <left | right | center>

textFont <font name>

textHeight <leading>

textSize <font size>

textStyle < bold | italic | underline | outline | shadow | condense | extend | plain>

Purpose: Controls font attributes of text painted with the Text tool.

When to Use Them: These five properties all represent settings in the font dialog box you can adjust when typing text with the painting Text tool. This gives you full control over the way painted text appears when a script types it into a card or background graphics layer.

Parameters to each of the properties should be self-explanatory in the list above, since the terms should be familiar to you by this point. When you set the TextSize property, HyperCard automatically sets the TextHeight (leading) property to approximately one-third again as large. If the default leading is acceptable, you won't have to adjust the TextHeight property. The TextStyle property may have any number of the parameters listed as possible styles. Simply list them as comma-separated parameters to the textStyle property.

Examples:

```
get the textHeight
set the textFont to New York
set the textSize to 14
set the textHeight to 16
set the textAlign to center
set the textStyle to condense, underline
```

You Try It: Type the following messages into the Message Box in a blank card of any stack. After a Set message, type a few words of paint text to see the results of the new setting. To type the next command, click the text insertion cursor inside the Message Box and press the Clear key to remove the previous message.

```
choose text tool
get the textFont
it
```

```
set the textFont to Chicago
set the textAlign to right
set the textStyle to underline, extend
set the textFont to Geneva
set the textSize to 9
set the textStyle to plain
choose browse tool
```

Stack, Background, and Card Properties

In this section we cover properties for stacks, backgrounds, and cards because these three objects share many properties in common. For each property, we'll identify which objects it applies to.

cantAbort <true or false>

Purpose: Controls whether the user may abort a script by typing Command-period.

Object: Stack.

When to Use It: There are many instances in which it is important to prevent a user from stopping a script in progress. This occurs primarily in self-running applications that run unattended in locations where everyday folks access information in the stack. Aborting a script in progress can disrupt the flow of the program and put it into a state that makes it unusable for the next person. By setting CantAbort to true, you disable the built-in HyperCard facility of stopping any script in progress by typing Command-period.

This is a dangerous property to set if you are still constructing your stack, because it gives you, as author, no way of stopping an accidentally runaway script. The setting remains in effect even if you close the stack.

Examples:

```
set cantAbort of this stack to true
set cantAbort of stack "Preferences" to false
```

You Try It: One way to see how frustrating it will be to set CantAbort to true and not be able to stop a script is to try it in a button script. Create a card button on a blank card of any stack, and enter the following script:

```
on mouseUp
    -- set cantAbort of this stack to true
    repeat with x = 1 to 1000
        put x
    end repeat
end mouseUp
```

With the CantAbort line commented out, click the button, and stop the handler with Command-Period when you tire of seeing numbers increase in the Message Box. Next, remove the comment hyphens from the script, and click the button. No matter what you do—short of turning off or restarting the Mac with the Reset Switch or performing a System 7 Force Quit (Command-Option-Escape)—you won't be able to stop the script. Fortunately, this is a finite loop, and the handler stops after 1000 cycles.

cantDelete <true or false>

Purpose: Controls whether an object can be deleted.

Objects: Stack, Background, Card.

When to Use It: This property allows you to perform from HyperTalk the same action as checking or unchecking the Cant Delete checkbox of a card, background (in their respective info dialog boxes), or stack (in the Protect Stack dialog). This property for any given object is either True (locked) or False (delete-able).

Any handler that creates a new stack or background should probably set the CantDelete property to true for that new object, unless it is a transient object. Cards need be protected only when the deletion of a particular card would be catastrophic, as in a single card containing scripts that perform special calculations.

A handler may turn off CantDelete if it is safe to free up an object for deletion either by the handler or the user. Change this property only in controlled situations—in which deletion of objects is either under control of the handler or the user will be prevented from accidental deletion of a crucial stack, background, or card. Any protected object presents a dialog box alerting the user to the fact that he or she can't delete the protected object.

Examples:

```
get cantDelete of this stack
set cantDelete of card 2 to true
set cantDelete of this bkgnd to false
```

You Try It: In any stack, set the CantModify property of the stack, background and any card. Then check the Protect Stack, Background Info, and Card Info dialog boxes to see the results in the Can't Delete checkbox settings. Try setting the CantDelete property of another, distant card in the same stack. Then go to that card and inspect the setting of the Can't Delete box of the Card Info dialog box.

cantModify <true or false>

Purpose: Controls whether a stack can be modified.

Object: Stack.

When to Use It: This property governs whether a particular stack may be changed by the user—including whether the stack may be deleted or compacted. When the CantModify property is set to true, the stack is locked. You can recognize a locked stack in a couple ways. First, the HyperCard menubar acquires a small padlock icon to the right of the rightmost menu title. Second, if you pull down the File menu, the Delete Stack and Compact Stack items are dimmed, indicating they are not available. The same is true for most of the Edit menu. Third, if you choose Protect Stack in the File menu, the Protect Stack dialog box indicates that the stack may not be modified.

When you set cantModify to true, cantDelete is also set to true. Conversely, when you set cantModify to false, cantDelete is also set to false, with one exception: If CantDelete is set to true *before* the CantModify property is adjusted, CantDelete is not affected when CantModify is set to false.

This property is cognizant of the condition of the stack. Therefore, if the stack resides on a locked disk (including CD-ROM) or is locked on an AppleShare network file server, then you may not set the CantModify property. In other words, the condition of the file outside of the control of HyperCard determines whether the property may be set.

Even when CantModify is set to true, a HyperTalk script may put text into fields, create fields and buttons, set field and button scripts, and draw pictures with the Painting tools. All changes you make with this property set to true are canceled the instant you close the card. Therefore, if you frequently rest HyperCard at a card that displays the current time (like the Home Card), you can reduce the wear and tear on your hard disk by setting CantModify to true when this card opens. The HyperTalk script will dutifully update the time, but the change won't be written to the disk each minute. And since it isn't important for the proper time to be in that field when you're not in the card, it's okay to discard changes when leaving the card.

Examples:

```
get cantModify of this stack
set cantModify of stack "Address" to true
```

You Try It: In any stack, type the two following lines into the Message Box, one at a time.

```
set cantModify of this stack to true
set cantModify of this stack to false
```

After each setting, notice the condition of the padlock icon in the HyperCard menubar. Also pull down the File menu to check the condition of the Protect Stack dialog box. Compare the states of the File and Edit menu items under both settings

cantPeek <true or false>

Purpose: Controls whether the user may peek at buttons and fields with the Command-Option and Command-Option-Shift key combinations

Object: Stack.

When to Use It: Experienced HyperCard users know about peeking at buttons and fields, and they often do it to examine the handiwork of other HyperCard authors. Peeking, especially at buttons, offers those who know the technique a quick way to discover where all buttons may be, including transparent buttons atop graphics that might not look immediately like buttons. Educational and childrens' stacks often encourage exploration by clicking on graphical objects. A stack's author may consider this method of finding the buttons almost cheating.

If you turn on the CantPeek property, the user will not be able to take a shortcut to see where buttons and fields are. This assumes, of course, that you also prevent the user from accessing the button and field tools, which grant immediate access to those objects. This property does not affect the availability of Command-Option shortcut keys to object scripts—sometimes called "peeking at scripts."

Examples:

```
get the cantPeek of this stack
set cantPeek of this stack to true
```

You Try It: After typing each of the following commands into the Message Box, try peeking at the buttons and fields:

```
set cantPeek of this stack to true
set cantPeek of this stack to false
```

freesize <bytes>

size <bytes>

Purpose: Reveals the amount of free space in the stack file and HyperCard's stack size on the disk (in bytes), respectively.

Object: Stack.

When to Use Them: These two properties are the same numbers that appear in the Stack Info dialog box as Free in Stack and Size of Stack. Size is the total size of the data and resource forks, while freeSize indicates the amount of disk space that can be recovered with compacting the stack. Unlocked stacks tend to grow larger than the exact amount of disk space required for the file, primarily for the sake of improved disk performance. But when a stack changes radically, such as after deleting objects or modifying object properties, the amount of free space in the stack file may grow quite large in proportion to the stack size.

While it is good practice to compact frequently changing stacks from time to time, you can also program the stack to compact itself upon closing when the FreeSize function returns a value that is excessive, like 25 percent of the stack size. After compaction (i.e., the next time the stack opens), performance will probably improve somewhat. Here is one way to carry out this idea:

```
on closeStack
    if freeSize of this stack ≥ size of this stack / 4 then
        put "Compacting stack..."
        doMenu "Compact Stack"
        put empty
        hide msg
    end if
end closeStack
```

This tidies up the stack whenever it closes and the FreeSize gets too big. These properties are read-only—you may not set them.

Examples:

```
put freeSize of this stack
put freeSize of this stack / size of this stack into bloatFactor
get size of stack "Address"
```

You Try It: You can try these properties from the Message Box. Look into the sizes of the current stack or any stack of your choosing. Compare the values with the reports in the Stack Info dialog box.

id <id number>

Purpose: Reveals the unique identifying number for the object.

Objects: Background, Card.

When to Use It: The ID of an object is a read-only property. HyperCard assigns the ID when it creates a background or card. While the other two ways of referring to an object (name and number) can change by various means, the ID number never changes. If a background or card is deleted, that ID number will not be assigned to another background or card. Also, the range of ID numbers applies to each object. Therefore, a background and a card may both have the same ID number, but because references to the ID property must contain a background or card expression (e.g., ID of card 39), there is never interference between the two.

You may extract three different versions of the ID property depending on modifiers you attach to the request. Here are examples of the syntax and their results:

```
id of this card
card id 2876
short id of this card
2876
long id of this card
card id 2876 of stack "HD-120:HyperCard Stacks:Home"
```

If you place the plain ID of an object into a container, you may then go to that object in a script with a simple Go command. Here is an example of the sequence:

```
get id of card "Invoice"
-- other stuff that may rename or sort cards
go to it
```

Both the plain ID and short ID of an object assume the current stack. The long ID includes the name of the stack containing the object. If you ask HyperCard to go to a card or object in a specific stack, and you are already in that stack, there is no error.

Examples:

```
put long id of this card into startCard
get id of background 2
get short id of card "Lesson 1"
```

You Try It: Type the following messages into the Message Box while at the Home card:

```
id of this card
short id of this card
```

```
long id of this card
get id of this bkgnd
it
set id of this card to 947 -- can't set this property
```

marked <true or false>

Purpose: Controls whether a card is marked for printing or navigation.

Object: Card.

When to Use It: When HyperCard marks or unmarks a card with the Mark and Unmark commands, it is actually setting the Marked property of an affected card. Therefore, if a Mark command is to mark all cards whose "Active Client" checkbox is checked, it sets the Marked property of those cards to true.

If a card is marked, it allows for quicker navigation to selected cards, with commands such as:

```
go to next marked card
```

Also, HyperCard's printing facilities let you print marked cards and reports from marked cards. These actions essentially check the Marked property of every card to see if data should be printed.

By giving you access to the Marked property, you can mark cards within a script other than with the Mark command. Setting the Marked property gives you more precise control over which card or cards are to be marked, including the option of marking cards that meet different criteria based on your scripts' observations or calculations of the current card's data.

Examples:

```
get the marked of this card
set marked of this card to hilite of bkgnd button "Active"
set marked of card "Summary" to true
```

You Try It: In the Addresses stack, type the following messages into the Message Box, and observe the results:

```
unmark all cards
set marked of this card to true
set marked of card 4 to true
go to next marked card
go to next marked card
go to next marked card
unmark all cards
```

name <object name>

Purpose: Controls the name of the object.

Objects: Stack, Background, Card.

When to Use It: You may read or change the name of any stack, background, or card object by calling the name property for that object. In the case of retrieving the name of the current object, simply specify which object you want, as in get the name of this background. Following the convention of the Get command, HyperCard places the response in the It variable.

When an object has a name assigned to it (all stacks automatically have names), the response includes the type of object and the object's name, the latter enclosed in quotation marks. Therefore, getting the name of the Home stack would leave

```
stack "Home"
```

in It. If an object does not have a name assigned to it, HyperCard returns the type of object and its ID number in It, as in background id 30.

You may obtain a shortened or longer name for the object by specifying *short* or *long* before the name property, as in short name of bkgnd button id 12. The short name gives only the object's name. The Home Stack's short name, for instance, is simply Home, without any quotation marks around it. The long name, on the other hand, gives you the position of the stack, background, or card in the HyperCard universe. A named card in a named background would return a long name property like this:

```
card "Set Up Card" of stack "HD-120:HyperCard Stacks:My Stack"
```

All named objects may have their name changed from a script by setting the name property to a new name. This also goes for stack files.

Examples:

```
get the name of this card
set the short name of background to "Forms 1"
get the long name of stack
```

You Try It: Type the following messages into the Message Box while at the Home Card:

```
name of this stack
short name of stack
long name of stack
get the name of this background
it
```

```
set the name of background to "Home Background"
name of background
name of prev card
name of card 5
```

number <number in sequence of like objects>

Purpose: Reveals the order of the object relative to similar objects.

Objects: Background, Card.

When to Use It: The number of an object is a read-only property. To change the order of backgrounds or cards within a stack, you must use other methods, such as the Sort command, to shuffle them. Because so many user actions can affect the order of cards (e.g., sorting, adding a new card, deleting a card), use this property carefully.

This property cannot tell you the ranking of a card within a certain background of a multiple background stack—a card has a number relative to the beginning of the *stack* only. If cards are grouped within their own backgrounds, however, you can calculate the location of the current card within the background (in case you need a counter, "Card 4 of 20," in a second background). Here's a script you can use:

```
put (number of this card - number of first card of this bkgnd) + 1 into cardCount
put "Card" && cardCount && "of" && number of cards of this bkgnd
```

The Number property returns only the number, regardless of modifier (short, long, abbrev).

Examples:

```
put number of this card into startCard
get number of background 2
get number of card "Lesson 1"
```

You Try It: Type the following messages into the Message Box while at the Home card:

```
number of this card
go next
number of this card
go next
number of this card
```

owner <bkgnd name or id>

2.1

Purpose: For cards, reveals the name (when available) or ID of the background to which the card belongs.

Object: Card.

When to Use It: This read-only property lets a script verify that a particular card is part of the desired background. Multiple cards from different backgrounds may have the same name or be shuffled after a sort. By checking the owning background, your script can branch accordingly.

If the owning background has a name, that information is returned from this property; otherwise the background ID is returned. Moreover, the values come in the same three varieties as name properties. The following table demonstrates the possibilities:

property	*named background ("Main")*	*unnamed background (ID 200)*
short owner	"Main"	bkgnd id 200
owner	bkgnd "Main"	bkgnd id 200
long owner	bkgnd "Main" of ¬ stack "HD:HC:Test Stack"	bkgnd id 200 of ¬ stack "HD:HC:Test Stack"

For application in scripts, the short version is recommended, as in:

```
if short owner of card 1 ≠ "Main"
then sort stack by bkgnd id
```

This script makes sure the first card is part of the "Main" background (perhaps after a sort of a different kind). If it isn't, then the stack is resorted by bkgnd ID (assuming "Main" has the lowest ID among all the stack's backgrounds).

Examples:

```
get owner of card "Table of Contents"
get owner of this card
```

You Try It: Open the Home stack, and then type the following message into the Message Box:

```
answer owner of this card
```

Use the right arrow key to visit each card of the stack, and press Enter or Return to view the owner of each card.

rect[angle] <left>,<top>,<right>,<bottom>

Purpose: Controls the rectangle of the card size for the stack.

Object: Card.

When to Use It: The Rectangle property of a card is different from the Rectangle property of a card window. Whereas the card window is the size of the viewing area, the card size is the active area on which we can place graphics, fields, and buttons. A card's Rectangle property is the one set by the Card Size part of a New Stack dialog box (also the Resize dialog box from the Stack Info dialog). This might get a bit confusing, because while the property is a card property, it actually affects the whole stack. The card's Rectangle property defines the card size for all cards in the stack.

A card's Rectangle property coordinates are measured relative to the rectangle of the card window. Card Rectangle properties always have 0,0 as the top left point. You may, however, resize the card's rectangle on the fly in a script. The hazard in doing this, however, is that if you have graphical elements in a background or card picture layer, those elements clipped by shrinking the card will be lost (buttons and fields are not lost), even if you grow the card rectangle later.

When to Use It:

```
get the rect of this card
set the rect of this card to 0,0,288,200
```

You Try It: Create a new, blank stack with a card size of a 9-inch Macintosh screen. Draw some graphics in the background so that every quadrant contains some art. Also add a few buttons and fields spread across the card. Now type the following messages into the Message Box:

```
put rect of this card into startRect
set rect of this card to 0,0,600,480
    -- scroll around on 9" monitor
set rect of this card to 0,0,352,210
set rect of this card to startRect
    -- outer graphics are gone!
```

reportTemplates <list of report templates>

Purpose: Reveals the names of report templates saved in a stack.

Object: Stack.

When to Use It: To reduce the possibility that your stack users may be confused by the Print Report dialog, you may wish to provide a friendlier front-end to your stack's report printing, particularly if you have prepared a number of report templates for your users. A separate card (or other device, such as an external window created with third-party tools like WindowScript) can display a list of all available templates in the stack. Use this property to derive that list for the users. The users may then select the template name, and the script can open report printing with that template.

Examples:

```
get the reportTemplates of this stack
get reportTemplates of stack "Addresses"
```

You Try It: Open the Addresses stack, choose Print Report from the File menu, and examine the long list of pre-formatted reports in the stack. Then close the stack and go to the Practice stack. Type the following command in the Message Box:

```
put reportTemplates of stack "Addresses" into field 2
```

script <object's script>

Purpose: Controls scripts from within a script.

Objects: Stack, Background, Card.

When to Use It: A remarkable feature about HyperTalk and the HyperCard structure is that scripts are self-modifiable. That means that a script may open any script (including itself) and make changes. A HyperCard author, therefore, may make some requests of the user the first time the user opens the stack and insert those preferences into scripts. The stack will be fully customized for the preferences of that user. A well-crafted HyperTalk script might even be designed so that it learns its user's habits and adjusts its scripts accordingly. The potential for self-modifying scripts is enormous.

When running a handler, HyperCard actually runs from a copy it stores temporarily in memory. That's how a script can modify itself without conflict.

Using the Get and Set commands with the script properties of stacks, backgrounds, and cards (as well as buttons and fields, below), one script can reach into another script and put any kind of text into that script. The procedure would be to first put the script from the object into a variable. Make all necessary adjustments to the script, and then set the object's script to the contents of the variable.

Examples:

```
get the script of this stack
set the script of card to empty
```

You Try It: To experiment with getting and setting a script, first create a new card in the Addresses stack. Then open its Script Editor and enter the following script:

```
on mouseUp
    beep 2
end mouseUp
```

Close the Script Editor and click once anywhere on the card (except in a text field). HyperCard should beep twice. Now type the following messages into the Message Box:

```
get the script of card
it -- all three lines are in It
put "flash 3" into line 2 of it
set script of this cd to it
```

Now click on the card. Since you replaced the beep with flashes, the beep instructions are no longer there. Open the card's script to see the changes.

scriptingLanguage <language name>

2.2

Purpose: Controls the language used for an object's script.

Objects: Stack, Background, Card.

When to Use It: The script of any object may be in any language installed in your system. The HyperTalk language is built into your copy of HyperCard. But you may also have additional scripting languages installed, such as AppleScript, installed as Open Scripting Architecture components (see Chapter 56). Your choices are normally visible in the popup menu at the top of every script editor window.

For the most part, you won't be setting the scriptingLanguage property of an object that already has a script in it. But if your script dynamically creates an object and assigns a script to it, you may need to change this property. The values are the straight text names, as presented in the script editor popup menus.

Examples:

```
get scriptingLanguage of this card
set scriptingLanguage of last card button to "AppleScript"
```

You Try It: Create a blank card in the Addresses stack, and type the following messages into the Message Box:

```
answer scriptingLanguage of this card
set scriptingLanguage of this card to "AppleScript"
```

Open the card's script, and notice that the Language popup menu has changed its value.

```
set scriptingLanguage of this card to "HyperTalk"
```

Open the card's script again, and see the change.

showPict <true or false>

Purpose: Controls the visibility of a background or card picture layer.

Objects: Background, Card.

When to Use It: While you can show and hide pictures in both the card and background domains by the Hide and Show commands, you may also set the showPict property of a card or background. The setting is either true or false. The availability of the property also lets you check for the condition of the picture at any given moment.

One reason to use this method of hiding and showing a picture is to reduce the length of a handler that toggles the picture on and off. For example, using the Hide and Show commands, the long way would be to use a combination of the ShowPict property and the commands, as in

```
on mouseUp
    if showPict of this card is true
    then hide card picture
    else show card picture
end mouseUp
```

This entire process may be sped up considerably by using the Boolean nature of the property—setting the property to the opposite of what it currently is, as in

```
on mouseUp
    set showPict of this card to not showPict of this card
end mouseUp
```

Therefore, if the current condition is true, the opposite of it is false (i.e., not true). You can set the property to what it currently is not.

Examples:

```
get showPict of this card
set showPict of bkgnd 2 to true
set showPict of card "Calculator" to false
```

You Try It: Use a blank card in the Addresses stack to draw some card-domain picture with the Painting tools. Then type the following messages into the Message Box:

```
set showPict of this bkgnd to false
set showPict of this bkgnd to true
set showPict of this card to false
set showPict of this card to not showPict of this card
```

With the last message in the Message Box, press Return several times, and notice how the card picture toggles on and off with each sending of this message.

Field Properties

Every field you create has dozens of properties that can be adjusted from a script. Most of these properties will be familiar to you as the settings in the Field dialog box and the Font dialog box you can reach from it.

autoSelect <true or false>

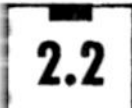

Purpose: Controls whether a locked field will automatically select clicked lines.

When to Use It: A field that is locked (i.e., lockText property set to true) lets the user click on the text. Nothing happens visually, however, when the click occurs. When you set this property to true (the same as checking the Auto Select button in the field's info dialog), the field selects (highlights) the entire line on which the user clicks. The field is then known as a *list field.* Setting this property to true also sets the dontWrap property to true, because you want lists to display each line of text as a single horizontal string of characters, even if the line extends beyond the right margin of the field. Setting the autoSelect property to false, however, does not automatically set the dontWrap property to false, because it is possible to have a field whose text doesn't wrap, while autoSelect is off.

Examples:

```
get the autoSelect of field 4
set autoSelect of field "Phone List" to true
```

You Try It: In the Practice stack, create a new card, and enter several lines of numbers or words into the top right field. Turn the field into a list field with these Message Box commands:

```
set lockText of field 5 to true
set autoSelect of field 5 to true
```

Click on various lines of the field to observe how the selection behaves. Then type the following message into the Message Box:

```
set autoSelect of field 5 to false
```

The field is still locked and dontWrap is set to true, but the automatic selection doesn't work. When you're finished, open the field's info dialog box, and uncheck Lock Text and Don't Wrap.

autoTab <true or false>

Purpose: Controls whether the user advances the text pointer from field to field with the Return key.

When to Use It: The AutoTab property corresponds to the Auto Tab setting in a Field Info dialog box. Because this property is primarily a concern of the person creating a stack, the property will rarely be changed in the course of running a completed stack. This is one property that should remain consistent for any given field while a user is entering information into a card.

Still, it is possible you'll need access to this property in a HyperTalk script. For instance, if you have created a series of fields in a new background and discovered that you forgot to set the Auto Tab checkbox in the fields, you can write a quick handler that sets the property for every field in the card. That handler would be

```
on fixIt
  repeat with x = 1 to the number of bkgnd fields
    set autoTab of bkgnd field x to true
  end repeat
end fixIt
```

This changes the AutoTab properties to all fields in the blink of an eye.

Examples:

```
get autoTab of field "Name"
set autoTab of field 3 to true
```

You Try It: From any stack, type the following message into the Message Box:

```
set autoTab of field 1 to true
```

Bring up the Field Info dialog box for that field to see the checkbox setting. Close the dialog and type the following into the Message Box:

```
set autoTab of field 1 to false
```

Reopen the dialog to see that the checkbox is now unchecked.

dontSearch <true or false>

Purpose: Controls whether a field is available for searching via the Find command.

When to Use It: The dontSearch property is the one controlled by the Don't Search checkbox in the Field Info dialog box. When this property is true, the Find command doesn't look at the text in this field during searches. Use the Set command to adjust this property when creating a new field from a script or setting a series of fields to be ignored for a Find command under script control. Unless you have a specific reason to let the Find command look for text in hidden fields, it is best to set the dontSearch property of hidden fields to true.

Examples:

```
get the dontSearch of field 4
set dontSearch of field "Code" to true
```

You Try It: In the Addresses stack, turn on the dontSearch property for the Name field with this Message Box command:

```
set dontSearch of field 1 to true
```

and try to search for a friend's name. You may still search for a telephone number, however. When you're finished, type this command into the Message Box:

```
set dontSearch of field 1 to false
```

so you may resume finding friends' names as before.

dontWrap <true or false>

Purpose: Controls whether text in a field wraps when a HyperCard line extends beyond the physical length of the field.

When to Use It: The default setting of a new field is to allow text to wrap (the dontWrap property is set to false). This should be the normal method of allowing users to enter running text in a field.

It becomes imperative to turn off word wrapping when lines of text are entered into a list in a field—a list that the user is likely to click on for navigation purposes. If a long line of text wraps, then the formatting and integrity of the line listing may suffer. By letting longer text flow off the right edge of the field, you make sure that each HyperCard line (one that ends with a return character) is on its own physical line as well. Setting the autoSelect property to true (which turns a locked field into a list field) automatically sets the dontWrap property to true.

Examples:

```
set dontWrap of field "Table of Contents" to true
set the dontWrap of field 1 to not the dontWrap of field 1
```

You Try It: Enter a long line of text in the first field of any card that displays multiple line fields. Then type the following messages into the Message Box while watching the text closely:

```
set dontWrap of field 1 to true
set dontWrap of field 1 to false
```

fixedLineHeight <true or false>

Purpose: Controls whether the line height of a field's text changes when the user modifies the font size of selected text.

When to Use It: As described in the chapter about fields, turning on the fixedLineHeight property prevents changes in a field's line spacing whenever a user chooses font sizes larger or smaller than the size specified in the field's font dialog box. It is unlikely that a script would change this once a field has been in use, but if your script generates a new field, and you wish to turn on the fixedLineHeight feature, then this is the property to set to do the equivalent of clicking the fixedLineHeight checkbox in the field dialog.

Examples:

```
get fixedLineHeight of field 3
set fixedLineHeight of last bkgnd field to true
```

You Try It: On a blank card in the Addresses stack, create a new card field that shows several lines. Type text into all lines of field 2, and change the font and increase font size of a few words in the second line. Now type the following messages into the Message Box, and observe how the appearance of the text in the field changes:

```
set fixedLineHeight of cd field 1 to true
set fixedLineHeight of cd field 1 to false
```

id <id number>

Purpose: Reveals the unique identifying number for the field.

When to Use It: The ID of a field is a read-only property. HyperCard assigns the ID when it creates a field. While the other two ways of referring to a field (name and number) can change by various means, the ID number never changes. If a field is deleted, that ID number will not be assigned to another field. Also, the range of ID numbers applies only to fields within one domain. Therefore, a background field and card field may both have the same ID number, but because references to the ID property must contain a background field or card field expression (e.g., ID of card field 4), there is never interference between the two domains.

There is only one variety of field ID (just the number, itself), even though HyperCard accepts modifiers (e.g., long, short).

Examples:

```
put id of field 4 into anchorField
get id of background field 2
```

You Try It: Type the following messages into the Message Box while at the Home card:

```
id of field 1
long id of field 1 -- same result
id of last field
```

left <integer>

top <integer>

right <integer>

bottom <integer>

topLeft <point>

bottomRight <point>

botRight <point>

width <integer>

height <integer>

Purpose: To retrieve or set specific coordinate dimensions of a button, field, or window.

When to Use Them: See discussion for these properties in the "Window Properties" section, above.

loc[ation] <left>,<right>

Purpose: Controls the center point coordinates of a field.

When to Use It: Unlike the location property of windows, the field Location property monitors the centerpoint of the field.

You have to be careful, however, when getting the location of the field to click the Browse tool as a means of setting the text insertion pointer flashing in a particular field for the user. If the field is a multiple-line field, the Click command will end up placing the text insertion pointer in a line other than the first line. In fact, that action will place return characters in every line above the insertion pointer (see the Rectangle property for a way around this).

You may set the Loc of a field to the result of a function. For example, to make a locked field follow the cursor around the screen, put the following handler in the field script:

```
on mouseStillDown
    set the loc of me to the mouseLoc
end mouseStillDown
```

The center of the field tracks the cursor as long as the mouse button is pressed.

Examples:

```
get the location of field id 4312
set loc of field 1 to 32,145
```

You Try It: Go to the Addresses stack and create a new card field on any card in the stack with the New Field menu command. Adjust its attributes to be a rectangle style and check the Show Lines box. Choose the Browse tool, and enter some text into the field. You'll use this field for other experiments about field properties below. Now type the following messages into the Message Box:

```
get loc of card field 1
it
add 50 to item 1 of it
set the loc of card field 1 to it
click at it
```

lockText <true or false>

showLines <true or false>

wideMargins <true or false>

Purpose: Controls the locked field, visible line, and wide margin features of a field.

When to Use Them: Authors of stacks whose contents are intended only for reading may wish to lock the fields after the text is typed into those fields. The HyperCard Help stacks, for instance, have locked fields, because it would not be particularly helpful for a user to change—intentionally or accidentally—the contents of the help cards.

If your stacks consist of many fields, you, as stack author, may hasten the locking and unlocking of all possible fields in the stack by writing a script that finds each background or card field, and changes the setting of the lockText property for every field:

```
on lockem
    repeat with x = 1 to number of bkgnd fields
        set lockText of field x to true
    end repeat
end lockem
```

Remember that when you lock a field, the Browse tool, when atop the field, remains as the hand, and the field can respond to mouse-related system messages.

The showLines and wideMargins properties are also available for setting from scripts. It is more likely that authors will modify these settings in the course of their stack development than in scripts the user will ever use, except when user scripts create new fields.

Examples:

```
get lockText of card field 4
set showLines of field "Text 1" to false
set wideMargins of field 3 to true
```

You Try It: Using the sample card field from the last experiment, place the Browse tool atop the field and watch it change as you type the following messages into the Message Box. Also watch other attributes of the field and text inside the field change with the commands.

```
set lockText of card field 1 to true
set lockText of card field 1 to false
set showLines of card field 1 to false
set wideMargins of card field 1 to true
```

multipleLines <true or false>

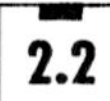

Purpose: Controls whether a list field allows multiple-line selections with the Shift key held down.

When to Use It: The multipleLines property is the same one selected with the Multiple Lines checkbox in a Field Info dialog. While the property may be set to either true or false at any time, it plays its role only when the field is set up as a list field (i.e., lockText, dontWrap, and autoSelect properties are all true). When this property is true, the user may select multiple lines in a list field by holding down the Shift key while clicking on various lines in the field. HyperCard allows only contiguous line selections.

Examples:

```
get the multipleLines of field 4
set multipleLines of field "My List" to true
```

You Try It: In the Practice stack, create a new card, and enter several lines of numbers or words into the top right field. Turn the field into a list field with these Message Box commands:

```
set lockText of field 5 to true
set autoSelect of field 5 to true
```

With the Shift key held down, click on various lines of the field to observe how the selection behaves. Then type the following message into the Message Box:

```
set multipleLines of field 5 to true
```

Shift-click again on the field, and notice how multiple lines are selected. When you're finished, open the field's info dialog box, and uncheck Lock Text, Don't Wrap, and Auto Select.

name <field name>

Purpose: Controls the name of the field.

When to Use It: You may read or change the name of any field by summoning the Name property for that field. Simply specify which field you want by field number or ID, as in name of field 4. If the field is a card domain field, the domain name must be part of the field name (for example, card field "Names"). Following the convention of the Get command, HyperCard places the response in the It variable.

When a field has a name assigned to it, the response includes the type of object and the object's name, the latter enclosed in quotation marks. Therefore, getting the name of a background field called "Address" would leave

```
bkgnd field "Address"
```

in It. If a field does not have a name assigned to it, HyperCard returns card field ID x or bkgnd field ID x in It.

You may obtain a shortened or longer name for a field by specifying *short* or *long* before the name property, as in get short name of field id 12. The short name gives only the object's name. The short name of the above example field, for instance, is simply Home, without quotation marks. The long name, on the other hand, gives you the position of the field in the HyperCard universe. A named field in a named background would return a long name property like this:

```
bkgnd field "Address" of card id 2388 of stack ¬
"HD-120:HyperCard Stacks:Addresses"
```

A named field may have its name changed from a script by setting the Name property to a new name.

Examples:

```
get name of field 1
set name of card field id 20 to "Special"
put the name of field id 9887 into field 2
```

You Try It: Type the following messages into the Message Box while in the Addresses stack.

```
name of field 1
name of field 2
set name of field 2 to "Say What?"
name of field 2
set name field 2 to "Telephone"
```

number <number in sequence of fields in the same domain>

Purpose: Reveals the order of the object relative to fields in either the card or background domains.

When to Use It: The number of a field is a read-only property. To change the order of fields within a stack, you must use other methods, such as the Bring Closer or Send Farther commands, to shuffle them.

The Number property returns only the number, regardless of modifier (short, long, abbrev).

Examples:

```
put number of cd field "Note" into noteNumber
get number of bg field 2
get number of field "Title"
```

You Try It: Type the following messages into the Message Box while in the Addresses stack:

```
number of field "Name"
number of field "Telephone"
```

partNumber <number in sequence of objects in the same domain>

2.2

Purpose: Reveals the order of the object relative to all field and button parts in either the card or background domains.

When to Use It: Adjusting the layer of a field by setting its partNumber is the fast, scriptable way that obviates the need for repeated issuing of the Bring Closer or Send Farther commands. HyperCard also lets you obtain the number of parts in either domain, which provides a shortcut for making a part the topmost part (the one with the highest number):

```
set partNumber of card field "Note" to number of card parts
set partNumber of bkgnd fld "Miscel." to number of bg parts
```

Examples:

```
get partNumber of bg field "Address 1"
set partNumber of field "Name" to 1
```

You Try It: Create a new card in the Practice stack, make three card fields (shadow style), and overlap portions of them so you can see how they layer. Then type the following messages into the Message Box:

```
partNumber of card field 2
set partNumber of card field 1 to 3
set partNumber of card field 2 to 3
```

rect[angle] <left>,<top>,<right>,<bottom>

Purpose: Controls the size and location of a field relative to the card window.

When to Use It: Because every field maintains information about the coordinates of its upper left and bottom right corners, you can retrieve those properties or set them in a script. Notice that because the coordinates are those of the Macintosh screen, you can both resize and move a field by one setting of the Rect property.

When you get the Rect property, HyperCard places four coordinate numbers into It. They represent the horizontal and vertical measures of the top left corner and the same for the bottom right corner. Each number is separated from others by a comma. When you set coordinates for the Rect property, the coordinates must be in this comma-separated format.

Get the Rect property of a multiple-lined field to find the location of the top left corner for clicking the text pointer at the top of the field. The experiment below shows you how to manipulate the property information in a variable to make the Click command work the way you expect.

Examples:

```
get rect of field "Entry"
set rect of field id 53819 to 34,150,134,250
```

You Try It: Create a shadow style card field on a blank Addresses stack, and type the following messages into the Message Box:

```
put the rect of card field 1 into myRect
delete item 4 of myRect
delete item 3 of myRect
click at myRect
set the rect of card field 1 to 20,20,100,300
```

script <field script>

Purpose: Controls a field script from within a script.

When to Use It: Using the Get and Set commands with the Script properties of fields, a script can reach into a field script and put any kind of text into that script. The procedure would be similar to that outlined for modifying stack, background, or card scripts, above.

Examples:

```
get the script of field id 43387
set script of field "Record Number" to empty
set the script of this background to the script of this stack
```

You Try It: To experiment with getting and setting a script, go to the Home stack and type the following messages into the Message Box:

```
put "on mouseUp" & return into scriptMaker
put "go next" & return after scriptMaker
put "end mouseUp" after scriptMaker
set the script of field 1 to scriptMaker
set the lockText of field 1 to true
```

Click on the card's title field. That field now has a script in it that instructs HyperCard to advance to the next card in the stack each time you click on the field. And that was done completely without opening the Script Editor to that field. Open the Script Editor to see the results of your handiwork.

scriptingLanguage <language name>

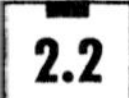

Purpose: Controls the language used for a field script.

When to Use It: The script of any field may be in any language installed in your system. The HyperTalk language is built into your copy of HyperCard. But you may also have additional scripting languages installed, such as AppleScript, installed as Open Scripting Architecture components (see Chapter 56). Your choices are normally visible in the popup menu at the top of every Script Editor window.

For the most part, you won't be setting the scriptingLanguage property of a field that already has a script in it. But if your script dynamically creates a field and assigns a script to it, you may need to change this property. The values are the straight text names, as presented in the Script Editor popup menus.

Examples:

```
get scriptingLanguage of field "Name"
set scriptingLanguage of last card field to "AppleScript"
```

You Try It: Create a blank card in the Addresses stack, and type the following messages into the Message Box:

```
answer scriptingLanguage of field 1
set scriptingLanguage of field 1 to "AppleScript"
```

Open the script of field 1, and notice that the Language popup menu has changed its value. Type the following into the Message Box:

```
set scriptingLanguage of field 1 to "HyperTalk"
```

Open the field script again, and see the change.

scroll <pixels>

Purpose: Controls the number of pixels a scrolling field has scrolled from the top of the text.

When to Use It: Each time a card with a scrolling field in it appears on the screen, its natural tendency is to display text starting with the first line. That may not be the desired effect for your card and stack design. By setting the Scroll property of a scrolling field, you can automatically advance the text further down the block.

The parameter to the Scroll property is the number of pixels from the very top of the text. If the position of scrolled text is to be saved for each card for the next time it comes into view, retrieve the current Scroll amount and store the value in a hidden field in the course of a closeCard message handler. In an openCard handler should be a corresponding Set command to restore the previous scrolled location.

Examples:

```
put the scroll of field "Description" into field "placeHolder"
set the scroll of field "Description" to 3 * the textHeight of field "Description"
```

You Try It: Create a new card field of any size and style on a blank Addresses stack card. Enter several lines of text into the card field such that the text runs below the bottom of the field. Then type the following messages into the Message Box.

```
set the rect of card field 1 to 100,100,250,200
set the style of card field 1 to scrolling
put the scroll of card field 1 into message
set scroll of card field 1 to 20
set scroll of card field 1 to 120
```

selectedLine[s] <chunk expression>

selectedText <text>

Purpose: Reveals the selection within a list field.

When to Use Them: (First of all, we offer our apologies to syntax purists, who will point out that what we call field properties here are, in truth, HyperTalk functions. The functions' behaviors, however, are far easier to understand in terms of field properties—which is how we refer to them in this section.)

List fields maintain their selections apart from other text selections on a card. Therefore, it is possible for the highlighted selection of a clicked line in a list field to persist even when a user selects text in an unlocked field. Moreover, the various text selection functions (Chapter 40) don't recognize a list field's selection as one of its "global" card selections. The selected-Line[s] (the "s" is optional) and selectedText properties let your script pick up the chunk expression of selected line(s) or the actual selected text in a list field.

The chunk expression returned for the selectedLine property is always a range of lines, even if only one line is selected. The following values are typical of those returned by this property:

```
line 3 to 3 of bkgnd field 6 -- one line
line 2 to 6 of bkgnd field 6 -- five lines
```

To obtain the actual text that has been selected, use the selectedText property. Its value is a return-delimited list when multiple lines are selected.

All fields have these properties, although only list fields make any use of them. Still, if a field is a list field at some time in its life, with some text selected in it, those values stay with the field, even if it becomes an unlocked field with no apparent selection. Both properties are read-only, and both return *empty* if there is no selection as a list field. To pre-select a line for the user, use the Select command, as in:

```
select line 3 of bkgnd field 2
```

And to clear a list field selection, use:

```
select line 0 of bkgnd field 2
```

Examples:

```
get the selectedLines of card field 4
get selectedLine of field "My List"
get selectedText of field "Report Formats"
```

You Try It: In the Practice stack, create a new card, and enter several lines of numbers or words into the top right field. Turn the field into a list field with these Message Box commands:

```
set lockText of field 5 to true
set autoSelect of field 5 to true
```

Temporarily, enter the following handler into field 5's script:

```
on mouseUp
    put selectedLines of me into temp
    put return & selectedText of me after temp
    answer temp
end mouseUp
```

Click and shift-click on various lines to see the results of the selection and the values returned by these two properties. When you're finished, open the field's info dialog box, and uncheck Lock Text, Don't Wrap, and Auto Select. Also remove the script from the field.

sharedText <true or false>

Purpose: Controls whether a background field's text is seen on every card of a background.

When to Use It: The SharedText property is the one controlled by the Shared Text checkbox of the Field Info dialog box. When turned on (set to true), you may enter text into that field (while in the background editing mode only) that will be visible on all cards of the background. With SharedText turned on, the field is not editable except in the background editing mode.

Shared text is of particular importance for those applications that will be translated into other languages. Place text for titles in a shared field rather than in the background graphic layer. When the stack is translated, the translator (localizer) will be able to change text for card and field titles without having to delete old art and fit new art to the space.

It is unlikely that you'll change this property from a script (other than as a stack author to change the property on bunch of fields), but remember that if you turn off SharedText, the user may enter information into the field for each card. By turning the SharedText property on and off under script control, you can toggle between a card-specific entry in the field and the shared text.

Examples:

```
get the sharedText of field "Title"
set the sharedText of field 3 to not the sharedText of field 3
```

You Try It: An experiment for this property is best done in a new stack of several cards. In this stack, create at least one background field, and check the Shared Text button in the Field Info dialog box. In the background editing mode, enter some text into the field. Choose the Browse tool, and type the following messages into the Message Box:

```
go next card -- same text
set sharedText of field 1 to false -- it's now editable
go next card
go first card
set sharedText of field 1 to true -- shared text comes back
```

style < transparent | opaque | rectangle | shadow | scrolling >

Purpose: Controls the field style.

When to Use It: Just as you manually adjust the style of a field in the Field Info dialog box, so can a script make the style adjustment by setting the style property. Parameters to the style property are the same style names that you find in the dialog box. Scripts that generate new fields for a user would be likely candidates for setting this property. The new field procedure might start with a doMenu "New Field" command, which brings up the default, transparent style. If the new field is supposed to be a rectangle field, the style of that new button would be set to "rectangle."

Examples:

```
get style of field 3
set style of card field id 4 to shadow
set style of field "ZIP" to transparent
```

You Try It: Use the card field from previous experiments in the Addresses stack, and watch the changes to the field after you type each of the following messages into the Message Box.

```
put the style of card field 1 into priorSetting
set style of card field 1 to shadow
set style of card field 1 to scrolling
set style of card field 1 to priorSetting
```

textAlign <left | right | center>

textFont <font name>

textHeight <leading>

textSize <font size>

textStyle < bold | italic | underline | outline | shadow| condense | extend | group | plain>

Purpose: Controls font attributes of a field.

When to Use Them: These five properties represent settings in the font dialog box you normally see by clicking the Font button in a Field Info dialog box. These properties give you full control over the way text appears in a field of your choice.

Parameters to each of the properties should be self-explanatory in the list above, since the terms should be familiar to you by this point. When you set the TextSize property, HyperCard automatically sets the TextHeight (leading) property to approximately one-third again as large. If the default leading is acceptable, you won't have to adjust the TextHeight property. The TextStyle property may have any number of the parameters listed as possible styles. Simply list them as comma-separated parameters to the TextStyle property.

You may also apply these properties to portions of text within a field. For example the following handler

```
on idle
    if the selection is not empty
    then set textStyle of the selectedChunk to bold
    pass idle
end idle
```

bold faces any text you select in a field on the card. Changing text attributes of a chunk within a field does not change the default text attributes of the field itself. When the receipient of these property settings is just a field expression (not a chunk expression), then the field's properties are affected.

Examples:

```
get textHeight of field id 9808
set textFont of field "Day 1" to Chicago
set textSize of card field 2 to 10
set textHeight of field id 1212 to 12
set textAlign of field id 1212 to right
set textStyle of field id 1212 to outline
```

You Try It: Use the card field from the previous experiments and type the following messages in the Message Box.

```
get textFont of card field 1
it
set textFont of card field 1 to New York
set textAlign of card field 1 to center
set textStyle of card field 1 to bold
set textFont of card field 1 to Geneva
set textSize of card field 1 to 9
set textStyle of card field 1 to extend, underline
```

visible <true or false>

Purpose: Controls the visibility of a field.

When to Use It: The Visible property is more likely to be used with the Get command than the Set command, because you can hide and show fields with the shorter Hide and Show commands. In practice, it will be more efficient for your script to simply hide or show a field regardless of its current visibility state. To test for whether a field's visible property is true or false would be a waste of HyperTalk's time. There is no penalty for hiding a field that is already hidden.

Examples:

```
get visible of field id 12
set visible of field "Help" to true
```

You Try It: Although it's a lot more typing than the Hide and Show commands, type the following Visible property messages into the Message Box in the stack and card you used for the other experiments in this section. When you're finished with the experiment, delete the card field.

```
visible of card field 1
set visible of card field 1 to false
visible of card field 1
show card field 1
```

Button Properties

Most properties of buttons are like those of fields, except for the special items that buttons, alone, have, such as their checkbox settings. You can also make changes to button text properties, which you cannot make from the Button Info dialog box.

autoHilite <true or false>

showName <true or false>

Purpose: Controls the highlight and name features of a button.

When to Use Them: If your scripts create new buttons for the user, you'll want to make adjustments just as you would from the Button Info dialog box. The Auto Hilite and Show Name settings are check-box settings in the Button Info dialog box. By setting these properties to true, the script does the same as checking these items.

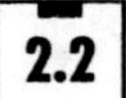

If you assign a button (most likely a radio button) to a family of buttons (with a family number greater than zero), the autoHilite property of that button is automatically set to true. That's because HyperCard takes over the highlighting of buttons within the family, unhighlighting all others when one is clicked.

Examples:

```
get autoHilite of button id 43
set showName of background button 1 to true
```

You Try It: For all experiments in this section, create a card button in any card of any stack you like. Use the New Button menu option to create the button, and leave the default settings the way they are. Now type the following messages into the Message Box.

```
put the showName of button "New Button" into msg
set showName of button "New Button" to false
set autoHilite of button "New Button" to true
    -- click on the button now
set showName of button "New Button" to true
```

left <integer>

top <integer>

right <integer>

bottom <integer>

topLeft <point>

bottomRight <point>

botRight <point>

width <integer>

height <integer>

Purpose: To retrieve or set specific coordinate dimensions of a button.

When to Use Them: See discussion for these properties in the "Window Properties" section, above.

enabled <true or false>

Purpose: Controls whether a button is active or not.

When to Use It: At various times within a stack design, it may be appropriate to prevent a user from clicking a particular button or group of buttons. In the realm of Macintosh user interface guidelines, the buttons should either be hidden from view or dimmed and inactive. This feature of HyperCard buttons is controlled by the Enabled property.

The default value for new buttons is for the Enabled property to be true. When the property is set to false, the button remains visible, but is dimmed (or "greyed-out"). The user may click on the button, but no system messages are sent to the button to trigger scripts or highlighting. If your stack changes the Enabled property for a bunch of buttons at one time, it is best to lock the screen prior to changing the property. The user then sees all buttons change their appearance at once.

As an alternative to setting the property directly, you may also use the Enable and Disable commands to perform the same action with a bit more script readability.

Examples:

```
get enabled of card button "Settings..."
set enabled of bg btn 2 to false
```

You Try It: Go to the Practice stack, and type the following message into the Message Box:

```
set enabled of bg btn 3 to false
```

Try clicking the disabled right arrow button. Now type:

```
set enabled of bg btn 3 to true
```

The right arrow now works. Perform the same tests with buttons 1 and 5 to see how icons are treated when disabled.

family <family number 0 through 15>

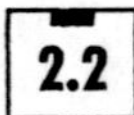

Purpose: Controls or reveals the family to which a button belongs.

When to Use It: The Family popup menu in a button info dialog box lets you assign the button to any of 15 families. For the sake of good interface design, this property should apply primarily to radio buttons, but it could also work well with a set of icon buttons that act like radio buttons (e.g., tool selectors). Use this property to detect in a script to which family a particular button belongs, if that information is necessary for your script. It is unlikely that a script would change the family of a button once it is established by the author, but a stack that creates a series of linked buttons on the fly would need to set the properties of each button.

To remove a button from its family, set the property to zero.

Examples:

```
get the family of bkgnd button 3
set family of last card button to 1
```

You Try It: Go to the Practice stack, and type the following message into the Message Box:

```
set family of bg btn 1 to 5
```

Open the left arrow button's info dialog, and notice that the Family popup menu has changed its value. Close the dialog, and restore the original value:

```
set family of bg btn 1 to 0
```

Open the button's dialog, and see the change.

hilite <true or false>

Purpose: Controls highlighting of a button.

When to Use It: You'll get and set hilite property of a button most often when you're in the checkbox and radio button styles. When a radio button is highlighted, it has a black dot in its center; when a checkbox is highlighted, it has an X in its box.

You may wish to highlight other button styles, depending on the function of the button and stack design. For example, if a card features a row of buttons, each of which links to a stack with a special function, you may want that stack's button to be highlighted when you are in that particular stack. The extra visual feedback reinforces in the user's mind which of the special function stacks he is in.

Examples:

```
get hilite of bkgnd button 1
set hilite of button "Choice 1" to true
```

You Try It: Choose the button tool and double-click on the new button used in the previous experiment. Change the style to the radio button style and return to the Browse tool. Now type the following messages into the Message Box to see how the hilite settings influence this style of button.

```
set hilite of button "New Button" to true
set hilite of button "New Button" to false
```

icon <icon number or name>

Purpose: Controls which icon art is attached to a button.

When to Use It: When a script creates a new button, it can assign an icon graphic to the button and turn the button into an icon button all at once by setting up the icon property with a valid icon number or name. Just as in the Button Info dialog box the entry of an icon number both assigns the art and makes the button an icon button, so too does the icon property influence a button from a script. An icon setting of zero removes icon art from the button and terminates the button's designation as an icon button.

The icon resource must be available to the current stack by being in the stack, Home stack, or other stack added to the message hierarchy. If you specify a name or number not available, HyperCard displays a blank space where the icon usually goes.

If your script is changing a button to an icon button, chances are that the button will also have to be resized to accommodate the art. The default new button size is usually not tall enough to show the entire icon graphic.

Examples:

```
get icon of button id 40
set icon of bkgnd button "Help" to 25002
set icon of bkgnd button "Help" to "Med Help"
```

You Try It: Since the new button you've been experimenting with will not be tall enough to accept icon art, select the button with the Button tool and adjust it so that it is approximately one inch square. Also open the button's dialog box to change the style to round rectangle. Then select the Browse tool and type the following messages into the Message Box.

```
put the icon of button "New Button" into message
set style of button "New Button" to round rect
set icon of button "New Button" to 1000
```

```
set icon of button "New Button" to 2002
set icon of button "New Button" to "Mac"
set icon of button "New Button" to 16735
```

id <id number>

Purpose: Reveals the unique identifying number for the button.

When to Use It: The ID of a button is a read-only property. HyperCard assigns the ID when it creates a button. While the other two ways of referring to a button (name and number) can change by various means (such as the Bring Closer command), the ID number never changes. If a button is deleted, that ID number will not be assigned to another button. Also, the range of ID numbers applies only to button within one domain. Therefore, a background button and card button may both have the same ID number, but because references to the ID property must contain a background button or card button expression (e.g., id of card button 4), there is never interference between the two domains.

There is only one variety of button ID (just the number, itself), even though HyperCard accepts modifiers (e.g., long, short).

Examples:

```
put id of button 4 into specialButton
get id of background button 2
```

You Try It: Type the following messages into the Message Box while at the Home card:

```
id of bg button 1
long id of bg button 1 -- same result
id of last bg button
```

loc[ation] <left>,<right>

Purpose: Controls the centerpoint coordinates of a button.

When to Use It: Like the Location property of fields, the button Loc property monitors the centerpoint of a button. By returning this location, you can make a script click in the center of the object with the Button tool to select the button. Then you can copy or cut the button into the Clipboard for later pasting on a different card or in a different stack.

You may set the Loc of a button to the result of a function. For example, to make a button follow the cursor around the screen, put the following handler in the button script:

```
on mouseStillDown
    set the loc of me to the mouseLoc
end mouseStillDown
```

The center of the button tracks the cursor as long as the mouse button is pressed.

Examples:

```
get the loc of button "Cancel"
set loc of field 1 to 200,150
```

You Try It: Type the following mouseUp handler into the Script Editor of the card button from previous button property experiments. Then click the button and watch what happens.

```
on mouseUp
    get loc of button "New Button"
    add 30 to item 1 of it
    set loc of button "New Button" to it
    choose Button tool
    click at it
    doMenu "Copy Button"
    go next card
    doMenu "Paste Button"
    go prev
    choose Browse tool
end mouseUp
```

name <button name>

Purpose: Controls the name of the button.

When to Use It: You may read or change the name of any button by summoning the Name property for that button. Simply specify which button you want by button number or ID, as in name of button ID 300. If the button is a background domain button, the domain name must be part of the field name (for example, bkgnd button "OK"). Following the convention of the Get command, HyperCard places the response in the It variable.

When a button has a name assigned to it, the response includes the type of object and the object's name, the latter enclosed in quotation marks. Therefore, getting the name of a background button called "Print Cards" would leave

```
bkgnd button "Print Cards"
```

in It. If a button does not have a name assigned to it, HyperCard returns card button id x or bkgnd button id x in It.

You may obtain a shortened or longer name for the object by specifying *short* or *long* before the name property, as in get short name of bkgnd button id 12. The short name gives only the object's name. The short name of the above example, for instance, is simply Print Cards, without any quotation marks around it. The long name, on the other hand, gives you the position of the button in the HyperCard universe. A named button in a named background would return a long name property like this:

```
bkgnd button "Help" of card id 30767 of stack ¬
"HD-120:HyperCard Stacks:Help"
```

A named button may have its name changed from a script by setting the name property to a new name.

2.2 The name of a popup menu style button becomes the label, or title, for the popup. We suggest assigning names ending in a colon, which makes the selected value in the popup menu appear as a value in a labeled field.

Examples:

```
get the name of button 3
set name of last bkgnd button to "Excel"
get name of button id 12123
set name of bkgnd btn 3 to "Style:"
```

You Try It: Use the card button from previous experiments in this section and type the following messages into the Message Box.

```
set name of button "New Button" to empty
get name of card button 1
it
set name of it to "Change"
```

number <number in sequence of buttons in the same domain>

Purpose: Reveals the order of the object relative to buttons in either the card or background domains.

When to Use It: The number of a button is a read-only property. To change the order of button within a stack, you must use other methods, such as the Bring Closer or Send Farther commands, to shuffle them.

The Number property returns only the number, regardless of modifier (short, long, abbrev).

Examples:

```
put number of cd button "Note" into noteButtonid
get number of bg btn 2
get number of bkgnd button "Home"
get number of card button id 3
```

You Try It: Type the following messages into the Message Box while in the Addresses stack:

```
number of bg button "Name"
number of bg button "Home"
```

partNumber <number in sequence of objects in the same domain>

Purpose: Reveals the order of the object relative to all field and button parts in either the card or background domains.

When to Use It: Adjusting the layer of a button by setting its partNumber is the fast, scriptable way that obviates the need for repeated issuing of the Bring Closer or Send Farther commands. HyperCard also lets you obtain the number of parts in either domain, which provides a shortcut for making a part the topmost part (the one with the highest number):

```
set partNumber of card button "Map..." to number of card parts
set partNumber of bkgnd btn "Next" to number of bg parts
```

Examples:

```
get partNumber of bg button "Home"
set partNumber of card btn "Previous" to 1
```

You Try It: Create a new card in the Practice stack, make three card buttons (roundRect style), and overlap portions of them so you can see how they layer. Then type the following messages into the Message Box:

```
partNumber of card btn 2
set partNumber of card btn 1 to 3
set partNumber of card btn 2 to 3
```

rect[angle] <left>,<top>,<right>,<bottom>

Purpose: Controls the size and location of a button relative to the card window.

When to Use It: Because every button stores information about the coordinates of its upper left and bottom right corners, you can retrieve those properties or set them in a script. Notice that because the coordinates are those of the Macintosh screen, you can both resize and move a button by one setting of the rect property.

When you get the Rect property, HyperCard places four coordinate numbers into It. They represent the horizontal and vertical measures of the top left corner and the same for the bottom right corner. Each number is separated from others by a comma. When you set coordinates for the rect property, the coordinates must be in this comma-separated format.

Examples:

```
get the rect of background button "Accept"
set rect of button id 802 to 15,300,65,330
```

You Try It: Use the card button from the previous experiments, and type the following messages into the Message Box:

```
get rect of button 1
subtract 10 from item 1 of it
add 10 to  item 3 of it
set rect of button 1 to it
```

script <button script>

Purpose: Controls a button script from within a script.

When to Use It: Using the Get and Set commands with the script properties of buttons, a script can reach into a button script and put any kind of text into that script. The procedure would be similar to that outlined for modifying field scripts, above.

Examples:

```
get script of button id 23
set the script of button "Cancel" to empty
```

You Try It: Use the previous card button, and type the following messages into the Message Box:

```
set script of button 1 to empty
put "on mouseUp"  & return & "beep 3" & return & "end mouseUp" into scriptHolder
set script of button 1 to scriptHolder
```

Click on the button. It should beep three times. Open the Script Editor to see the results of your handiwork.

scriptingLanguage <language name>

2.2

Purpose: Controls the language used for a button script.

When to Use It: The script of any button may be in any language installed in your system. The HyperTalk language is built into your copy of HyperCard. But you may also have additional scripting languages installed, such as AppleScript, installed as Open Scripting Architecture components (see Chapter 56). Your choices are normally visible in the popup menu at the top of every script editor window.

For the most part, you won't be setting the scriptingLanguage property of a button that already has a script in it. But if your script dynamically creates a buton and assigns a script to it, you may need to change this property. The values are the straight text names, as presented in the script editor popup menus.

Examples:

```
get scriptingLanguage of bg btn "Get Data"
set scriptingLanguage of last card btn to "AppleScript"
```

You Try It: Create a blank card in the Addresses stack, and type the following messages into the Message Box:

```
set scriptingLanguage of bg btn 1 to "AppleScript"
```

Open the script of the right arrow button, and notice that the Language popup menu has changed its value. Type the following into the Message Box:

```
set scriptingLanguage of bg btn 1 to "HyperTalk"
```

Open the button script again, and see the change.

selectedLine[s] <chunk expression>

selectedText <text>

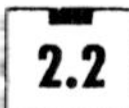

Purpose: Reveals the chosen item within a popup button.

When to Use Them: (Our apologies, again, about discussing these two HyperTalk functions as button properties, but they're easier to understand this way.) Popup style buttons regard their selected items as selections. For your script to determine the item within the popup menu that the user has selected, use either of these two properties.

The chunk expression returned for the selectedLine property refers to a single line of the contents of the button, such as:

```
line 3 of card button 3 -- one line
```

To obtain the actual text that has been selected, use the selectedText property.

All buttons have these properties, although only popup buttons make any use of them. Still, if a button is a popup button at some time in its life, with some item chosen, those values stay with the button, even if it becomes a radio button. Both properties are read-only, and both return *empty* if there is no selection. To pre-select an item for the user, use the Select command, as in:

```
select line 3 of bkgnd button 2
```

And to clear a pop-up button selection, use:

```
select line 0 of bkgnd button 2
```

Examples:

```
get the selectedLines of card button 4
get selectedLine of bg btn "Type:"
get selectedText of bg btn "Report Formats:"
```

You Try It: In the Practice stack, create a card button of the popup style. Enter several lines of words into the Contents field. Also enter the following handler into the button's script:

```
on mouseUp
    put selectedLines of me into temp
    put return & selectedText of me after temp
    answer temp
end mouseUp
```

Make selections in the popup button, and observe the returned values of these two properties. When you're finished, delete the button.

sharedHilite <true or false>

Purpose: Controls whether a background button (predominantly a checkbox or radio button style) maintains a highlight for single cards or for every card in the background.

When to Use It: Other than setting this property when creating a new background button from a script, it is unlikely you'll change the setting from a script. This setting is the same as the Shared Hilite checkbox in the Button Info dialog box. It applies only to background buttons.

When this property is turned on (true), the hilite for a button is displayed on all cards in that background. Therefore, a checkbox setting will appear on all cards. Turning this property off, however, lets the Hilite setting for each card be different. This is usually the preferred setting when radio and checkbox buttons are displayed on a series of cards, and their settings are unique for each card.

Examples:

```
get the sharedHilite of bkgnd button "Radio 1"
set sharedHilite of bkgnd button 3 to false
```

You Try It: The best way to experiment with this setting is to create a blank stack containing several cards and at least one background checkbox button. Then type the following messages into the Message Box:

```
set autoHilite of bg btn 1 to true
set hilite of bg btn 1 to true
go next card -- second card same as first
go next card
go first card
set hilite of bg btn 1 to false
set sharedHilite of bg btn 1 to false
set hilite of bg btn 1 to true -- or click on button
go next card -- second card different from first
go next card
go first card
```

style <transparent | opaque | rectangle | shadow | roundRect | checkBox | radioButton | ¬ standard | default | oval | popup>

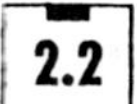

Purpose: Controls the button style.

When to Use It: Just as you manually adjust the style of a button in the Button Info dialog box, so can a script make the style adjustment by setting the Style property. Parameters to the Style property are the same style names that you find in the dialog box. Scripts that generate new buttons for a user would be likely candidates for setting this property. The new button procedure might start with a doMenu "New Button" command, which brings up the default, round rectangle style. If the new button is supposed to be a radio button, the style of that new button would be set to "radioButton."

Examples:

```
get style of button id 50989
set the style of bkgnd button 4 to transparent
set style of button "OK" to roundRect
```

You Try It: Use the card button from previous experiments and watch the changes to the button after you type each of the following messages into the Message Box.

```
get the style of card button 1
it
set style of button 1 to checkBox
set style of button 1 to radioButton
set style of button 1 to standard
set style of button 1 to default
set the style of button 1 to it
```

textAlign <left | right | center>

textFont <font name>

textHeight <leading>

textSize <font size>

textStyle < bold | italic | underline | outline | shadow | condense | extend | plain>

Purpose: Controls font attributes of a button's name.

When to Use Them: Although Button fonts can be set from the Font and Style menus (with a button selected), you can also modify them with these five text properties. The settings are the same as you normally find in a font dialog box.

Parameters to each of the properties should be self-explanatory in the list above, since the terms should be familiar to you by this point. TextAlign applies to all styles except checkboxes and radio buttons. When you set the TextSize property, HyperCard automatically sets the TextHeight property to approximately one-third again as large. Since button names can be only one line, however, the TextHeight property is not used. The TextStyle property may have any number of the parameters listed as possible styles. Simply list them as comma-separated parameters to the TextStyle property.

Examples:

```
set textFont of button id 3 to Chicago
set textSize of button "OK" to 10
set textAlign of bkgnd button 3 to right
set textStyle of button "Help" to italic, extend
```

You Try It: Use the card button from the previous experiments and type the following messages in the Message Box.

```
set icon of button 1 to zero
put the textFont of button 1 into message
set textFont of button 1 to Geneva
set textAlign of button 1 to right
set textStyle of button 1 to outline, extend
set textFont of button 1 to New York
set textSize of button 1 to 9
set textStyle of button 1 to italic
```

titleWidth <pixel count>

2.2

Purpose: Controls the width (in pixels) devoted to the title of a popup button.

When to Use It: If a script creates a new popup button, it can adjust the amount of space devoted to the button's title (to the left of the popup). Button info dialogs provide a field for entering a value, or you can drag the divider of the button with the Button tool. The value is in pixels, which is not easily convertible from the length of the button's name (which appears in the title). Therefore, this property gets tricky to set on the fly with a name supplied by the user.

Examples:

```
get titleWidth of bg btn "Report Format:"
set titleWidth of card button "Type:" to 41
```

You Try It: Create a blank card in the Addresses stack and a new card button of the PopUp style. Name it "Select:", and give it a starting Title Width of 60. Then type the following messages into the Message Box:

```
answer titleWidth of cd btn 1
set titleWidth of cd btn 1 to 50
```

Open the script of card button 1, and notice that the Title Width field has changed its value.

visible <true or false>

Purpose: Controls the visibility of a button.

When to Use It: The Visible property is more likely to be used with the Get command than the Set command, because you can hide and show buttons with the shorter Hide and Show commands. In practice, it will be more efficient for your script to simply hide or show a button regardless of its current visibility state. To test for whether a button's visible property is true or false would be a waste of HyperTalk's time. There is no penalty for hiding a button that is already hidden.

Examples:

```
get visible of background button 2
set visible of bkgnd button "Itinerary" to true
```

You Try It: Although it's a lot more typing than the Hide and Show commands, type the following Visible property messages into the Message Box in the stack and button you used for the other experiments in this section. When you're finished with the experiment, delete the card button.

```
visible of button 1
set visible of button 1 to false
visible of button 1
show button 1
```

From properties, we now move onto HyperTalk's built-in functions.

CHAPTER

37

INTRODUCTION TO HYPERTALK FUNCTIONS

In our discussions directed at HyperTalk authors so far, the two major areas we've been looking at are objects and commands. Commands are the first words in HyperTalk script lines. HyperTalk also contains many words in its vocabulary that let you retrieve information about internal system workings, like the clock and the location of the cursor on the screen, plus information about text in containers. At the same time, HyperTalk lets you perform many math operations, which end up coming in very handy, even if you tend to shy away from math. Finally, HyperTalk provides a number of predefined constants—plain words that stand in for important values your scripts need from time to time. The next eight chapters focus on all these items—elements that make up the balance of what most scripts require. About the only other knowledge you'll need to get rolling on HyperTalk scripts is information on how HyperTalk makes decisions in your scripts. We cover that in Chapter 46.

For now, we'll demonstrate all the other parts of HyperTalk that fill out your scripts. We'll divide the discussion into three broad categories: functions, operators, and constants. The format we'll use is the same as for commands and properties in the last several chapters, so you'll have a chance to experiment with each item when we explain it.

Functions

The first point we must make about functions is how they differ from commands. At first glance, they may appear to be quite similar, since you can type commands and functions into the Message Box and have something happen in either case. But in actuality, commands and functions are very different, both in the way HyperCard treats them and the way you incorporate them into your scripts.

By and large, commands are orders directed at something. Whether you type a command into the Message Box or put it into a script, a command tells HyperCard to carry out some action. It may be putting some information into a field or locking the screen. When you issue a command, it affects or changes the state of some entity—a container, an object, a tool, a menu item, the screen, the system. The key word, then, is *action.*

A function, on the other hand, does not provoke action. Instead, it retrieves the current status of an entity and tells you what that status is. Nothing about that entity changes as the result of peeking at it with the function, although it may change later or on its own. For example, several

HyperTalk functions look at the internal Macintosh clock to tell you things like today's date or the current time (according to the settings of the internal clock). The function only tells you what those settings are at the instant it looks at the clock. The clock, of course, continues to tick away at its steady pace. If you want an update on the clock's status, you use the function again.

The answer that a function produces for you is called its *result.* Another common way to express how a function operates is to say that a function *returns* a certain kind of value, like the date or the location of the cursor on the screen. Understanding how a function returns its result is of fundamental importance.

Using Functions in Scripts

The name of a function essentially acts as a substitute in a script line for the type of information it returns. For instance, if you wish to design a stack that automatically places the current date into a card's field on the creation of a new card, the newCard message handler would look like this:

```
on newCard
    put the date into field "Date"
end newCard
```

Let's examine what happens in the command line. The Put command, as you'll recall, requires two parameters: an expression and a destination container. The destination parameter you'll readily recognize as being a field, named "Date." According to HyperTalk syntax for this command, the expression parameter must be either a text string, an arithmetic expression, or the content of any container.

The convenient property about the date function is that it returns a text string (in the form 3/4/94). A function's underlying mechanism lets us substitute the function name (the date) in the command line where we'd normally type in a text string. As HyperCard encounters the function name in the script, it practically says to itself, "OK, this is a function, so let's use its returned result as the parameter here."

Whenever a command parameter calls for a text string, you can substitute a function. All HyperTalk functions return text strings (although many results are entirely numbers). We repeat: All HyperTalk functions return text strings that can be used as text parameters for HyperTalk commands. All you do is plug in the function where the parameter belongs.

HyperCard functions may be written in a script (or typed into the Message Box) in a few ways, according to some simple rules based on the *arguments* following the function name.

An argument is like a parameter, and usually consists of a piece of information the function needs to calculate. If a function is calculating the sine of 50, for example, the number 50 is an argument to the sine function; if a function calculates the average of five numbers, then the average function is said to have five arguments.

If a function requires one argument or no arguments, then the form may be either of two ways: (1) the function name preceded by the word "the"; or (2) the function name followed by the argument in parentheses. In the case of the latter, if there are no arguments, then you type a left and right parenthesis without any spaces or characters between them. Here are examples of valid functions

```
the sin of 50
sin (50)
the date
date()
```

When a function expects two or more arguments (or a variable number of arguments), then you may use only the parentheses style, with arguments inside the parenthes is separated by commas. Here's what some of these functions look like

```
max (10,30,40)
average (3,6,12,9,8)
```

In our discussions of functions in the next several chapters, we'll show the function name in the "the" style wherever possible. This form is more natural sounding in a script and is thus more true to the spirit of HyperTalk.

In scripts, functions must not be surrounded by quotation marks. If they are, they are viewed as a text string consisting of the function name. Therefore, if you were to issue the following command,

```
put "the date" into field "Date"
```

HyperTalk would put the words *the date* into the field. Just plug in function names as if they were a regular part of the HyperTalk language—because they are.

You can test the type of information that virtually any function returns by typing the function into the Message Box. Since the function substitutes for some internal Macintosh or HyperCard value, you simply type the function name (and the prefix "the" or with parentheses around its arguments), and HyperCard instantly shows you its result.

To show you all the HyperTalk functions, we provide the following reference chapters. We've divided the functions into six subject areas: time and date functions; keyboard and mouse functions; text functions; math functions; system environment functions; and script functions (including user-definable functions). We strongly suggest you work your way through every function, even if you won't necessarily use them all right away. The more you are aware of the powers available to you, the more likely you are to think of ways to use them. In later chapters, we'll apply most of these functions to real-world HyperCard applications.

CHAPTER 38

TIME AND DATE FUNCTIONS

• Beginner	•• Intermediate	••• Advanced
date	seconds	
time	ticks	

If you plan to use HyperCard to help organize time, the HyperTalk time and date functions will become some of your most valuable programming aids. You'll have access to the internal Macintosh clock and a few different formats for this information. Typically, you'll also call upon the Convert command to perform additional time and date arithmetic.

• the date

• the abbreviated | abbrev | abbr date

• the long date

Returns: The current date, as maintained by the internal Macintosh clock.

When to Use Them: Many stacks in a business environment will need some form of date stamping, often upon creation of a new card or when information is updated on an existing card. Any one of the three date function formats should prove workable.

The shortest of the three formats is the function, *the date*, which presents the date in a format like 8/4/94. One level higher in completeness is *the abbr date*, which has a format like Thurs, Aug 4, 1994. At the high end is *the long date* function, which spells out everything, as in Thursday, August 4, 1994.

The long date is the function to use if you need only the current day of the week or month in textual form. Rather than build long scripts that painstakingly convert the numbers of the day of the week into each day's text, simply extract the desired component from the long date's results. For example, if you need only the day of the week, use the long date function as a parameter to the command, as in

```
put first item of the long date into field "Day of the Week"
```

Similarly, for the month, extract only the first word of the second item of the long date, as in

```
put first word of item 2 of the long date into field "Month"
```

These two methodologies will prove to operate much faster than any other approach (but may not work correctly in other languages).

Treat the results of these functions as straight text. You won't be able to perform any date arithmetic with these functions directly. Use the Convert command and its seconds or dateItems formats to perform date calculations.

Examples:

```
put the long date into field "Date"
put the abbrev date into it
open file the date
```

You Try It: Type the following functions and messages into the Message Box from any stack:

```
the date
the abbr date
the long date
first word of the long date
item 2 to 3 of the long date
```

• the time

• the long time

Returns: The current time as determined by the Macintosh clock.

When to Use Them: Both time functions will probably get a lot of use if the kinds of stacks you design involve managing time during the day. Time-stamping the creation of a new card in a stack is a popular application.

Your choice of function depends on the format you prefer. The *time* function presents time in the format 3:03 P.M. if you've selected 12-hour time in the Date & Time control panel (System 7), 15:03 if you've selected 24-hour time. If you want the seconds to appear in the results, use the *long time* function, which returns in the formats 3:03:15 P.M. in 12-hour time or 15:03:15 in 24-hour time.

Treat the results of these functions as straight text. You won't be able to perform any time arithmetic with these functions directly. Instead, convert the results of these functions to seconds or dateItems for calculation.

Examples:

```
put the long time into field "Start Time"
ask "Starting Time?" with the time
```

You Try It: Type the following functions and messages into the Message Box from any stack:

```
the time
the long time
put "Experiment started at " & the long time
```

•• the seconds

•• the secs

Returns: Total number of seconds since 0:00:00, January 1, 1904.

When to Use Them: Use the seconds function when you need an accurate counting of seconds within a HyperCard application. The internal Macintosh clock uses January 1, 1904 as the starting point of its time-and date-keeping. As a result, the number of seconds returned by this function is enormous—in the billions.

Since the measure is from a constant starting point, you can compare the total elapsed time in seconds between any two points in the life of a HyperCard application, even when the computer is turned off between sessions.

Examples:

```
put the seconds into field "Hidden"
subtract the secs from elapsedSecs
    -- elapsedSecs is a local variable
```

You Try It: Type the following functions and messages into the Message Box from any stack:

```
the seconds
put the secs into temp
temp
the secs - temp
the seconds / (365.25*24*60*60) -- how many years since 1904
```

•• the ticks

Returns: The number of 1/60th seconds since the last system start-up.

When to Use It: All the while the Macintosh is running, it keeps track not only of the ongoing time according to the clock, but also the number of tick intervals (1 tick = 1/60 of a second) since the machine was last turned on. In other words, each time you turn on your Macintosh, the system starts counting ticks from zero. When you turn off the machine, the tick counter stops, and the number of ticks is erased.

In practice, the Macintosh sometimes misses a heartbeat as far as the tick counter goes. This may occur during disk drive access or during the flow of information through the serial ports. Therefore, the tick counter should not be deemed a reliable time counter over the length of a typical Macintosh work session. If you need accurate timings for long periods, use the other functions that take readings from the internal clock.

Examples:

```
put the ticks into counter -- counter is a local variable
divide field 3 by the ticks
```

You Try It: Type the following functions and messages into the Message Box from any stack:

```
the ticks
put the ticks into howMany
howMany
the ticks - howMany
the ticks - howMany -- see how quickly they tick!
```

Next we go to mouse and keyboard functions.

CHAPTER

39

KEYBOARD AND MOUSE FUNCTIONS

• Beginner	•• Intermediate	••• Advanced
mouseH	commandKey	clickH
mouseV	optionKey	clickV
mouseLoc	shiftKey	clickLoc
	mouseClick	
	mouse	

A second important group of functions lets your scripts obtain information about the current status of the screen cursor and modifier keys (Shift, Option, and Command) on the keyboard. As with many of the functions, these functions end up being used as decision aids for a HyperTalk script. Although we haven't delved into decision-making yet, you'll get a gentle introduction to the basic concepts in this chapter as you see how decisions in scripts are based on the condition of keyboard modifier keys or the location of the cursor.

• the mouseH
• the mouseV
• the mouseLoc

Returns: Coordinate locations (relative to the current HyperCard window) of the hot spot of the screen cursor.

When to Use Them: The need for summoning the screen coordinates of the cursor may not seem obvious at first. But in many advanced HyperTalk programming situations, a well-crafted script can perform wonders with one button that might otherwise require dozens.

For example, if a card features a list of To Do items, you might wish to add a column next to the items so you can check off each item when completed. One method to allow the user to check off an item with the mouse would be to put individual buttons over each check box. That, however, could add twenty or more buttons to the card. As an alternative, you could create one large button over all the check boxes. Then use the script to retrieve the coordinates of the Browse tool when the user clicks the mouse (on mouseUp). Depending on the vertical coordinate along the column, the script could fill in the appropriate line with a check mark character. One button, one script. We'll show you how to do this later when we modify the To Do stack started in Chapter 19.

HyperCard's Home stack contains a script that utilizes all three mouse location functions to help you find coordinates on the screen for other purposes (such as setting locations or rectangles of objects). That handler, called xy looks like this:

```
on xy
    set cursor to cross
    repeat until the mouseClick
        put the mouseLoc && "  horz:" & the mouseH && "  vert:" & the mouseV
    end repeat
end xy
```

By typing xy into the Message Box, you start this handler, which continues to show the mouse location until you click the mouse button.

So, you see, there are several opportunities to use the mouse location functions. The three you have available let you obtain the horizontal (the mouseH), vertical (the mouseV), and both coordinates (the mouseLoc). When you request a single coordinate, the function returns just the one number. When requesting both coordinates, the mouseLoc function returns coordinates in the proper HyperTalk format for multiple parameters —separated by commas—with the horizontal coordinate first.

We mentioned above that the coordinate returned by the functions is where the cursor's hot spot is. One of the design parameters of any cursor is the pixel that represents the action point of the cursor. For example, when the arrow cursor is in the menubar, the hot spot is the very tip of the arrow. That is the pixel that must be in the menu title for you to pull down the menu. In the Browse tool, the hot spot is the very point of the index finger (see Figure 39–1). That's where you should point to find the location of a screen object with the mouseLoc function.

Figure 39–1. The Browse tool's "hot spot" is the reference point for HyperCard's mouse location functions.

Examples:

```
show button ID 200 at the mouseLoc
if the mouseV > 120 and the mouseV < 140 then put "OK" into line 3 of field 2
show message at the mouseV + 25,the mouseH + 25
```

You Try It: Type the following messages into the Message Box from any stack. Move the mouse around and try the same messages to get a feel for the coordinate system of the HyperCard screen.

```
the mouseV
the mouseH
the mouseLoc
put the mouseLoc into temp
show message at temp
add 50 to item 1 of temp
add 100 to item 2 of temp
show message at temp
```

•• the commandKey

•• the optionKey

•• the shiftKey

Returns: Up or Down, depending on the state of the key at the time the function runs

When to Use Them: The Command, Option, and Shift keys are called *modifier keys* in Macintosh programming parlance. They get this name because, according to Apple's Macintosh User Interface Guidelines, you can modify an operation by holding down one of these keys while pressing any other key or the mouse button. We've seen how the Shift key modifies the letters of the alphabet to capitals. Most of us have also experienced how the Command key alters the behavior of most keyboard keys when we wish to perform one of the keyboard menu shortcuts programmed into applications like HyperCard. The commandKey, optionKey, and shiftKey functions give you the same power when programming in HyperTalk.

The primary way to use these functions is to test whether any of these keys is pressed when the mouse button is pressed (mouseDown) or released (mouseUp)—usually in a button script. Generally speaking, the button script will follow a specified path if none of these keys is pressed. If you want a certain button to perform double, triple, or quadruple duty—perform related but decidedly different operations when clicked—you can program the script to follow a different path, depending on which modifier key is pressed along with the mouse button.

Here's what the skeletal structure of a quadruple-purpose button's script would look like:

```
on mouseUp
  if commandKey is down then
    -- carry out the command-key version of this button
  else if optionKey is down then
    -- carry out the option-key version of this button
  else if shiftKey is down then
```

```
        -- carry out the shift-key version of this button
    else carry out the plain version of this button
end mouseUp
```

You don't have to set traps for each of the modifier keys in such a script. If you have only one alternate, say for the Option key, you would only test for the Option key. Even if the Command or Shift keys were held down, the script would *fall through* to the plain version of the button, because the script ignores the condition of the other two keys.

You can also trap for the simultaneous pressing of two modifier keys. A script to do that for both the Shift and Command keys would look like this (you can try it in a button script):

```
on mouseUp
    if the shiftKey is down and the commandKey is down
    then beep 4
    else beep 1
end mouseUp
```

If you hold down both modifier keys and click on the button, the script will beep four times. With only one or no modifier keys held down, you'll get only one beep.

All three functions return the text responses "up" or "down," which can be put into containers. This is good to know, because in a long button script, you should place the test for a modifier key at the start of the script. If the test is later in the script, the user might remove his finger from the modifier key before the script gets to the modifier key function. For the function to return a "down" result, the modifier key must be down when the function acts. Therefore, consider testing for the modifier key(s) first and placing the results of the test in a local variable that can be used later in the script, such as:

```
on mouseUp
    put the optionKey into keyState
    -- keyState is the local variable
        .
        .
        .
    if keyState is down then
        -- carry out the option key modified version
    else
        -- carry out the regular version
    end if
end mouseUp
```

As you design your stacks and lay out the buttons on the cards, always look for possibilities of ganging up functions on fewer screen buttons. Too many buttons can make the screen look cluttered and confusing to the user. At the same time, however, make sure that the functions you apply to the same screen button are logically connected. For example, an unmodified click of a button may create a new card in a stack; a shift-click of the same button may delete the current card. And then, if there is a pattern to the modifier keys' actions to your buttons, maintain consistency throughout your environment. For instance, if you set an option-modified button in one stack to mean that the stack branches to a different background and searches text right away, then keep that system going throughout the environment you establish for your users.

Examples:

```
if the shiftKey is down then doMenu "Delete Card"
put the commandKey into command -- local variable
if the optionKey is down then update
    -- "update" is a message handler
```

You Try It: Most of what we've been showing you about the modifier keys require incorporating the functions into decision-making scripts (see Chapter 46). From the Message Box, however, you can see the effect of pressing the modifier keys on the functions. Type each of the messages below into the Message Box in any stack. Press Return to execute each message twice. The first time, don't hold down the designated modifier key when pressing the Return key; the second time, keep the key pressed when you also press the Return key. You'll see that the modifier key must be down while the function runs for the function to return the "down" result.

```
the optionKey
the shiftKey
put optionKey into temp
temp
```

•• the mouse

•• the mouseClick

Returns: Up or Down for the mouse; true or false for the mouseClick.

When to Use Them: We'll talk about these two functions together, because they both relate to actions the user takes with the mouse button. In some cases, the two functions are interchangeable (although the construction of the decision-making HyperTalk code differs slightly), but there is a distinct difference between the two.

The Mouse function should be used when an indication of the current state of the mouse button is required. If the mouse button is down at the instant HyperTalk executes the function, the function returns the text word "down." If the mouse button is up, the function returns the word "up." A fun example of this function is to write the following card script:

```
on mouseDown
    repeat while the mouse is down
        show message at the mouseLoc
    end repeat
end mouseDown
```

This script starts when you press the mouse button on the card (not in a text field, however). As long as you keep the mouse button pressed, HyperCard draws the Message Box wherever the cursor is on the screen. The repeat construction (explained in Chapter 46) keeps requesting the mouse function and executes the next line, provided the mouse function returns "down" as the result.

The MouseClick function returns either "true" or "false." One of the best ways to use this function is trap for the click of the mouse button. In other words, a script might keep repeating itself until the user clicks the mouse button. You can try this by setting up the following message handler in a card or background script:

```
on beeper
    repeat until the mouseClick
        beep
        wait 5
    end repeat
end beeper
```

Then type *beeper* into the Message Box. This starts the script going. It will continue to repeat the beep and wait loop until the mouseClick function returns a true. A press of the mouse button will make that happen, thus ending the repeat and the message handler.

Notice that the mouseClick function returns a true upon pressing the mouse button. It doesn't wait for the mouse button to be released.

Examples: See above.

You Try It: Be sure to try the examples shown above. They demonstrate the dynamics of these two functions. Unfortunately, you can't experiment with these two functions from the Message Box except with the mouse button released. As long as the mouse button is down, you won't be able to send the message in the Message Box. Still, type the two functions into the Message Box to see how HyperCard responds with the mouse up.

```
the mouse
the mouseClick
```

••• the clickH

••• the clickV

••• the clickLoc

Returns: The coordinates (relative to the current HyperCard window) of the last mouse click (at the cursor's hot spot), regardless of current cursor position.

When to Use Them: Because it is so easy to move the cursor on the screen, even accidentally after clicking the mouse, it's nice to know that HyperCard keeps track of the location of the last time you clicked. Especially if you need to use the mouse coordinates in an extended mouseUp message handler, the cursor may have long moved from the original point by the time the script gets to the coordinate call (making the mouseLoc function useless). While you could save the mouseLoc coordinates at the beginning of the script, the clickLoc function saves you from that step.

As a rule, then, whenever you need to retrieve the screen location of a mouse click within a script, use clickLoc instead of mouseLoc. The fast mousers in your user constituency will appreciate it.

Like the mouseLoc, the clickLoc returns screen coordinates separated by commas. The horizontal coordinate comes first.

The clickH and clickV functions let you retrieve just the horizontal or vertical coordinate if that's all you need for some computation.

Examples:

```
show field "Help" at the clickLoc
if the clickH > 300 then answer "Too far right."
```

You Try It: One easy way to try this function is to click the mouse at the upper left corner of the screen and type the clickLoc into the Message Box. You should get the coordinates 0,0. Then move the mouse around the screen without clicking the mouse button and type the clickLoc again into the Message Box. The location stays the same. Click the mouse button with the cursor somewhere near the middle-left edge of the screen. Then type the following messages into the Message Box from any stack.

```
put the clickH into x
put the clickV into y
add 300 to x
add 20 to y
show message at the clickLoc
show message at x,y
```

CHAPTER 40

TEXT FUNCTIONS

• Beginner	•• Intermediate	••• Advanced
length	clickChunk	charToNum
number	clickLine	numToChar
	clickText	offset
	selectedChunk	
	selectedLine	
	selectedText	
	selectedField	
	selectedLoc	
	foundChunk	
	foundLine	
	foundText	
	foundField	

HyperTalk includes three types of text functions. One type lets you learn about the characteristics of text inside a container. Another lets you extract information about user interaction with a field. The last type accommodates conversion between ASCII values and characters. This last type is offered as a convenience to experienced programmers. Fortunately, even for them there is little need to get "down and dirty" into ASCII code, since HyperTalk has simpler ways of handling the most-used control characters.

Some of these text functions have arguments attached to them. Therefore, for this section, we include a discussion about arguments for each function.

• the length of <chunk expression>

Returns: The number of text characters in a text chunk.

When to Use It: Whenever your script needs to know the total number of characters in a variable, text field, line, item, or other container, use the length function. It counts the total number of characters (that is, including invisible return characters) in a container.

The length function may be used to establish an endpoint for text analysis. You can also use it to validate the length of an entry into a small text field. For example, if you set up narrow text fields on a card form, you might want to limit the number of characters that a user can enter into the boxes. While the actual number that will fit varies with the proportion of skinny-to-thick letters (most Macintosh fonts are proportionally spaced), you could select an average length that will fit comfortably in the box. Your script would be a handler triggered by the closeField message. In that message handler would be a section like the following:

```
if the length of field "Name" ≥ 25 then
   beep
   put "The name must be fewer than 25 characters"
end if
```

As with most other functions, you can place the results of the length function into a variable or other container and use it for further calculations in the script.

Arguments: The sole argument of the length function is the chunk expression whose text it is to measure. Remember that a chunk may be any text field, local or global variable, the Message Box, the special local variable, It, or a selection. You can also substitute an actual text string as the argument, but that wouldn't seem to make much sense in a HyperTalk script: If you already know the text, you certainly know its length and don't need a HyperTalk script to figure it for you.

Examples:

```
put the length of field 3 into howLong -- a local variable
if the length of title > 50 then beep
put the length of field 2 / 6 && "words" into message
```

You Try It: For this experiment, it will help if you have access to a card with different-length text strings. You can use the Addresses stack, create a blank card, and type one long string into field 1, a shorter one into field 2. Then type the following messages into the Message Box:

```
the length of field 1
the length of line 1 of field 1
the length of field 2
put the length of field 1 into temp
put "Field 1 has about" & temp / 6 & " words in it."
```

• the number of <chunk components> of <expression>

Returns: The number of chunk components (e.g., characters, items, lines) in a specified expression.

When to Use It: When performing analyses on text in a container, you usually need the maximum number of components before you can set up a repeating script structure (see Chapter 46). Once you have the maximum number of words, for example, the repeating structure can begin looking at word 1, continue with word 2, and so on, until the word count equals that of the total number of words in the container. Then the repeating structure can stop.

Another application occurs frequently in multiple-lined fields. If your script needs to add a new item to a list in a field, it cannot predict how many items will already be in the list when it makes its addition. The script can use the Number of Lines function to find out how many lines are occupied with text. Then the script can put the new text in the maximum number of lines plus one. Here's how such a script would look:

```
on mouseUp
    ask "Any additions to the list?"
    put number of lines in field "List" into counter
    put it into line counter + 1 of field "List"
end mouseUp
```

You'll discover that once you can retrieve the total number of text components in a container or any expression, you can gain quick access to specific parts of the text.

(See Chapter 42 for using the Number function with objects.)

Arguments: Any valid component name works in the first argument. This includes *chars*, *words*, *lines*, and *items*.

For the second argument, any valid expression is accepted, including other functions. Most of the time this argument will be a field (identifiable by field name, number, or ID number) or a local variable.

Examples:

```
put the number of lines of field 12 into fieldLines
    -- local variable
put the number of items of it into howMany
    -- local variable
put the number of chars of first word of field 1 into it
```

You Try It: Artificial though it may be, you'll use the Message Box to experiment with the Number function. Create a new card in the Addresses stack and type any kind of information into the first field, including text on many lines, and some series items separated by commas. Now type the following messages into the Message Box.

```
the number of lines of field 1
the number of chars of field 1
the number of words of field 1
the number of items of field 1
put the number of words of field 1 into theWords
    -- "theWords" is a one-word variable
put the number of chars of field 1 into theChars
put "Field 1's average word is " & theChars / theWords ¬
    & " characters long." into message
```

•• the clickChunk

•• the clickLine

•• the clickText

Returns: The actual text, chunk expression, and the line number of the text in a field last clicked by the user.

When to Use Them: If you need to capture information about where in a field the user clicks, these are the functions that can tell you lots of information about the text at the click location.

The clickText function returns the actual text clicked on by the user. The Group text style plays a role in the value returned. If the text is not part of a text group, then HyperCard returns the text of the complete word (i.e., the first word, last word, or everything between spaces), no matter where in the word the user has clicked. If two or more words are grouped together (e.g., by selecting the text and choosing the Group font style), the clickText function returns the text of the contiguous group. This is a valuable hypertext power if you are creating such an environment.

A more detailed description of the clicked text can be retrieved with the clickChunk function. The syntax of the returned value is as follows:

```
char <number> to <number> of card | bkgnd field <number>
```

As with the clickText function, if the text clicked on is not part of a group, then the chunk is for the whole word clicked on; if the word is part of a text group, then the chunk expression is for the entire group. You can use the results of the clickChunk function to select text clicked on by the user. Here is a way to highlight text clicked on by the user:

```
select the clickChunk
```

This works even if you have a grouped bunch of text on multiple lines.

But to select the entire line, like when you click on a name in a scrolling list, you may use the clickLine function. This function returns information about the entire line containing the text clicked on by the user. The syntax is as follows:

```
line <number> of bkgnd field <number>
```

Bear in mind that these lines are HyperCard lines—any amount of text to the left of a return character, no matter how many physical lines the text occupies in a field. If you group more than one line together, the clickLine function returns the first line of the group.

Examples:

```
the clickLine
put word 2 of the clickLine into lineNum
get the clickText
```

You Try It: The Click functions work even long after you've clicked a field and moved the mouse elsewhere. Therefore, at any time you may type the functions into the Message Box and see the results. If you click in an unlocked field, move the mouse to an area outside a field and click (even on a button). Then try the functions. Also try grouping some text and see the results for all three functions.

•• the selectedText

•• the selectedChunk

•• the selectedLine

•• the selectedField

•• the selectedLoc

Returns: The actual text, the chunk expression, the line number, and the name of the field of whatever text is selected in a field; the coordinate point of the beginning of the selection.

2.2

When to Use Them: Before describing these functions, it is important to distinguish between types of selections. For the most part, a HyperCard card can have only one piece of text selected at a time. In other words, as you tab from field to field, the text of only one field can ever be highlighted at one time. Selecting text in field B de-selects text in field A. As a result, the functions in this section, when used without any object identifiers, refer to that one possible selection—kind of a global selection for the card.

In contrast to this, two special types of objects—list fields and popup buttons—may also have selections of their own, which work completely independently from the global selection. A list field (locked, auto-selected) maintains its selection (whatever the user clicks on) even while other text in unlocked fields may be selected. Similarly, a choice in a popup button persists, even though other stuff on the card may be selected. You can essentially regard the object-specific selection information as properties of those objects, and we discuss these applications of the selectedText and selectedLine functions among field and button properties in Chapter 36.

To summarize, a plain

```
the selectedText
```

refers to the global selection, while

```
the selectedText of field "Report List"
```

refers to the special selection within that list field.

The functions described in this section refer to the global kind of selections on a card, such as the kind created manually by holding down the mouse button and dragging the text cursor across text in a field. Whichever way text is selected, you may want a script (probably in a button) to do something with that text. For instance, you may want to bring the contents of that selected text into a variable. Or you may want to know where in the field that text is located so you can replace it or determine if the selection is the one your handler expects it to be.

The SelectedText function returns the same information—the contents of the selection—as the Selection container. You may either get the contents of the Selection or use the selectedText function. Neither form is preferred over the other, but the selectedText version may be easier to remember since it now has three related functions.

The next three forms of this function return not the text, but rather information about where the text is located. The selectedChunk function returns an expression in the form

```
char <number> to <number> of card | bkgnd field <number>
```

In other words, it gives you the chunk expression equivalent of the selected text, plus the field number. Notice that the field is designated by its number (not its ID number). While it is often hazardous to refer to one field (out of many) by its number rather than something more permanent like its ID number or name, this is not a big issue in this instance. Since you use this function inside a handler, it's not likely that the handler will change the field order between the time you use this function and have to do something to text in that field. The field number should be good, as long as your handler does not delete the field or otherwise adjust the field order.

HyperCard considers a flashing text insertion pointer as a selection—one of zero length. To depict a zero-length selection as a chunk expression requires a bit of a twist. The expression is in the form *char b to char a of a field*, where *char b* is the character immediately after the pointer and *char a* is before the pointer. Thus, if the pointer is between the "r" and "C" of "HyperCard" in a one word field, the SelectedChunk function would return

```
char 6 to 5 of field 1
```

The SelectedLine function returns the line number and field number in the form

```
line <number> of card | bkgnd field <number>
```

You are free to extract the line number from the expression that this function returns, and with that, perform some actions on the selected line of a field.

The SelectedField function returns the number of the field holding the selected text. The form is

```
card | bkgnd field <number>
```

Again, the field is referred to by its number, not is ID number.

Which one of the location-based functions you use depends on how much information you need to derive from the selection. Use the function for the unique information it provides. While you can derive the field number from all three, if that is the only information you need, then use the simplest form, SelectedField.

Examples:

```
get the selectedText
put the selectedChunk into where
put word 2 of the selectedLine into lineNumber
get the selectedField
```

You Try It: Because you cannot manually select text in an unlocked field and then type into the Message Box, create a card button on a fresh card in the Practice stack. We'll use the top left field as the place for selecting text. Here's the script for the button:

```
on mouseUp
    put the selectedText into line 1 of output
    put the selectedChunk into line 2 of output
    put the selectedLine into line 3 of output
    put the selectedField into line 4 of output
    answer output
end mouseUp
```

Type two lines of text into the top left field. Be sure to type carriage returns between the lines to guarantee that there are two HyperCard lines in the field.

Finally, use the mouse to select various parts of the text in the field and then click the mouse button. Observe closely how each function reacts to the text selection.

•• the foundText

•• the foundChunk

•• the foundLine

•• the foundField

Returns: The actual text, the chunk expression, the line number, and the name of the field of whatever text is inside the outline box as a result of a Find command.

When to Use Them: Whenever you issue a Find command in a script, these functions let you derive the text or the location of the found text in the field—the text inside the rectangle outline after a successful search. Being able to derive the location of found text allows the programming in HyperTalk of search-and-replace scripts.

The extent of the text encircled by the Find command is largely dependent upon the variation of that command you issue. For instance, if you use the plain Find command, specifying two words as the search string, HyperCard encircles only the first word it finds on a card. Whatever is in the box is the foundText, and its location is returned by the other functions. The text and location of the second word is not readily available. In contrast, if you perform a Find Whole on two words, both complete words are encircled in the box. Details about both words are available through these functions.

The foundText function returns the contents of the text inside the box. If you say

```
Find "and"
```

in your script, HyperCard would stop on a card whose field contains the name "Andrew." In fact, the way the Find command works, the entire word would be encircled in the box (Find Chars or Find String would limit the box to the "and" characters). Thus, the FoundText after this Find command would return the entire name, "Andrew."

The other three forms of this function return not the text, but rather information about where the text is located. The foundChunk function returns an expression in the form

```
char <number> to <number> of  card | bkgnd field <number>
```

In other words, it gives you the chunk expression equivalent of the found text, plus the field number. Notice that the field is designated by its number (not its ID number). The foundChunk function in the following script plays a key role in a search-and-replace operation:

```
on mouseUp
    put 0 into counter
    ask "Search for what string?"
    if it is empty then exit mouseUp
    else put it into findString
    ask "Replace '" & findString & "' with what?"
    if it is empty then exit mouseUp
    else put it into replaceString
    if findString = replaceString then exit mouseUp
    repeat forever
        set cursor to busy
        find whole findString
        if the result is not empty
        then exit repeat
        else do "put replaceString into" && the foundChunk
        add 1 to counter
    end repeat
    if counter is zero
    then answer "No occurrences were found."
    else answer "Replacement of" && counter && "occurrences complete."
end mouseUp
```

The foundLine function returns the line number and field number in the form

```
line <number> of card | bkgnd field <number>
```

You are free to extract the line number from the expression that this function returns, and perform some actions on that line of the field. Let's say we have a membership roster stack that lets the user enter searches for partial names—the user isn't sure if someone's name on the roster is "Andy" or "Andrew." Rather than browse through cards of possible matches, the script gathers a list of matches for display in a field on a different card. The script, via an Ask dialog, prompts the user for a string to search. If the user types "And," HyperCard can locate the line of each match for the first name. Knowing the line of the matching string, the entire line may be copied into a local variable. That local variable accumulates a list of all possible matches. When all matches are found, the script goes to a special card with a scrolling field in it. There, the contents of the local variable are shown, with an on-screen list of all possible matches.

The foundField function returns the number of the field holding the found text. The form is

```
card | bkgnd field <number>
```

Again, the field is referred to by its number, not its ID number.

Which one of the location-based functions you use depends on how much information you need to derive from the found text. Use the function for the unique information it provides. While you can derive the field number from all three, if that is the only information you need, then use the simplest form, foundField.

If a Find command fails to locate a match in the stack, then any of these four functions will return empty. In any case, these functions must be used after Find commands in scripts. They do not work with Find commands issued from the Message Box.

Examples:

```
put the foundText
put the foundChunk into where
put word 2 of the foundLine into lineNumber
```

You Try It: Since these functions require that a Find command be executed in a handler before the functions are called, experiment with these functions in a card button in the Addresses stack. Here is a button script that will let you experiment with three different types of Find commands:

```
on mouseUp
    ask "Find what string?"
    if it is empty then exit mouseUp
    else put quote & it & quote into searchString
    answer "What kind of 'Find'?" with "String" or "Whole" or "Plain"
    if it is "Plain" then put empty into searchType
    else put it into searchType
    do "find" && searchType && searchString
    answer the foundChunk -- try other 'found' functions here
end mouseUp
```

This handler displays the results of the foundChunk function in an Answer dialog after each find. This function is perhaps the most revealing about how Find works and what characters are considered "found." For further experiments, substitute other functions for the foundChunk to see how they report the text or location of found text in a field.

••• the charToNum of <character>

••• the numToChar of <ASCII value>

Returns: The charToNum returns the ASCII value; the numToChar returns the actual character.

When to Use Them: These two functions are direct opposites of each other. The charToNum function converts a keyboard character into its ASCII value; the numToChar function converts an ASCII value into a character as it appears on the screen when typed from the keyboard.

Both functions have ready application when it becomes necessary to work with characters that you cannot normally access from the keyboard—primarily control codes at the bottom end of the ASCII value table. Most of these codes are for use with printers and telecommunications devices, although several of them find their way into standard files, such as the Tab and Return characters. Fortunately, for the common control codes, HyperCard provides constants in the form of plain words that we can plug in for those characters (see discussion about constants later in Chapter 45).

One special character you might be interested in is the Apple character that appears at the top of the Apple menu. This character is not available from the keyboard in any fashion, but it is ASCII character 20 in the Chicago font. Therefore, if you wanted to use this character in a text field set for the Chicago font, you'd have to send a message like this:

```
put numToChar of 20 into field 2
```

The numToChar function is also useful when you need to send control characters out to text files (or out the serial port with the help of external commands that control the serial port). For example, if the file format you are writing to requires an ASCII 29 value as a delimiter character, you can write that character out to the file, like this:

```
write numToChar(29) to file myFile
```

Another application for these two functions is converting uppercase to lowercase letters and vice versa. Since an uppercase letter and its lowercase counterpart have different ASCII values (separated by a value of exactly 32 across the entire alphabet), you can make conversions quite simple in a script. Here's an example of how a script would convert lowercase text in a field to all uppercase:

```
on convert                      -- message handler name
  repeat with x = 1 to the length of field 2
                                -- repeat for each character
    put the charToNum of char x of field 2 into temp
                                -- get ASCII value
    if temp >= 97 and temp <=122 then
                                -- if it's in lowercase range
      put temp - 32 into temp
                                --  put it in uppercase range
      put the numToChar of temp into char x of field 2
                                -- replace lower with upper
    end if
  end repeat
end convert
```

In this case, the two functions were used in tandem: once to convert the character to the ASCII value for the arithmetic; the second time to convert the result back into the character for the text string. Try this on a blank Addresses card. Place this script in the card's script, and type a mixture of uppercase and lowercase letters into the second field. Then type convert into the Message Box. Watch as each lowercase letter is turned into its uppercase equivalent.

Arguments: The argument for the charToNum function is any character you can type from the keyboard or any nonkeyboard character that was put into a container via the numToChar function at an earlier time. When the character is not one you can type from the keyboard, it usually appears as a small rectangle. Because this argument can be any keyboard character you can use alternate characters, like the ones available by pressing the Option and Shift-Option keys. Choose Key Caps from the Apple desk accessory menu and press the Option key to see some of the alternate characters. The text character *must* be in quotes.

For the numToChar function, the argument is any ASCII value from 0 to 255. If you specify a number above 255, HyperCard automatically subtracts 255 (or multiples of 255) so you have only one set of characters, the first 256 available largely from the keyboard.

Examples:

```
put the numToChar of 27 before field 3
put the charToNum of "æ" into temp -- option-apostrophe
```

You Try It: The sample script above is a good experiment to try yourself. You may also do some conversions via the Message Box to help you get the feel of these two functions. Type the following messages into the Message Box from any stack.

```
the numToChar of 167
the charToNum of "a"
the charToNum of "b"
the charToNum of "B"
put the charToNum of "A" into temp
add 32 to temp
put the numToChar of temp into message
```

••• offset (<expression>, <expression>)

Returns: The starting position of a text string within another text string.

When to Use It: Because the information that HyperCard stores in its fields and in its object names is so dominated by text (despite HyperCard's heavily graphical environment), it is important to have the flexibility to perform a full array of analyses on the text. One of those analytical tools is the Offset function.

With this function, you can compare any piece of text (which may be a text string or the contents of a container) against the entire content of a container. The function returns a number corresponding to the number of the character at which the test string starts. Let's see how this works.

If field 1 of a card contains the text "Crime and Punishment," you can try a couple of offset functions on it to see what it comes up with. If you were to type into the Message Box

```
offset ("Crime", field 1)
```

the result comes back as 1, because "crime" starts at the first character of field 1. If you then type

```
offset ("and", field 1)
```

the result comes back 7, because "and" starts at the seventh character of the field's text. You can also test for the occurrence of single letters. Therefore, if you type

```
offset ("i", field 1)
```

the result is 3. The function stops at the first occurrence, so it won't find the second letter "i" in "punishment."

Chances are that you will use the offset function in the same script with one or more other text functions in your analyses. For example, if you wish your script to capitalize a word in a container, you would first find the starting location of that word with the offset function. Then you'd work with the characters one at a time and change from lowercase to uppercase with the charToNum and numToChar functions (below). You'd have to put the capital letter into the lowercase letter in the container, so the offset function would help in giving you the starting character number.

Because the Offset function returns a single number, you can use it to help you construct chunk expressions. For example, if you get the long name of a stack (e.g., stack "HD-120:HyperCard Stacks:Home"), and want to remove the characters up to the first quotation mark, you might use the following construction:

```
get the long name of this stack
delete char 1 to offset(quote,it) of it
```

Then, to extract the volume name, you need to get the first character of it to the character just before the colon separator character:

```
put char 1 to offset(":",it) - 1 of it into volumeName
```

The Offset function's return value, minus 1, is the last character of the hard disk name.

In these constructions, it is common to accidentally omit the second reference to the text (of it in the above examples).

Arguments: Both arguments to the Offset function may be straight text, but the more likely scenario will be for both to be containers. The first expression will probably be in a local variable, and the second expression will be either in a field or another local variable. If you use a plain text string as either or both arguments, be sure each string is in quotation marks.

Examples:

```
put offset (field 5, field 1) into temp -- local variable
put offset ("Boston", field "Cities") into it
```

You Try It: The Offset function is not one you're likely to use from the Message Box, but you can experiment with it just the same. By following the messages below, you'll put a text string into a variable and then perform some offset functions about it. Type the following messages into the Message Box from any stack.

```
get "When in the course of human events..."
it
offset ("course", it)
put word 6 to 7 of it into temp
temp
offset (temp, it)
offset ("events", it)
offset ("events", temp)
```

In the next chapter, we shift gears from text to numbers—math functions.

CHAPTER

41

MATH FUNCTIONS

• Beginner	•• Intermediate	••• Advanced	SANE	
random	sum	value	abs	ln
			annuity	ln1
			atan	max
			average	min
			compound	round
			cos	sin
			exp	sqrt
			exp1	tan
			exp2	trunc

As you've seen, you can go pretty far with HyperTalk without ever getting into advanced math. In fact, you may not ever need the functions in this chapter. But for more experienced programmers or those who are comfortable with things like logarithms and compound interest, HyperTalk has many built-in functions to aid in those calculations.

A few of the math functions require the full treatment that we give to functions in other chapters. A majority, however, are self-explanatory, and we'll treat them in a way that will help those familiar with the functions to use them quickly. We'll start with the more in-depth functions first.

• the random of <upper bound integer>

Returns: Random number between 1 and upper bound.

When to Use It: While business applications are not necessarily a likely target for a random number generator, many kinds of entertainment and education applications are. HyperTalk lets you request a random number between 1 and any number up to 2,147,483,646.

In an educational application, the random number may be used in interactive math quizzes, so that not every problem is the same when the same user comes to the application repeatedly. In an entertainment program, the random number generator can mix up the pattern of the game to keep it fresh.

You don't have to use the random function when you wish the user to advance to a random card in a stack. For that task, the *go to any card* message is the desired route.

Examples:

```
put the random of 12 into field "Dice"
if the random of 31 is 11 then put "This is your lucky day"
if the minute is the random of 60 then beep
```

You Try It: First try typing the random of 100 into the Message Box several times to get an idea of how random the random number generator really is.

Then type the following handler into a new card script in the Addresses stack. Then type dice into the Message Box.

```
on dice
    repeat until the mouseClick
        put "The roll is: "& the random of 6 && the random of 6
    end repeat
end dice
```

•• the sum of <number list>

2.2

Returns: Sum of all numbers in the argument.

When to Use It: This function may be used as a shortcut to the Add command or addition operators, particularly when the values you need summed are in a comma-delimited list. The list of values may be in any container (variable, field, button) but if the container holds more than one line of values, only the first line is evaluated. Moreover, the list may be a list of any valid expressions (e.g., a series of selectedText properties of popup buttons whose values are all numbers).

Examples:

```
put sum(10,20,30) into field "Total"
if sum(fld 1, fld 2, fld 3) > 60 then beep
```

You Try It: Create a new card in the Practice stack, and enter numbers into the first three lines of the upper left field. Then type the following command in the Message Box:

```
answer sum(line 1 of fld 1, line 2 of fld 1, line 3 of fld 1)
```

••• the value of <expression>

Returns: The value of an expression.

When to Use It: Information is stored in a container strictly as text information. That includes individual numbers and numbers linked together by operator signs like plus, minus, and so on. Therefore, if a container holds the text, 4 * 5, HyperCard sees it as a string of five characters: a 4, a space, an asterisk, a space, and a 5. There are times, however, when you need to know the calculated value of an expression like that when it is stored in a container. The Value function forces that extra evaluation. Here's an example.

On a card that resembles a scaled-down spreadsheet, there are 12 fields set up in a grid, as illustrated in Figure 41–1. Each field is named with its cell designation, like A1, B2, and so on. Near the bottom of the card is a place for you to type in the formula that will ultimately calculate the desired result of the numbers you type into various cells. So, you might type

```
field "A1" + field "A2" + field "A3"
```

into the formula field. That container now holds the text of the formula, but does not perform any of the arithmetic implied in the string. For that, you would have another cell, named "Answer," into which the value of the formula field goes when you click the Calculate button. That button's script would be:

```
on mouseUp
    put the value of field "Formula" into field "Answer"
end mouseUp
```

The value function performs whatever calculations are in the container specified in its argument and returns that answer. That answer, of course, becomes text again when it is placed into the destination container.

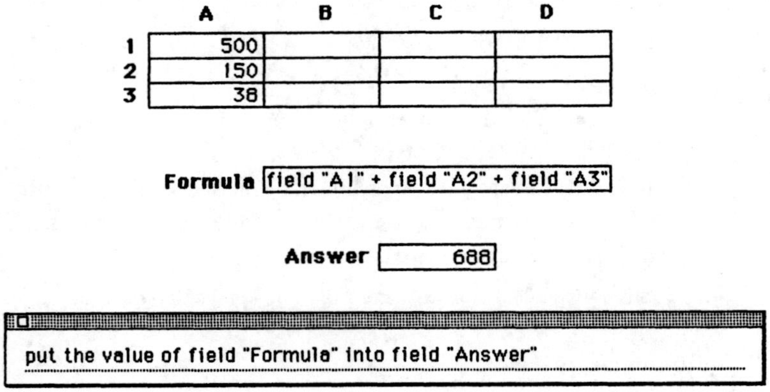

	A	B	C	D
1	500			
2	150			
3	38			

Formula field "A1" + field "A2" + field "A3"

Answer 688

```
put the value of field "Formula" into field "Answer"
```

Figure 41–1. The text in the "formula" field needs to be evaluated to get the result. Use the Value function.

Arguments: The sole argument for the Value function must be a valid expression, whether it is entered directly into the argument (for example, the value of "12/5"), is the result of a function or comes from a container.

In the case of a function or property that returns a quoted string, the Value function treats the string differently than you might expect. For example, when you retrieve the long name property of a stack, the property comes back with something like this: stack "HD-40:HyperCard Stacks:Home." If you wish to extract just the pathname without the quotes, then use this construction:

```
get the value of word 2 of the long name of this stack
```

The Value function interprets all text in the quotes as a single word, the value of which is the string without the quotes. Remember this technique whenever working with quoted text data.

Example:

```
put the value of field "Formula" into it
```

You Try It: The best way to experiment with the value function is to place arithmetic expressions in a card's field and type `the value of field x` into the Message Box, where x is the number of the field. Notice that the Message Box is a special container in this regard, because if you type an arithmetic expression into it, HyperCard automatically calculates the value of that container—hence the built-in calculator capability of HyperCard.

SANE Functions

The following functions will be familiar to experienced Macintosh programmers, because they are most of the math functions in the Standard Apple Numerics Environment, or SANE. The internal-number crunching that these functions perform is actually built into the Macintosh ROM and System.

In describing the following functions, we elect to use the alternate format for designating functions—the function name and parentheses. Those HyperTalk programmers who are familiar with the purpose of these functions should feel comfortable with the format. Just the same, you may use the *the* function style for all functions that take fewer than two arguments, as in `the cos of 40`.

abs (number)

Returns: The absolute value of the number parameter.

Example:

```
abs (-23) returns 23
```

annuity (periodic rate, number of periods)

Returns: The present value of one payment unit. Internally, this function performs the following calculations:

To calculate the present value for the actual payments of an annuity, multiply the result of the annuity function times the amount of a single periodic payment.

Example:

annuity (0.1,12) returns 6.813692

atan (angle in radians)

Returns: The arctangent of an angle.

Example:

atan (25) returns 1.530818

average (number list)

Returns: The average of the numbers presented in a comma-separated list.

Example:

average (10,20,30) returns 20

compound (periodic rate, number of periods)

Returns: The future value of a periodic payment unit. Internally, this function performs the following calculation:

compound(r,n) = $(1 + r)^n$

To calculate the future value of an actual investment, multiply the results of the compound function by the periodic payment.

Example:

compound (0.1,12) returns 3.138428

cos (angle in radians)

Returns: The cosine of an angle.

Example:

cos (50) returns 0.964966

exp (number)

Returns: The natural (base-e) exponential.

Example:

exp(4) returns 54.59815

exp1 (number)

Returns: The natural exponential minus 1.

Example:

```
exp1(4) returns 53.59815
```

exp2 (number)

Returns: The base-2 exponential.

Example:

```
exp2(5) returns 32
```

ln (number)

Returns: The natural (base-e) logarithm of the number.

Example:

```
ln(4) returns 1.386294
```

ln1 (number)

Returns: The natural log of 1 plus the number, as in ln(1 + x).

Example:

```
ln1(4) returns 1.609438
```

max (number list)

Returns: The highest value in a comma-separated list of numbers.

Example:

```
max(20,50,30,49) returns 50
```

min (number list)

Returns: The lowest value in a comma-separated list of numbers.

Example:

```
min(20,50,30,49) returns 20
```

round (number)

Returns: The nearest whole number.

Example:

```
round(12.5) returns 12, while round(12.51) returns 13.
```

sin (angle in radians)

Returns: The sine of the angle.

Example:

sin(75) returns - 387782

sqrt (number)

Returns: The square root of the number.

Example:

sqrt(144) returns 12

tan (angle in radians)

Returns: The tangent of the angle.

Example:

tan(33) returns -75.313015

trunc (number)

Returns: The next lowest whole number of a number.

Example:

trunc(4.825) returns 4

CHAPTER

42

SYSTEM ENVIRONMENT FUNCTIONS

•Beginner	••Intermediate	•••Advanced
number of objects	menus	diskSpace
sound	screenRect	heapSpace
systemVersion	stacks	stackSpace
tool	windows	selectedButton
version		

A number of HyperTalk functions give you information about the current system environment. This includes information about the disk, memory, monitor, plus data about the HyperCard version you're using. Also in this category are functions to tell you about the number of various objects in the current stack or on the current card.

- the number of [card | bkgnd] buttons
- the number of [card | bkgnd] fields

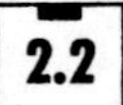

- the number of [card | bkgnd] parts
- the number of cards [of <bkgnd expression>]
- the number of marked cards
- the number of backgrounds
- the number of menus
- the number of menuItems of <menu expression>
- the number of windows

Returns: The number of specified objects.

When to Use Them: A common application that uses the total number of objects is when you need to set up a repeat loop to adjust each item in the stack or card. The total number of objects is used as the maximum number of times the repeated procedure should be done.

For example, let's say you wish to store information in one card that draws information from field 1 of every card in a small stack. The task of the script would be to retrieve the text from each card's field 1. For the script to know how many times to do this, it uses the number of cards function to obtain a count of the cards. The script would look something like this:

```
on accumulate
    repeat with x = 1 to the number of cards
        put field 1 of card x after field "Summary"
    end repeat
end accumulate
```

As you'll learn more in Chapter 46, the repeat construction shown above initializes the local variable, x, and assigns the value of 1 to it at the outset. In the next line of the script, HyperTalk recognizes the variable as a valid card number. The next time through the repeat construction, the local variable, x, is automatically incremented by 1 to a value of 2, and the Put command works on card 2. This repetition continues until x equals the value returned by the number of cards function. After that, the repeat cycle ends, and so does the handler in this case.

You may also limit the card counts to a single background. If, instead, the inner line of the repeat loop, above, said

```
put field 1 of card x of bkgnd "SubTotals" after field "Summary"
```

the Card x counter would stick to cards within the SubTotals background. Therefore, no matter how the cards were sorted, the repeat loop keeps looking for data only within the desired background card style.

A special version of the Number of Cards function lets you instantly retrieve the number of cards whose Mark property is set to true. This may help you navigate to marked cards in a repeat loop, like this:

```
repeat with x = 1 to the number of marked cards
    go to marked card x
    -- do stuff on the marked card
end repeat
```

Use the number of buttons and the number of fields functions carefully. If you don't specify a domain, the fields count will be background fields; the buttons count will be card buttons. To get the number of fields on a card, the function must read the number of card fields. Background buttons are counted by the number of bkgnd buttons (bkgnd and background are synonymous throughout HyperCard). If you want a grand total of both background and card layer objects, you'll have to perform that arithmetic in the script, as follows:

```
the number of background buttons + the number of card buttons
```

2.2

The same goes for uncovering the number of parts (all buttons and fields). If you don't specify card or background in the function call, you get the number of parts in the card domain.

The Number of Menus function lets you establish the number of standard or custom menus. In the count is included the Apple menu. One possible application would be to use this function to help you determine the current state of an application, particularly if the menu composition changes from section to section. If the number of menus is 7, you may wish the program to delete the last menu before moving to another section.

Another variation of this function allows you to obtain the number of items in a particular menu. You must supply a valid menu expression (name or number) as an argument to this function. The number of menu items includes dividing lines.

The last version, the Number of Windows function, returns the total number of windows that exist as far as HyperCard can determine. The number includes all windows that HyperCard considers ready and available for display, including the Message Box, Tools and Patterns palettes, the Message Watcher, and the Variable Watcher.

Examples:

```
put the number of background buttons into temp
set name of card field id 20 to "Field " & the number of fields
if the number of cards > 100 then beep
```

You Try It: Use the Home card for this experiment, because it contains both background and card objects. Show the Message Box and type the following messages into it.

```
the number of cards
the number of cards of this bkgnd
the number of cards of bkgnd 2
the number of card fields
the number of background fields
the number of card buttons
the number of background buttons
the number of card parts
the number of bkgnd parts
the number of bgs
the number of menus
the number of menuItems of menu "File"
the number of windows
```

• the sound

Returns: Done if no Play command is active; the name of the sound resource playing.

When to Use It: Whenever your script issues the Play command (see Chapter 27), you can think of it as instantaneously sending all the note parameters to a separate section of the Macintosh to be carried out. That means that as the music is playing, the script continues to move on to the next line. If you want the script to halt while the music plays, your script should find out when the music is completed before proceeding. The Sound function helps with that task.

Used primarily in conjunction with the Wait command or "repeat" decision constructions (see Chapter 46), the sound function returns the name of the Play command's voice parameter while the music is still playing. Once the music finishes, the function returns "done." A typical script construction would look like this:

```
on mouseUp
    play <parameters for long music>
    wait until the sound is not "done"
    -- further commands
end mouseUp
```

One reason you'd want to hold up further execution during a Play command's music is that some disk drives may interfere with the tonal quality of the Play command's sound. A command after the Play command in the script may access the disk drive. A floppy disk will cause momentary garbling of the sound when accessed during play. A SCSI hard disk should not interfere with the sound. But if you don't know what kind of hardware the users of your stack may be using, play it safe by trapping for the sound function after a play command.

Examples: See above.

You Try It: If you type the sound into the Message Box, it will return "done" as long as no music is playing. To see the function return a voice name, go to the Play command's help card in the HyperCard Help stack. Show the Message Box and drag it so you'll have access to the sample sound buttons on the card. Before clicking a button, type the sound into the Message Box. Now click a button and press Return to test the function. The name of the voice will appear in the Message Box.

• the systemVersion

2.1

Returns: A number representing the version of system software running on the Macintosh.

When to Use It: A number of features in HyperCard versions 2.1 and later (especially Apple events and open scripting) require System 7. By checking for the systemVersion in your openStack handler, you can advise the user whether the system is compatible with these advanced features in your stack.

Even though some versions of the system may be depicted elsewhere with multiple decimals (e.g., 6.0.5), the systemVersion function returns a straight decimal version (e.g., 6.05), so your scripts can perform numeric comparisons, as in:

```
if systemVersion < 7 then
    answer "Sorry, but this application requires System 7" && "or later."
    go back -- leave the stack
    exit to HyperCard
end if
```

This function does not distinguish the Performa versions of System 7 (normally denoted by a trailing "p") from System 7 for other Macintosh models.

If the System 7 features of HyperCard are not necessary for your stack, but offer enhanced functionality, you can also check the system version at various places to bypass the System 7-related features of your stack:

```
< statements>
if systemVersion ≥ 7 then
    <System 7-related statements>
end if
<statements>
```

Examples: See above.

You Try It: Type the systemVersion into the Message Box to see the version currently running and how HyperCard reports it in decimal form.

• the tool

Returns: The full name of the currently chosen tool (e.g., "browse tool").

When to Use It: By checking the currently chosen tool, your scripts can determine the current state of HyperCard based on a user's choices (or a tool chosen under script control). In a graphically based HyperCard stack, you may ask the user to choose a paint tool before clicking a button that uses that tool. If you only want the user to choose only a rectangle or circle, the if-then-else construction to check for that would look like this:

```
if the tool is "circle" then
    -- do circle drawing
else if the tool is "rectangle" then
    -- do rectangle drawing
else answer "Choose only the circle or rectangle tool."
```

If your scripts let the user adjust the tool, and you want to return to the Browse tool, it is fastest to just give the command (choose browse tool), rather than testing whether the current tool is the Browse tool. If-then-else constructions are slower than an overt command.

Examples:

```
get the tool
if the tool is "button tool" then makeNewButton
```

You Try It: From any card, tear off the Tools palette, and show the Message Box. Click on several of the tools, and type *the tool* into the Message Box to see how HyperCard responds.

• the version [of HyperCard]

• the long version [of HyperCard]

• the version of <stack expression>

Returns: Version information about HyperCard or a stack.

When to Use Them: If your stacks are created with HyperCard version 2.2 and take advantage of any commands, functions, or properties new to that version, then your stack should test for whether the user is running HyperCard 2.2. If the user tries to run your 2.2-specific stack on earlier versions, error messages will crop up, because those versions of HyperCard won't understand the new words you're using in your scripts.

The best way to test for the version of HyperCard is to do so in the openStack handler. Such a handler would look like this:

```
on openStack
   if the version of HyperCard < 2.2 then
      answer "Sorry, HyperCard 2.2 or later is required."
      go Home
   end if
end openStack
```

The Version function returns what you could call the "version family number" of the user's HyperCard application. For example, all incarnations of HyperCard 1.2—the buggy 1.2, the official releases 1.2.1, 1.2.2, and 1.2.5—all respond with plain "1.2." That makes the value a legitimate number, which may be compared numerically against some value, like the version you're working with.

The Long Version returns an 8-digit number that comes from the vers resource attached to HyperCard. For HyperCard 2.2, that value is

```
0220xxxx
```

which indicates version 2.2. The rest of the digits are reserved for later use. At the moment, there is little reason to call the Long Version function.

You may also determine the version of a stack. The function returns a five-item result that reveals information about:

- The version of HyperCard used to create the stack
- The version of HyperCard that last compacted the stack
- The oldest version of HyperCard used to modify the stack since its last compaction
- The version of HyperCard that last modified the stack
- The time and date, in seconds, of the most recent stack modification

Each of the first four items—HyperCard versions—are in the same 8-digit format as the Long Version of HyperCard function value. If the version referred to is earlier than 1.2, the value will be 00000000.

If a stack had been created with version 1.0.1 and had been recently compacted with HyperCard 1.2.5, the Version of the stack function would return a value like this:

```
00000000,01258000,01258000,01258000,2667909870
```

The last item will be as many digits as required for the number of seconds, as read from the Macintosh internal clock. This value may be converted to other time formats if you desire.

By checking the version of HyperCard last used to compact the stack, you can make sure your stacks remain up to date by having them compact the stack under versions higher than the last compaction. Major upgrades, such as from 1.2 to 2.0, automatically trap for this discrepancy and alert you about updating the stack. But for intermediate upgrades, a test on your own will keep the stack functioning with the kind of performance provided by whatever new version of HyperCard comes around.

Examples:

```
the version
the long version
the version of HyperCard
the version of this stack
the version of stack "Projects"
```

You Try It: From any stack, type the following commands into the Message Box.

```
the version
the version of HyperCard
the long version
the version of this stack
the version of stack "Addresses"
```

•• the menus

Return: A return-delimited list of all menus currently visible in the menubar.

When to Use It: While the number of menus function tells you how many menus are in the menubar, this function provides the names. If you need to check the presence of one or more menus, then use this function to retrieve the current names. An alternate method of testing for the presence of a menu is to use the There Is operator (Chapter 44).

By returning a return-delimited list, this function is useful when you wish to save the current state of the menus, perhaps recording them in a hidden field for later comparisons.

Examples:

```
the menus
put the menus into field "menuState"
if last line of the menus is "Window" then...
```

You Try It: For this experiment, it is best to have a scrolling field available in a card. Create a simple stack with a single background field, called "output." Then type the following message into the Message Box:

```
put the menus into field "output"
```

•• the screenRect

Returns: The coordinates (left, top, right, bottom) of the rectangle of the screen containing HyperCard's menubar.

When to Use It: With the proliferation of so many different screen sizes attached to Macintoshes, you never know how large a screen will be using your stacks. Generally, this doesn't make a difference in an interactive way, because you should create your stacks to run on all sizes of monitors.

One case in which the size of the screen might be of value to your stack is in the placement of the Message Box. The default location of the Message Box is near the bottom of the HyperCard window. This allows Macintosh Classic style computers to display the Message Box atop the card, all within the 512 × 342 pixel screen. But if you'd prefer that users with larger monitors have the Message Box below the HyperCard window, then use the ScreenRect function to determine upon opening the stack how large the monitor is.

On a Macintosh Classic, the ScreenRect function for the internal monitor returns the value

```
0,0,512,342
```

meaning that the screen begins at coordinate 0,0 for the top left corner, and ends at coordinate 512,342 for the bottom right corner (actually in the order of right, bottom). In virtually every case, the top left coordinate will be 0,0. What will distinguish a larger, external monitor from the internal Macintosh monitor will be either of the right or bottom coordinates. If you test the last coordinate, and find that it is greater than 342, then the user has a larger monitor.

Other common display sizes are 512 × 384 (low-cost color monitor), 600 × 400 (most PowerBooks) and 640 × 480 (Apple RGB and AudioVision 14 monitors). It should be a safe bet that if you adjust the location of the Message Box based on a screen size greater than 512 × 342, the location will work for all screens your stack will encounter. Such a handler would look like this:

```
on openStack
    get last item of the screenRect
    if it > 342 then set loc of msg to 20,355
end openStack
```

For most PowerBook screens (item 4 of the screenRect = 400), you may wish to adjust the Loc of the card window up (to 64,19), and show the Message Box at approximately 20,345. If your stack launches to another application, be sure your Resume handler also performs this test. Otherwise, the Message Box will go back to its default location when the user returns from the external application.

Examples:

```
get the screenRect
get item 3 to 4 of the screenRect
```

You Try It: Unless you have access to more than one size monitor, you'll be limited to trying this function on your single screen. Type the function into the Message Box and you'll see the coordinates of your monitor's opposite corners.

•• the stacks

Returns: A return-delimited list of pathnames for all stacks currently open.

When to Use It: Unlike the stacksInUse property, which reveals the names of stacks inserted into the message hierarchy, the Stacks function lists all open stacks. An open stack is usually visible in a window (although an open stack's window may be hidden). With this information, you can create a window management system in a custom menu, much like other applications offer in a Windows menu, as in

```
put the stacks into menu "Windows"
```

Examples:

```
get the stacks
get line 1 of the stacks
```

You Try It: Type the following message into the Message Box and you'll see the list of all open stacks:

```
answer the stacks
```

•• the windows

Returns: A return-delimited list of all current windows by name.

When to Use It: This comma-delimited list includes not only the visible HyperCard stack windows on the screen, but hidden windows that are available, such as the Message Box, Tool palette, Variable Watcher, and Message Watcher. An important use of this function is for your script to determine whether a particular external window (such as one created with the Picture command) is on-line. You can use the Contains operator to find if a window is present, as in

```
if the windows contains "My Picture" then...
```

The list displays the windows in layer order receding from the viewer's eye. For example, from the Home stack with no other stacks open, the Windows function returns:

```
Message
Variable Watcher
Message Watcher
Scroll
FatBits
Pattern
Tool
Home
```

Notice how all the palette style windows, which live in the palette layer, are listed before the Home window, which is in the document layer.

Examples:

```
put the windows
if last item of the windows is "Home" then...
```

You Try It: Type the following command into the Message Box:

```
answer the windows
```

••• the diskSpace

Returns: The amount of free disk space (in bytes) on the current volume or any other mounted volume.

When to Use It: Your scripts need to be aware of available disk space in only a few instances, such as just before opening a text file for importing or exporting data, prior to sorting, and prior to compacting the stack. In other words, if an operation is going to take up space on the disk, you may wish to check the diskSpace function first. If the returned number of bytes is smaller than your operation requires (e.g., at least twice the Size of the stack for sorting or compacting) then you can alert the user that this operation cannot be performed on the current disk, and then bypass the operation in the script. Employing a strategy for disk management is needed much more for stacks operating on floppy disks than on a hard disk.

2.2 Without any parameters, this function returns the free disk space on the startup volume. But you may also specify any other mounted disk volume to have HyperCard get that volume's free space.

Examples:

```
get the diskSpace
get the diskSpace of disk "DannyBook"
if the diskSpace > size of this stack * 2
then doMenu "Compact Stack"
```

You Try It: Simply type the diskSpace into the Message Box to see the current amount of free space on the current disk. Insert a floppy disk of your choice, noting the name of the disk. Then type the diskSpace of disk <name> into the Message Box, substituting the disk's real name for <name>.

••• the heapSpace

••• the stackSpace

Returns: The size, in bytes, of Macintosh memory locations called the application heap and the stack.

When to Use Them: These functions tell you something about what's going inside the part of memory that runs HyperCard. The heap is generally used to store active portions of the application program, temporary data, the clipboard, copies of handlers while they're running and copies of XCMDs while they're running. When you select a Painting tool, the Paint buffers load into the heap. The stack (not related to HyperCard stacks in any way) is another memory zone, traditionally used by programs to store pending instructions and other very low-level items rarely noticed by the program's users. Both memory zones are constantly changing, so you may not receive the same values with two successive readings of these functions.

Of these two functions, the heapSpace is usually the more useful when debugging scripts, although regard it only as an approximate value. The heapSpace function typed into the Message Box can tell you approximately how much contiguous space there is in the heap zone of HyperCard's memory partition. Occasionally, running an XCMD (or having an XCMD end in an error) or moving resources around leaves insufficient heap space for opening the Painting tools. In rare, severe cases, there won't be sufficient heap space to perform the simplest HyperTalk commands. In practice, you'll probably be able to open Painting tools with less memory, because 88K of the tools' buffers don't need a contiguous heap zone. The real hazard, however, is when the heapSpace nears 32,000. HyperCard will balk at continuing with so little space. Your scripts may check for the heapSpace prior to opening the Painting tools and deny access if the function returns a value less than 120,000. When the heap zone gets too small to perform needed operations, the best way to recover the space is to quit HyperCard and restart from the Finder.

Examples:

```
put the heapSpace
if the heapSpace < 50000 then exit to HyperCard
```

You Try It: To see how the Painting tools gobble up heap space, type `the heapSpace` into the Message box with the Browse tool selected. Then choose a Painting tool, and see the difference in the heap value.

●●● the selectedButton

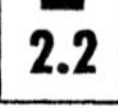

Returns: The name of the currently highlighted button within a designated button family.

When to Use It: It is often important to uncover which button in a radio button cluster is selected. The slow way would be to work through a repeat loop that examines the hilite property of each button in the group. The selectedButton function, however, speeds the process, because you can ask it to supply you with the descriptor of the highlighted button within a button family.

You must supply and domain and the family number as an argument to the function, as in:

```
get the selectedButton of bkgnd family 2
```

Both the card and background domains may have up to 15 families, so it is vital that you specify which domain family you want.

The value that comes back from this function is a valid button desciptor, such as:

```
card button 2
```

You may then use the returned value as a valid button expression. For example, you can obtain the short name of a selected button in a single statement:

```
get short name of the selectedButton of bg family 3
```

In a script that makes if-then decisions based on the chosen button in a radio cluster, this could help simplify the readability of the script:

```
get short name of the selectedButton of bg family 2
if it is "Fred" then
    -- do Fred stuff
else if it is "Jane" then
    -- do Jane stuff
end if
```

Examples:

```
answer the selectedButton of cd family 2
get the selectedButton of bg family 1
```

You Try It: Create a new card in the Practice stack. Then add three card radio buttons named Larry, Moe, and Curly. Assign all three to family 1. Then add the following handler to the card script:

```
on mouseUp
    answer "You selected" && short name of the selectedButton of card family 1
end mouseP
```

This handler will trap the mouseUp messages from the radio buttons, and show reveal whose button you clicked.

Coming next is the last chapter on functions, covering those that help scripters.

CHAPTER

43

SCRIPT-RELATED FUNCTIONS

• Beginner	••Intermediate	•••Advanced
result	target me	destination param paramCount params

The seven remaining functions are of importance to scripters, because they reveal information about processes occurring inside a script. One of these, the Result, is used frequently, because it carries news about whether another command was carried out correctly.

• the result

Returns: Indications that a Find, Go, Ask, Answer File, Ask File, Open, Convert or other command failed.

When to Use It: HyperTalk provides a bit of what is commonly called error-trapping when a script attempts to execute one of several commands and is unable to do so. Failure to find a match, for instance, causes the Result function to return not found. Failure to find a card specified in a Go command causes the result function to return no such card. If the failure to accomplish a command affects the way your message handler proceeds, insert the Result function in a statement immediately following the command. When the action is successful, the Result function returns empty.

Trapping for the Result function prevents HyperCard from displaying its regular error message for commands like Go or Convert. This keeps your script and interface running more smoothly.

As part of an if-then-else construction (Chapter 46), the Result function will let your handler take whatever action is necessary to make the handler run smoothly after a command failure. As part of a Find command, the Result function might be used like this:

```
on mouseUp
    find message
    if the result is not empty then
        ask "Sorry, I couldn't find that." with "OK"
        exit mouseUp
    end if
    ...
end mouseUp
```

The best way to handle the Result function is to simply test for the presence of any string that the function might return. Since the function returns an empty string on successful command execution, you can test whether the Result is empty. If not, the message handler can branch to an error-handling script elsewhere, as in:

```
if the result is not empty then doError
```

Here, the error-handling message handler is called *doError*.

Examples: See above.

You Try It: Create a temporary button on the Home card with the following script. Then click the button to begin the handler, and click the mouse button a couple times to see the results of the three commands.

```
on mouseUp
    find the seconds
    put "find ->" && the result
    wait until the mouse is down
    go card 20
    put "go 20 ->" && the result
    wait until the mouse is down
    go card 2
    put "go 2 ->" && the result
end mouseUp
```

•• the target

Returns: The name or ID number of the object receiving the last message along the HyperCard hierarchy.

When to Use It: With this function you can discover which object received the current message. For instance, if you click on a background button named "Daily," the Target function returns: `bkgnd button "Daily"`.

With HyperCard making this information available as a message works its way along the hierarchy, it is possible to use that information to direct execution of a script. For example, you might set up a card in your Home Stack with several icon buttons representing stacks you've designed. If you name the buttons with the stack names, you only need one message handler—in the card object—to link those buttons to their respective stacks. The card handler would read:

```
on mouseUp
    get short name of the target
    go it
end mouseUp
```

The first command puts the button's short name—the same as the desired stack name—into it, because the button became the target when you clicked it. Then the Go command uses the button's name as its parameter.

You can keep adding new stacks' buttons to this card without ever writing another linking script between a new button and its stack.

Examples:

```
send "mouseUp" to the target
get the name of the target
```

You Try It: If you try typing the target into the Message Box, it will always return the current card's ID number, because that's where the Message Box sends all its messages. To see a different result from this function, create a new button in a stack and enter the following script into it:

```
on mouseUp
    put the target into message
end mouseUp
```

When you click on the button, the button name (if you assigned one) or ID will appear in the Message Box.

•• target

•• me

Returns: The contents of the object last receiving the current message (target) and the current object (me).

When to Use Them: Before HyperCard 1.2, the words *target* and *me* referred strictly to objects, rather than their contents (in the case of fields). For example, the following handler

```
on closeField
    put the target
end closeField
```

puts the name of the field, not the contents of that field, into the Message Box. If you wanted to obtain the contents of the field by referring to the target, then you had to get the value of the target.

The reason you'd even bother with the target nomenclature doesn't become evident until you place a single closeField handler in a background to take care of the closing of several fields on the card. Instead of having the identical closeField handler in each field, a single handler in the background will trap all closeField messages initially sent to each field. You may then obtain the name of the field (via the target function) to identify which one closed. For example,

```
on closeField
    get the target
    if it contains "Amount" then recalc
end closeField
```

only recalculates (recalc is a custom handler elsewhere in the card, background or stack) when a field whose name contains the word "Amount" closes—is the initial target of the closeField message.

All this still holds true for HyperCard 1.2 and up, but you may now have more direct access to the contents of the field, both retrieving its contents or putting something in it. The syntax is the word Target without the leading *the*. Target is a container. You can put its contents into another container, such as a field or variable. You can also put any text into that container.

Target refers to the contents of the object that first received the system message. For instance, in a background closeField handler like this one:

```
on closeField
    put target into temp
    ...
end closeField
```

the text that goes into that local variable, temp, is the text from the field just closed. Working in the other direction, let's say you have a column of fields, each named "Amount" plus the number of the cell, as in "Amount 1," "Amount 2," and so on. If you wanted to make sure that all number entries are adjusted to dollars and cents, a single closeField handler in the card or background could take care of it all. Here it is:

```
on closeField
    get the target -- the NAME of the target field
    if "Amount" is in it then -- do only for "Amount" fields
        set numberFormat to "0.00"
        add zero to target -- the CONTENTS of the target field
    end if
    pass closeField
end closeField
```

Notice how you can treat Target just like a container, in this case the field that just closed. Adding zero to the contents of the field with numberFormat set to "0.00" formats the number in that field to two places to the right of the decimal.

Another word in the HyperTalk vocabulary gains similar powers: Me. Previously, you could use Me in an object's own handler to derive properties of the object, as in:

```
on mouseUp
    set the hilite of me to not the hilite of me
end mouseUp
```

This handler toggles the hilite property of a button with each click of that button. The handler, however, must be in the object's own script. Since

Me refers to the object in which the handler appears, placing the above handler anywhere but in a button script would be meaningless.

For fields, however, you may use Me as a container that holds the contents of the field. For example, if a user is supposed to enter a date into a field on a card, you may want to make sure all dates are stored in that field in a particular date format. To guarantee that, and then to lock that field, you might use the following handler:

```
on closeField
    convert me to long date -- the CONTENTS
    set the lockText of me to true -- the OBJECT
end closeField
```

In this case, Me (without the "of") refers to the contents of the field—the very field in which this handler is located. You can still refer to the object to get or set properties of that object, but the syntax is

```
set the <property> OF me to <setting>.
```

In the last closeField handler, you could have also used Target instead of Me in both cases. In an object's own handler, Target and Me are interchangeable. Generally, we use the Target syntax in handlers that might intercept messages from several related objects, while using Me in an object's own handlers. Reading aloud a script of an object in which there are references to itself or its contents makes more sense with Me than with the Target syntax. Wherever possible, write scripts that make sense reading them aloud.

Examples: See above.

You Try It: These pseudo-functions (they exhibit behavior different from other functions, yet do return values) work only in object scripts. Re-create the examples, above, in fresh objects on a blank card to experiment with them.

••• the destination

2.2

Returns: Pathname of the stack to which the user is about to switch.

When to Use It: When creating a multiple-stack system, it is often helpful to know if the user is navigating to another stack within that system or heading for some other stack. If the user is staying within your system, you don't have to close down certain elements behind the scenes, such as custom menus, shared stacks, and global variables. Closing these things down and starting them upon re-entry into your system can take time. But if you know that the destination is within your system, your closeStack, suspend-Stack, openStack, and resumeStack handlers can bypass those time-consuming steps.

A good way to make this even easier in a multiple-stack environment is to make a unique character series part of the names of all stacks within the system. For example, in a personal information manager program produced by Concentrix Technology, Inc., the stacks all begin with the letters "CT" and a bullet symbol (Option-8) followed by a descriptive name for the stack, such as "CT•Calendar 1994." With a series of stacks bearing these characters, we could set up a universal user-defined function that gives us the information we need:

```
function leavingSystem
    if the destination contains "CT•"
    then return false
    else return true
end leavingSystem

on closeStack
    if leavingSystem() then
        -- stuff here to shut down system-wide items
    end if
end closeStack

on suspendStack
    if leavingSystem() then
        -- stuff here to shut down system-wide items
    end if
end suspendStack
```

To test for a specific stack name, you can extract just the stack name from the returned pathname value of the destination function:

```
set itemDelimiter to colon
put last item of the destination into headingTo
set itemDelimiter to comma
```

The good news is that HyperCard can give us this information even before the current stack closes or suspends (e.g., when a user clicks on another open stack window). This lets us clean up or not, depending on where we're headed.

Examples: See above.

You Try It: Create a small stack with the following stack script.

```
on openStack
    global mySystemStacks
    put "Practice, Addresses" into mySystemStacks
end openStack
```

```
on closeStack
    if leavingSystem() then flash
end closeStack

on suspendStack
    if leavingSystem() then flash
end suspendStack

function leavingSystem
    global mySystemStacks
    set itemDelimiter to colon
    get last item of the destination
    set itemDelimiter to comma
    if return & it & return is in mySystemStacks -- uniqueness
    then return false
    else return true
end leavingSystem
```

Close the new stack and reopen it. Also open in separate windows the Practice, Addresses, Appointments, and Home stacks. Arrange the windows so you can click on each of them to activate them without entirely covering up your new stack. Then navigate from your stack to each of the stacks. Your new stack's window flashes when you click on the Practice and Addresses stack, because they are considered part of the multiple stack system.

••• the param of <parameter number>

••• the paramCount

••• the params

Returns: The text of the parameter specified by <parameter number>; the number of parameters; and the complete list of parameters to the current message, respectively.

When to Use Them: These three functions can contribute a substantial amount of power to your scripts, because they allow you to retrieve parameters that you send with your scripts. This requires a bit of explanation.

Most of the message handlers described so far in this book have been those that trap for system messages that HyperCard sends to various objects in the hierarchy—things like mouseUp, openCard, and so on. But there is an entirely different class of messages: messages that your scripts send to other message handlers that carry out tasks you design.

Let's say that you have designed a card with five fields in it. Let's also say that you want all text in each field to be all uppercase. In case the user forgets to type in uppercase, you plan to include a script in each field that will convert lowercase letters to uppercase letters automatically when the user advances to the next field (that is, on closeField). As we saw in our explanation of the charToNum and the numToChar functions, the conversion routine takes several lines of HyperTalk instructions. While you could write the complete conversion routine in each field's script, there is a shortcut: Put the conversion routine in a stack or background script, and let the field scripts branch to the single conversion routine whenever they need it.

Such a background script might trap for the message *toUpper*. Its message handler, then, would begin with *on toUpper* and finish up with *end toUpper*, as shown below:

```
on toUpper
    repeat with x = 1 to the length of field 3
        get the charToNum of char x of field 3
        if it >= 97 and it <=122 then
            subtract 32 from it
            put the numToChar of it into char x of field 3
        end if
    end repeat
end toUpper
```

Since the field script is located in an object very low in the hierarchy, its toUpper message would first go to its own object and then work its way up the hierarchy until the background message handler, on toUpper, traps it. When the conversion is completed, the original script in the field object continues on.

But there is a special problem with this kind of subroutine. The toUpper message handler needs to know which field it should convert. You solve that by sending a field number, ID, or name as a parameter along with the convert message, as in *toUpper 3* for converting field 3. Inside the toUpper message handler, then, you can retrieve the parameter with the help of one of these three functions and insert the number in the appropriate parts of the convert script, as shown below:

```
on toUpper
    put the param of 1 into whichField
    repeat with x = 1 to the length of field whichField
        get the charToNum of char x of field whichField
        if it >= 97 and it <=122 then
            subtract 32 from it
            put the numToChar of it into char x of field whichField
        end if
    end repeat
end toUpper
```

In the script for field number 3, then, would be the following message handler:

```
on closeField
   toUpper 3
end closeField
```

The number 3 will be used by the toUpper message handler as the number of the field to convert to uppercase.

These three functions, then, give your scripts access to parameters that are sent along with messages. Here's how they differ.

The Param function lets you extract a known parameter from the list. In the above example, only one parameter was sent along with the message, but that's not always the case. For example, if you send parameters specifying the location of an object on the screen, there will be two parameters in the message, separated by commas (such as, (50,75)). By specifying a parameter number in the function's parameter (in the <parameter number>), your script can pick out a single parameter and act on it, if necessary. The param of 0 is the message name; the param of 1 is the first parameter of the message; and so on.

If your script needs the entire message, complete with parameters, then the Params function (notice the "s" on Params) returns the entire message. By putting the complete message into a container, like a variable, you can then dissect the parts as needed.

Lastly, to help in extracting multiple parameters from a series of many parameters, you can use the Paramcount function to determine the total number of parameters in the message. As with most other functions that return the total number of something, the Paramcount function will most often find itself at home as a counter within a repeat construction (see Chapter 46).

Examples:

```
put the params into fullMessage -- a local variable
show message at the param of 1,the param of 2
add 100 to item the paramcount -1 of fullMessage
```

You Try It: Working with these functions from the Message Box won't be too helpful in your understanding of these functions. It's more important that you try the toUpper message handler shown above and understand its workings.

Since menu commands send some parameters (the menu item and the menu name), you can try a short card script that displays the results of each parameter function in a field on a blank Practice stack card. Type the following script into a blank card's Script Editor. Then choose menu items like Message, Find..., or desk accessories, which don't move you from the card. Compare the values of each function type.

```
on doMenu
    put empty into field 1
    put "The paramCount function returns"&& the paramCount into line 1 of field 1
    put "The params function returns"&& the params into line 2 of field 1
    repeat with i = 0 to the paramCount
        put "Param" && i & " is" && param(i) into line i+3 of field 1
    end repeat
    pass doMenu
end doMenu
```

User-Defined Functions

You aren't restricted to HyperCard's built-in functions. You may create your own to perform any frequently used calculations in your work. User-defined functions, just like HyperTalk functions, return values and may be used like any HyperTalk function in your message handlers.

To define a function, you type it into an object script in the following form:

```
function <function name> [ argument [, argument [, ... ]]]
    <command>
    <command>
    return <value>
end <function name>
```

Here's a sample function you might find useful in your stacks:

```
function dayOfWeek date
    get date
    convert it to long date
    return item 1 of it
end dayOfWeek
```

To use this function, type dayOfWeek("11/12/94") into the Message Box. You could also say put dayOfWeek(the date) into field 1, just like any valid function. Note that user-defined functions must be called with the parenthesis form, not the "the" form.

Here is another function you can use to calculate factorials of numbers (for example, factorial 5 = 5 * 4 * 3 * 2 * 1):

```
function factorial n
    if n <= 2 then return n
    else return n * factorial (n-1)
end factorial
```

This example serves double duty, because it demonstrates not only a function definition's basic structure, but also a doubling back on itself (*recursion*) by calling itself. This type of recursion is allowed, because it is finite.

If you create or discover functions that might apply to many stacks, you'll be best off to place the scripts for those functions in your Home Stack. Since function calls follow the same hierarchy through the HyperCard system that messages do, you'll want the functions to be in a place accessible to all stacks.

Also, make your own functions as general as possible—avoid referring to specific objects or conditions. Generalizable functions can be reused in other stacks quite readily. They can also be shared with other HyperTalk programmers.

CHAPTER 44

OPERATORS

If there is one part of computer programming that usually frightens newcomers, it's math. We hope, however, that you've seen how much you can accomplish without getting deeply into mathematics. In fact, most HyperTalk programming requires little more than a basic working knowledge of arithmetic. In this chapter, we explain each of the operators you use in HyperTalk scripts to perform math and mathematical comparisons (for example, whether one value is greater than another).

These operators behave very much like functions. They return values, either the result of the actual math performed or a true/false determination. Like a function, the result may then be placed into a container. You'll see many examples of what we mean in the following operator descriptions.

+ (plus)

Returns: The sum of two numeric values.

When to Use It: The Plus operator lets you sum two numbers together in an arithmetic expression. You can add two straight numbers, any container that evaluates to a number, any function that returns a number, or any combinations thereof.

Examples:

```
put item 3 of the long date + 2 into field "Future"
show message at param 1 + 25,param 2 + 25
put field 1 + field 2 + field 3 + field 4 into field "Total"
```

You Try It: Type the following messages into the Message Box from any stack:

```
put 10 into temp1
put 500 into temp2
temp1 + 1
temp1 -- the container doesn't change
put temp1 + 1 into temp1
temp1 -- now it changes
temp1 + temp2
add temp1 to temp2
temp1
temp2
add temp1 + temp1 to temp2
temp2
```

– (minus)

Returns: The difference between two numeric values.

When to Use It: The Minus operator lets you subtract two numbers in an arithmetic expression. You can subtract two straight numbers, any container that evaluates to a number, any function that returns a number, or any combinations thereof.

Examples:

```
put item 3 of the long date - 1 into field "Last Year"
put "almost" after the number of words - 1 in field id 770
```

You Try It: Type the following messages into the Message Box in any stack:

```
put 500 into big
put 5 into small
big - small
small - big
subtract small from big
big
small
add small - 5 to big
big
small - 5
```

* (multiply)

Returns: The product of two numeric values.

When to Use It: The Multiply operator (the asterisk character, Shift-8) lets you multiply two numbers together in an arithmetic expression. You can multiply two straight numbers, any container that evaluates to a number, any function that returns a number, or any combinations thereof.

Examples:

```
put field "Monthly Rate" * 12 into field "Annual Rate"
put 2 * 2 * 2 into field "Two Cubed"
```

You Try It: Type the following messages into the Message Box in any stack:

```
put 10 into x
put 5 into y
x * y
put x * y into it
it
add y + y to y
y
multiply x by y
x
y
```

/ (divide)

Returns: The quotient of two numeric values.

When to Use It: The Divide operator lets you divide two numbers in an arithmetic expression. You can divide two straight numbers, any container that evaluates to a number, any function that returns a number, or any combinations thereof.

Examples:

```
put field "Total Year" / 365 into field "Per Day"
put x / y into z -- three local variables
```

You Try It: Type the following messages into the Message Box in any stack:

```
put 100 into big
put 5 into small
big / small
small / big
put big / small into it
it
put small & " is 1/" & big / small & "th of " & big
```

= (equals)

is

<> (does not equal)

≠

is not

Returns: True or False, based on an arithmetic comparison of two expressions or containers.

When to Use Them: The Equals and Is operators may be used interchangeably. When comparing two expressions or containers placed on either side of the operator, HyperCard evaluates whether the two items have the same value. If so, the operator returns true. If not, the operator returns false.

The other three operators, also interchangeable with each other, test for whether the items on either side are not equal. If they evaluate to different numbers, the operator returns true. If the items are the same, then the operator returns false. To type the first of these operators, type the less than symbol (<) followed immediately by the greater than symbol (>) without any space in between. For the second "does not equal" symbol, a common math symbol, hold down the Option key and press the equals key. The "not equals" character appears in most fonts, but not all. Even if the symbol doesn't appear, the character's number is duly logged, so you don't have to see it to use it. The symbol does appear, fortunately, in the font used for HyperTalk scripts, so feel free to use it there.

Examples:

```
if field 1 = field 2 then ask "Should both fields be the same?" with "Yes" or "No"
if x ≠ 0 then put 0 into x
repeat while the hour is 9
if field "Year" <> the year then beep 2
```

You Try It: Type the following messages into the Message Box from any stack:

```
put 100 into temp1
put 100 into temp2
put 99 into temp3
temp1 = temp2
temp1 is temp2
temp1 <> temp2
temp1 ≠ temp2
```

< (less than)

<= (less than or equal to)

≤ (less than or equal to)

> (greater than)

>= (greater than or equal to)

≥ (greater than or equal to)

Returns: True or False, based on an arithmetic comparison of two expressions, containers, functions, or any combinations thereof.

When to Use Them: These four operators (two have alternate versions) let you test for greater precision of a comparison than just whether two numbers are or are not equal to each other. They let you test for a value being in a range, like whether a number is less than 10 or greater than 100.

The addition of the equals sign helps you in the definition of the limit of the range. This is especially helpful when the limit is defined by a function, whose value you never know beforehand. If you want to know if a variable is less than or equal to the current minute (as derived from a dateItems conversion), you can do that. If the current minute should not be in the limit, then use the simple less than operator. (To define both an upper and lower limit to a range, see the And operator).

To type the special single character symbols for less than, greater than, or equal to, type Option-comma and Option-period, respectively. These symbols may be more familiar to you from your math training.

Almost every application of these operators will be in repeat and decision-making constructions, as detailed in Chapter 46.

Examples:

```
if field 3 < 0 then put 0 into field 3
repeat while item 5 of field "Time" <= 5
if item 3 of the long date > 2000 then put "Reset your clock" into message
```

You Try It: Type the following messages into the Message Box in any stack:

```
put 100 into temp1
put 100 into temp2
put 50 into temp3
temp1 <= temp2
temp2 <= temp1
temp3 >= temp1
temp3 <= temp1
temp1 + temp3 >= temp1 * 2
```

div (divide and truncate)

mod (modulo)

Returns: Div returns the whole number of times one number is divisible by a second; Mod returns the remainder left after dividing one number by a second.

When to Use Them: These two functions come in much handier than you might think at first (that is, unless you're a seasoned programmer and already appreciate their importance). When you divide one number by another, there is a good chance that the result will not be a whole number, but usually a number and a decimal, like $5/2 = 2.5$. But in the way we learned division in the second grade, the problem resolves to an answer of 2 with a remainder of 1 (see Figure 44–1). These div and mod functions let you isolate the whole number and the remainder of a division problem.

```
    2
2 ) 5
   -4
    1
```

Figure 44–1. Division the way we learned it in grade school.

If we take a new problem and apply each of the functions to it, you'll see the distinction between the two. The problem is that we are reviewing a project schedule that extends over a fixed number of days, 98. We also know that the project schedule started counting on a Sunday sometime back. What we want to know first is how many weeks the 98 days account for. For that answer, we use the Div operator. Solving for 100 div 7, the answer comes to 14. In one operator, we both divide 100 by 7 and strip away the decimal part of the answer, since we're only interested in knowing the total number of weeks. Of course, this response tells us only the number of full, seven-day weeks. We don't know if there were any extra days into the eighth week. That's what the Mod operator finds for us.

By solving for 100 mod 7, the answer comes to 2. If we had simply divided 100 by 7, the answer would have been 14.2857 weeks. How many days is 0.2857 weeks? The Mod operator tells us that it is exactly 2. So the project took 14 weeks and 2 days. Not only that, since we know the project started on a Sunday (day 1 of the first week), the project ended on a Monday (day 2 of the 15th week).

Examples:

```
put "$" & (amt div 1) & "." & (amt*100 mod 100) into money
if it mod 2 is zero then put "Even" into field 2
```

You Try It: Type the following messages into the Message Box in any stack:

```
put 100 into temp1
put 103 into temp2
temp1 div 5
temp2 div 5
temp1 mod 5
temp2 mod 5
temp2 div 5 & " with a remainder of " & temp2 mod 5
50 div -10
50 mod -10
```

Validation Operators

HyperTalk includes operators that allow the scripter to check the validity of data or objects before a script does further processing. These can be very important when a user has the ability to input information or change objects in the course of using your stack. Good programming practice supports the checking of user-entered data if bad data can mess up the program. For example, if your program requires a number for calculation, then a letter could cause a script error—something you should guard against at all cost. Use these operators when bad data or missing objects will upset your stack's functional flow.

is a[n] <type>

is not a[n] <type>

Returns: True or false depending on the outcome of the comparison between the content of the left side of the equation and one of the predefined data types on the right.

When to Use Them: Valid <type> parameters are: number, integer, point, rect, date, and logical (Boolean). If users of your stack enter data into fields, and that data becomes part of calculations or other data sensitive manipulations, you should trap for the validity of the data in a closeField handler for that field. The farther away from the actual calculation you trap for data entry errors, the smoother that calculation will go. Otherwise, you'll spend much execution time checking the validity of each component during the calculation handler, and you'll have to add a bunch of code to tell the user which field is the bad data culprit. By that time, the source material for the data may no longer be around for the user to check it.

Here's an example of a closeField handler checking for the entry of a number:

```
on closeField
    if target is not a number then
        answer "You must enter a number only."
        select text of me
    else pass closeField
end closeField
```

This handler selects the suspect text, so that the next character keystrokes replace the selection. This is not enough, however, because the user could click on a button or something to de-select the field's text. You should couple this handler with an exitField handler to trap for cases in which the contents of the field don't change between opening and closing. Since the closeField handler already has all the code, the exitField handler could be:

```
on exitField
    closeField
end exitField
```

The other time it's wise to test for the validity of entered data is after an Ask command. This command presents a dialog box for user input. If the resulting operations rely on any one of the predefined types, then perform the test, display an Answer dialog if there is a problem, and re-display the Ask command again. Here's one way to take care of this situation:

```
on mouseUp
    repeat
        ask "Please enter your account number."
        if the result is Cancel then exit mouseUp
        if it is a number
        then exit repeat
        else answer "Sorry, not a valid number. Try again."
    end repeat
end mouseUp
```

This handler keeps the user in a loop until either a valid number is entered or the Cancel button is clicked in the Ask dialog box.

Data validation is a sign of good programming. Use this operator liberally to keep your user from accidentally or intentionally throwing your handlers off track.

Examples: See above.

You Try It: Type the following messages into the Message Box in any stack:

```
"A" is a number
125 is an integer
125 is a point
"20,20" is a point
"0,0,100,100" is a rect
the date is a date
true is a logical
```

there is a <thing>

there is no <thing>

there is not a <thing>

Returns: True or false depending on whether the <thing> exists as far as HyperCard can tell.

2.2

When to Use Them: These operators test for the presence of items that your script needs to work with. The <thing> parameter must be a valid expression representing any of the following items:

menu	field
menuItem	part
window	disk
stack	folder
background	file
background picture	program
card	document
card picture	scriptingLanguage
button	

In general, you only need to check for the existence of an item if the user has control over the existence in the normal course of using the stack. For example, let's say you create an address book stack that is so customizable that it invites users to adjust the names of text fields, even though you supply a default set of fields with names like First Name, Last Name, Company, and so on. If one of the operations you build into the stack takes information from the Company field, it is quite possible that the user may delete the Company field or change its name (a government employee may change "Company" to "Agency," for instance). Since the order of fields may also change, you cannot rely on the field number as a link to the Company field data. In this case, you would test for the existence of the Company field before trying to fetch any of its data:

```
if there is a field "Company"
then [do normal stuff]
else [tell me which field to use]
```

If the field does not exist, then perhaps your script asks the user to click on the field to use instead. Be prepared to provide pathnames for files and stacks if the files are in folders other than the one HyperCard occupies.

But perhaps the most popular application of these operators is to check for the existence of an item before attempting to create another item with the same name. In the address book example, above, if you automate the process of creating a new field with the help of Ask dialog prompts, you can do a quick test immediately after the user enters a new field name to see if that field already exists before creating the field and setting the name to the one entered by the user. If you didn't test for that beforehand, HyperCard would allow a duplicate field name. It's much better for your script to trap the existence of the object and offer the user a way to revise the entry. The same goes for checking the existence of stacks, files, menuItems, and windows before attempting to create another instance of the same named object. Bear in mind that numerous HyperCard windows "exist" even if you cannot see them, such as the Tools, Patterns, FatBits, Scroll, and other windows.

2.2

HyperCard makes a distinction between documents and files in the way it looks for their existence. In the case of documents and applications, HyperCard uses the search paths from the Home stack to see if the designated file is available in those paths. If it is not, you don't see the "Where Is" dialog; the operator simply returns false. For files, HyperCard doesn't use any stored pathnames, so it is best to define the pathname as the file descriptor in the statement (e.g., `there is a file "HD120:Documents:Letter to Joe"`). Without a full pathname, HyperCard assumes the folder containing HyperCard contains the named file.

If your stack relies on the presence of AppleScript (or other scripting language), then your openStack handler should verify its existence before you let the user get too far. If the desired language isn't available, then alert the user about what is needed to use the stack, and then exit the stack.

Examples:

```
if there is no field "Name" then doMenu "New Field"
if there is no menu "Special" then create menu "Special"
if there is a window "Picture" then...
if there is a file "Text Data" then open file "Text Data"
if there is a disk "HD120" then...
```

You Try It: Type the following messages into the Message Box in the Home stack:

```
there is a stack "Home"
there is no stack "Home"
there is a card "Home Card"
there is a file "HyperCard"
there is a window "Tools"
there is not a window "Patterns"
there is a menu "Home"
there is a menuItem "Open Stack..."
there is a scriptingLanguage "AppleScript"
```

Miscellaneous Operators

The remaining operators are a mixed bag of logical, text, and command operators.

and

or

not

Returns: And and Or return true or false depending on the logical relationship between two comparison expressions; Not returns the opposite of the logical result of a comparison expression.

When to Use Them: All three of these expressions are used primarily in repeat and decision-making constructions (see Chapter 46). They are sometimes called Boolean operators, because they're based on Boolean algebra, a math system founded by George Boole in the nineteenth century.

The And operator lets you establish two comparison criteria, both of which must be true for the operator to return true. If one of the comparisons is false, then the operator returns false. In other words, condition A must be true *and* condition B must be true for the whole statement to be true.

You have a few important ways to apply this tool. For example, you can specify a range of numbers within which a comparison figure must be before a certain procedure is carried out. If you want the script to beep when a number in a field is between 10 and 20, the conditional test would look like this:

```
if field 1 >= 10 and field 1 <= 20 then beep
```

Notice that on either side of the And operator is a complete comparison statement, including the field number and the math range. Both sides must be complete statements, as shown. You cannot use if field 1 >= 10 and <= 20 then beep. The script doesn't remember the field 1 part for the second comparison.

If you change the direction of the less than and greater than signs in the above conditional construction, you can test for a number that is outside the range of 10 to 20, as follows:

```
if field 1 < 10 and field 1 > 20 then beep
```

indicating that the number is out of the desired range.

You may also test for two completely different conditions, both of which must be met for the operator to return a true. For instance, you may insist that one field have a number greater than 100 while a second field has specific text in it. Such a test would look like this

```
if field 1 > 100 and field 2 is "Pounds" then...
```

In other words, any two comparisons may be used on either side of an And operator. The key is that both must evaluate to true if the And operator is to return a true.

The Or operator is similar to the And operator, but only one of the two comparison expressions must be true for the Or operator to return true. Therefore, the expression

```
3 < 100 or 5 = 20
```

returns true, because the first comparison, that 3 is less than 100, is true. Even though 5 = 20 on its own returns false, the Or operator returns a true because at least one of the two comparisons is met. If both are met, the Or operator still returns a true. If neither comparison returns true, the Or operator returns false.

The Not operator works with only one comparison and turns its result into the opposite. Therefore, if the comparison

```
20 > 10
```

returns true on its own, the comparison preceded by the Not operator, as in

```
not (20 > 10)
```

returns false. In other words, the Not operator returns what the following expression is NOT. If it's not true, then it must be false, and vice versa.

You'll see these expressions frequently in Chapter 46 where we demonstrate the conditional constructions.

Examples:

```
if field 1 is true or field 2 is true then put true into answer
repeat while theHour > 10 and theHour < 11
    -- theHour is a local variable
```

You Try It: Type the following messages into the Message Box in any stack:

```
put 1 into temp1
put 100 into temp2
temp1 > 0 and temp2 > 0
temp1 < 0 and temp2 > 0
temp1 < 0 or temp2 > 0
temp1 < 0 or temp2 > 100
temp1 = 1
not (temp1 = 1)
```

& (concatenate)

&& (concatenate and space)

Returns: The combined text string from two individual text strings.

When to Use Them: The Concatenate operators are demonstrated frequently in chapters about HyperTalk commands. Generally speaking, the Concatenate operators link two text strings together into one string. This is used primarily as a way of combining text components from diverse sources before putting the result into a container, like a field or variable.

A practical application of concatenation revolves around a system of naming cards in a stack in such a way that you can assemble the card name from various components before going to the card. At one stage of development of a world traveler's stack, for instance, cards with country maps contained a row of buttons linking to information cards about that country. The button scripts assembled the name of the information card from two sources: the first item of a hidden text file containing one or more country names, and a text string in the button script representing the type of card, such as Currency or Air Travel (Figure 44–2).

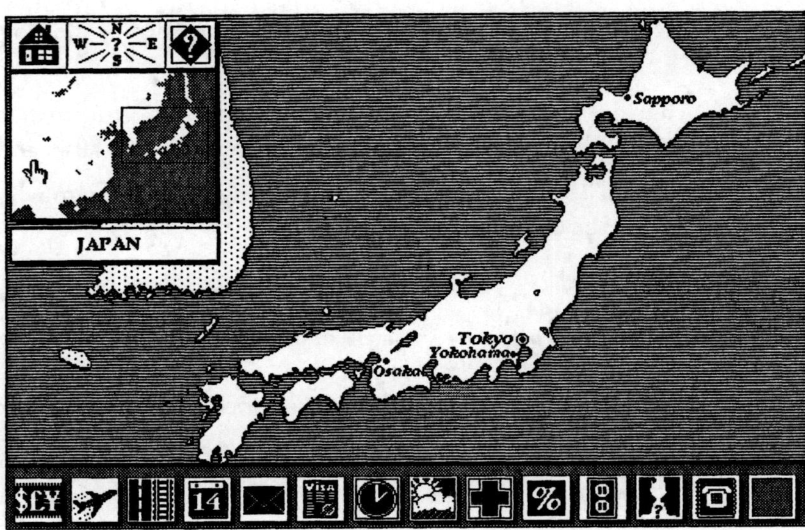

Figure 44–2. In this travel stack, the button scripts linking country maps to information cards for currency, air travel, and so on use the Concatenate feature of HyperTalk.

When the user clicked on the Currency button in the Japan card, the button script assembled the information card's name by concatenating the country name, Japan, and a three letter code for the Currency card, "Cur." The script looks something like this:

```
on mouseUp
   put item 1 of field "Country Name" & "Cur" into goName
   go to card goName in stack "Currency"
end mouseUp
```

Over in the Currency stack, Japan's card was named "JapanCur," and HyperCard zipped to that card as quickly as it could.

Since the Concatenate operator, by itself, abuts two pieces of text without any spaces, HyperTalk includes a shortcut to adding a space between the pieces: the double ampersand operator. This operator works just like the regular Concatenate operator but also inserts a space between the pieces.

You can also link more than one concatenation together in a script line as well as a mixture of single and double ampersands. It's not uncommon to see constructions like

```
field 1 && field 2 & field 3
```

in a script.

Examples:

```
put item 1 of the long date && item 2 of the long date
open file the date & the time
```

You Try It: Type the following messages into the Message Box in any stack:

```
put "Howdy" into temp1
put "Doody" into temp2
put temp1 & temp2 into message
put temp1 && temp2 into message
put "It's the " & temp1 && temp2 & " Show!"
```

contains

is in

Returns: True or false, depending on whether one text string is in another.

When to Use Them: You'll find times in your script writing when you want to test whether a certain character, word, or phrase is included in a container like a field or variable. For such a test, use the Contains operator. The syntax is as follows:

```
<container> contains <text to look for>
```

meaning that the first parameter holds the text through which you wish to look for a match of the second parameter. The alternate syntax is

```
<text to look for> is in <container>
```

For example, let's say that field 1 contains the text, "Larry, Moe, and Curly." The following expression,

```
field 1 contains "Moe"
```

returns true. But the expression

```
field 1 contains "Sarah"
```

returns false. The operator performs strictly a text-matching task, ignoring whether the parameters are valid words or items. Therefore, the expression

```
field 1 contains "r"
```

returns true, although this fact doesn't tell you a lot, since there are three instances of the letter r in the container.

Examples:

```
if field "date" contains the long date then...
repeat while temp contains the time
if field "checkmark" contains "√" then go card id 1655
```

You Try It: Type the following messages into the Message Box in any stack:

```
put "Four score and seven years ago..." into speech
speech contains "four"
speech contains "4"
speech contains " " -- a space between quotes
speech contains "r s" -- r, space, s
"four score" is in speech
```

within

Returns: True or False depending on whether a specified coordinate point is inside the boundary specified by a set of rectangular coordinates.

When to Use It: Perhaps the most common use of this operator is to test for whether the cursor is in a particular area on the screen, including atop a button or field rectangle. The syntax for using this operator is as follows:

```
<point expression> is [not] within <rectangle expression>
```

A point expression is any expression that offers two coordinate numbers separated by a comma, such as

```
100,150
topLeft of field 1
loc of bkgnd button "OK"
```

Similarly, a rectangle expression is any expression that offers four coordinate numbers separated by commas, such as

```
100,150,300,300
rect of field 1
rect of bkgnd button "OK"
```

Don't, however, use this operator when a mouseWithin handler is possible.

Examples:

```
the mouseLoc is in rect of bkgnd button "OK"
topLeft of field 3 is not in "200,200,300,300"
```

You Try It: Position the cursor atop the Name & Address field of any card in the Address stack. Then type the following messages into the Message Box.

```
the mouseLoc is within rect of field 1
the mouseLoc is within rect of field 2
the mouseLoc is within rect of card window
```

-- (comment)

Returns: Nothing. HyperTalk skips the script line.

When to Use It: While it's true that HyperTalk scripts are in more of a natural language than most programming languages, it is still an excellent idea to place comments in your scripts to help you find sections or long scripts or remind you later of the technique used to carry out a particular operation. When you type two hyphens in a script line (even as the first characters of the line), HyperTalk skips over the words following them on the line. This is where you can place your comments about the script.

If your stacks are going to be used and customized by other people, then be as helpful as you can by providing many clues in your scripts regarding techniques and philosophies about your stack and script-design decisions. You might even include instructions in the script for ways of customizing certain parts of it.

While debugging a script, it is often helpful to comment-out lines to isolate problems. The Script Editor's Comment and Uncomment menu items affect all selected lines in a flash.

Examples:

```
put 1 into x -- x is local variable, used for counter.
    -- this section calculates the metric conversion...
```

You Try It: Typing comments into the Message Box is a waste of time, since nothing happens. We have been using comments so liberally throughout this book that they should be rather familiar to you by now.

Precedence

While we've covered all the HyperTalk operators, there is one aspect about them that is not obvious. If more than one operator or more than one type of operator is located in a single script line, HyperTalk obeys strict rules as to which operators are evaluated first—and it doesn't go from left to right. The rules are based a lot on algebra (don't run away!) and can be summarized here.

HyperTalk performs operations in this order:

1. Operators within parentheses are performed before those outside parentheses.
2. minus sign (for a negative number), Boolean not, there is [not] a[n], within
3. ^ (to the power)
4. * / div mod
5. + -

6. & && (concatenate)
7. > < <= >= ≤ ≥ contains, within, is [not] in, is [not] a[n]
8. = <> ≠ is, is not
9. and
10. or

What this all means is that HyperTalk picks apart a line of script and calculates each operator in accordance with the priorities listed above. No script line will contain all these operators, but HyperTalk still adheres to the list.

The importance of understanding *precedence*, as it is called, can be demonstrated in a simple comparison of two formats for the same arithmetic expression:

a. 4 * 5 + 10
b. 4 * (5 + 10)

Because of HyperTalk's rules of precedence, expression (a) would evaluate to 30. Expression (b) evaluates to 60. That's quite a difference for the addition of a couple parentheses, but those parentheses can help you direct HyperTalk to interpret your intention (which was, in this case, to add 5 to 10 before multiplying the result by 4).

A lot of HyperTalk's precedence rules are almost automatic. For example, the way you've learned about the And and Or operators, you pretty much expect the other arithmetic operators to have been completed before the anding and oring is performed. That's exactly how the rules are already set. The important thing to remember is that when you assemble complex arithmetic expressions (including those using containers as numbers), you should run a simple test with small values like 1 and 0 to be sure the expression is evaluating correctly. If they're not, you may need to add a set of parentheses or two to force HyperTalk into following your lead on how to evaluate the expression.

CHAPTER 45

CONSTANTS

HyperTalk simplifies the entry of certain values that are normally difficult to get to from the keyboard, like the values for the Return or Tab characters and an empty string. These characters are given plain language words that substitute for the longer, more cumbersome ways of expressing them. For instance, inserting a tab character between field entries in a Write To File command would normally require knowing the ASCII value of the Tab character and performing a numToChar conversion. Instead, HyperTalk gives you a constant, called Tab, which you use in the script as if it were a standard text character.

In this section, we examine each of the constants HyperTalk provides its programmers. Some constants—like true, false, up, and down—HyperCard uses to convey information at the return of a function or operator.

true
false
up
down

When to Use Them: If you've studied HyperTalk functions and operators, you've seen that HyperCard uses these four constants frequently. True and False are often the result of comparison operators, while Up and Down represent the condition of various keyboard keys and the mouse button at the time a function executes.

But HyperCard doesn't have a monopoly on these functions. You are free to use them as you see fit. In fact, programmers commonly apply the True and False constants to set variables so that they behave as markers for where they've been. For example at the beginning of a long script, the programmer may set a variable to true (`put true into marker`). If the script includes a decision point (see Chapter 46) and the execution proceeds down one path, the script in that path may set the variable to false. Later in the script, where execution continues regardless of intervening paths, the script can test the variable. If the variable returns false, the script knows one path has been taken and can then act accordingly. This methodology is often called setting flags, because the variable, by its true or false setting, flags the script as to which route the script has followed.

Also, as you'll see in Chapter 46, any variable set to true or false can substitute for a longer comparison operation that also returns true or false.

Therefore, instead of saying `if marker is true then beep`, you can simply say `if marker then beep`. The variable "marker" by itself returns its content, which could be true or false. That meets the requirement of the conditional construction.

Examples:

```
if the optionKey is down then go card id 100
repeat while marker
if the shiftKey is down and the sound is done then go Home
```

You Try It: The right way to experiment with these constants is in the context of if-then structures. Since you cannot execute if-then structures from the Message Box, place the following handler in a new button script in a blank card of the Practice stack. Then click the button while holding down one or more modifier keys.

```
on mouseUp
   put "The Option Key is " & the optionKey into line 1 of field 5
   put "The Command Key is " & the commandKey into line 2 of field 5
   put "The Shift Key is " & the shiftKey into line 3 of field 5
   if the optionKey is down or the commandKey is down or the shiftKey is down
   then put "Modifier(s) in effect." into line 4 of field 5
   else put empty into line 4 of field 5
end mouseUp
```

empty

When to Use It: The Empty constant is the same as the null text string (that is, two quotation marks with nothing in between, ""). Not only is it easier to put an empty constant in a container to clear it, but it is also more natural-sounding in a script to test for whether a container is empty than to bother with the null string.

Examples:

```
put empty into field 1
if field "Name" is empty then ask "Enter Name:"
```

You Try It: Type the following messages into the Message Box while viewing a blank card in the Practice stack:

```
put "hello" into field 1
put empty into char 2 of field 1
put "everybody" into line 2 of field 1
put empty into line 1 of field 1
```

quote

When to Use It: If you've ever tried to place a quotation mark in a field or variable, you probably were frustrated, because HyperCard sees a quote mark as the beginning or end of a text string. You couldn't place a quotation mark inside two quotation marks. That's why HyperCard has a quote constant. It substitutes for a quotation mark in a text string when that string should contain the quotation mark.

Example:

```
put "Say " & quote & "Hello" & quote & " to everybody."
put "Coordinates: " & field 3 & quote && field 4 & """
```

You Try It: Type the following messages into the Message Box in any stack:

```
put "He said, "My name is Joe." " into message -- not allowed
put "He said, " & quote & "My name is Joe." & quote into message
```

return

space

tab

When to Use Them: These three constants substitute for keyboard characters. Return and Tab are used most often in the Write to file command. In typical scripts built around the Write to file command you must insert field and card (record) delimiters. This assures that the external Macintosh application can read the information from the text file created by HyperCard.

If information in a text field needs additional spaces between items, a script can use the Put command and the space constant to insert a space where necessary. The alternative would be to put a text string consisting of quotation marks surrounding one or more spaces. The difficulty with that construction is that it becomes very difficult later to determine exactly how many spaces are between the quote marks. With the space constant, you can tell exactly how many are there, because there is one constant per space.

Examples:

```
put space & space & space after word 1 of field 3
read from file "Database" until tab
write return to file "Expense Report"
```

You Try It: Use a blank card in the Practice stack for these experiments. Type the following messages into the Message Box:

```
put "Three blind mice. See how they run." into field 1
put space & space after word 1 of field 1
put return after word 1 of field 1
put return before word 2 of field 1
put return before word 3 of field 1
```

colon

comma

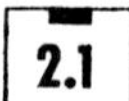

When to Use Them: These two constants represent their respective characters, and were added to the vocabulary as readability enhancements for itemDelimiter property values. The default value of this property is a comma, and the most common value for setting this property is the colon, to help parse file path names.

Examples:

```
set itemDelimiter to colon
set itemDelimiter to comma
```

You Try It: See the discussion of the itemDelimiter property in Chapter 36 for suitable experiments.

formfeed

linefeed

When to Use Them: The formfeed and linefeed constants are control characters usually used for printers (although some communications services respond to the linefeed character). These two characters are not available from the keyboard, so HyperCard provides a way to send them primarily to text files you create with the Write command.

A Linefeed character (ASCII value 10) differs from return. On telecommunications terminals (and also on the old teletype machines), a Return character sends the print cursor (or printhead) to the left edge of the screen (or page) without advancing to the next line. To advance the cursor (or paper) to the next line, the Linefeed character command is required. Today, most printers automatically insert a Linefeed command when they receive a Return command (this ability is one of the settings of the small DIP switches inside dot-matrix and letter-quality printers—laser printers don't need to bother). If you find that the text files you write from HyperCard cause the printer to print text all on the same line without advancing the paper, either change the printer's switch setting or include a Linefeed character along with the Return character in the printing script.

Formfeed is another character (ASCII value 12) that causes the paper to advance to what the printer considers to be the top of the next page. The need for this constant will be rare, but it is here if you need it.

Examples:

```
write return & linefeed to file "Print File"
write formfeed to file "Pages and Pages"
```

You Try It: Since you cannot see these characters on your HyperCard screen, there is little need to experiment with them here. To prove these constants are legitimate ASCII characters, however, type the following messages into the Message Box:

```
the charToNum of lineFeed
the charToNum of formFeed
```

This concludes our discussions about functions, operators, and constants. There is one more fundamental subject area you should know about before we get into some sample HyperTalk applications: control structures. That's the subject of the next chapter.

CHAPTER 46

HYPERTALK CONTROL STRUCTURES

Much of what we, as humans, do every day can be described in terms of what HyperCard calls *control structures.* The two basic structures involve (1) making simple decisions and (2) repeating actions with slight variations.

In the course of a day, you make many decisions, most of them unconsciously. For instance, if the television set is too loud, then you turn the volume down. If it is getting dark, then you turn on a light. If it is a nice, warm day and if you have a free moment, then you'll step outside for a breath of fresh air. You may make thousands of these if-then decisions per day. HyperCard, too, can make if-then decisions.

A number of daily tasks are repetitive actions. Again, you probably don't recognize such tasks as being repetitive. But, even while you're reading this book, you're performing a repetitive task: reading one word or phrase at a time, then advancing your eye to the next word or phrase. You continue repeating this action until you finish the book or stop reading because you're tired or have something else to do. The same can be said for paying bills from a checkbook. The basic action, writing a check, is repeated until all the bills are paid or your checkbook balance is zero. Some details of each step in the repetition are different, like the payee and the amount, but the basic action is still repeated. HyperCard allows you to program similar kinds of repeated actions, allowing for slight modifications at each step.

The HyperTalk syntax provides several construction options for if-then and repeat control structures. Each has a specific purpose that affects the flow of logic through a HyperTalk script. We'll discuss each one in detail, following a format similar to what you saw for commands and functions earlier.

Rather than offer separate experiments for you to try, we'll show you real-life examples in each discussion, which you can place in button or card scripts to try yourself. These constructions generally involve multiple-line scripts, so the Message Box approach is out of the question. All examples will be presented in such a fashion that you can write them into card scripts attached to blank cards in the Address stack. Each sample script will be a complete message handler with its own name. To try the script after typing it into the card's Script Editor, type the name of the message handler into the Message Box (for example, if the message handler starts with *on fourTimes*, then type fourTimes into the Message Box). HyperCard, as you'll recall, sends the message from the Message Box to the current card.

If-Then Decision

All HyperTalk if-then constructions have one important characteristic in common. Each one begins by testing whether a certain condition is true. By that we mean that whatever expression is under test, it must evaluate to either a "true" or "false." If the result is true, HyperTalk progresses down the special path set aside for it whenever the expression returns true. If the result is false, HyperTalk ignores the special path and zips to the next regular line in the script. This process is pictured in Figure 46–1.

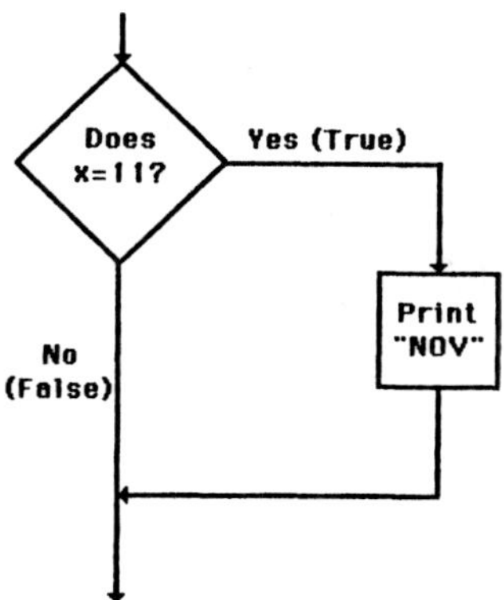

Figure 46–1. The result of a decision is either true or false. A script can perform different or extra steps based on the results of a decision.

If you think back to the last chapters, which covered functions, operators, and constants, you'll recall that a few functions and many operators return either a true or false. Any one of those expressions may be used in the test part of an if-then construction. You'll commonly test for things like: whether a container is equal to (or less than or greater than) a certain value; whether a container is empty; whether a container holds a specific text string; whether two containers are equal (or less than or greater than) each other. You may also test directly for the true or false setting of properties, like whether a button is highlighted.

All if-then constructions, therefore, begin with the word "if," followed by the true/false expression and the word "then." Here are some examples of this prefix:

```
if x < 3 then...
if item 3 of the long date > 1994 then...
if field 3 <> field 1 of card id 7067 then...
if field "Name" is empty then...
```

With the help of the And and Or Boolean operators, you can set more than one expression for the true/false test. For example, if you want HyperTalk to execute some special instructions only if the current year is between 1990 and 2000 (inclusive), you could first put item 3 of the long date function into It. Then set up the following prefix to an if-then construction:

```
if it ≥ 1990 and it ≤ 2000 then...
```

Following the rules of the And operator, the expression will return a true only if the year is 1990, 1991, . . . ,2000. You can use the Or operator to allow execution of the special code only if the month function returns 1990 or 2000 in the following prefix:

```
if it is 1990 or it is 2000 then...
```

Using the Not operator, you can test for all conditions except one. All years other than the one specified will divert to the command(s) following the "then" part of the construction:

```
if it is not 1984 then...
```

While all the if-then constructions share the true/false structure, what distinguishes each of the three is what happens after the "then." That's what we'll focus on in the descriptions of each if-then construction.

if...then

Formats:

```
if <true> then <command>

if <true>
then <command>

if <true> then
    <command>
    <command>
end if
```

When to Use It: This is the simplest of the if-then constructions. It presumes that you have an alternate command path set for instances in which the true/false expression returns true. When the true/false expression returns false, the alternate command path is not carried out.

When you have a short, single command as the alternate path, use the simple, one-line if...then format. When the one line command is a long one, it may be more convenient to use the second format. When multiple commands apply to the alternate path, use the third format. The HyperTalk Script Editor automatically indents commands beneath the *if* statement. But also notice that multiple command lines require an *end if* marker to let HyperCard know that it has reached the end of the *if* commands.

A <command> is any HyperTalk command statement that you would normally put at the beginning of a script line. Use this construction whenever your script needs to make some kind of simple adjustment whenever a certain condition is true.

Examples:

```
on insert
    if field 1 is empty then put the long date into field 1
    get item 3 of field 1
    if it < 1990 then put "Your clock may be off"
end insert

on openCard
    if field 1 is empty then
        put the long date into field 1
        put the time into line 2 of field 1
    end if
    ask "Is the current time " & line 2 of field 1 & " correct?" with "OK" or "No"
    if it is "No"
    then put "Please adjust time in Control Panel."
end openCard
```

if...then...else

Formats:

```
if <true> then <command> else <command>

if  <true> then <command>
else <command>

if <true> then
    <command>
    <command>
else <command>

if <true> then <command>
else
    <command>
    <command>
end if

if <true> then
    <command>
    <command>
else
    <command>
    <command>
end if
```

When to Use It: Use the if-then-else construction when you have two possible side paths for HyperTalk after a decision, one path for true, one for false. When the expression returns true, HyperTalk pursues the first path (the one after the "then"); when the expression returns false, HyperTalk pursues the second path (the one after the "else"). Figure 46–2 illustrates this execution path.

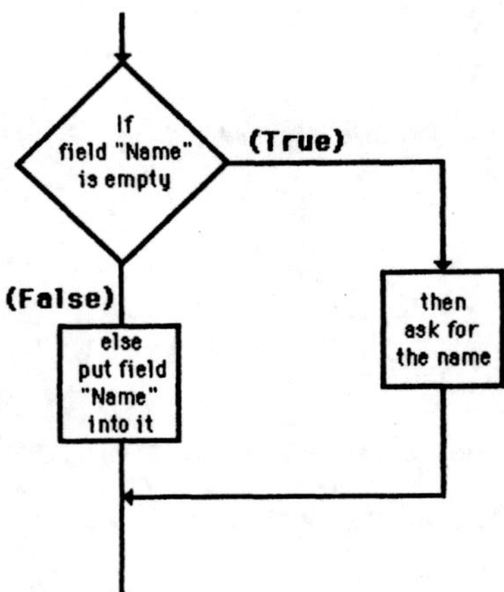

Figure 46–2. An if-then-else construction lets your script perform two distinct operations based on the results of a decision.

You can use this construction even if you have only one command for each condition or different numbers of commands for each. Since the true/false expression will return one of those two possibilities, the script will execute one of the two banks of commands before proceeding through the script.

Only when the *else* part of the construction contains multiple command lines do you need the *end if* marker, as in the last two formats, above.

Example:

```
on quiz
    put empty into message
    ask "What is another name for Britain?"
    if it is "England" or it is "United Kingdom"¬
    or it is "U.K." then put "Correct" into message
    else
        beep
        answer "Sorry. Try again"
    end if
end quiz
```

Nesting If-Then Decisions

You may place an if-then construction within another if-then construction—a format called nesting. It's not uncommon to require nested if-then constructions, because the world is not black-and-white (or true-and-false). Even when something tests to be true, it may still undergo further scrutiny to help narrow the decision process.

The best way to observe this is to watch it in action inside a real script. The following message handler presents a dialog box requesting whether you wish to know how many days are in the current month. It then reads the current month from the Macintosh clock and makes further determinations before presenting the reply in another dialog box.

```
on hathMonth
    answer "Do you wish to know how many days in this month?" with "Yes" or "No"
    if it is "Yes" then
        get the date
        convert it to dateItems
        put item 1 of it into year
        put item 2 of it into month
        if month is 4 or month is 6 or month is 9 or month is 11
        then put 30 into howMany
        else put 31 into howMany
        if month is 2 then
            if year mod 4 = 0
            then put 29 into howMany
            else put 28 into howMany
        end if
        answer "This month has " & howMany & " days in it."
    else answer "Just thought we'd ask"
end hathMonth
```

This may seem to be an extreme case, but it does demonstrate that you can nest if-then constructions quite deeply, mixing single and multiple command line constructions as needed. And, despite what seems to be many lines of code, HyperCard goes through its paces rather quickly. Try the message handler above to see for yourself. Place it in a card script and type hathMonth into the Message Box.

Replicating Case Statements

Other programming languages, such as Pascal, offer a construction that speeds branching to any number of possible conditions. For example, if a user can respond to a dialog box with the letters A, B, or C, the program branches to do a special operation for each response: in the case of A, do this; in the case of B, do that; etc. Pascal calls these CASE statements.

HyperTalk doesn't have an explicit CASE statement facility, but you can replicate the its action by a stream of if-then-else constructions. Using the dialog response problem above, here's one way to handle it in HyperTalk:

```
on caseTest
    ask "Please enter A, B, or C."
    if it is not empty then
        if it is "A"
        then doAStuff
        else if it is "B"
        then doBStuff
        else if it is "C"
        then doCStuff
        else answer "You didn't enter the right letter."
    end if
end caseTest
```

This construction is reasonably compact, and follows in the spirit of the CASE statement.

Repeat Constructions

HyperTalk offers five different repeating control structures from which to choose: Repeat Forever, Repeat For, Repeat Until, Repeat While, and Repeat With. While their uses are quite different, they share two common characteristics.

The first characteristic is that in the same line as the repeat command you will be providing information that controls when the repetition is to end. Sometimes the repetition ends after a specific number of times; at other times, the repetition ends only upon a certain condition being met, a condition that changes each time through the repetition. Repetitions like these are sometimes called loops, because the execution of the instructions runs in circles until it can break out of the cycle.

The second characteristic has to do with the ending of the repeat construction within the script. The End Repeat statement must be entered on its own line at the close of the repeat grouping. This is like a marker to HyperTalk so that it knows how far down the script to go before looping back to the beginning of the repeat construction.

Now we can look at each repeat construction in detail.

repeat [forever]

Format:

```
repeat [forever]
    <command>
    <if-then-exit repeat>
end repeat
```

When to Use It: This is a common but potentially dangerous repeat construction. While the syntax indicates that the loop will go on forever, you obviously don't want that to be the case. The point is that the controlling factor is not some condition attached to the Repeat statement, but something else that takes place inside the loop. Once the condition is met, the program flow jumps out of the loop with the Exit Repeat statement (described more fully later).

If the if-then condition is never met, the repeat loop will go on forever —or at least until you stop script execution with Command-period (as long as CantAbort is false), type Command-Option-Escape in System 7 to Force Quit HyperCard, or turn off your Macintosh. Use this construction only when the statements inside the repeat loop govern whether the loop should continue. This is different from the Repeat Until or Repeat While constructions, which trigger their loop escape by conditions that accumulate during the loop cycles.

Examples:

```
on readFile
    put empty into importText
    open file "myText"
    repeat
        read from file "myText" for 5000
        if it is empty then exit repeat -- no more in the file to read
        else put it after importText
    end repeat
    close file "myText"
    put importText into field "External Text"
end readFile
```

repeat for

Format:

```
repeat  [for]  <number of times> [times]
    <command>
    <command>
end repeat
```

When to Use It: This repeat construction repeats the indented commands a fixed number of times. The <number of times> parameter may be a plain number, an arithmetic expression, or a container (provided the container evaluates to a number).

Examples:

```
on addCards
    ask "How many new cards do you want?"
    repeat for it
        doMenu "New Card"
        put "This is a new card" into field 1
    end repeat
end addCards

on showTime
    put "Hooray for HyperCard!"
    repeat 10 times
        put space before msg
    end repeat
    repeat  20 times
        put space before word 3 of msg
        beep 1
    end repeat
    repeat 20 times
        put empty into char 21 of msg
    end repeat
    repeat 10 times
        put empty into char 1 of msg
    end repeat
end showTime
```

repeat until

Format:

```
repeat until <true>
    <command>
    <command>
end repeat
```

When to Use It: In the Repeat Until structure, the indented commands are executed until an expression returns a "true." In other words, if the expression returns a true the first time, none of the indented commands are executed. But if the expression is false, the loop starts and continues until the expression returns a true.

Obviously, the commands inside a Repeat Until construction must have some effect on the factors in the true/false expression. If nothing about that expression changes, the loop will drone on endlessly. In fact you will have caused what is known as an endless, or infinite, loop. The only way to break out of an infinite loop is to hold down the Command key and press the period key. That key combination halts a HyperTalk message handler in its tracks.

A common application for Repeat Until is to keep a loop going while waiting for a mouse click. There doesn't have to be a command between the *repeat* and *end* repeat parts of the construction. If you include no command lines between the start and end of a repeat, the repeat loop keeps cycling very tightly until the true/false expression returns true.

Examples:

```
on jumpWeeks -- best demonstrated in Appointments stack
    repeat until the mouseClick
        get number of this card
        go card (it + 7)
        wait 1 second
    end repeat
end jumpWeeks
```

repeat while

Format:

```
repeat while <true>
    <command>
    <command>
end repeat
```

When to Use It: The Repeat While construction is essentially the opposite of the Repeat Until construction. In this case, the indented commands are carried out as long as the true/false expression remains true. If it is false to begin with, HyperTalk will skip right past it.

As with Repeat Until, your indented commands must have some effect on the items being compared or measured in the true/false expression. If these factors never change, then your script will be in an infinite loop.

Examples:

```
on tunes
    put the random of 60 into note
    if note < 40 then put 40 into note
    if note mod 2 is not zero then add 1 to note
    repeat while note ≤ 82
        put note
        play "Harpsichord" temp 700 note
        add 2 to note
    end repeat
end tunes
```

repeat with

Format:

```
repeat with <variable> = <low number> to <high number>
    <command>
    <command>
end repeat
```

```
repeat with <variable> = <high number> down to <low number>
    <command>
    <command>
end repeat
```

When to Use It: While the Repeat With construction may seem like the most complicated of the four, it is perhaps the most commonly used. With this construction, you can both initialize a variable and set bounds for it. Each time through the loop, the value of the variable is increased or decreased by one. The loop continues cycling until the value of the variable equals that of the second number.

This is so valuable because you can use the variable within the indented commands to perform actions on any numbered group of objects or components. Therefore, if you initialize a variable "a" and give it the bounds 1 through 5, each time through the loop you can issue a command like put the date into field "Date" of card a. The first time through the loop, the date goes into card 1; the second time through, the date goes into card 2; and so on.

Parameters for either boundary number may be a plain number, an arithmetic expression, a function, or a container. Therefore, if you wish to perform an operation on every field in a card, the repeat construction would start out like this:

```
repeat with x = 1 to the number of fields
```

Then, within the indented commands, the instructions calling for a field designator would look like this:

```
put empty into field x
```

The beauty of this repeat construction is that you can condense an awful lot of HyperTalk code into just a few lines by repeating the same code over and over, but incrementing (or decrementing) the object or container designator each time. Whenever you notice that a script repeats the same commands to similar kinds of objects, you probably have a candidate for condensation with the Repeat With construction.

When deleting a series of objects in a repeat loop, always use the second version, which counts backwards. You'll want to delete from the highest number to the lowest, because deleting the first item rearranges the order of the remaining items—the second item becomes the first, as the repeat loop deletes only the item it sees as the second item.

Example:

```
on makeCards
    ask "Please enter the starting date:" with the date
    convert it to seconds
    put it into start
    ask "Please enter the ending date:"
    convert it to seconds
    put it into finish
    put finish - start into howLong
    divide howLong by 24*60*60 -- seconds per day
    repeat with count = 1 to howLong
        doMenu "New Card"
        put "Day " & count into field "Which Day"
        put start into field "Date"
        convert field "Date" to long date
        add (24*60*60) to start
    end repeat
end makeCards
```

Modifying Repeat Execution Order

Normally, within a repeat construction the commands are executed in the order in which they appear. That's as it should be. But there may be times when you might not want the cycle to include some commands. In other words, you'd like the cycle to skip the remaining commands and start over at the top of the cycle, incrementing the counter, if it's the Repeat With construction. HyperTalk has a keyword statement that does that: Next Repeat.

You can also exit a repeat construction in the middle of it, if a condition you're looking for is met before execution reaches the bottom and starts over. The keyword statement that takes care of that is Exit Repeat.

next repeat

When to Use It: You can set up any valid conditional test (if-then) within the indented commands of a repeat construction, in such a way that a test returning true executes the Next Repeat statement. A skeletal repeat script set up this way would look like this:

```
repeat until <true>
    <command 1>
    <command 2>
    if <true> then next repeat
    <command 3>
end repeat
```

HyperTalk would start following the repeat commands as usual. If the conditional test after command 2 proves true, the Next Repeat statement tells HyperTalk to loop back to the top of the repeat and start over without executing command 3. If the repeat construction had been the Repeat For or Repeat With, the counter would have increased by 1.

The Next Repeat statement is used to trap a special case in a repeat loop and prevent further commands within the repeat to be executed. A practical application for this construction is within a repeat with loop in which you want the counting variable (that is, the "x" in repeat with x = 1 to 100) to increment by numbers other than 1. If, for instance, you want to use the counting variable only when it is even, you could place an if-then statement at the very beginning of the repeat loop that tests whether the counter mod 2 is not zero. If it's not (meaning the counting variable is an odd number), then do a next repeat without performing any other commands in the loop. Experienced BASIC programmers will recognize this method as an equivalent to the REPEAT...STEP construction.

Example:

```
on plan
  repeat with count = 1 to 14
    if count mod 7 is 0 then
      put "No scheduled work on Sundays" into line count of field 2
      next repeat
    end if
    put "Day " & count into line count of field 2
  end repeat
end plan
```

exit repeat

exit <handler name>

When to Use Them: You may also test for a condition within a repeat loop that is different from the one the repeat is looking for. For example, the repeat may be waiting for a mouse click all the while some math is going on within the indented commands. If you want to exit the repeat without a mouse click when the math reaches a certain value, you'd test for that value and issue the Exit Repeat command. The skeletal construction looks like this:

```
repeat until the mouseClick
  <command 1> -- does things to the contents of field 3
  <command 2>
  if field 3 > 100 then exit repeat
  <command 3>
end repeat
```

In this case, the loop stops before a mouse click if the content of field 3 grows to over 100. This is assuming, of course, that the commands in this loop have some effect over field 3 during the execution of the loop.

It also turns out that the Exit command is rather universal, covering message handlers in general. Within a message handler situation, the Exit statement comes in quite handy when the script reaches a condition that makes the rest of the handler superfluous. When the handler exits, then it's all through. See also "Exit to HyperCard" in Chapter 35.

Examples:

```
on mouseUp
    if the heapSpace < 120000 then
        answer "Not enough memory for painting tools."
        exit mouseUp
    end if
    choose spray tool
    ... -- more commands
end mouseUp
```

pass <message>

When to Use It: Occasionally, you will want to trap a HyperCard system message or other kind of message whose primary handler is way up the HyperCard hierarchy. If you'd like to add some extra feature to the handler or trap the message when it has a particular parameter (like a menu item name), issue the special command, and then send the message on its way up the hierarchy, as if it had never been trapped. You send it on its way with the Pass keyword.

The one parameter to the Pass keyword is the name of the message that you originally trapped for. For example, if you have a button script that traps for mouseUp and there is a background script also for mouseUp, your button script would trap the mouseUp message first. After it has done its thing, it may then pass the mouseUp message to the next level up the hierarchy. When the background mouseUp message handler gets the mouseUp message, it will not know that the message had been intercepted anywhere along the path.

Trapping for some menu items and passing the rest is a popular application for the Pass keyword. Since the doMenu system message comes with a parameter consisting of the name of the menu item and the menu, you can perform operations in a handler for one or more menu items. But you must also pass the message to HyperCard so it can respond to other menu items.

If you don't pass doMenu, the system message would be forever trapped in the handler—one method, by the way, of protecting read-only stacks from saboteurs.

Examples:

```
on doMenu whichItem
   if whichItem is "Help"
   then go card "Custom Help"
   else pass doMenu
end doMenu
```

This concludes the discussion about HyperCard's control structures. In the following chapters, we'll look at more advanced authoring tools and techniques. Later, we'll be applying the concepts learned in the preceding chapters. Together, we'll build some practical HyperCard applications, while you learn more about the commands, properties, functions, operators, constants, and control structures in action.

PART IV

HYPERCARD AUTHORING TECHNIQUES

CHAPTER

47

INTERPRETING “HYPERCARD HELPER” MESSAGES

You may have expected the title of this chapter to use the expression "Error Messages," because the dialog boxes that present them are often an unpleasant sign. They indicate that something went wrong. They seem to imply that you made a mistake someplace.

We believe that is the wrong perspective. That you inadvertently left out a character from a HyperTalk script or didn't realize that your disk was filling up is hardly cause for anyone—much less a computer—to point a finger at you saying: "You are wrong." No one is immune to a slipped digit or forgotten character.

But that's precisely why these messages are in HyperCard, and why they show up when something isn't perfect. They're not there to scold you, but to point out that something isn't quite right and needs your attention. Moreover, the wording of most messages is clear enough to direct you to the spot in a script or to your last manual operation so that they really help you figure out what needs investigation.

Therefore, we call these messages HyperCard Helpers. Use them as if they were suggestions from a kindly teacher. They won't solve the problem, but they guide you and prompt you to figure out what the missing character or word is. The purpose of this chapter, then, is to list the *most common* HyperCard Helpers, and explain why they occur and what to look for in solving the mystery—in other words, typical problems and typical solutions. They are presented in alphabetical order, so feel free to use this chapter as a reference when you're building stacks or experimenting with HyperCard.

A printing error has occurred; the print job cannot be completed.

Problem: Something has happened at the printer end or in communication between printer and computer that tells HyperCard all is not well. A printing session in HyperCard is called a *print job*. When this message occurs, all printing activity ceases, and the print job is closed.

Solution: Check your ImageWriter or StyleWriter for paper-out conditions and make sure the printer is "on-line." LaserWriter printers usually provide their own clues in the AppleTalk window or Print Monitor dialog about printer problems, so you won't see this message as a result of paper-out indications. Check that the Chooser is set to the correct printer, and double check all cabling between Macintosh and printer.

Already have a local variable named " ".

Problem: If you declare your global variables (with the Global keyword) other than at the top of a handler, there is the possibility that you will declare a global variable name that you've used earlier in the handler as a local variable. HyperTalk prevents you from declaring a global variable in a handler if you've used that same name for a local variable earlier in the same handler.

Solution: Declare global variables early in the handler, and then be sure you use unique names for local variables later in the handler.

An error has occurred in the LaserWriter. Turning the printer off and back on again might clear up the problem.

Problem: This message, specifically for the LaserWriter, lets you know that something has gone awry inside the memory or control circuitry of the LaserWriter. Sometimes, trying to print before the LaserWriter is ready causes the printer to "hang."

Solution: Do as the message says. Turning the printer off, waiting for about 5 or 10 seconds, and then turning it back on again usually clears up the problem. In the most severe case, you may also have to restart your Macintosh and the printer.

An icon with that ID already exists in the current stack. Replace existing icon?

Problem: In the Icon Editor, you have tried to save an icon with an ID number of another icon with that same number already in the stack. Icon resources in the same stack must have unique ID numbers.

Solution: The dialog box that contains this message also includes a button choice for renumbering the icon you're trying to save. If you don't want to overwrite the other icon, then let the Icon Editor renumber it for you (it assigns another random ID number that is not used by other icons in the stack) by clicking the Renumber button. If you click the OK button, the old icon will be replaced. The Cancel button halts the save process entirely.

Can have "else" only after "then".

Can have "then" only after "if".

Problem: Keywords in an if-then-else construction are out of their normal order.

Solution: Look for balance in the construction. Follow any of the formats shown in Chapter 46.

Can't delete last card of protected background.

Problem: You tried to delete the last card of a background whose Can't Delete Background box is checked in a background's Info dialog box.

Solution: If you wish to delete the last card of a protected background, first uncheck the setting of the Can't Delete Background checkbox in the background's Info dialog box.

Can't delete last card. Use delete stack instead.

Problem: You are trying to delete the single card remaining in a stack. You cannot delete a stack by removing the last card, even if the card or background is unlocked.

Solution: Use Delete Stack to remove the stack from your disk. Delete Stack is not undoable.

Can't delete protected card.

Problem: The Can't Delete Card checkbox in the card's Info dialog box is checked. The card is considered protected while that checkbox is checked.

Solution: To remove the card, first uncheck the setting of the Can't Delete Card checkbox in the card's Info dialog box.

Can't DIV by zero.

Can't MOD by zero.

Problem: The DIV and MOD operators must be followed by an integer value, but not zero. If you are using an expression to evaluate to this value, it is not evaluating to an integer.

Solution: Test for the actual value of the expression prior to making the DIV or MOD call. If the expression is in a variable, use the debugging tools (Chapter 48), including the variableWatcher, to step through your program and check the value of that variable along the way.

Can't edit script of HyperCard.

Problem: Your script tried to open the script editor for HyperCard. HyperCard does not contain scripts.

Solution: Be sure your Edit Script command is calling an object that can contain a script.

Can't find menu item "".

Problem: The name of a menu item specified in a DoMenu command is either misspelled or not available.

Solution: First, be sure the menu item is spelled correctly in your DoMenu command. Menu items with three periods after them must be represented in the argument to the DoMenu command with those three periods, as in doMenu "New Stack..." Next, check to make sure the user level setting gives you access to the menu. A userLevel of 2 (Typing), for instance, won't grant you or HyperTalk access to any menu item in the Objects menu nor to items left out of the shortened File and Edit menus at this user level. Third, make sure the menu item specified in the command is not dimmed. A protected stack, for example, dims the Compact Stack and Delete Stack menu items in the File menu. When a menu item is dimmed, HyperCard cannot find it, even if you send the DoMenu command directly to HyperCard. Finally, if the DoMenu command is to a custom menu item, be sure that item has been added to the menu before calling its DoMenu command.

Can't get that property.

Problem: You are attempting to retrieve a property setting that doesn't make sense to HyperCard, usually due to not specifying the correct object along with the property name.

Solution: If a property is a global or painting property, do not specify any object. The command would be something like get userLevel or get lineSize. If a property is a window, stack, background, card, field, or button property, use the appropriate object expression after the name of the property, as in get scroll of field ID 12 or get script of this stack. Also, be sure the property you're requesting for an object is indeed a property of that object. Consult the property listings in Appendix C for quick reference.

Can't modify this script.

Problem: You tried to edit a script in a locked stack.

Solution: If the padlock icon appears in the menubar, then the stack is locked by Protect Stack dialog setting (Can't Modify Stack checkbox) or by virtue of being on read-only storage media (locked floppy disk, locked file in a network, or CD-ROM). On eraseable storage (e.g., hard disk or unlocked floppy disk), you may be able to change the Protect Stack dialog settings (provided they're not password protected) to allow modifications to the script and other parts of the stack.

Can't modify this stack.

Problem: The stack is protected, either physically (on locked media) or by property setting from HyperTalk or the Stack Info dialog box.

Solution: If the stack is on a CD-ROM, is locked on a local area network, or is on a locked diskette, you won't be able to modify the stack without changing the userModify property setting. If the stack is locked, and the UserModify property is set to true, you may make changes to a card, but those changes disappear the instant you go to another card or stack. If you must modify the stack, and it is neither password protected nor on a locked disk, then uncheck the Can't Modify Stack checkbox in the Protect Stack dialog box. If the stack is password protected, you will not have ready access to this dialog box without the password.

Can't set that <object> property.

Problem: You attempted (a) to set a property that doesn't belong to the named object or (b) to set a property that may only be retrieved but not set.

Solution: Compare the arguments to your Set command against the property quick reference listings in Appendix C. Be sure that the property you are requesting is one of those available for the object you're specifying. For instance, you may not set the userLevel property of a stack, because that is a global property. The other cause of this message is trying to set a read-only property. For instance, you may not adjust the ID of an object in HyperCard, so setting that property will result in this message.

Can't understand "".

Problem: HyperCard doesn't recognize the first word of a statement line as a valid command or key word; HyperCard cannot evaluate a function because its argument is of an incorrect type.

Solution: Perhaps the most common HyperTalk Help message, it also points directly to the source of difficulty: the first word of a HyperTalk statement or function.

For command words, usually the problem is a misspelling or a word that is not a HyperTalk command at all. Remember, all HyperTalk script statements begin with a HyperTalk (or XCMD) command verb. From the Message box, you may also type in functions, preceded by the word "the." If the function name is misspelled, then the Help message comes back saying it can't understand the function name.

Properties of all objects may be retrieved by typing their names (and objects) into the Message Box. Global property names by themselves result in this Help message; but global names with the HyperCard object name (e.g., *userLevel of HyperCard*) return the property values to the Message Box without complaint.

Can't understand arguments of "".

Problem: HyperCard does not recognize either a function's parameter as a valid type or something in a command line after the command name.

Solution: This is a more difficult problem to trace than the plain "Can't understand" message, unless you use the Script button in the help message's dialog box to point to the problem in a script. A command statement may have multiple arguments, as in a chunk expression (e.g., char 3 of word 2 of line 6 of field ID 1982). Without a little help, you'll need to check each parameter very carefully for misspelling, missing spaces, or missing words. If there is a flaw in a HyperTalk script line, a click of the Script button from the Help dialog box will bring you to the location in the script where HyperCard balked. The text insertion pointer will be flashing immediately before or after the word HyperCard couldn't digest. In particular, look for incorrect adverbs (an "in" that should be an "into" or vice versa; literal text that requires quotes around it), missing arguments (forgetting the number or style to set a particular property), or missing object names (leaving out the field expression following a chunk expression; omitting an object name when getting or setting a property). If you still encounter difficulty, compare the arguments to the command of that line against the examples shown in the *Handbook* section for that command. Also, check variable names against the list in the next message description.

Expected a variable name but found " ".

Problem: A script attempted to use a HyperTalk reserved word as a local or global variable name.

Solution: To prevent confusion internally, HyperTalk prohibits users from naming variables the same as any reserved word. Not all words in the HyperTalk vocabulary are reserved for this purpose. Here is a list of words you may not use for variable names (a few are not reserved words in the true sense, but they may still not be used as variables, because their meaning is confused with valid containers or chunk expressions):

abbr	four	quote
abbrev	fourth	repeat
abbreviated	function	return
after	global	second
and	if	selection
any	into	send
before	is	seven
colon	last	seventh
comma	lineFeed	short
contains	long	six
div	me	sixth
do	message	space
down	mid	tab
eight	middle	target
eighth	mod	ten
else	msg	tenth
empty	next	then
end	nine	third
exit	ninth	three
false	one	true
fifth	or	two
first	pass	up
five	pi	zero
formFeed		

If you are trying to put a value into a variable with any of these names, choose a different name, one not on the list of "reserved" words.

Expected " " here.

Problem: HyperTalk was expecting a certain type of value, character, or expression in an argument, but encountered something else.

Solution: Before clicking the Script button when you see this Help message, pay close attention to what the message says it expected and what it found. The message offers big clues as to what's troubling the script. The types of values or characters you often see in this message are:

signed integer

unsigned integer

floating point value

true/false value

arithmetic value

of

(

A signed integer is any positive or negative whole number but not zero and not displaying any digits to the right of the decimal; a floating point value may be any value, including fractional values represented by decimal values; a true/false value is any expression that evaluates to True or False; an arithmetic value is any number.

When you click the Script button, the text pointer shows you where the trouble value or character is. Most often, the missing character is a parenthesis in a math expression or the word "of" in a chunk expression. Use the variableWatcher debugging tool (Chapter 48) to see what values HyperCard encounters. If you need an integer, use the Round or Trunc functions to evaluate the variable to an integer prior to use or to set the numberFormat to "0" (if previously set to another format with places to the right of the decimal earlier in the handler) and add zero to the value prior to its use in the statement.

Expected "end if" after "then".

Problem: The handler has at least one more If or Repeat construction requiring an End statement than there are End statements.

Solution: When you click the Script button on the help message dialog box for this message, you may not be shown the location of the difficulty. Instead, the text insertion pointer will be flashing at the top of the script. It's up to you to locate where the extra End statement(s) is needed. In a complex handler with many nested if-then and Repeat constructions, look first to be sure that all Repeats have balancing End statements. Then look for If-then-else constructions to see if any ending Then or Else segments are more than one line long—these require End statements. Nested if-then-else constructions can sometimes get complicated and therefore require explicit End If statements when you might not normally use one. For example, in the following construction:

```
if Tarzan = 1 then
    if Jane = 2
    then put "Me Tarzan, you Jane" into field "Name"
else put "Names unknown" into field "Name"
```

A press of the Tab key in the Script Editor will show this construction to be incomplete, even though the internal if-then construction appears to have correct syntax. The problem is that the Else statement is ambiguous: Does it belong to the outer or inner if-then construction? To clear up the ambiguity, you *must* be more explicit in the constructions. If the Else statement belongs to the inner if-then construction, then the syntax becomes:

```
if Tarzan = 1 then
    if Jane = 2
    then put "Me Tarzan, you Jane" into field "Name"
    else put "Names unknown" into field "Name"
end if
```

But if the Else statement belongs to the outer if-then construction, you must artificially end the inner construction, as follows:

```
if Tarzan = 1 then
    if Jane = 2
    then
        put "Me Tarzan, you Jane" into field "Name"
    end if
else put "Names unknown" into field "Name"
```

Typically, omissions of End statements can also be detected before running the handler, because HyperTalk won't be able to balance the entire handler. The End statement of the handler will not be flush left if any control structure in that handler is missing a crucial ingredient. Always press the Tab key when finished writing a handler, and check the End statement to make sure all is well within.

Expected "end if" after "else".

Expected "end if" after "if".

Expected end of line after "end if".

Expected end of line after "end repeat".

Expected "end repeat" after "repeat".

Problem: There is an imbalance in an if-then or repeat control structure.

Solution: With all control structures being of rather rigid structures (even within the wide latitude HyperTalk offers), HyperTalk can detect when an if-then-else construction is missing its "then," or when a statement tells it to exit a repeat structure when there is none. Typically, all the omissions indicated by these help messages can also be detected before running the handler, because HyperTalk won't be able to balance the entire handler. The End statement of the handler will not be flush left if any control structure in that handler is missing a crucial ingredient. Always press the Tab key when finished writing a handler, and check the End statement to make sure all is well within. If not, look for the conditions indicated in this help messages. Even if you cannot locate the problem right away, you can test the handler and let the help message guide you to the trouble spot.

External commands and functions cannot have more than 16 parameters.

Problem: Your script is trying to pass more than 16 parameters to an XCMD or XFCN (Chapter 52).

Solution: Since no XCMD or XFCN resource will ever be written to require more than 16 arguments, it is clearly a case of miscounting the number of arguments being passed along to the external code. Remember that arguments are separated by commas, and no argument may contain a comma unless the comma is inside quote marks.

Failed to " ". Stack may be corrupted.

Problem: HyperCard detects a corrupted card or background.

Solution: The cause of this problem has to do with HyperCard's internal management of objects and memory. Only when an object's space in the stack file gets "out of alignment" (i.e., it's not an even multiple of bytes required by HyperCard) does this message pop up. Frequent compacting greatly reduces the likelihood of corrupted cards and backgrounds. If you have a stack in its pristine form and can predictably cause this message to occur, Apple's HyperCard Team would like to see both versions of the stack.

To work around this problem, you'll need to create a new stack and copy as much as you can from the old to the new. If the problem is a bad card, use the following handler in the corrupted stack to copy cards on either side of the bad card to a new, empty stack you've created.

```
on transfer
    repeat with x = number of this card to the number of cards
        go to card x
        put x -- shows you which card number you're on
        doMenu "Copy Card"
        push card
        go to last card of stack "Pyramid II"
        doMenu "Paste Card"
        pop card
    end repeat
end transfer
```

Run this handler until you reach the bad card (the handler will stop). Then go to the card after the bad one and restart the handler.

There is also a stack, called Recover, produced by the HyperCard team, and readily available in public domain collections of HyperCard stacks (user groups and bulletin boards). This stack automates the process more fully.

Failed to compact stack. Disk is full.

Problem: Compact Stack requires free space on the disk of approximately double the size of the current stack.

Solution: To compact the stack, you must remove or archive unused files on your disk to make space for the compaction process. HyperCard writes the compacted version of the stack to another part of the disk in a file with a temporary name, while the original version is still safely stored on disk. When the compact is successful, the new file is renamed to the old stack name, while the original file is removed from the disk directory.

Failed to create a new card.

Failed to create a new stack.

Failed to paste card.

Failed to sort this stack.

Problem: Insufficient disk space to accommodate creation of new card or stack or to write a sorted copy to disk. Other operations triggering a "Failed to..." message indicate insufficient disk space.

Solution: Free up disk space on the current volume by deleting (or archiving) unneeded files, or save a copy to a floppy disk and retry the procedure on the copy. If there isn't enough disk space to accommodate these operations, there certainly won't be enough to compact the stack to free up space.

Failed to delete stack. Stack is protected.

Problem: You tried to delete a stack while the Can't Delete Stack checkbox in the Protect Stack dialog box is checked. This box is also checked when the stack is on a write-protected medium, like a locked floppy disk or CD-ROM.

Solution: You may delete stacks when they are stored on eraseable media, like a hard disk or unlocked floppy disk. Open the Protect Stack dialog box and uncheck the Can't Delete Stack checkbox. If the user level is set to Browsing or Typing, hold down the Command key before pulling down the File menu to bring the Protect Stack menu choice into view. If the stack is password protected, you won't be able to change this setting without the password or a password defeat utility available on most Macintosh bulletin boards or from HyperCard user groups.

Failed to delete stack. It is the current Home stack.

Problem: You tried to delete the Home stack. Since HyperCard must have a stack named Home available to it, you may not remove it from within HyperCard.

Solution: Don't try deleting this stack. HyperCard will allow you to delete any stack named Home that is not the current Home stack. The Home stack that HyperCard finds on startup remains the "official" Home stack for the duration of the HyperCard session, even if you later open a second Home stack in a different folder.

Failed to export paint. Existing file is not a MacPaint document.

Problem: You tried to export a HyperCard picture to a file with the same name as a non-MacPaint document on your disk.

Solution: Because exporting pictures from HyperCard creates a MacPaint document, you may overwrite only other MacPaint documents of the same name. Either delete the original file on the disk (in the Finder or via desk accessory products, such as CE Software's DiskTop) or re-do the operation, specifying a different file name.

Fields can't hold more than 30000 characters.

Problem: You attempted to put more than 30,000 text characters into a field.

Solution: The exact number may vary by a few characters, but this is a limit that cannot be extended by compacting the stack. Divide the text into smaller chunks and distribute the text across multiple cards. Remember, too, that scripts have the same size limit, while variables may be larger when HyperCard has ample RAM to roam. Fields have one more limit: 32,000 vertical pixels occupied by text in the field. In other words, if the line spacing of your text is 12 pixels, then a field may contain no more than 2,666 lines, even if the lines are short, and the number of characters is considerably less than 30,000. These limits are imposed by the TextEdit routines in the Macintosh Toolbox, upon which HyperCard must rely for localization purposes.

File " " is already open.

Problem: You attempted to open a text file with the Open File command, when that file has been opened earlier in the same HyperCard session.

Solution: A file need be opened only once to do multiple reads and writes. If you need to start reading the file from the beginning again, then close the file and reopen it. You may do this as many times within a handler as is needed.

Got error " " while trying to " ".

Got file system error " ".

Problem: The Macintosh File System is reporting difficulty reading or writing to the current disk volume. The error number is a Macintosh System error number.

Solution: These negative numbers in the range -33 to -61 relate disk problems not connected to HyperCard. Obvious problems are trapped by HyperCard and presented by way of its own Help messages, explained elsewhere in this chapter. For your reference, however, here are all possible File System errors and their numbers. If you see any of these errors, there may be a serious problem with your disk drive or diskette, although sometimes quitting and restarting HyperCard solves the problem.

Error Number	*Error Indication*
-33	Directory full
-34	Disk full
-35	No such volume
-36	I/O error
-37	Bad name
-38	File not open
-39	End of file
-40	Tried to position to before start of file
-41	Memory full or file won't fit
-42	Too many files open
-43	File not found
-44	Disk write protected
-45	File is locked
-46	Volume is locked
-47	File is busy
-48	Duplicate filename
-49	File already open with write permission
-50	Error in user parameter list
-51	Refnum error
-52	Get file position error
-53	Volume not on line (was ejected)
-54	Permission error
-55	Drive volume already on-line at MountVol
-56	No such drive
-57	Not a Mac disk
-58	Volume belongs to an external File System
-59	File system 'system trouble' error
-60	Bad master directory block
-61	Write permission error

If a file system error occurs and you don't understand the nature of the error, it will be out of your control anyway. Disk problems may sometimes be remedied with the help of disk maintenance utility software, such as Symantec's *Norton Utilities for the Macintosh.*

HyperCard does not have enough memory to continue.

Problem: At idle time, HyperCard determined that there is insufficient memory to perform even simple HyperCard operations.

Solution: HyperCard "bails out" after this message, returning you to the Finder or "unexpectedly quitting." Something happened to gobble up enough heap space to reduce the largest available block to less than 32K—an extremely low heapSpace reading. Moving resources and aborting some XCMDs midstream can occasionally leave the heap so fragmented that no block is larger than 32K, causing this problem. If the problem persists, increase the memory partition for HyperCard, and launch it as the first application so it grabs all the memory listed intne Preferred size listing of the System 7.1 Get Info dialog for HyperCard.

"" is not an application.

Problem: A script tried to open an application, but supplied a valid file name for something other than a Macintosh application. If the file name were not valid, you would receive, instead, the Where is...? standard file dialog to help HyperCard locate a file it can't find in the Applications pathname list.

Solution: If you want to open a document and its application, then use the Open <document> with <application> syntax. But if just the application is your target, then make sure the application file name is not the same as a data (or other) file in an Applications pathname that HyperCard finds before locating the application file. Remember that HyperCard checks the pathnames from the Applications search path card of the Home stack for a roadway to that file name in the order listed on that card.

No open file named "".

Problem: In reading from or writing to a text file, the file name specified does not match a file currently open.

Solution: First check to make sure that the file of that name was opened earlier in the handler and has not been closed in the meantime. File messages like this one usually close all opened files, and they'll have to be reopened before they may be read from or written to. Second, be sure the name of the file you're reading from or writing to is identical (including pathname, if any) to the one opened earlier in the handler.

No such card.

Problem: A command cited a card in the current stack by number, ID, or name that does not exist.

Solution: The first item to check is whether the card expression used to cite that card is entered correctly. If the reference is to a number, be sure you have your card number and ID numbers straight. Card numbers, recall, tend to change as the stack is sorted or has cards added to or removed from it. A card name may be misspelled. If you wish to go to a certain card and find it gone, that card may have been important enough to lock in its info dialog box so that it couldn't be accidentally deleted.

Importantly, this Help message does not appear if a script attempts to go to a nonexistent card. Instead this message comes back as the Result of the Go command. Unless your scripts test for the result of a Go command, you won't be alerted that the card was not found.

Not a scrolling field.

Problem: You tried to set the scroll of a field whose style is not scrolling.

Solution: If the field should be a scrolling field, then change its Style setting in its Info dialog box or its Style property with HyperTalk. If the field is not supposed to be a scrolling field, do not try to set this property. You won't be able to get the scroll property of a nonscrolling field, either.

Not enough memory to...

Problem: There is not enough free memory to perform the indicated operation.

Solution: As with any insufficient memory condition, there are only a couple seemingly rash solutions.

To free up memory space, you'll have to quit HyperCard. Restarting HyperCard from the Finder will start you out fresh. If you are running MultiFinder or System 7, be sure that you have allocated at least 800K of memory to HyperCard. It actually prefers 1000K or more, especially if you are using Color Tools, the audio palette, or the Picture command. Assign a larger memory partition, and launch HyperCard first so it grabs its preferred amount.

Not handled by target program.

Problem: You tried to send an Apple event that the target program is not wired to interpret.

Solution: The HyperTalk Send command sends a dosc Apple event, which not all programs respond to. Use an Open Scripting language to access the application's Apple events.

Nothing to copy. Try background.

Problem: You tried to copy a card picture selection with nothing in the selection.

Solution: Often this message comes because you meant to be in background editing mode before choosing the Select painting tool to select part of a picture. Simply choose Background from the Edit menu before selecting the picture.

Only start and stop using can change the stacksInUse.

Problem: You tried to set the stacksInUse property with the Set command.

Solution: Use the Start Using and Stop Using commands instead.

Out of memory.

Problem: The Macintosh has insufficient memory to carry out a HyperTalk handler.

Solution: This problem occurs primarily on very large handlers—those nearing 30,000 characters, but sometimes with much smaller handlers in otherwise tight memory situations. To find out how large an object's script is, type the following into the Message Box (using the name of your object):

```
length of script of <object expression>
```

This will reveal how many characters are in the entire script. If the number is above 20,000 consider breaking up the handler into smaller components. HyperCard loads the contents of an entire handler into a special section of memory, which has limits, even on multi-megabyte RAM Macintoshes. If you break up your handlers, that should prevent this memory condition.

Some large XCMD-based add-ons to HyperCard, such as Reports, occupy a great deal of memory while they are running. You may obtains Out of Memory indications while trying to print a report. Executing handlers within Reports (like CardSelected and CardUpdate handlers) may indicate errors when in reality there isn't enough memory for them to carry out valid HyperTalk commands. Quit HyperCard and assign a larger memory partition in its Get Info dialog box in the Finder.

Show Background Picture?

Show card Picture?

Problem: You are trying to edit a background or card layer picture while the ShowPict property of that picture is false.

Solution: You can choose any Painting tool while the picture of the current domain is hidden, but the instant you try to apply the tool to the picture, one of these messages appears. You must show the picture before you may add to that picture layer. If you elect not to show the picture from this message, you will not be able to draw on the picture layer. The layers are independent, so you may work on a background picture layer while the card picture is hidden.

Sorry, there isn't enough memory to print from HyperCard.

Problem: There is insufficient memory to load the printer driver information.

Solution: See "Out of Memory" messages for solutions to such memory conditions.

Sort by what?

Problem: The argument to the Sort command has been omitted or incorrectly stated.

Solution: The Sort command syntax includes the word "by" followed by optional modifiers (ascending/descending, and text/numeric/international/datetime) and an expression. Typically that expression is a field expression, but it may also be a background expression (to keep all cards of the same background together), a HyperTalk function (e.g., the length of a particular field), or even a user-defined function that establishes the sort key for each card "on the fly." If the expression is invalid, you'll receive this message: "" was not a valid expression for this card." Typically, the Sort by What message comes as the result of omitting the "by" of the syntax.

That tool is not available at the current user level.

Problem: The UserLevel global property is set too low for the desired tool.

Solution: Even when a particular tool is set by a HyperTalk script, the UserLevel global property must be set to the level that supports that tool. The most typical hindrances come when a script needs to draw with the Painting tools, but the UserLevel is set to Typing (2). Before calling a Painting, button, or field tool, be sure the UserLevel property is set correctly. This may be done in the openStack handler or just prior to using the tool.

There is no <object>.

Problem: HyperCard cannot locate a button, field, or background object named in a HyperTalk command.

Solution: This Help message appears whether you call the object by number, ID number, or name, and specifies in its description the way it sought the object. One common mistake is to call an object by its ID number when you mean its number (or vice versa). It is also possible to misspell the name of an object if you're accessing it by name. Bear in mind when referring to objects by number or ID number in a Repeat loop (in which the counting variable is used to make up part of the object designation) that the number must be an integer. If the numberFormat property has been adjusted to something with places to the right of the decimal, HyperTalk will append the decimals to the Repeat loop counting variable when summoning the object, as in card ID 47.00. This will bring up the Help message, and you'll see how HyperTalk is evaluating that counting variable to a noninteger.

This operation can't continue because an error occurred:

Problem: This is the equivalent of a script error that occurs when a stack has been saved as an application.

Solution: If the error does not occur when running the stack within HyperCard, then try increasing the memory partition of the standalone. Otherwise, you should be able to recreate the error in the stack version with a little help from the description in this error (it tells you the error and the name of the handler—but not its object). A likely cause is that the userLevel property was not adjusted in the stack to account for the standalone's default setting of 2.

Too much recursion.

Problem: A handler or series of handlers is calling itself too many times, or may be in an infinite loop.

Solution: Recursion is like something that keeps folding back on itself. In a HyperTalk script, it could take the form a doMenu handler that traps for the "New Card" menu item. After performing some special extra preparation for creating a new card, it then uses the statement *doMenu New Card* in the hopes of actually creating the new card. This last statement, however, merely restarts the on doMenu handler all over again. This is caught in an infinite loop, and no new card ever gets created. Of course, HyperTalk recognizes this very quickly, and throws up this Help message.

Tracing the point of recursion may not always be simple, especially if the recursion takes place across two or more handlers. In the case of the menu situation, above, the handler must *send "doMenu New Card to HyperCard"* to break out of the object hierarchy, and get the message to HyperCard where it belongs. In more complex situations, print out the handlers you suspect are in the way, and follow execution carefully line by line. If you find yourself coming 'round and 'round, you know you have a recursion problem, and must find a way out of it.

The most common recursion sources are in open<Object> handlers, especially openCard handlers. Typically the problem is that a command in the openCard handler goes to another card that is also governed by the same openCard handler (which goes to another card...). The domino effect is certain. If your goal, for example, is to have your stack automatically cycle through a series of graphical introductory cards before getting to the actual title card, the following *background* handler is guaranteed to cause a recursion problem:

```
on openCard
   visual effect dissolve
   go to next card
end openCard
```

Instead, you should but a handler in the *card* script of the very first card as follows:

```
on openCard
   repeat 5 -- assuming five next cards including the title card
      visual effect dissolve
      go to next card
   end repeat
end openCard
```

Experienced programmers may actually desire recursion under controlled circumstances for special kinds of math. For now, there is no way to turn off this recursion trapping that HyperTalk performs.

User level is too low to edit script.

Problem: You are trying to gain access to an object's script while the User-Level global variable is set to 4 or less.

Solution: As with accessing any tool, HyperCard must be set to the proper level before the Script Editor will open. Even if your own UserLevel setting (i.e., the setting in the User Preferences card of your Home stack) is set to 5, the author of the stack you're using may have locked the user level to below 5 to prevent you from looking into scripts. If access to a script of such a stack is important, remember that you can put the script of any object into a global variable and put the contents of that variable into a field of the same or other stack for perusal. There are also stack utilities that extract scripts and print them out for you. Script Report is an excellent tool for this purpose as well as checking your own stacks' scripts.

Other HyperCard Helper messages are generally clear enough to point you in the right direction toward a solution. Very often, the debugging tools described in the next chapter round out your problem solving.

CHAPTER

48

DEBUGGING HYPERTALK SCRIPTS

HyperCard's built-in Script Editor includes a companion debugging environment that greatly simplifies debugging particularly nasty entanglements. Through a series of windows atop the card window, you can watch the stack in action as well as see a microscopic view of what's going on inside a handler at each execution.

Distinguishing Compiler from Run-Time Errors

Before you can start taking advantage of the HyperTalk debugger, it's vital that you understand the difference between syntax errors that prevent a script from compiling and execution errors caused by other reasons. Only the second type may be examined with the debugger.

Compiler syntax errors make themselves known by the error alerts that have only two buttons: Cancel and Script. This means that the script has not been compiled or run yet: no values have been entered into any variables nor have any commands been carried out. Generally, the kinds of errors involved at this stage are misspelled words, the wrong preposition, or a missing parameter.

A run-time error, on the other hand, presents an error dialog with three buttons: Debug, Cancel, and Script. Seeing this dialog is a good sign in a way, because it means that there were no syntax errors in the script. Part of the script may have executed (up to the line prior to the one containing the error), and the error has something to do with values of expressions, container contents, object identifiers, and the like. That's where the debugger helps out.

Overview

The debugging system consists of three different types of windows (Figure 48–1). The most obvious window is the Script Editor window. Here you watch a highlighting rectangle indicate which line of the script is next in line to be executed. The second window, the Variable Watcher, is particularly important when values of local and global variables change in the course of a handler's execution. The third window, the Message Watcher, is usually of more value to see which messages are being sent during normal execution of a script.

The debugger and the two Watcher functions can act independently, so you can have either (or both) Watcher window open without the debugger running. You'll want to turn on the debugger to monitor handler execution line by line.

You turn on the debugger by setting a *checkpoint* in a handler. To experienced programmers in other environments containing debuggers, a checkpoint may be better known by its more traditional name, *breakpoint.*

Because you can use the Watcher windows independently of the debugger, we'll start by describing what they do and how they work. Then we'll get more deeply into the methods of setting checkpoints and what options are available in the debugger.

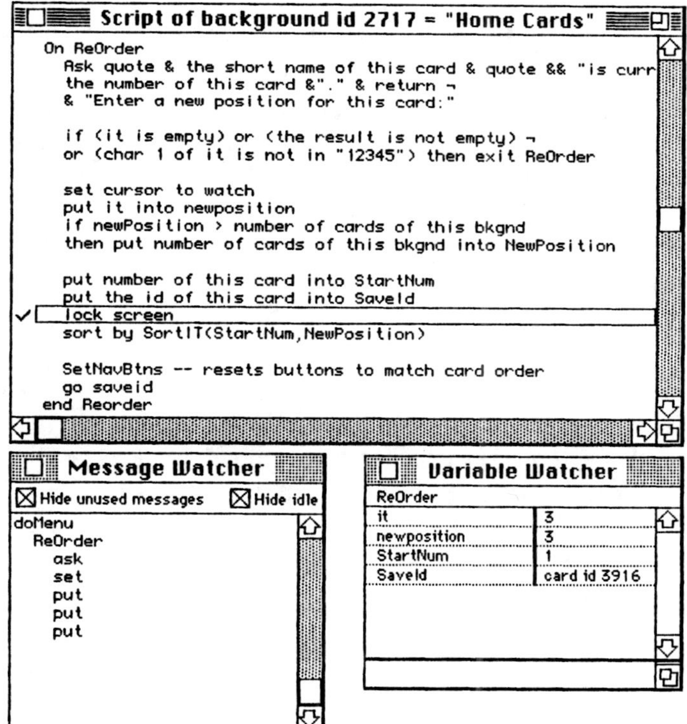

Figure 48–1. The three components of the HyperTalk debugging system (clockwise from top): Script Editor, Variable Watcher, and Message Watcher.

The Message Watcher

To turn on the Message Watcher independently of the debugger, enter the HyperTalk command

```
show window "Message Watcher"
```

either into the Message Box or in a handler (if you wish the window to appear and begin tracking messages in the middle of a handler). A shortcut handler is also in the Home stack, so you can show the Message Watcher by typing

```
mw
```

into the Message Box and pressing Return.

The Message Watcher can display two kinds of messages in its window: active and unused. An active message is one that actually does some work or triggers an action; an unused message is sent (usually by the system), but no handler intercepts it along the hierarchy.

One example of an active message is any system message that has a handler intercepting it along the way. Therefore, a mouseUp message, when intercepted by a mouseUp handler, is listed in the Message Watcher window. Any command inside a handler—including any Put or Set command —is also an active message, because it was sent by an active handler and does, in fact, carry out work. The Message Watcher always displays active messages as long as message watching it turned on.

An unused message generally consists of system messages not intercepted by a handler. Therefore, if you have no idle handler in your stack, the steady stream of idle messages sent by HyperCard pass by unused. A checkbox in the Message Watcher window lets you choose whether unused messages should be displayed. An unused message appears in the window inside parentheses.

Because the Message Watcher window holds only the last 2048 characters of messages sent through the system, you probably want to ignore unused messages for most debugging purposes. Seeing unused messages can be valuable, however, if you want to verify that a particular system message is being sent as you expected it (perhaps it's coming in a different order than you thought).

While the unused messages are being displayed, you'll see a steady stream of idle messages being listed (unless the cursor happens to be atop a button or field). Again, because of the limited storage capability of the Message Watcher, you may wish to prevent unused idle messages from taking up space. Clicking the Hide Idle checkbox keeps those idle messages from being listed. Because HyperCard opens (but doesn't show) the Message Watcher window at startup, you may consider modifying the getHomeInfo or startup handler in the Home stack to set the hideIdle property of the Message Watcher window to true—making the setting your personal default setting.

Let's examine how the Message Watcher displays messages in both the active and unused message modes. We'll use a simple pair of handlers—a mouseUp handler which calls a user-defined function handler—to show how the Message Watcher indents the various messages for easy reading and tracing. Here are the two handlers:

```
on mouseUp
    answer "Calculate the number of days left in the year?" with "Cancel" or "OK"
    if it is "OK"
    then put daysLeft() into cd field 1
end mouseUp

function daysLeft -- in the current year
    put the date into today
    convert today to dateItems
    put item 1 of today + 1 & ",1,1,0,0,0" into nextFirst
    convert nextFirst to seconds
    convert today to seconds
    return (nextFirst-today)/(60*60*24)
end daysLeft
```

By turning on the Message Watcher before clicking the button containing these handlers, we'll get a complete list of the messages sent during execution of this script, as shown in Figure 48–2.

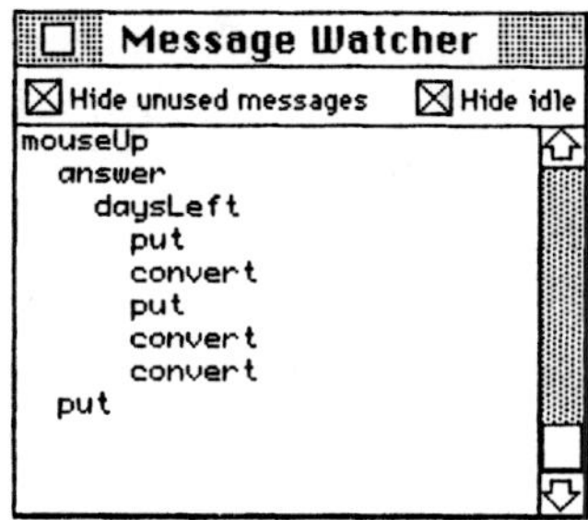

Figure 48–2. The Message Watcher catching active messages.

The first system message, mouseUp, is at the left margin, indicating that it is not called by any other handler. It is a kind of primal message. Indented on the next line is the Answer message, which is the first command of the mouseUp handler. We said earlier in our very first discussions about messages that a HyperTalk command in a handler is sent as a message, therefore the Answer command is also the Answer message.

The if-then construction is not sent as a message. Technically, these are HyperTalk keywords, not commands, and keywords don't appear in the Message Watcher.

Indented once again on the next line of the Message Watcher is the name of the user-defined function, called daysLeft. Messages that trigger other handlers are indented to help you locate them in what could be a long series of standard HyperTalk command messages. Below and indented once more are all the messages inside the daysLeft function. These are all standard HyperTalk commands, so they are displayed at the same indentation level. Notice that the Return keyword at the end of the function is not listed as a message.

As the last message of the script execution, the Put command is back at the indentation level identical to the Answer command that opened the handler. If you look at the actual handler, these two commands are at the same level, so should be displayed as such, even though it may look to be disjointed from the nested messages of the function handler. A series of messages are not always symmetrical, as statements in a HyperTalk handler must be.

Figure 48–3 shows all the active and unused messages being sent in the action of clicking the button containing the two handlers (the window has been artificially elongated in the illustration to show you the entire sequence of messages). It starts with the series of idle messages, followed by mouse movement to the button. The mouseDown message is followed immediately by the mouseUp message, which is an active message. The rest of the messages are the same as before until the handler ends. Then a mouseLeave message and ensuing stream of idle messages show that everything is back to normal.

The Message Watcher is particularly helpful when tracing execution of handlers that call other handlers, especially if the calling goes two or more layers deep. By watching the messages go by, you may discover that a particular subhandler is being called more often that you thought it was being called. You may also discover where bottlenecks in complex scripts are occurring. While the speed of the handler execution is slowed somewhat while the Message Watcher logs messages, you can get a visual feel for what parts of the script are taking longer than others. If you discover such a slow area in the script, then perhaps it's time to examine that part more closely to see if there are ways to streamline execution. Overall, it should prove useful to work through a nearly completed stack with the Message Watcher window open and see how smoothly your handlers are working.

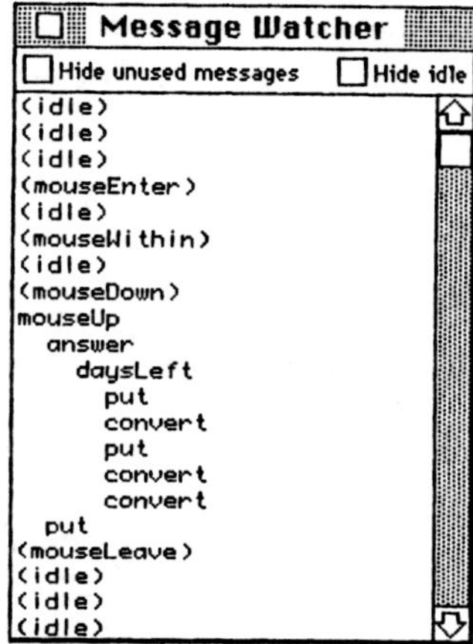

Figure 48–3. The Message Watcher displaying both active and unused messages.

The Message Watcher is a read-only window. You may select text in it for copying or cutting, but you may not edit the contents. A script, however, can write to the window. By setting the nextLine property of the Message Watcher window (Chapter 36), a script can insert any text you please. The purpose of this is to let you mark spots in the list of messages with things like markers (e.g., "made it to Point A"). But in addition to plain text, you can write any expression to the window, including HyperCard and user-defined functions. For example, if you are running timing tests on various parts of your handlers, you can set the nextLine property with the Ticks function to display the elapsed time at various points. An even more sophisticated user-defined timing function could calculate the number of ticks between instances of setting the nextLine property:

```
function timer
    global lastTick
    if lastTick is empty
    then put 0 into lastTick
    put lastTick into oldTick
    put the ticks into lastTick
    return lastTick - oldTick
end timer
```

Then, in strategic places in your script (e.g., before and after calls to subhandlers), insert the following line of debugging code:

```
set nextLine of "Message Watcher" to timer() & return
```

Before you run the handler the next time, show the Message Watcher, and you'll see timings that you can use as comparison values when you make modifications to subhandlers to improve performance.

The Variable Watcher

The second watcher window lets you peek at the values of global and local variables at different times. Like the Message Watcher, you can turn on the Variable Watcher by showing its window:

```
show window "Variable Watcher"
```

This command may be entered into the Message Box or from within a script. If the Variable Watcher window is not showing before you turn it on, the window appears on screen. A Home stack handler offers a shortcut by letting you type

```
vw
```

into the Message Box to show the window, as well.

Unlike the Message Watcher, the Variable Watcher window is split into three panes (Figure 48–4). One pane, at the upper left, shows a list of all variables that apply to the current moment (sometimes it's globals only, other times it's variables within a handler). To its right is the pane that displays the current values of those variables. The bottom pane lets you edit the contents of a variable at any instant. To resize any pane, place the cursor atop the black line separating two panes. The cursor changes to a double line with arrows indicating possible drag directions (similar to window pane cursors in programs like Excel and Word). Click and drag on the line until the panes are at the desired size. You may resize the entire Variable Watcher window by dragging the grow box at the lower right corner. The size of the window and the locations of the bars may be set by adjusting the rect, hBarLoc, and vBarLoc properties of the Variable Watcher window (Chapter 36).

When you turn on the Variable Watcher from the Message Box, it lists only global variables, because at idle time those are the only variables in effect. Global variable names are displayed in bold face in the top left pane. Local variables (shown when the debugger is on, and you are stepping through scripts) are shown in regular font style.

To the right of the variable's name is the first line of the variable's contents. If the variable consists of more than one line (e.g., the list of stack pathnames), an ellipsis (...) appears to the right of the first line's contents.

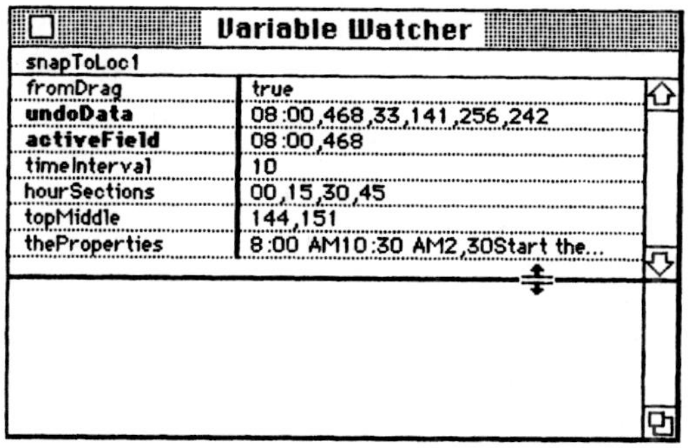

Chapter 48-4. The Variable Watcher has three panes. The top pair show variable names and current values. The bottom pane allows editing of variable values.

Click on the variable name or its contents line to see the full variable values in the bottom pane of the Variable Watcher window (Figure 48–5). Adjust the size of the window or the pane divider line as needed to view the contents. You may change the contents of a variable by simply typing a new value and either pressing the Enter key or closing the window by clicking the close box. The new value appears in its place to the right of the variable name in the window. You may also copy and paste values to or from the lower pane.

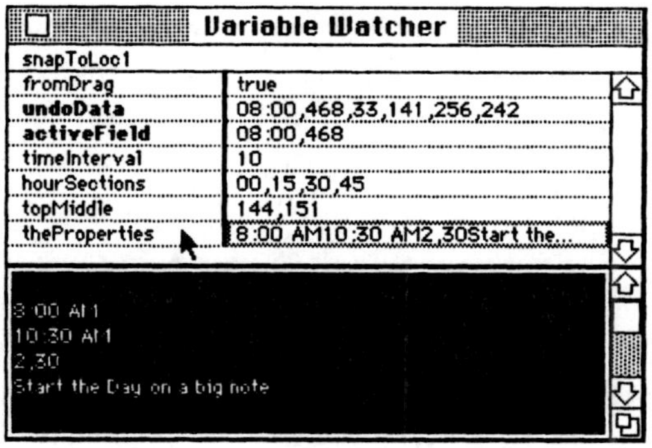

Figure 48–5. Clicking on a variable name or value places the value in the lower pane for viewing (multiple-line variables especially) and editing.

If the debugger is not running while a script executes, the contents of the Variable Watcher are essentially locked (you don't even see whatever local variables may be in use). When the handler finishes, any changes to the global variable values show up in the Variable Watcher window at that time. To see variable values change dynamically, you'll have to set a checkpoint in a script, and step or trace through a script with the Variable Watcher window open.

Starting the Debugger

As mentioned earlier, the primary trigger for the debugger is a checkpoint in a script. The built-in debugger offers two types of checkpoints. One is a *permanent* checkpoint, which you may put in as many places of a script as you like. The command

```
debug checkpoint
```

is the so-called permanent checkpoint. It's only permanent because the checkpoint is saved along with the script when you quit HyperCard.

A *temporary* checkpoint may be inserted while in the Script Editor. Place the cursor anywhere in a script line, and choose Set Checkpoint from the Script menu. A checkmark appears in the left margin of the window on that line. A keyboard shortcut is holding down the Option key and clicking the cursor anywhere on a script line. Option clicking again on that line removes the checkpoint. Shift-Option clicking on a checkpointed line removes all temporary checkpoints. Temporary checkpoints are not saved when you quit HyperCard.

You may also start the debugger any time a script is running by typing Option-Command-Period. This may not be accurate enough for you if you wish debugging to start at a specific point in a script. If you think your handler is caught in an infinite loop, however, the keyboard method is an excellent way to dive straight into the script at the trouble spot.

When the debugger starts, the script window for the object containing the executing handler pops open. In the Script Editor window, a rectangle surrounds the next line of the script to be executed. Choose Variable Watcher from the Debugger menu to show the Variable Watcher window. Any global or local variables the have been declared in the current handler are listed in the Variable Watcher window. Global variables declared in the handler (if any) are shown at the top of the variable list in boldface.

Finally, any script error triggers a dialog box that includes a Debug button. Clicking that button starts the debugger with the problem line already selected. At the point of a stopped script, with the debugger running, you have several options as displayed in the Debugger menu. Let's examine each of these.

Step (Command-S)

By repeatedly typing Command-S, you may execute the script one line at a time, giving you as much time as you need between lines to examine variable values in the Variable Watcher window or to monitor the condition of your HyperCard stack. On smaller screen Macintoshes, you may have to resize the script and variable windows small enough to see changes in the card window underneath. The rectangle in the Script Editor shows you what line will be executed with the next press of Command-S. Stepping through a handler is limited to the current handler only. If you also want to step through the lines of handlers called by the current handler, then choose Step Into, below.

Step Into (Command-I)

An alternative to the Step command is the Step Into debugger command. This version follows the script execution line by line, even if the execution branches to another handler in the same or different object. When branching takes you to another object (e.g., a button handler calls a function handler in the stack script), the Script Editor window for that second object comes to the screen so you can follow it line by line.

The Variable Watcher tracks only variables that apply to whichever handler is working at the moment (the handler name appears at the upper left corner of the Variable Watcher window). For example if a mouseUp handler branches to a stack script function handler, the Variable Watcher's contents changes to the variables in the function handler. When execution returns to the mouseUp handler, all variable values for that handler reappear, just as they were when the branch occurred.

Trace

When you trace a script execution, the debugger window stays open, but the handler proceeds near its normal pace. You can watch the rectangle in the script window zip through the script, branching to other handlers where necessary. On fast Macintoshes, you won't be able to see much of the detail (even though Variable Watcher keeps pace with current values), but you'll be able to see at a glance what parts of if-then-else constructions, for example, are executed. Adjust the Trace Delay (next page) if you wish to view the Trace while in motion.

The real value of setting Trace in action is that the debugger stays active so you may then stop the Trace action by typing Command-S or Command-I to let you examine a part of the script line by line. Therefore, tracing is a convenient way to speed up script exams by zipping through parts of a long script that don't need close inspection.

Trace Into (Command-T)

The preferred alternate to the Trace command is the Trace Into command. It performs just as the Trace command does, but also steps into subhandlers called by the current handler. The Trace Delay setting affects this operation as well.

GO (Command-G)

Once you've checked out a part of a script and want to set the rest of the script in action, use the Go command to turn off the debugger and let the script carry on. The Go command brings the card window to the front, and resumes regular script execution as if the debugger had never been started. Another checkpoint in the script or Option-Command-Period will restart the debugger.

Trace Delay...

Because tracing through a script may run too fast for you to see what's being executed, you may adjust the time (in ticks) between the execution of each line of HyperTalk. Choosing this command presents a simple dialog box that lets you type a number representing the number of ticks to wait between each HyperTalk line. The default setting is zero.

Set Checkpoint (Command-D)

This is the same command that appears in the Script Editor menu. The only difference is that in this case, you don't have editing access to the script. Only the debugger rectangle marks the line to which a temporary checkpoint should be added. If the line already has a checkpoint, then the menu item reads Clear Checkpoint. Even with the debugger in effect, however, you may set a temporary checkpoint at an unhighlighted line by Option-clicking on that line.

Abort (Command-A)

Aborting the debugger stops the debugging process, but leaves the current script window(s) open for you to edit. The text insertion pointer is also in the line that was to be executed next (i.e., the one with the rectangle around it while the debugger was active). You may also abort with the Command-period keyboard command.

Script Errors and the Debugger

The Debug option in script error dialogs gives you an excellent way to learn more about your problem, especially if the script error is caused by an erroneous variable value. By seeing the values of variables at the instant of the script problem, you can determine which variable is the troublemaker. Then set a temporary checkpoint at the first use of the variable in the script, and run the handler again. Now you'll be able to step through the handler seeing the evolution of the variable value along the way.

By combining two techniques:

- Interpreting HyperCard Helper messages
- The HyperTalk debugger (including the watchers)

you have a powerful set of debugging tools at your disposal. Mastery of them will make your stack authoring go much faster.

CHAPTER

49

TIPS ON IMPORTING AND EXPORTING DATA

Moving text and graphics information between HyperCard and other programs is, if nothing else, flexible. Text transfers are accomplished by way of scripts, which can read or write text data in as many ways as there are formats. Graphics transfers benefit from the universal Macintosh bit-map formats that all paint-type programs share.

Text Transfers to HyperCard

In Chapter 32, we described the Read From File HyperTalk command and provided a sample script that can be used unmodified to import most database and spreadsheet information. The principles behind the format of information stored as text-only data are quite simple.

When you save an Excel spreadsheet as a text file, for instance, it stores information in cells along a row as individual text items with tab characters between them. The rightmost cell in a row, however, has a carriage return following it. Therefore, if you wish to import a row of numbers into fields of a single card, you must first prepare the card so there are enough fields for the number of cells in the row. Then write the import script in such a way that it reads until a tab (which puts the imported text into It) puts the contents of It into a particular field, and continues the reading and putting (but into subsequent fields on the card) until it reaches the return character at the end of the row. At that point, the import script should go to the next card in the stack and repeat the reading and putting process for that row and card.

Importing text from a database has a similar feel to it. In FileMaker Pro, for instance, you can choose an Export Records option. In the subsequent Save dialog, a popup menu of choices includes an item named Tab-delimited file. This turns the text-only data into the same text-only format that Excel generates.

When importing text from a word processing document (presumably into a large or scrolling HyperCard field), you should first save the original document in a text-only format. HyperCard cannot directly read the custom file formats of word processors, but it does recognize the common language of Text Only (ASCII). If your word processor, like Microsoft Word, gives you a choice of saving with return characters (line breaks) at the end of each line or at the end of each paragraph, choose the paragraph setting. This will let the text attributes of your HyperCard fields take care of word wrapping and line lengths within the field. Then write a short HyperTalk script that reads text until a return character. That will put a single paragraph into a field.

If you want more than one paragraph per field, you may either read from the file for a fixed number of characters or read until HyperCard encounters an unusual keyboard character that you must insert at the end of the text-only document section. For example, if the text contains no special symbols, you can place an "@" symbol at the end of each block you wish to be read into a single HyperCard field. The script, then, would read from the file until that symbol. From there, the script may read another block into another field on the same card, or progress to the next card in the stack and read the next block—that depends on how you intend to manipulate the data in your stack.

Exporting Text

The rules for exporting data are very similar to the rules for importing text. The sample script in the Write to File command discussion of Chapter 32 should get you started. The important point to remember when writing your export script is how the program receiving the information expects the data to be formatted.

If the destination program is a spreadsheet, like Excel, then write tab characters at the end of each field's data—or data that will be going into a single spreadsheet cell. When the data is to go into the next row of the spreadsheet, write a return character before the next batch of tab-delimited data.

Databases are to be treated in the same way. They usually expect tabs between data that will be going into individual fields, and return characters between records. In the script line that actually writes the contents of a field to the file, you can concatenate a tab or return character like this:

```
write field 1 & tab to file "Transfer File"
```

When exporting long blocks of text that will go into a word processing document, all you need to do is write the field to the file. Observe, however, how subsequent fields will be written to the file. If you do not specify any return characters between fields, they will be run on in the text file generated by HyperCard. To separate the fields by more traditional paragraph separation, write two return characters to the file after each block. Each return character you send advances the cursor one line down the destination document.

If you need to export control characters that are not available from the keyboard, you may write those characters with the help of the NumToChar function. For example, if you need to write an ASCII character 29 as a field separator, the syntax for writing one field and ASCII 29 would be:

```
write field 1 & numToChar(29) to file "Transfer File"
```

As with any text-only transfer in the Macintosh, none of the font attributes of the source document are stored with the characters. When you load the exported text into your word processing document, you may then assign font attributes as you see fit. Also, depending on the program you're using, you will probably have to save the document with a different name in the word processing program's own file format. Because the text-only document and the word processed document are different file types (something that the Finder keeps an eye on), you won't be able to save the specially formatted file to the same name as the text-only file you used for the transfer. Therefore, consider exporting documents to an intermediate file name you won't be needing later.

Open Scripting Solutions

A more direct solution, which obviates the need for saving data to an intermediate text file, is to write an AppleScript or similar script to transfer data between HyperCard and any other scriptable application. If you perform these kinds of data transfers regularly, then the effort that goes into such a script—scarcely more difficult than the HyperTalk scripting described above—will pay for itself quickly.

Because the arrangement of data users may wish to transfer into and out of HyperCard can vary widely, we refer you to the application shown in Chapter 66. This application, while devoted to showing multi-user sharing of a FileMaker Pro database file, provides a number of workable AppleScript segments for extracting FileMaker data from a record and inserting it into a HyperCard card's fields. The stack also extracts HyperCard field data and writes it to a FileMaker record. These examples should go a long way to get you started in composing a custom script for your specific importing and/or exporting needs.

Newton Transfers

Personal Digital Assistants (PDAs), such as the Apple MessagePad, are likely candidates for one end of data transfers to and from the Macintosh. The prescribed method is to use dedicated connection software, such as Apple's Newton Connection Kit, as the primary intermediary between

PDA and Mac. Version 2.0 and later allows for the import and export of tab-delimited data files for built-in Newton applications (Names, Dates, and Notes). Therefore, it still requires moving data into and out of HyperCard via HyperTalk scripts.

Later versions of the Newton Connection Kit are expected to offer access via OSA scripting to an extent that such scripts will be able to synchronize new HyperCard stack data into an existing set of data stored in the virtual Newton in the Connection Kit (which then gets transferred en masse to the Newton). To assist in the reconciliation of multiple copies of data, it is a good idea to build your stacks with fields containing unique ID numbers (or you can let the card ID do the trick) and date stamping of changed data. For example, a closeField handler in the stack's background script could put the seconds into a hidden date stamp field on the card.

Importing Existing Printed Text

Because HyperCard is often used as a publishing medium, it is common to wish to transfer a printed version of material you've prepared to HyperCard. It can be done without retyping the material, but requires the assistance of an scanner and optical character recognition (OCR) software.

Using a combination of the Apple Scanner and software such as Caere Corp.'s OmniPage, the Macintosh can easily translate printed text into text files. Once the text is in a file, you may then copy and paste the data into HyperCard or write an importing script to do the work for longer chunks of text.

For longer chunks of text, the tendency is often to put it all into a single scrolling field. If at all possible, try to divide your large text blocks into card-length pieces so that the user may see an entire card's text without having to scroll a field. It is more fulfilling for users to move from card to card (especially with visual effects) than to scroll through pages of text.

Serial Port Input/Output

While HyperCard doesn't have built in facilities for controlling the Macintosh serial port, there are some serial port add-ons (XCMD resources) available from outside sources. The Apple Programmers and Developers Association offers a set of external resources for reading and writing data through either the modem or printer ports. Another, more complete kit, CommsTalk (Full Moon Software), includes support for not only straight text transfer with other computers, but also file transfer with error checking protocols, such as XMODEM and ZMODEM (see Chapter 58).

With control over the serial port, you can script connections and data transfers either via a serial cable or modem to other serial devices or even mainframe computing services, such as CompuServe. Other serial port possibilities include any external device that offers a serial (RS-232) port, such as the X-10 system for controlling home lighting and appliances or even sophisticated hobby train sets and amateur radio equipment. All you need to know is the commands that such equipment responds to and what commands, if any, it sends back to monitor the device's status. Also see Chapter 54 on controlling videodisc players from HyperCard.

Graphics Transfers

Whenever you choose a painting tool from the Tools palette, the File menu gains two new items, Import Paint and Export Paint. These menu items are your windows to monochrome bit-mapped graphics in other paint-type programs, such as SuperPaint (when pictures are saved as MacPaint files).

To export a HyperCard screen, choose any painting tool and then Export Paint from the File menu. You are presented with a standard file dialog box requesting a name for the MacPaint file you wish to create. This export picture includes not only the graphics layers of the card you're viewing, but also the contents of the fields. Field text, of course, will be converted into bit maps in the MacPaint document. Also, the picture will be placed in the upper left corner of the MacPaint document, just as a Command-Shift-3 screen dump is.

All painting programs can load MacPaint documents, so even if you have one of the newer graphics programs, you will still be able to load and modify the picture exported from HyperCard.

Importing MacPaint-formatted documents is just as simple. The one limitation you should be aware of is that the source graphics document must have its content in the upper left corner of the page. In other words, when HyperCard imports a picture, it takes a one-screenful bite from the top left corner—the same spot to which it exports pictures.

Don't forget, too, to watch the graphics layer into which the imported graphic is to go. Imported graphics generally come in as opaque graphics layers. If you wish it to be transparent—to let background fields and buttons on the card show through—immediately select the entire screen (use the A Power Key) and press the T Power Key for transparency. You may also import or export graphics under HyperTalk control with the Import Paint and Export Paint commands, described in Chapter 32. All other factors about location on the MacPaint page and layering apply to these graphics transfers as well.

Using Copy and Paste, you may also transfer object graphics (PICTs) from programs like MacDraw Pro. Be aware, however, that the instant you paste a PICT into HyperCard, it becomes a bitmap. In other words, what may be a draggable, growable, easily modified object in MacDraw, becomes a collection of pixels in the card or background picture layer in HyperCard.

Transferring Images to HyperCard

Several technologies are available that facilitate moving images into HyperCard. Images can take the form of printed graphics and photographs or even live images. Displaying animated graphics and live video is a separate discussion, reserved for Chapter 54. We'll be concentrating here on static images that can be displayed as HyperCard pictures in the background or card picture layers.

When we talk about HyperCard pictures, we are limited to the resolution of the HyperCard and Macintosh screen—approximately 72 dots per inch. This is substantially less than the resolution of most source material, but as good as it gets on standard Macintosh displays. Printing these images (i.e., printing the cards) also prints at the coarse resolution. Images are not PostScript, so printing on a LaserWriter won't improve the resolution any. With Graphic Smoothing turned on in the Page Setup dialog, however, laser printing helps fill in the jagged edges.

One of the simplest ways to grab an image from paper and transfer it to HyperCard is with the HyperScan stack that comes with Apple scanners. HyperScan controls all Apple scanners directly from HyperCard. You may preview a page before specifying exactly which part you'd like to scan and bring into HyperCard (Figures 49–1 and 49–2). Once you've performed the scan, HyperScan provides control over brightness and intensity of the image prior to letting you save it as HyperCard art.

Other scanners, like Caere Corporation's OmniScan, allows you to scan images into the Macintosh, but not directly into HyperCard. The process becomes more lengthy (scanning first, and then copying the art into your HyperCard stack), but the hardware cost is substantially less than a desktop scanner.

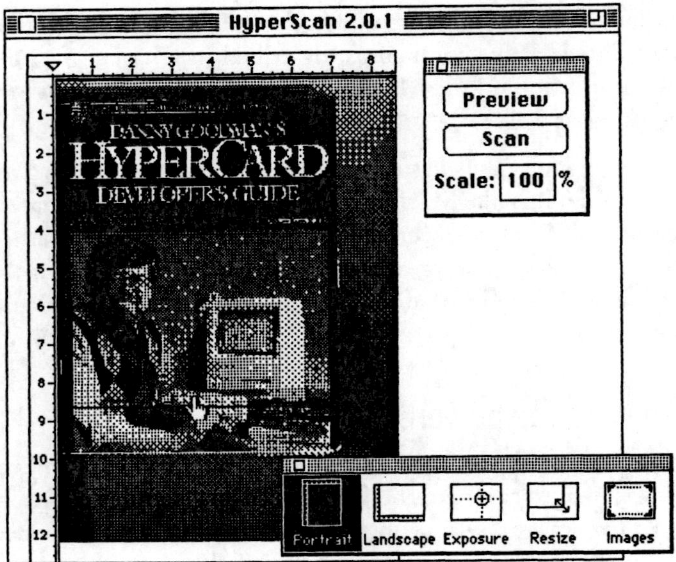

Figure 49–1. In HyperScan, you may preview the scan, and specify the rectangular area to carefully scan. Here we scan a cover of a vintage book.

Figure 49–2. After selecting the area to scan, you instruct HyperScan to do a full scan, after which it places the graphic into a temporary holding place for further adjustments and, finally, a direct export to a stack of your choice.

Capturing static images of three-dimensional objects or live video snapshots is also possible with the right hardware add-ons. These add-ons are called *video digitizers*, and usually consist of a hardware box or Nubus Card that connects to a video source (camcorder, VCR, electronic still camera). Quadra AV models have the requisite hardware built in. The hardware converts a video signal to digital signals that the Macintosh can display on the screen and store as files. Most of the software that comes with digitizers are not HyperCard-based, so you must capture the video image, save the image as a MacPaint or PICT file, and then import or copy the image to the desired HyperCard paint layer. Most monochrome digitizers also capture images in multiple gray levels (when using gray-scale or color monitors), which produce much better looking images than you will get when transferred to HyperCard. HyperCard does not display gray-scale images in its picture layers.

Using color digitizers, you can also capture color pictures. These then become the color PICT files that HyperCard displays with the Picture command from HyperTalk (Chapter 30). The Picture command also displays gray-scale PICTs captured on monochrome digitizers.

In the next chapter, we look at another way of getting information out of a stack, with enhanced application of HyperCard's report printing facilities.

CHAPTER

50

ADVANCED REPORT PRINTING

In Chapter 4, we surveyed HyperCard's report printing facilities from the point of view of a non-scripter. But with an application of HyperTalk scripting, report printing becomes far more powerful via the same dialog boxes we saw earlier. The extra power comes not in the form of fancy graphics, but rather in the way a report format can extract and massage information that goes into the fields in a report template.

Report Printing Commands

The Open Report Printing command description in Chapter 34 details how a script can select from any of the 16 possible report templates stored within a stack. Understanding how these commands work is vital to making the report printing function of a stack transparent to the user—the primary goal of scripting report printing. Therefore, be sure you are conversant in the following commands:

```
open report printing with template <template name>
print <card>
close printing
copy template
```

Report Item Info

The true power of report printing takes place in the deeply nested Report Item Info dialog boxes (Figure 50–1). These dialogs contain the details about what each report item is to print from a card.

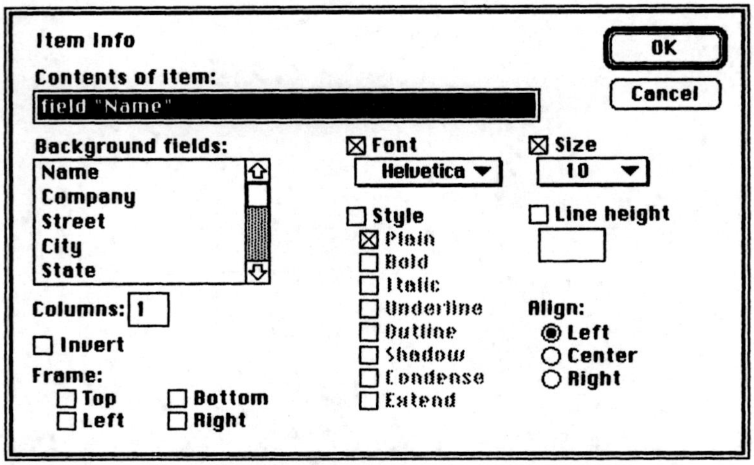

Item Info
OK
Contents of item:
field "Name"
Cancel
Background fields:
Name
Company
Street
City
State
Font
Helvetica
Size
10
Style
Plain
Bold
Italic
Underline
Outline
Shadow
Condense
Extend
Line height
Columns: 1
Invert
Frame:
Top
Bottom
Left
Right
Align:
Left
Center
Right

Figure 50–1. Report Item Info dialog box.

In Chapter 4, we directed non-scripting users to select one of the background fields listed in the dialog to assign data from a desired field to the printed field item in the report template. That's fine if the data you want to print in an item is the straight data from the field. But there can be much more.

Notice that when you select a field in this dialog, its descriptor is placed in the Contents field. That descriptor is the same one you would use in a script to obtain the data from that field. What is not obvious, however, is that you may place *any* HyperTalk expression into the Contents field. That includes global variables, quoted strings, HyperTalk functions, and user-defined functions. We'll demonstrate each of these possibilities.

Global Variable Data

In one stack we designed, we had a complex report printing problem. The stack, called *Which Mac Should I Buy?* (available on-line from ZiffNet/Mac), led a user through a decision process to narrow the choice of a Macintosh model to four prospective models. The user could then print out a comprehensive table of features for the four models.

For purposes of stack efficiency in other areas, the data about the Mac models was scattered about in some oddly formatted hidden fields. Moreover, the user could choose four from dozens of possible models, so assigning specific fields to the report template would not work anyway.

The solution was to create an elaborate handler that assigned the desired data to global variables. These variables were then assigned to carefully laid-out report items in the template. Figure 50–2 shows the main layout screen. Because this report was not going to be printing data from multiple records (as in a database), there was a single report record, filling the entire page.

In Figure 50–3, you can see a portion of the full-page-sized record, with numerous report item rectangles defined. The report title is a field whose Contents consists of the quoted string. Each of the other report items prints the contents of a global variable. Figure 50–4 shows the report item dialog for the item that prints the Macintosh model name at the top of the first column, machine1. We've assigned special text formatting to these column header fields. If the global variables have not been defined by running the script that defines them, then their names (and not sample values) appear in the report items in the dialog, as illustrated in Figure 50–3.

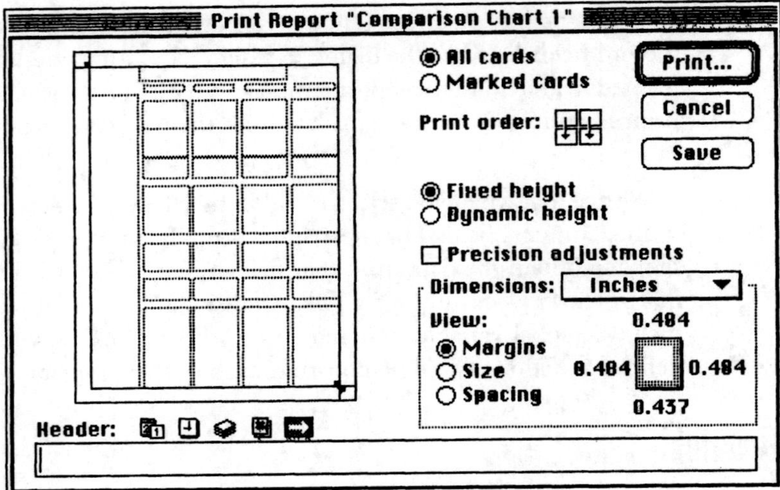

Figure 50–2. The Print Report dialog for the global variable report.

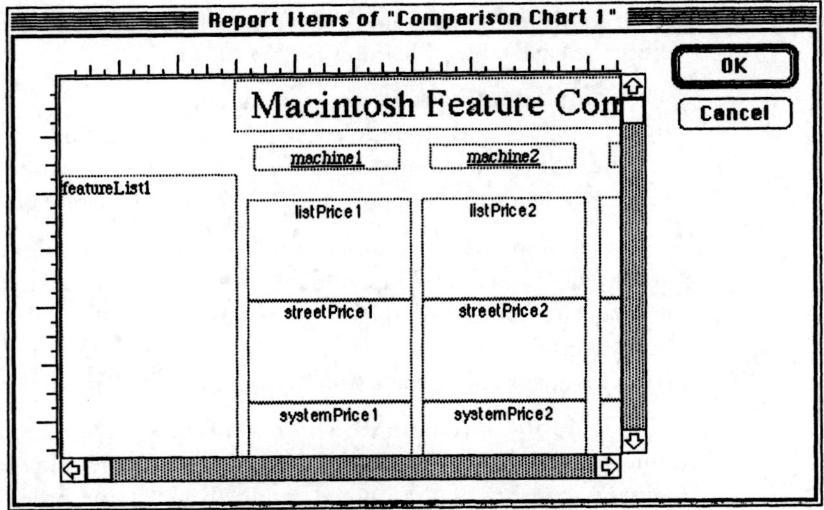

Figure 50–3. The Report Layout dialog.

A portion of the final printed report appears in Figure 50–5. While repeating the script that performed the printing would be meaningless without understanding the inner workings of the stack, we will share some segments that could prove useful for your scripts.

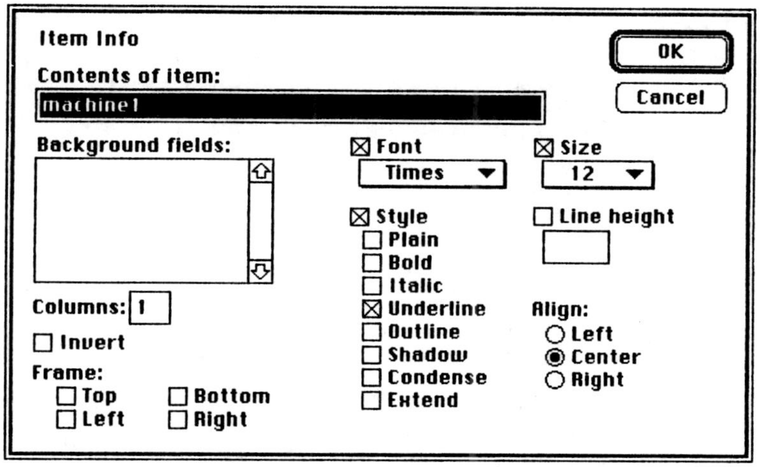

Item Info
Contents of item:
machine1
OK
Cancel
Background fields:
☒ Font
Times
☒ Size
12
☒ Style
☐ Plain
☐ Bold
☐ Italic
☒ Underline
☐ Outline
☐ Shadow
☐ Condense
☐ Extend
☐ Line height
Columns: 1
☐ Invert
Frame:
☐ Top ☐ Bottom
☐ Left ☐ Right
Align:
○ Left
◉ Center
○ Right

Figure 50–4. The Report Item dialog for one field.

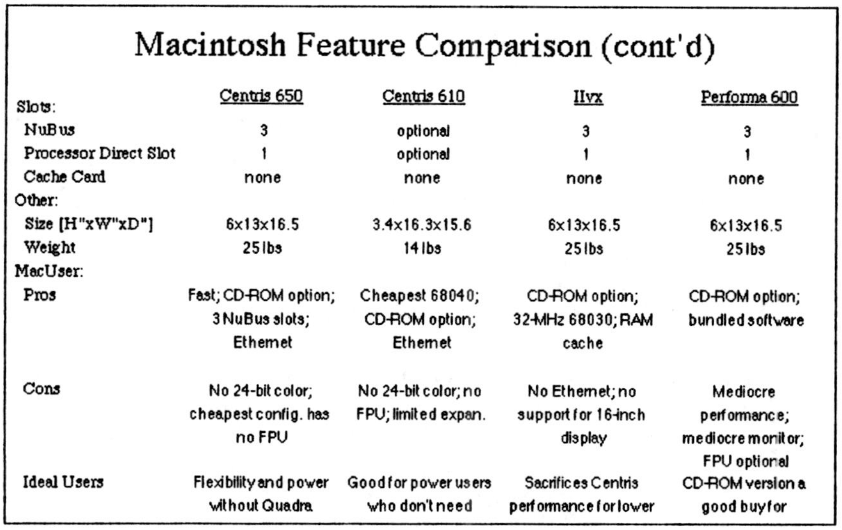

Macintosh Feature Comparison (cont'd)

	Centris 650	Centris 610	IIvx	Performa 600
Slots:				
NuBus	3	optional	3	3
Processor Direct Slot	1	optional	1	1
Cache Card	none	none	none	none
Other:				
Size [H"xW"xD"]	6x13x16.5	3.4x16.3x15.6	6x13x16.5	6x13x16.5
Weight	25 lbs	14 lbs	25 lbs	25 lbs
MacUser:				
Pros	Fast; CD-ROM option; 3 NuBus slots; Ethernet	Cheapest 68040; CD-ROM option; Ethernet	CD-ROM option; 32-MHz 68030; RAM cache	CD-ROM option; bundled software
Cons	No 24-bit color; cheapest config. has no FPU	No 24-bit color; no FPU; limited expan.	No Ethernet; no support for 16-inch display	Mediocre performance; mediocre monitor; FPU optional
Ideal Users	Flexibility and power without Quadra	Good for power users who don't need	Sacrifices Centris performance for lower	CD-ROM version a good buy for

Figure 50–5. A portion of the final report.

One problem was to initialize all those global variables. The report, which actually covered two templates over two pages, used no fewer than 50 global variables—an extreme case to be sure. Because 48 of those globals were actually four versions of 12 globals, we set up the initialization in a repeat loop:

```
repeat with x = 1 to 4
  set cursor to busy
  do "global machine" & x
  do "global listPrice" & x
  do "global streetPrice" & x
  do "global systemPrice" & x
  do "global CPU" & x
  do "global RAM" & x
  do "global Video" & x
  do "global Ports" & x
  do "global SlotsOther" & x
  do "global Pros" & x
  do "global Cons" & x
  do "global Users" & x
end repeat
global featureList1,featureList2
```

After filling the globals with their data, we then had to print the two reports in a row. Here is the part of the script that did that:

```
open report printing with template "Comparison Chart 1"
print this card
close printing

open report printing with template "Comparison Chart 2"
print this card
close printing
```

Notice the critical importance of printing a single card. That command in each template forces HyperCard to plug the data into the report fields for one copy of the report, even though all the data had been extricated from HyperCard fields earlier while filling the global variables.

Afterward, we felt it was worthwhile emptying the values of those globals. There were so many of them that they could occupy memory that may be needed elsewhere. Again, we put the chore into a repeat loop, employing the Do keyword:

```
repeat with x = 1 to 4
  set cursor to busy
  do "put empty into machine" & x
  do "put empty into listPrice" & x
  do "put empty into streetPrice" & x
  do "put empty into CPU" & x
  do "put empty into RAM" & x
  do "put empty into Video" & x
  do "put empty into Ports" & x
  do "put empty into slotsOther" & x
  do "put empty into Pros" & x
  do "put empty into Cons" & x
  do "put empty into Users" & x
end repeat
```

This example is probably far more complex than you'll need. But it more than demonstrates the value of using global variables for some or all of the fields in a report when field-by-field mapping just doesn't work.

HyperTalk Functions

Another kind of expression that can go into a report item is the value returned by any HyperTalk function. Some of the most obvious examples are date and time functions. Figure 50–6 shows the contents field of a report item set to the long date, and the resulting appearance in the layout screen.

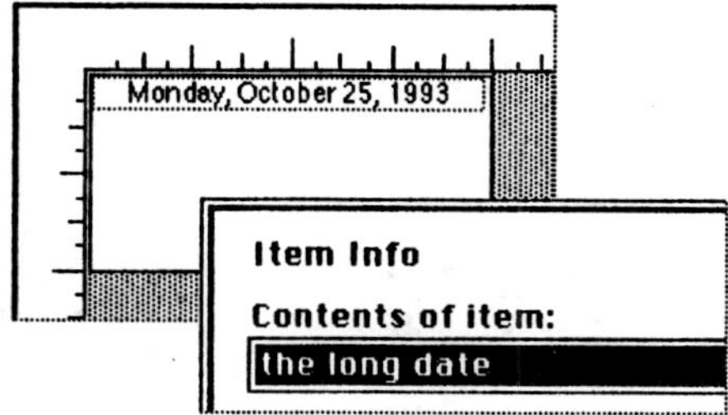

Figure 50–6. Assigning the long date function to a report item.

If the report is one that prints data from multiple cards, then the template places the value of the function in each report record on the page. If you just want a time or date stamp to cover the entire page, then use the facilities in the header for placing that information there.

User-defined Functions

By far the most powerful aspect of report printing is the ability to assign a user-defined function to a report item. Any function you write into the card, background, or stack script can be called for any report item. Whatever value that function returns is what gets printed in the item. Figure 50–7 shows what the Contents field of a report item would look like for a function called "lookup." In this case, a field is passed as a parameter to the function. If there were no parameters, the function would appear with empty parentheses.

User-defined functions have virtually no limit to their data gathering powers. They may perform calculations or text manipulation of information in fields of the current card. A function could even look up data in a remote database on a network via a SQL link (if you are so connected). The function may summon an AppleScript script that passes data from a HyperCard field to another program, massages that information in the other program, and returns entirely different values.

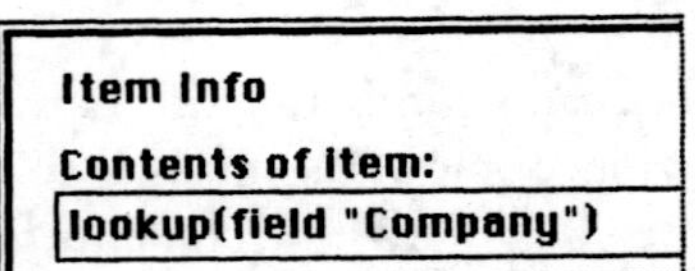

Figure 50–7. A report item that prints the returned value of the lookup user-defined function (passing a field as an argument).

Borders

2.2

Report items are transparent. In other words, if you lay out two report items atop one another, any data from the bottom one will show through the data in the top one. Of course, you wouldn't want text from one field to overprint text in another field, but that's not to say you can't use this behavior to your advantage.

Because you can assign borders to report items, it is possible to create items whose sole job is to print nice rectangular borders around areas of your report. By careful placement of items, you can create multiple-line thickness borders as well. Figure 50–8 shows a variation of a mailing label report record. Three extra report items were created to print a custom border around each label. The border consists of two single-line borders abutted to each other, with a third border 2 pixels inside the outer ones.

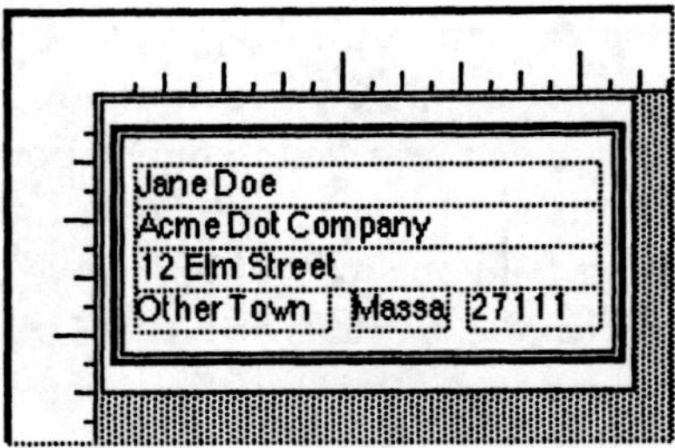

Figure 50–8. Three extra report items produce the fancy border around each mailing label.

To create one of these borders, begin by generating a new item. Position it as best possible, and then double-click it to view its item dialog. At the lower left of the dialog, assign whichever border lines you like—checking all four boxes if you want a complete rectangle border. The most important part, however, is typing a single space into the Contents field. Without this space (or some other invisible character other than empty), the report item and its border won't appear on the report. And because these report items are transparent, you may create them in any order.

Despite the lack of graphics in HyperCard's built-in reports, you can produce some intriguing reports with a little experimentation and scripting.

CHAPTER

51

HOME STACK AUTHOR UTILITIES

The team that created the 2.x generation of HyperCard also built a lot of stacks for themselves. It's not surprising, therefore, that they would build several helpful shortcuts into the Home stack that they—and we—could use in stack development. In the stack script of the Home stack are 16 handlers that all HyperCard scripters should be aware of.

I've divided these handlers into two categories. The first consists of those that could lighten day-to-day development: handlers to call from the Message Box as shortcuts to longer (or mouse-prone) processes. The second group consists of handlers that you may find useful to call from your scripts. All of these handlers have been in all versions of the Home stack (including the HyperCard "Light" version that was bundled with Macintoshes for a time) since the release of HyperCard 2.0. If a user has any unadulterated HyperCard 2.x Home stack running, then these handlers should be there.

If you look into the Home stack script (or any script in an Apple-released stack), you'll notice that some comment lines have small triangle symbols in them. These symbols are there to alert anyone who may be creating a localized (non-U.S. English) version that the HyperTalk statement contains text that probably needs translating. By and large, they affect things like dialog boxes or other interface items that involve text. If your Macintosh is running the U.S. English system, then you can ignore these symbols.

Development Shortcuts

When you see the handlers in this group, you'll recognize that their creators were looking for shortcuts to their own stack development. They're all one- or two-character shortcuts that you type into the Message Box. For these to be most efficient, you should turn on Blind Typing in the Home stack's Preferences card. That way you won't have to display the Message Box to issue any of these commands.

C, B, S

These three one-character commands stand for "card," "background," and "stack", respectively. Type any one of these characters into the Message Box and press Return or Enter to view the information dialog box for the current object. This is the same as choosing Card Info, Background Info, or Stack Info from the Objects menu.

It helps to know that these three handlers do more than just issue a doMenu command to show the dialogs. Here's the script for the card info dialog:

```
on c -- Δ type "c" into message box
    -- Requires handlers: setUserLevelFive,restoreUserLevel
    put the tool into saveTool
    choose browse tool
    setUserLevelFive -- so the menu item will be there
    doMenu "Card Info..."
    restoreUserLevel
    choose saveTool
end c
```

Since you cannot reach these object dialogs when a tool other than the Browse tool is selected, these handlers save the current tool into a local variable (saveTool) for restoration once you close the info dialog. They also use two other utility handlers (described below) to make sure the user level is set to 5. The previous user level (if different) is also restored once the info dialog goes away.

While you can reach the script of any of these objects directly by typing Option-Shift and the respective letter, you can also hold down the Shift key while pressing Enter or Return with any of these commands to view the script for that object. This mimics the behavior of holding the Shift key while selecting the menu items in the Objects menu.

MW, VW

Two helpful windows for debugging purposes are the Message Watcher and Variable Watcher. Although HyperCard automatically opens these windoids when it starts up, they are normally hidden. The mw and vw messages trigger handlers that take care of otherwise long commands to show the windows. Here are the handlers:

```
on mw -- Δ type "mw" into message box
    -- Requires XWindow: Message Watcher
    show window "Message Watcher"
end mw

on vw -- Δ type "vw" into message box
    -- Requires XWindow: Variable Watcher
    show window "Variable Watcher"
end vw
```

Both of these windows are actually XCMDs that are built into HyperCard at the factory. Windows created by XCMDs are often called XWindows (external windows)—hence the comments in the scripts.

SS, SearchScript

The searchScript handler has been in the Home stack since the first release of HyperCard, but the ss shortcut, which triggers searchScript, was added at 2.0. SearchScript is a very useful development tool, particularly when an object's script extends over several screens in the Script Editor window.

The purpose of the searchScript handler is to let HyperCard scour the script of every object in a stack for any text string you wish to locate. Therefore, if you need to change a variable or object name in several places throughout the stack, you can let this handler find those places for you, instead of manually checking perhaps hundreds of kilobytes of scripts. The larger a stack's script collection becomes, the more valuable this tool.

SearchScript is one of few handlers in the Home stack collection to accept parameters. It has two. The formal syntax is:

```
searchScript [<stringExpression> [,<stackExpression>]]
```

Although the first parameter shows itself as being optional, all it means is that if you leave it out, the handler prompts you for the string to locate. Typically, you use this command to search the current stack. By specifying a stack name as the second parameter, however, you can search a different stack. This may be helpful if you have created a multi-stack environment and some utility scripts of your own, which call this handler.

Given the ss shortcut, the most convenient way to get this command working for you is to type the command, a space, and the string into the Message Box, as in:

```
ss "on openStack"
```

The handler searches scripts of the stack's objects in the following order:

```
stack
background 1
background 1's buttons (starting with 1)
background 1's fields (starting with 1)
    (continuing through all backgrounds)
card 1
card 1's buttons (starting with 1)
card 1's fields (starting with 1)
    (continuing through all cards)
```

The handler simply checks whether the specified case-insensitive string is contained in that object's script (which means you can search for "on opens" to locate "on openStack"). If it's there, then the handler opens the script window for that object. Unlike the debugger, searchScript does not scroll to the first appearance of the string. But it does fill a HyperCard global variable (ScriptFindString), which is what the Script Editor's Find system uses. With the text in that global variable, you can instantly issue the Find Again (Command-G) command to locate the first instance of the string. You should continue pressing Command-G until you've made it all the way through the script to catch every instance of the string.

While inside the Script Editor, the handler is in suspended animation. You can edit the script as you like. But when you close the script window, the handler continues to course its way through the rest of the stack. You can stop it at any time by typing Command-Period. When complete, the handler displays a dialog alerting you to the fact (Figure 51–1).

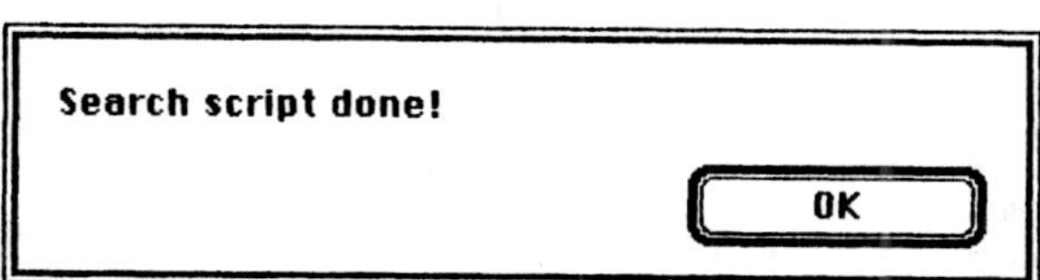

Figure 51–1. The alert that searchScript has completed its survey of the entire stack.

XY

Another handler that's been in HyperCard since the beginning is the xy handler. Typing this command into the Message Box turns the cursor into a crosshair, and the pixel coordinates of the pointer appear in the Message Box. Here's the handler that makes it happen:

```
on xy -- Δ type "xy" into message box to obtain mouse coordinates
  set cursor to cross
  repeat until the mouseClick
    put the mouseLoc && "  horz:" & the mouseH && "  vert:" & the mouseV
  end repeat
end xy
```

The handler was beefed up in a later version to provide a more understandable readout, specifying precisely which number is the horizontal and which the vertical. Figure 51–2 shows a typical reading in the Message Box.

Use this utility to help you measure art or find screen locations that you wish to put into scripts. For example, if you are scripting an animation by repositioning an icon button, you can use the xy tool to figure your locations for the path of the button. Jot down the series of desired coordinates, and then enter them into your script.

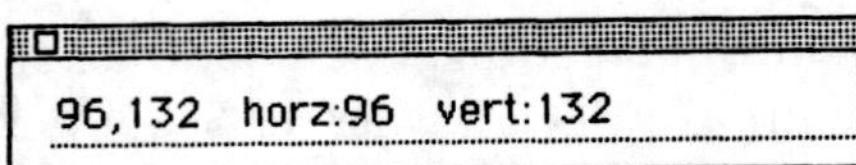

Figure 51–2. The xy handler shows the screen location of the cursor in real time.

SE

Occasionally, it may be necessary to adjust the font family or size of the Script Editor window. If so, the se handler offers somewhat of a shortcut to making the changes. The values for these characteristics are stored in global properties (scriptTextFont and scriptTextSize). This handler provides a more friendly interface to setting these properties:

```
on se -- Δ type "se" into message box
   -- Requires XWindow: Script Editor
   ask "Set script editor font type to:" with "Monaco" -- Δ default value
   if the result is "Cancel" or it is empty then exit se
   set scriptTextFont to it
   ask "Set script editor font size to:" with "9" -- Δ default value
   if the result is "Cancel" or it is empty then exit se
   set scriptTextSize to it
end se
```

When you type the command, the handler presents two dialogs that request font family and size desires. Unfortunately, the limitations of the Ask dialog box don't allow presentations of popup lists of available fonts or sizes, so you must type the complete name of an installed font family. Any changes you make affect only new script windows you open, and these property settings are forgotten when you quit HyperCard.

Scripting Library Handlers

Six other handlers act like libraries, which your scripts can call to help with common scripting tasks. While you can rely on these handlers being in the vast majority of Home stacks (in case you distribute your stacks to others), it is possible that some HyperCard owners have removed them from their stacks or modified their behavior. If you plan to distribute your stacks to a wide audience, it's probably best to replicate these handlers (if needed) in your own stacks. You'll definitely have to do this if you distribute the stack as a standalone—none of this chapter's Home stack handlers are built into a standalone stack.

AllowInterruption, DisallowInterruption

Two handlers toggle the cantAbort stack property. Their scripts are as follows:

```
on disallowInterruption -- so can't stop scripts while running
    set cantAbort of this stack to true
end disallowInterruption

on allowInterruption -- so can stop scripts while running
    set cantAbort of this stack to false
end allowInterruption
```

The wording of these handler names are inverse to the cantAbort property: The positive-sounding allowInterruption sets the property to false. But by reducing the property setting statement to a single command, you may find yourself blocking the user from aborting critical handlers or handler fragments. See the discussion of this property in Chapter 36 for more details.

SetUserLevelFive, RestoreUserLevel

Many tasks executed by scripts require that HyperCard be at user levels above the default Level 2. Users of your stacks may have never ventured into their Home stack (or know the "magic" incantation for the HyperCard Player's Home stack) to adjust their user level's above 2.

To head off potential script errors, you should set the userLevel property to 5 upon opening (and resuming) your stack. And, as a good scripter, you should also restore the previous user level upon closing (or suspending) the stack. The setUserLevelFive and restoreUserLevel handlers take care of these tasks:

```
on setUserLevelFive -- some things need this userLevel
    global SvLvl
    put the userLevel into SvLvl
    set the userLevel to 5
end setUserLevelFive

on restoreUserLevel -- use after setUserLevelFive
    global SvLvl
    if SvLvl is a number then set the userLevel to SvLvl
end restoreUserLevel
```

Notice that these handlers share a global variable, called SvLvl. One handler saves the previous level to this variable; the other handler restores the userLevel property to this value.

LastHCItem

While the addition of the itemDelimiter property to HyperCard makes the lastHCItem Home stack function somewhat obsolete, the script for this function is nevertheless an interesting one. It is a case of exercising HyperTalk's recursive abilities.

The function is designed to extract the last item of any string, given any single-character delimiter (presumably something other than comma, for which the "last item of x" would suffice). Here is the handler:

```
function lastHCItem delim,theText
    -- returns the portion of <theText> that follows the last <delim>
    if delim is in theText then
        put lastHCItem(delim,char offset(delim,theText) + 1 ¬
        to length(theText) of theText) into theText
    end if
    return theText
end lastHCItem
```

Notice that the handler calls itself, returning whatever remains in the string beginning with the character following the first instance of the delimiter character. This won't generate a recursion error, however, because it will not become an infinite process—the string is modified at each invocation, and eventually something will fall out, returning the value to the original calling statement.

If you wish to use this function, here is an example of how to extract the file name from a pathname:

```
answer file "Choose a file:"
answer "The file name is:" && lastHCItem(colon,.it)
```

This method is much more compact than setting and restoring the itemDelimiter property, as shown in Chapter 36.

CheckHCFont

The checkHCFont function is in the Home stack primarily for HyperCard's initial check of system fonts as it starts up. But it uses an XFCN (fontExists) that could be helpful to your stack if it requires a nonstandard System font (this XFCN is not built into standalone stacks, however). To summon this function, you must provide a font family name and at least one font size, as in:

```
checkHCFont ("Toronto",12)
```

To specify multiple font sizes, you must provide them in a quoted string of items, as in:

```
checkHCFont ("Toronto","12,18")
```

The function returns the name of the font family and whatever sizes are missing. If the font and sizes are already installed then the function returns empty. Here is the script of the function:

```
function checkHCFont theFont,pointSizes
    -- Requires XFCN: FontExists
    -- returns a list of font sizes needed but not in the system
    put empty into missing
    -- steps through each point size passed in
    repeat with count = 1 to the number of items in pointSizes
        put item count of pointSizes into theCurrentPtSize
        if not FontExists(theFont,theCurrentPtSize) -- if can't find it
        then put theCurrentPtSize & "," after missing
    end repeat
    if missing is not empty then
        put theFont & space before missing
        delete last char of missing
        put return after missing
    end if
    return missing
end checkHCFont
```

To see how HyperCard, itself, handles the issue, examine the checkForMissingFonts handler in the Home stack script. This is the source of the message about the missing Palatino font that many users of older or stripped down systems encounter when starting HyperCard.

Your Own Utilities

These helpful utilities supplied by Apple should be an inspiration to you for creating utilities of your own design. There is lots of script space available in the Home stack for utilities that you find useful.

Here is one utility I've found useful in positioning windows according to global (i.e., screen) coordinates. As an enhancement to the xy handler, this one, called gxy, provides both global and local coordinates as you drag the mouse around the screen. Here's the handler:

```
on gxy
    set cursor to cross
    repeat until the mouseClick
        put the mouseLoc into globalLoc
        add left of cd window to item 1 of globalLoc
        add top of cd window to item 2 of globalLoc
        put "global:" && globalLoc && "    local:" && the mouseLoc
    end repeat
end gxy
```

Figure 51–3 shows a typical display in the Message Box while this handler runs.

Figure 51–3. The results of the gxy handler.

It becomes easy to identify what kinds of utility scripts you need. When you notice yourself typing the same long commands over and over in the Message Box, you have identified processes that can be reduced to one- or two-character commands. The ability to build your own development tools within HyperCard is one of its appeals.

CHAPTER

52

INTRODUCTION TO EXTERNAL RESOURCES

HyperCard is like the base model of an automobile. As it comes from the factory, it does its job well, and comes with enough features built in to make it quite useable without modification. But you can also add accessories that give HyperCard features that are important to you. Just as you may add a ski rack to your car because you're a skier, so too in HyperCard you can add sounds or icons because they'll help you make HyperCard the special-purpose tool you need.

Six types of accessories are commonly added to HyperCard stacks. Three of them will probably be familiar to you just from your exposure to HyperCard and other Macintosh applications: cursors, icons, and sounds. Fourth is an accessory called a *palette.* The Navigator palette built into HyperCard (type `palette "Navigator"` into the Message Box to see it) is one example. The fifth accessory type, a picture, works with the palette, as we'll see later on. The last kind of accessory comes in two flavors, called *external commands* (XCMDs) and *external functions* (XFCNs). Usually lumped together under the heading of XCMDs (and generally pronounced "ex-commands"), these accessories are capable of extending the power of the basic HyperTalk language beyond what's built inside. To use the auto metaphor, they can turn the base model auto into a family station wagon, a racy sports car, a limousine, or a recreational vehicle. In other words, XCMDs build on the foundation of HyperCard and let it do special-purpose things not offered in the base model.

Resources—The Building Blocks

The internal facility that lets you add these accessories is called the *resource* —the clever invention of the original Macintosh design team. Its first purpose was to simplify the programming and localization of Macintosh applications for different countries and spoken languages. Certain visible attributes of a program, such as menu bars and dialog boxes, are maintained as elements separate from the main program code. Thus, a simple modification to a menu item or the size of a dialog box could be made quickly by modifying the resource, instead of digging into hundreds of pages of code and recompiling the entire program (a process that, in the early days, could take one-half hour). A resource could be modified with a separate program, called a Resource Editor. One such program, ResEdit (pronounced REZ-eh-dit), is still a popular tool among Macintosh programmers and the curious.

A Macintosh file may consist of two files, called a data fork and a resource fork. Even when both forks are present in a file, the Macintosh file system presents them in Finder listings as a single unit.

The data fork generally contains information that we enter into a document. Typically, a word processing document file consists of a data fork only, without a resource fork at all. The characters we type in and the formatting specifications we choose are saved in the file as data.

The resource fork of a file generally consists of items other than user-entered data. A Macintosh application program, for example, contains nothing but resources, including the code for the program. This code is rarely editable, because it has been compiled into machine code from a higher level programming language, such as Pascal, C, or Assembler.

HyperCard stack files represent instances in which a file may contain both a data fork and a resource fork. The data fork consists of the text in the fields, the pictures, and the specifications of every object in the stack. But we can also add resources that let us change the cursor, introduce new icon art for buttons, play new sounds, and extend the vocabulary of HyperTalk. If you've used the Font/DA Mover utility (System 6.0x) or shifted fonts and sounds around in System 7, then you've already had experience shifting resources around.

It is safe to visualize resources as kinds of objects (not HyperCard objects) that you can attach to stacks as you need them. There is even a useful utility packaged with HyperCard that helps in that task: the Resource Mover in HyperCard's Power Tools stack.

About Resource Mover

Resource Mover is a HyperCard-based utility that emulates the operation of a useful tool, called ResCopy, written for early HyperCard authors by Steve Maller (while he was at Apple Computer). Steve had the insightful notion that users would want to shift resources in and out of stacks quickly. At that time the only viable tool was the ResEdit programmer's tool, which not many non-programmers understood. He came up with a system of moving resources around stacks with the same kind of user interface as the Font/DA Mover. The Resource Mover version does most of what ResCopy did in its prime.

Figure 52–1 shows what the Resource Mover card looks like in the Power Tools stack. The two scrolling fields become viewers to lists of resources in two stacks. To view the resources of any stack, click the Open button beneath the field, and locate the stack in the file dialog box. To move resources, you must have two stacks open at the same time.

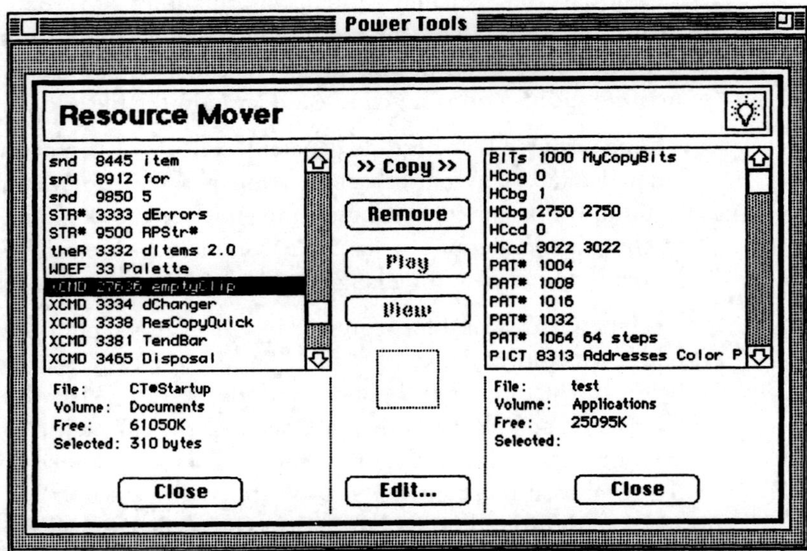

Figure 52–1. Resource Mover, from the Power Tools stack, provides a familiar interface for copying resources between stacks.

Notice that each resource has a four-character leading identifier—the resource type name. There are a couple dozen standard resource names. The ones we'll be concerned with here are

Identifier	*Meaning*
CURS	cursor
ICON	icon
'snd '	sound
PLTE	palette
PICT	picture
XCMD	external command
XFCN	external function

Resources also have numbers—a unique number for each resource type in the file. Optionally, a resource may have a name.

When you select a CURS resource from the list (by clicking on it in the field), the active cursor changes to the cursor art of that resource so you can see what it's like to work with that cursor (Figure 52–2). Selecting an ICON resource displays the icon art in the dotted box in the center of the Resource Mover window (Figure 52–3).

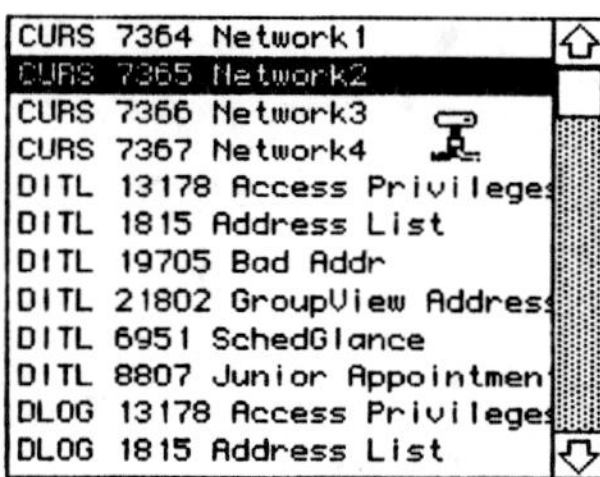

Figure 52–2. Selecting a cursor resource changes the active cursor so you can see how it looks as you drag the mouse. Click the mouse button to restore the Browse tool.

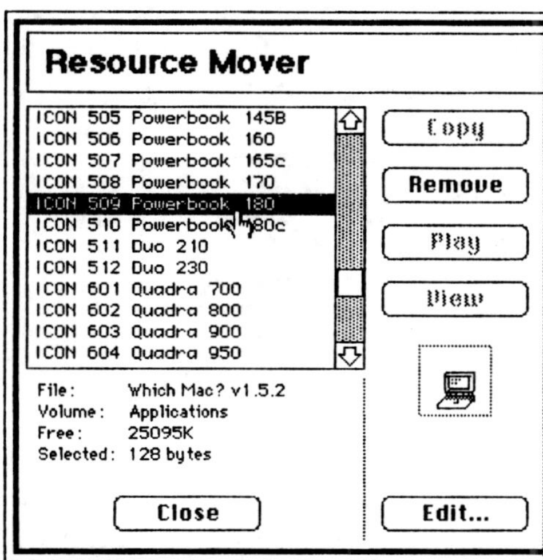

Figure 52–3. Selecting an icon resource displays that icon in the small box.

The type name for sound resources are the three lowercase letters "snd" and a space. Most sounds may be tested from within Resource Mover. Simply select a sound resource and click the Play button (Figure 52–4).

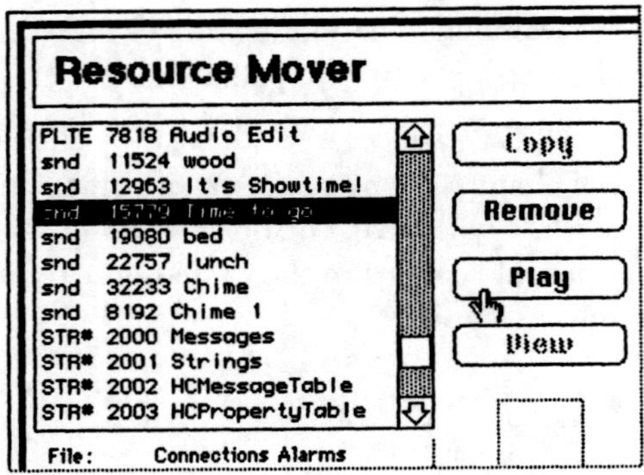

Figure 52–4. You can play most sound resources within Resource Mover by selecting them and clicking the Play button.

Any resource of any HyperCard stack may be renumbered or renamed with ResCopy. The Edit button leads to a sequence of dialog boxes for renumbering or renaming a selected resource (Figure 52–5). While two resources of the same type may have the same name, they may not have the same number. Since some calls to resources, such as setting the cursor, may use names, you should avoid duplicate names of resources within the same resource type. As for assigning resource numbers, numbers below 129 are usually reserved for applications and Macintosh system use. To be on the safe side, specify numbers between 129 and 32767.

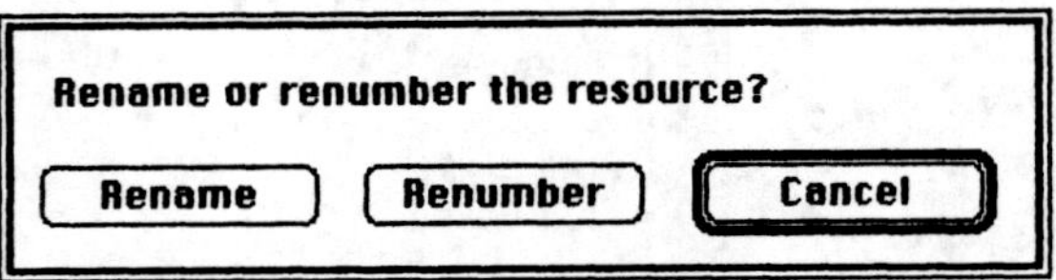

Figure 52–5. The Edit button lets you rename or renumber a selected resource.

To copy a resource from one stack to another, open both stacks in their respective ResCopy windows. Select the file you wish to copy. The Copy button comes alive, with arrows pointing in the direction of the possible copy. Click the button to duplicate that resource in the other stack. Selecting a resource and clicking the Remove button deletes that resource from the stack.

Font Resources

You may have noticed that we have not said anything about font-related resources yet. In early versions of HyperCard (especially in system software versions prior to System 6), it was not uncommon for stack authors to attach custom fonts to a stack. That practice is no longer wise. Changes in the way the System treats fonts makes the likelihood of font conflicts between your stacks and system fonts very good. Morever, because the System font overrules in such conflicts, the desired effect of your font may be wasted on some users. If you stacks require custom fonts, then deliver those fonts as font suitcase files for the user's installation into the System (System 6.0.x) or the Fonts folder (System 7.1). Attaching any kind of font resource (FONT, FOND, or NFNT) is asking for trouble if your stacks will be used by a wide number of people.

Cursor Resources

A cursor resource is one of the simplest graphical resources on the Macintosh. It consists of information about pixels inside an 16 × 16 pixel square —the size of a standard Macintosh cursor. Those pixels are either black or white, and the pattern of those black and white pixels is what determines the shape of the cursor.

Creating or editing cursors takes some skill in understanding the interaction of what is called "mask" and "data" elements of the cursor graphic. The appropriate tool for editing cursors in an interactive way is ResEdit. You should be prepared to dig through *Inside Macintosh* a bit to see exactly how mask and data work to allow cursors to appear as they do on white, gray, and black backgrounds.

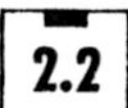

While you are free to add cursors for temporary display as a handler executes, the browse cursor always returns at idle time. This browse cursor, however, is editable with a tool such as ResEdit. Whatever you design for the browse cursor, it must be CURS resource ID number 128. This resource is also editable and assignable for standalone stacks.

Icon Resources

Even though HyperCard comes with 170 icons for attaching to buttons, there is a strong desire among users to add icons. Common requests are for icons from applications programs or custom icons.

So strong was this demand that an icon editor is now a part of HyperCard. See Chapters 11 and 17 for further instructions on creating and editing ICON resources with HyperCard's own Icon Editor program.

Sound Resources

Adding to the hypermedia aspect of HyperCard is its abilities to play digitized, sampled sound that is in the format of a 'snd ' resource. Once a sound is in resource form, you may use the HyperTalk Play command to play back the sound at different pitches and durations. Digitized voices, especially for educational stacks, sound very real, compared to machine-sounding voice of MacinTalk.

The Audio Palette that comes in the bundled Audio Help stack (Figure 52–6) is a fine way to experiment with recording sounds. With Audio Help in the message hierarchy (two Audio menu items appear at the bottom of the Edit menu), you can record and partially edit sounds that can be saved directly into the current stack as the proper 'snd ' resource for the Play command.

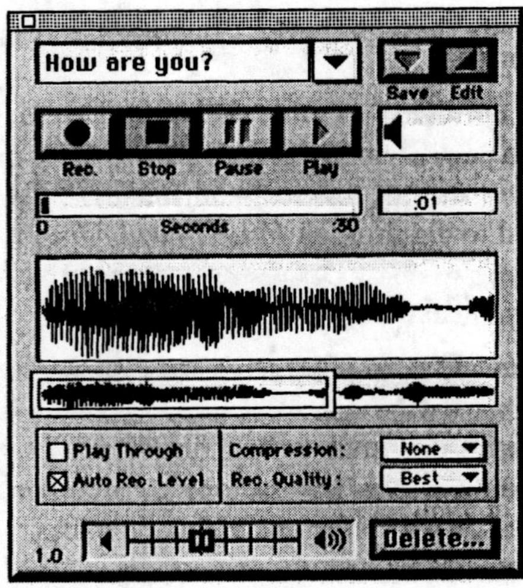

Figure 52–6. The Audio palette, expanded to view the editing facilities.

Employ digitized sound judiciously, not gratuitously. Make sure the sound conveys information or imparts an important effect. Users of other programs that include digitized speech are already tiring of meaningless voices on productivity products that say "Welcome" when you start them or "Have a nice day" when you quit. Also, if you are trying to synchronize music or voice with a free-running stack, test it carefully to be sure everything is synchronized correctly.

PLTE and PICT Resources

We'll discuss these two resource types together because they work in tandem to produce floating palettes atop your HyperCard stacks. A sample palette, called Navigator, comes already installed in HyperCard so you can see how the palette mechanism works.

You have two ways to create these resources. The more complex method involves working with ResEdit (Resource Edit) and another programmer's utility called RMaker (Resource Maker)—both of which come with most programming languages, like Think Pascal and Think C. While a full explanation of how these programs work is beyond the scope of this book, we'll still show you how to use them to create PLTE and PICT resources.

The simpler way is to use the Palette Maker card in HyperCard's Power Tools stack. With Palette Maker, you work with directly manipulating active areas on a make-believe palette, and then let the stack create and install both the PLTE and PICT resources in the stack of your choice.

Let's look at the Navigator palette. If you type `palette "Navigator"` into the Message Box, you see the Navigator palette (Figure 52–7). The palette is displayed in a windoid style window (like the Tools palette), and consists of two basic layers. In the back is a static picture—a PICT resource—which must contain every element that you expect the user to see. Palettes can work with color and gray-scale PICTS as well, provided the stack will be running only on color or gray-scale monitors.

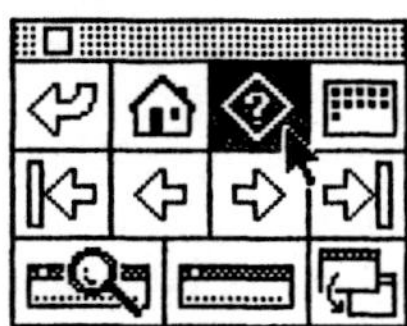

Figure 52–7. The Navigator palette as the user sees it.

The PLTE part of the windoid consists of specifications about where button areas are to be and what message is to be sent to the current card when the user clicks each "button." The PLTE resource, therefore, lists the rectangles of each button area and the one-line HyperTalk message to be sent from each.

Palette buttons may be specified in the PLTE resource to behave in different ways. The highlighting of a button may be either a complete inversion of the pixels within the rectangle (the same as highlighting a HyperCard rectangle icon button, for example) or just a two pixel line highlighted around the border of the button. This latter highlighting method is called *framing*. Whichever setting the palette is designed with applies to all buttons on the palette.

The entire palette of buttons may also be set to be either *action* or *state* buttons. Action buttons, like in the Navigator palette, highlight when you click and hold the mouse button with the cursor atop the button. The highlight goes away upon release of the mouse button or when you slide the cursor outside of the button's rectangle. As the name implies, this type is best for palette buttons that initiate immediate actions, like navigating from card to card. State buttons, on the other hand, remain highlighted after you click the mouse button. This behavior is like HyperCard's Tools palette: when you select a tool, its icon stays highlighted, and that tool remains in effect. Therefore, the state type of palette is best for controls that set modes that remain in effect until the user chooses another. In fact, that calls an important distinction between the two types. You may click the same action button over and over to perform the action over and over. But no matter how many times in a row you click a state palette button, it performs the action (e.g., changing modes) only the first time you click it.

This leads us to another feature of palettes. In the PLTE resource definition, each button may have a one-line message attached to it. This message is sent each time the button is clicked (unless the palette is of the state variety, and the button is already highlighted). The Navigator palette messages, for instance, are all doMenu commands, because these items mimic the items in the Go menu. But the messages may also be calls to user-defined handlers and functions.

On the PICT resource side of palettes, you can let the Palette Maker stack do the work for monochrome pictures. Or, you can use ResEdit to create color and grayscale PICT resources derived from other graphics programs. Here's how to use ResEdit for this task:

1. Create your art with the painting tools, select it with the Select tool (and with the Command key held down to make sure you copy only the active art area), and copy the art into the Scrapbook.
2. Open ResEdit and locate the Scrapbook file in the System Folder.

3. Double-click the Scrapbook file, and you'll see a text listing of the different kinds of resources in the file.
4. Double-click on the PICT listing.
5. Click once on the picture you just copied into the Scrapbook, and choose Copy from the Edit menu. You may now close the Scrapbook and System Folder windows.
6. Locate the stack file where you want the palette, and open that stack file. If there is no resource fork, you'll be prompted as to whether ResEdit should create one; click OK to create that fork.
7. Choose Paste from the Edit menu. The PICT resource will be added to your stack. Double-click on the PICT listing to verify it's there.
8. Choose Get Info from the File menu. The resulting dialog box lets you name and number the PICT resource. Give this resource the same name and number as your PLTE resource.
9. If you're using ResEdit version 2.1 or later, choose Save from the File menu and Quit. Otherwise, close the windows until ResEdit asks whether you wish to save changes; click OK.

The Palette Maker is much easier to negotiate, particularly if the PICT resource is nothing more than art you can create with HyperCard's painting tools. You can still use it with PICT resources (including color and gray-scale PICTs) created from other programs or via the ResEdit method described above. Create individual palettes by simply drawing the art and creating card buttons over the art as they would work in the palette (Figure 52–8). Into each button's mouseUp handler goes a one-line statement, which the palette button will execute.

When you click on the button that creates the palette, an XCMD (see below) built into the stack creates the PLTE and PICT resources and adds them to the Power Tools stack. Another button installs the resources to the desired stack. If you replace the PICT resource created by the Palette Maker stack with another PICT with the same name (with a tool such as ResEdit), you can have your color or gray-scale art behind the palette's buttons.

To show the palette, simply type `palette` and the name of the PLTE resource into the Message Box. Optionally, you can position the palette in the HyperCard window by adding coordinates in the command. The syntax is:

```
palette <palette name>,<horiz>,<vertical>
```

where <horiz> and <vertical> are coordinates for the upper right corner of the active area of the palette window. You may hide a palette by clicking the close box on the palette's top bar or from HyperTalk by sending a message to the window:

```
close window <palette name>
```

Palette windows, being in the windoid layer (in front of the document layer where the HyperCard card windows are), disappear if you switch to another application in MultiFinder/System 7. They reappear in the same location when you reactivate HyperCard.

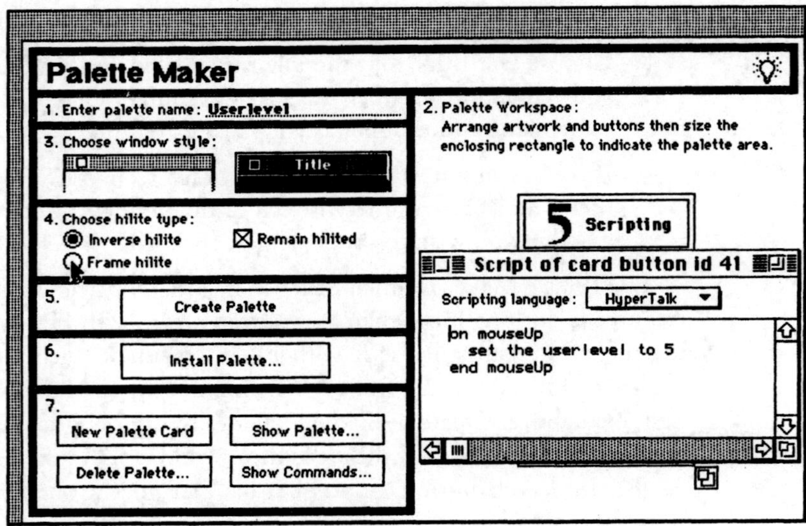

Figure 52–8. Creating a palette with the help of the Power Tools stack's Palette Maker.

Typical uses for palette windows are for icon button shortcuts for menu items and other commands. Because the palette is moveable, you can devote more of the card window's space to information handling rather than navigation or command buttons. Remember, too, that examples like HyperCard's built-in Navigator palette have all iconic art beneath the buttons, you can turn any art into a button, including a list of text items, as if in a permanently pulled-down menu.

XCMDs

External commands and functions are essentially vocabulary words that you add to HyperTalk so that your stacks can do something that HyperTalk can't provide. The purpose of leaving HyperCard open ended (*extensible* is the technical term) is that a user can add a special purpose command or function which would not be of value to the mainstream HyperCard user. Rather than burden us all with loads of rarely used commands and functions, HyperCard offers us a broad-based vocabulary. When the special need arises, it can be added by attaching an XCMD resource to the stack.

Most XCMDs are written in a language that can be compiled into a Macintosh code resource. Languages that qualify are Think Pascal, Think C, MPW Pascal, C, or Assembler, and System Technology's HyperBASIC compiler. As you might imagine, writing an XCMD is not as easy as writing a HyperTalk script. You must be familiar with the external language, Macintosh programming, and the inner workings of XCMDs and HyperCard.

Serving as a middle ground is CompileIt! (Heizer Software), written by Tom Pittman. This HyperCard-based application compiles HyperTalk scripts into XCMD or XFCN resources, offering speed enhancements on certain types of operations. See Chapter 58 for further details.

There are also dozens of XCMDs available from user groups and bulletin boards. A few collections of commercial XCMDs are also available. If you receive an XCMD that is already in a HyperCard stac, you may use the Resource Mover to move these XCMDs into your stacks or into your Home stack. Because the commands and functions added by these external resources are viewed by HyperCard as new words in the vocabulary, they follow the object hierarchy just as HyperTalk commands and functions do. Therefore, if an XCMD is in the Home stack, it may be accessed by any stack; if the XCMD resource is in a single stack, that command is available only in that stack.

To use an XCMD or XFCN written by someone else, you must know its syntax, just like you need to know HyperTalk's vocabulary syntax. Most XCMDs require one or more parameters. All parameters must be separated by commas, just like HyperTalk command parameters. External function arguments must be in parentheses, just like user-defined functions in HyperTalk.

CHAPTER

53

ADDING COLOR TO HYPERCARD STACKS

Without a doubt the feature for which HyperCard developers have been most clamoring is color. While HyperCard 2.2 does not have color integrated into its core, it does come with a bundled color solution. Color Tools uses an entirely different technology from the Colorize HC public domain add-on that appeared a few years ago. With Color Tools, simple color can be worked into any stack without a speck of scripting, while more advanced applications of color in complex stacks can be scripted, if necessary.

Rather than rehash the Color Tools documentation stack in this chapter, we will explain the basics of how the tools work and demonstrate some applications of color to familiar stacks as examples of how to use color wisely. Classy use of color requires restraint, which may be difficult at first if you haven't yet dabbled in creating color applications.

Color Tools Overview

Following a practical trend in HyperCard tools, all the power of the tools remains in the Color Tools stack, which enters the message passing hierarchy when the tools are engaged with the Home stack button (on the Stack Tools card). When you turn on Color Tools in the Home stack, an extra menu, named Color, is added to the menubar.

The tools are for stack authors. Users of stacks containing color see nothing different in their menubars or Home stacks. Once you use Color Tools to build even the tiniest spec of color into a stack, the stack contains everything it needs to display color, provided the user has enough memory set aside for HyperCard's partition.

RAM Time

Color is a memory hog in any application. For example, if you consider a 512 × 342 pixel Classic-sized card, a total of 175,104 pixels comprise that space. For a program to display that many pixels in plain old HyperCard monochrome, it takes one bit per pixel, or 21,888 bytes. If you turn each pixel into one capable of 256 possible colors (requiring 8 bits per pixel to differentiate among the colors), then we're up to approximately 175K just for the display you see on the screen. For the sake of performance, HyperCard maintains copies of the screen in memory (called buffers), which only further increases the program's memory demands.

The bottom line is that HyperCard needs more memory for color than for monochrome. For development purposes, it's a good idea to adhere to

Color Tools' request for a 4-megabyte partition for HyperCard. In practice, however, Classic-sized colored stacks can usually function well in 2500 KB or less.

Color Editing Mode

The Color menu contains only two items. The first, Open Color Tools, puts you into color editing mode, with a set of menus and colorful palette dedicated to working with color (see Figure 1 in the color section). The buttons across the top of the palette offer a visible clue that Color Tools works with color in four ways: color added to buttons; color added to fields; color pictures (from PICT resources and files); and color rectangles.

While in color editing mode, you still have access to a few HyperCard actions, such as opening scripts via keyboard shortcuts (e.g., Option-Command-S to view the stack script). But by and large, the color mode precludes clicking on buttons to effect their actions or editing fields.

Color Layers

The power of Color Tools is hidden from stack authors and users alike. One XCMD, called AddColor, manages a database of color layers that you assign to your stack. Information about the layers is quietly stored in additional resources in a colored stack. When asked to color a screen, the XCMD matches the visible buttons and fields with other color layers assigned to a particular card or background, and then draws the colors where specified.

This is perhaps a gross oversimplification of the technology behind Color Tools, but it serves its purpose to help authors learn them. Think of each color layer as a distinct object. While color assigned to a button, for example, is not a property of that button, the AddColor XCMD does its best to keep the button and its corresponding color object together. Occasionally, a color and its object may momentarily appear to be disconnected. For example, if you assign a color to a button with Color Tools, then close Color Tools, you might then move the button with HyperCard's button tool. It seems kind of weird at first, but the color stays where it was, while the button follows your drag. Choosing Update Screen from the Color menu, however, triggers the AddColor XCMD to realign the button's color to its object—and the internal color database is also updated accordingly. Of course, a more convenient way to move a just-colored button or field is to move the object while in the button or field tool of the Color Tools palette. These tools move the object and its corresponding color object at the same time.

Automatic Scripts

When you insert color of any kind into a stack, Color Tools generates or modifies essential scripts it needs to make sure color is drawn. The following system message handlers are created or added to in the stack script:

```
openStack
closeStack
openCard
closeCard
```

In a fresh stack with no stack script, the following script is generated for you:

```
on openCard
    send "colorMe" to this card
end openCard

on closeCard
    lock screen
end closeCard

on colorMe
    AddColor colorCard,stamp,30
end colorMe

on openStack
    AddColor install
end openStack

on closeStack
    AddColor remove
end closeStack
```

The added scripts are minimalist. They essentially turn on the AddColor XCMD on openStack, awakening it for further commands; turn off AddColor upon closing the stack; force the color to be drawn on any openCard; and a lock of the screen upon closeCard to prevent the ugliness of seeing the color being drained from a card just before it closes.

Scripters should note the colorMe handler. This is the handler you can call from various places that may require a redraw of color, such as when you show or hide an object on the card. The handler calls one of AddColor's commands to update the card (the same as choosing Redraw Screen from the Color menu). Additional handlers that call colorMe are also inserted into the card or background scripts if you color any objects in those domains. If you have a relatively simple stack, without any handlers for these system messages in objects other than the stack script, then you probably won't have to write a word of HyperTalk code to make your color design work in the stack.

When to Script Color

In addition to worrying about redrawing the screen when objects hide and show themselves, you can script a wide variety of color functions with the tools. A lot of the commands associated with the AddColor XCMD (the commands are parameters to the single XCMD) let you recreate in script what you do manually with the color palette and menus. Therefore, if part of your stack entails creating new buttons or fields for users, then these new objects may be colored in the process by asking the AddColor XCMD to color a specific button or field. For example, here is a short script fragement that creates a background button and then assigns a color to it:

```
set editBkgnd to true
doMenu "New Button"
set editBkgnd to false
choose browse tool
put id of last bg btn into btnID
set rect of last bg btn to 100,100, 150,150
set name of last bg btn to "Jerry's Button"
AddColor addButton,bg,btnID,"20000,40000,32000"
```

The one statement that summons the AddColor XCMD is all that is needed to apply a specific color (designated by the red, green, and blue values) to a particular button. The AddColor XCMD and the database take care of the rest.

Scripts may also change colors of an existing color object. Therefore, it is possible under script control to both animate a button object and/or shift its colors, such as changing the shade of a highlighted or disabled button. Carefully chosen color shifts, themselves, can appear to bring an object to life. Similarly, you can assign a sequence of PICT resources to an object to create one type of animation.

Limitations

Color Tools don't provide everything a designer might want in the way of colorizing facilities. For example, color applied to objects such as buttons and fields covers the entire region of the object. Unless you apply a color PICT (file or resource) to an object, the effect is still that of a single color and black. Moreover, you won't get colored icons or different colors for a highlighted version of a button by assigning flat colors to a button (although PICTs can do this). Nor is there a provision for colored, editable text. Even the effect of colored paint text must be done in an underlying PICT, rather than a colorized version of text you enter with the HyperTalk painting tools.

Most of these limitations are addressed in third-party color solutions.

Dreaming in Color

The power that Color Tools provide can be as dangerous as it is exciting. The danger isn't to the stack or information therein, but rather to a user's aesthetic sensibilities. If you thought it was easy to get carried away with multiple fonts, wait until you start experimenting with color.

Before applying color to stacks, it is a good idea to look around existing Macintosh software to see how the pros do it. That may be stretching it, because not everyone is a pro, even in much released commercial software. Apple has researched in depth the subject of color in user interface elements. The results of their studies appear in much of what you see in color application to System 7's own items. One important fact you should notice is that color rarely carries information. Rather, it can enhance a presentation or make a drab presentation more pleasing, but color is rarely, if ever, the focus of attention.

For example, while some third-party shareware products offer outrageous color combinations for Finder elements, Apple's own choices in items such as Label colors or Window colors are rather subtle. Figure 2 in the color section shows an Apple colorized Finder window and icons colored with each of the possible Label menu colors. First notice how the grays of the window elements are the dominant shades. Color appears in only a few place for gentle highlighting. In the icons, despite very bright colors appearing in the Label menu, far subtler shades are applied to the icons. The shades are distinctive enough to serve their purpose of providing visual clues as to the relations of similarly colored icons.

Apple Colors

Of the 256 possible colors in the standard palette, Apple has found that only a handful work particularly well for Finder icons. These colors can be seen directly on your screen if you have ResEdit, and open any ICl8 resource. The Apple color palette and sample icons using those colors are reproduced in Figure 3 in the color section. If you are stumped over colors to use in a stack, consider reducing your choices to shades similar to these time-tested colors.

That's not to say you can't use any shade or combination in your stack. But over the years, a sense of high quality appears to come from sparse use of pastel shades, with ample use of gray shades. Even on the DOS and Windows side of the personal computing street, colors have tamed substantially from the blaring colors of DOS applications to a more pastel look in Windows. Bright colors tend to be limited to tiny patches employed for emphasis or breakup of boredom, but with care, the days of bright red screens with yellow letters are behind us.

Applying Color Tools

In this section, we'll demonstrate two ways to design a colorful stack with Color Tools. The first uses color objects for everything except two icons (for which we use one tiny PICT resource); the other uses a large PICT resource to serve as the background art for the stack. So you have an accurate point of reference, we've used the Addresses stack, which ships with HyperCard as a starting point. Figure 4 in the color section shows the layered version. The purpose of coloring the stack was to dress it up a bit, including making the first two telephone dialing icons red, since they would be the most important numbers.

Color Layering

When dealing with color layers it's important to think about how colored areas and objects are layered. In the case of the Addresses background, the actual background picture consists of the dotted fill pattern, plus the rectangle for the text entry information and the button panels. Although the picture is one HyperCard layer, visually we have three distinct layers to deal with: the dotted background pattern, the entry card, and the two button panels. Since we want to give each of these layers a different color, we must think of them as distinct object layers—the colors we assign to each will, in fact, be distinct layers.

It's perfectly permissible to create the color layers in any order and then re-order them via the familiar Bring Closer and Send Farther items in the

Color Tools' Items menu. No matter how you do it, however, it will likely be unsettling at first to draw a color layer that covers the entire background in a single shade, as we did with the first dark gray rectangle. But when we then created a new color rectangle, colored the pale yellow, and positioned it atop the data entry card, things started to make sense. The yellow layer completely covered the dark gray layer, yet allowed the HyperCard background art (the dividing lines) to show through. We finished the rectangles by creating two new ones in a lighter gray for the button panels (see Figure 5 in the color section).

We selected a light purple shade for the buttons in the top button panel. Since these were rectangle buttons, a color would fill the objects nicely, allowing their names to show through. To make these clickable areas look more like buttons, we chose a two-pixel bevel, which is also part of the Color Tools choice in the button's color info dialog.

Because coloring an icon button does not color the icon, but rather the entire rectangle specified for the button, we couldn't apply a color to the top two telephone dialing icon buttons. Instead we created a color version of the icon as a PICT resource (see below about how to do this) and attached that resource to the stack. Using the PICT tool of Color Tools, we place two copies of the red phones in the position of the icons. Closing the Color Tools, we opened the two buttons' info dialogs, and set the icon of each to None. This allowed the red of the PICT object to show through.

A Popup Field

This stack presents an interesting twist, which Color Tools handles very nicely. When the user clicks the Show Notes button, a hidden scrolling field appears atop the regular data entry area (see Figure 6 in the color section). To enhance the contrast between this note field and the entry card, we want to assign another color to it. To do so, we must first display the field, and then show the Color Tools palette. Here we applied a more vibrant yellow to the field.

A popup field like this presents a problem, however. The color object associated with the field won't automatically appear or disappear with the field. We must communicate to the AddColor XCMD that the screen needs redrawing based on the current visibility of objects. Therefore, it become vital to modify the script of the Show Notes/Hide Notes button to lock the screen prior to changing the field's visibility status, and then calling ColorMe to redraw the screen. The modified handler is:

```
on mouseUp
    lock screen -- we won't see the field until it's colored
    toggleNotes (not visible of Bkgnd field "Notes")
    colorMe
end mouseUp
```

Since we lock the screen in this handlers, it will assist performance if we also modify the toggleNotes handlers (in the background) to remove or comment out its own lock and unlock statements. They become redundant and time consuming. In the process, however, we lose the visual effect that was originally in there. Instead of calling ColorMe (with its plain visual effect), we can replace that command with a more direct call to the AddColor XCMD:

```
on mouseUp
    lock screen
    toggleNotes (not visible of Bkgnd field "Notes")
    if visible of bkgnd field "Notes" then
        addColor "colorCard","fromLeft",10
    else
        addColor "colorCard","fromRight",10
    end if
end mouseUp
```

In a stack with dynamic actions, such as this, it is important to test all possibilities for objects being hidden and shown with missing calls to redraw the screen. Don't be surprised if you must insert an occasional ColorMe call in handlers that make transitions.

The PICT Way

To demonstrate another way of handling color that affects an entire background, we created a color PICT resource (information below) that contained virtually all the color information necessary for the Addresses stack. Once the PICT was safely stored as PICT resource (it could have also been a PICT file), it was placed into the background. Prior to doing that, we removed much of the original background art. Figure 53–1 shows what was left in the background.

By creating all the art in a background PICT, we were able to accomplish some additional touches. They include colorizing what look to be icon buttons (see Figure 7 in the color section). In truth, the icons were removed from the HyperCard buttons, and replicas were drawn into the background PICT. We were able to apply color to just the icons, such as the arrow buttons, the two lower panel icons, and the two red telephone icons. We were also able to dress up the dividing lines surrounding the field names. Instead of the monochrome dotted lines of the original, we used an attractive gray tone.

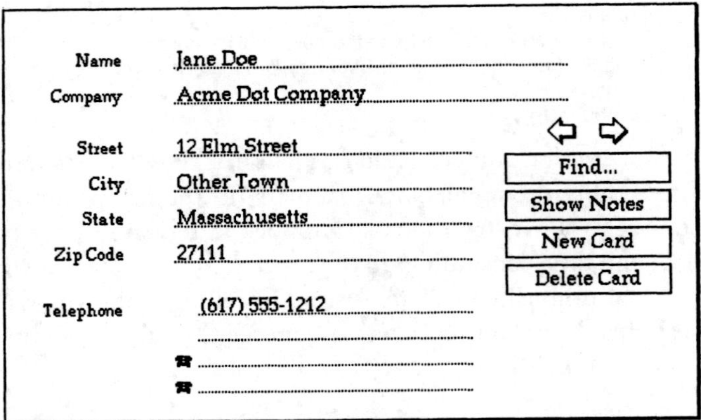

Figure 53–1. All that's left in the modified background of the Addresses stack in preparation for the PICT.

Although we did not replicate Color Tools' button bevelling abilities in the PICT, we could have easily done so, selecting desired light and dark shades of the main color to create the three-dimensional look. A better compromise would be to add button color layers atop the PICT, and let Color Tools do the work of the bevel effect.

The PICT wouldn't be able to help out with the popup field, however. The same technique we used in the earlier version would apply here, along with any changes to scripts.

If stack size is a consideration, then the use of color PICTs may make a stack larger than you'd like. For example, in our Addresses stacks, here is how the various versions came out in file size:

Style	*Stack size*
No Color	57K
Layers	94K
PICT	156K

The increase from the uncolored stack to the layered version is all in the handful of resources required for controlling and maintaining the color information. But the color PICT for the background of this 416 × 256 pixel background is 67K.

Memory is also a consideration when deciding between PICT and rectangle color. For example, in the Addresses stack, addition of rectangle color (plus two tiny icon PICTs) makes the stack occupy 31,924 bytes more than the uncolored original. The PICT version occupies yet another 31,576 bytes of heapSpace. In other words, rectangle colorization places much less of a burden on the user's HyperCard (or stack application) memory partition.

You can clearly do more with PICTs, such as introduce textures and other artistic effects that aren't possible with the rectangular layers, so it is probably best to reserve PICT applications to those that need it. Many of the knock-out screens in the Color Tools stack are PICT resources.

You'll face less of a size penalty and gain a lot of pizzazz by combining smaller color PICTs with large swaths of color rectangles. Designing icon buttons as PICTs can be fun, and when they are on the order of the 32 × 32 pixel HyperCard icons, they take up very little disk or memory space.

PICT Files vs. Resources

The choice between coloring backgrounds and objects with PICT files or with PICT resources is a matter of personal taste. Color PICTs can get pretty big, but if your stack is using a PICT, it ends up being more a question of whether the stack is self-contained or if it is comprised of two or more files.

An advantage of PICT files is that it is easier to modify a PICT file and immediately see the results by re-opening the stack. Moreover, the stack may be more easily customized by users, even if they don't have a developer version of HyperCard. All they need to do is replace your PICT files with PICT files of their own, provided they have the same names.

For ease of distribution of a stack, however, a single file consisting of the stack and PICT resources makes good sense. There is less chance that the user will lose or misplace one of the PICTs, possibly harming the aesthetic brilliance of your design. The Color Tools stack, with its fancy title card and demo art, utilizes embedded PICT resources, making a complex color job a no-brainer for the user. PICT resources also tend to load much faster than the disk access required for PICT files, so performance also leans toward PICT resources.

Creating PICTs

HyperCard comes with monochrome painting tools, which produce only bitmapped paintings, so you should look outside for color graphics programs. You can use a number of the venerable products, such as MacPaint 2.0, SuperPaint, and Studio/8. But if you think you might have some talent in the graphics area (or want to explore whether you do), you should look into some of the more fully-featured graphics programs.

In today's graphics products, you can spend anywhere from less than $100 to many hundreds for high-end products. A lot also depends on whether the art you want to create is completely self-generated, or adapted from scanned photographs or art. Many computer graphics designers regard Adobe Photoshop as King of the Hill. With add-on products, such as Kai's Power Tools 2.0, it is possible to create eye-boggling effects. Ray Dream Designer is also highly regarded for its 3D effects. For the more budget minded, BrushStrokes (Claris Clear Choice) has plenty of graphics power.

Whatever program you choose, be sure it can save files in the PICT format. Encapsulated PostScript (EPS) files won't help you.

Matching Colors

When working with Color Tools, you can double-click a color object layer to get its info dialog, like the one shown in Figure 8 in the color section. Color in this tool is specified by Red-Green-Blue (RGB) values. Double-clicking on the color sample displays the familiar Macintosh color wheel, from which you may manually or graphically select a special color.

If you try to create a PICT to match a color you see or create in Color Tools, you may discover that the graphics program refers to RGB values by percentage. That percentage is the value within the 0-to-65,535 range of Color Tools and color wheel RGB values. Therefore, a 50% Blue value is 32,767. To match the colors perfectly, you may have to perform the percentage calculations yourself.

Getting PICTs into Resources

Even with a great piece of art in a graphics program, you still need to transfer that art to a PICT resource in your stack. Few graphics programs export their pictures as resources, so it takes a little manual work.

The New Picture menu command in Color Tools presents a dialog that allows you to import PICTs from other files (Figure 53–2). This includes PICTs from graphics program documents that are saved in the PICT format. This works fine if the PICT in the file is no larger than the size of the PICT (i.e., no white space surrounding the art). Importing a PICT with white space around it brings the white space with it (increasing the disk space size of the resource, too), and you cannot crop that white space away.

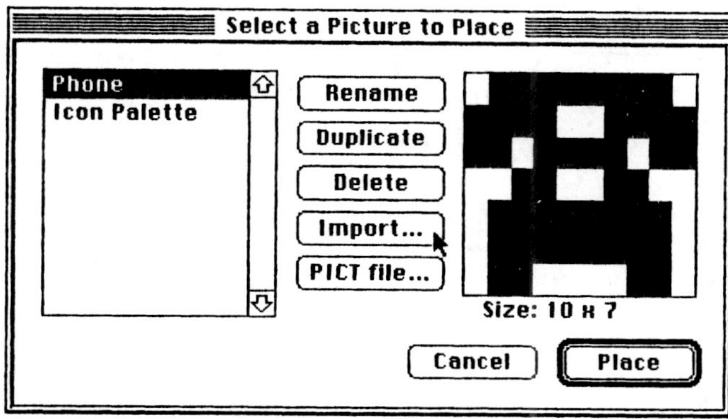

Figure 53–2. PICT importing in Color Tools.

Copying PICT Selections

When the PICT has undesirable white space around it (and you don't want to edit the file) or if you just want part of a larger PICT as one of your resources, you can use a resource editing tool, such as ResEdit. The ideal setup is to have both the graphics program and resource editor open at the same time. Resource editors cannot edit the resource fork of a stack that is already open in HyperCard, so you'll have to close the stack in the interim (but leave HyperCard running so you can quickly open the stack to check out the results). In our example, we'll use ResEdit to demonstrate the process.

1. In the graphic program, use the selection tool to select just the rectangular region containing the art you want.
2. Choose Copy from the Edit menu.

   Regardless of the file format of the graphics file, the Clipboard will contain at least a PICT copy of the selected art.
3. Switch to ResEdit, and be sure the resource fork of the stack is open.

If you get an alert advising that a resource fork doesn't exist, click the button that creates the resource fork. Depending on the format of the data in the Clipboard, you can sometimes just choose Paste at this point, and ResEdit will paste the PICT into a new PICT resource. Should that fail, you can choose Create New Resource from the Resource menu. Scroll through list of types, select PICT, and click OK (Figure 53–3). This action both creates the resource (empty for now) and opens the PICT resource browser.

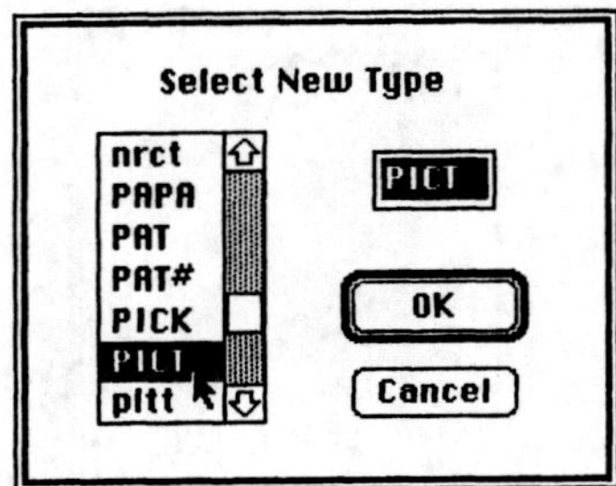

Figure 53–3. Creating a new PICT resource.

ResEdit's PICT browser (Figure 53–4) shows miniature (and sometimes distorted) representations of each PICT resource in the open file.

Figure 53–4. ResEdit's PICT browser.

4. Choose Paste from the Edit menu to get the Clipboard PICT into the new resource.

   If you double-click on the miniature resource, a viewing window appears, showing the PICT in life size.

5. Importantly, you must assign a name to the PICT for Color Tools to let you insert it into a color object. To do this, select the PICT in the browser, and choose Get Resource Info from the Resource Menu.
6. In the resulting dialog (Figure 53–5), enter a name into the Name field.

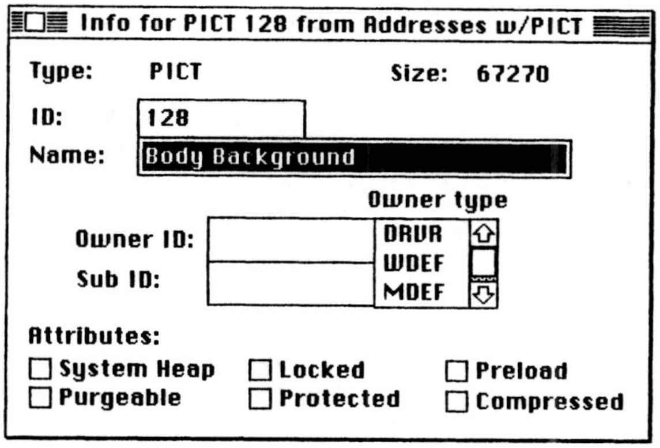

Info for PICT 128 from Addresses w/PICT

Type: PICT Size: 67270

ID: 128

Name: Body Background

Owner type

Owner ID: DRVR

Sub ID: WDEF

MDEF

Attributes:

☐ System Heap ☐ Locked ☐ Preload

☐ Purgeable ☐ Protected ☐ Compressed

Figure 53–5. Name the PICT.

Be sure the name is something you could identify from a blind list of PICT resource names in your stack. Ignore all other settings in this dialog.

7. Choose Save from the File menu, and close all windows related to your stack.

You can now switch to HyperCard, open the stack, and use Color Tools to place the PICT resource.

Screen Capture of PICTs

One other method may of interest to you if you intend to create PICT resources out of composite elements of your video screen. A screen capture utility, such as Flash-It! (Nobu Toge) is an excellent tool for specifying a desired rectangular area to capture. Among its user choices is one that lets you capture the area to the Clipboard. From there, you can go into ResEdit, and create a PICT resource with a simple Paste.

InColor—Style Sheets for Stack Color

Heizer Software offers a third-party color tool for stack authors that goes beyond Color Tools bundled with HyperCard. InColor comes with a host of carefully tuned textures and color palettes that can be applied to backgrounds, fields, and buttons. Like Color Tools, InColor comes in a stack that is inserted into the message passing hierarchy for authoring purposes. Memory requirements are also about the same.

The full developer version of InColor lets you define style sheets for how you'd like color applied to a background and its objects. For example, you may develop a number of well-tuned color schemes for the way different button and field styles should be treated on a card. Once you save the style sheet, you can later color everything on the card with a single command to apply the style sheet to all objects.

Beyond the style sheets, InColor (both versions) come with palettes of high-quality textured PICTs that can be applied to any background, button, or field. With a textured background, for example, you can assign a complementary color to a field, but instruct the color to blend with the background texture. Figure 9 in the color section shows a version of Chapter 61's CalcuVertor colorized in a matter of minutes with InColor. If the settings had been in a style sheet, the stack would have been colorized in a couple of seconds.

InColor and Color Tools work well with each other. Since you can perform some tasks in each that the other cannot do (or do as easily), you may want to colorize part of a stack or background with one tool, and finish the job with the other. When user opens the stack, both color tools will kick in to do their jobs.

Use Color Wisely

These and other third-party color tools (HyperTint, HyperGASP, and QuickColor) let authors give color to what had been a largely monochrome HyperCard world. If you're unsure about how best to use color, look for examples and models in other successful programs. You will probably discover that simplicity and subtlety are far more effective than loud splashes of color.

CHAPTER

54

HYPERCARD MULTIMEDIA: ANIMATION, SOUND, AND VIDEO

Of all the applications areas that have attracted HyperCard authors, multimedia has received perhaps the most attention. What's interesting about this phenomenon is that multimedia really isn't an applications area. It is better described as a method of presenting and capturing information with the help of multiple media: combinations of text, static graphics, animation, sound, and even live video. Multimedia stimulates our senses of sight and hearing in ways that hadn't previously been possible on a personal level before (we don't have any readily available hardware add-ons or XCMDs to tickle our senses of touch, taste, and smell—yet).

Multimedia Applications

The world will outgrow the Silicon Valley hype about multimedia when multimedia's powers work their way into mainstream information-handling applications. With the built-in hardware tools of the Macintosh and software facilities of HyperCard and accessory products, we can start adding multimedia facets to otherwise boring applications today. In time, users will find productivity applications interesting to use and more inviting because of the extra senses touched by the program's author. There's no reason a straight business or instructional application can't be in their own ways entertaining—at least enough to encourage the user to come back and work some more with the program.

Animation can work its way into many types of applications, even subtly, to add to the information presented to the user. In training and simulation stacks, a series of cards flashed on the screen can give the appearance of moving objects.

For example, a classic and still one of the best free-standing HyperCard applications ever designed was called the Boston Macworld Kiosk stack (once available through APDA, but now out of print). It ran on Macintosh SEs scattered around the display floor of the Boston Macworld Expo in 1987, at which HyperCard was introduced. To catch the attention of passersby in the aisles, a series of title cards displayed what looked to be a rotating planet Earth. When the user clicked on the spinning globe, as instructed, further animation appeared to zoom the user from outer space through the atmosphere down to the eastern seabord, Massachusetts, Boston, and eventually to an information desk in the lobby of the exposition hall. On that table were graphic representations of publications, like a booth directory, lists of restaurants, conference schedule, and so on.

If that stack were being done today, there would be a number of multimedia enhancements. For instance, when the user checks into a company's offerings at the show, a prerecorded video segment in the form of a QuickTime movie might play in a small window on the card listing the company and its products. A digitized audio message might also reveal some last minute information for show goers. Speaking into a microphone attached to the Macintosh, the user might leave a voice mail note for a friend; a video camera could even capture the user's face and display it with the voice note.

Even in a less flashy stack, multiple media can add to the information flow to or from the user. For instance, an animated cursor during a lengthy computation lets the user know that something is actually working, and the computer has not frozen. Or perhaps you wish to call attention to a numbered item in a list. Let a prerecorded digitized audio segment tell the user which item to look for.

The hardest part of working with these readily accessible multimedia tools is that it is easy to overdo it. There is a fine line between multimedia that adds value, and multimedia that is too cute for words. Don't trivialize multimedia just to show off. Make it work for the application and the user.

Let's now look at several techniques for adding animation to your stack, followed by a discussion of digitized sound and QuickTime movies.

Animation Techniques

HyperCard itself offers a number of animation techniques that let you convey remarkable effects. Most of these techniques are variations on the method that makes images on film seem to dance before our eyes. A succession of frames at a reasonable speed fools our mind's eye into believing the images move smoothly on the silver screen. Several HyperCard animation techniques accomplish the same end, but by different means of flashing successive "frames" on the Macintosh screen.

Animating Cursors

As discussed in the Chapter 36 section on global properties, you can turn the cursor into a spinning beachball by repeatedly setting the cursor to busy within a handler. Each time you set the property, HyperCard rotates the beachball one-eighth of a turn. Unfortunately, animating cursors of your own creation isn't as simple as repeatedly setting the cursor property to the same cursor over and over.

In the nature of creating a movie, you must create a series of cursors with a slightly different arrangement of elements. When flashed in quick succession, the cursors appear to come alive. Changing the cursor must be done with the Set command to set the cursor property to whatever cursor resource (type CURS) ID number or name you wish to display at any point in an animation sequence.

Creating cursors is fairly easily done with ResEdit, the resource editing utility program (available from most Macintosh user groups and APDA). Since a cursor is no larger than 16 pixels on a side, the resource template in ResEdit lets you click away to make pixels in that grid black and white (Figure 54–1). Work in the window to create each cursor in FatBits style. A normal size representation is shown in the Pointer rectangle. Another series of patterned areas lets you see how the design will appear when the cursor is dragged atop various patterns and black space. This is largely a factor of the "mask," which can be created most simply by dragging the Pointer version to the Mask square (although you may modify the mask pixels individually if you like). Choose Get Resource Info from the Resource menu while the cursor is open to change the name or ID number (more on that in a moment).

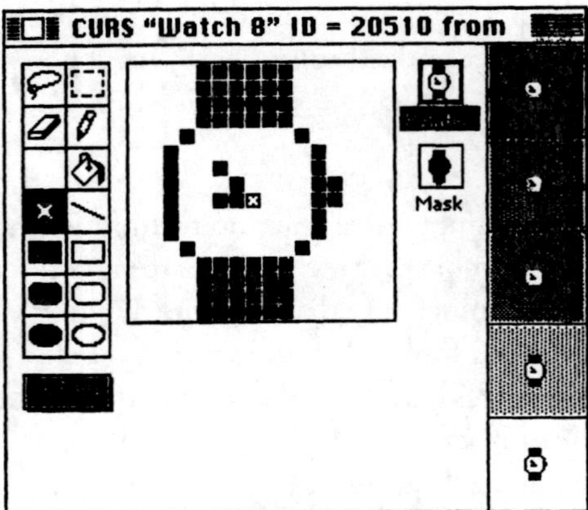

Figure 54–1. In ResEdit, you create cursors pixel-by-pixel, and drag the Pointer version to the Mask box to ensure good readability atop various patterns.

Figure 54–2 shows a series of cursors that, when animated in order, look like the minute hand is rotating around the watch. This is a variation of the plain watch cursor that can be found in the Macintosh system. Using ResEdit, here are the steps to creating these cursors (always backup a file before working on it in ResEdit):

1. Make a copy of your System file.
2. Start ResEdit and open the System file copy.
3. Open the CURS resource from the list of all resources.
4. Select the watch cursor.
5. Choose Copy from the Edit menu.
6. Close the System file's windows.
7. Still in ResEdit, open the stack file into which you wish the cursors to go (the stack cannot be open in HyperCard at the same time). If the stack has no resource fork (its little file icon in the ResEdit file listing will be empty inside), you'll be asked to create one. Do so.
8. Choose Paste from the Edit menu to drop in the watch cursor.
9. Double click the CURS resource listing in the ResEdit window. A window with a graphic list of cursors appears.
10. Click on the new cursor and choose Get Resource Info from the Resource menu. Change the name to "Watch 1."
11. For each of the remaining seven cursors, choose Duplicate from the File menu. The duplicate cursor will be automatically selected. Double-click on the new cursor to display the editing window. Carefully remove the pixels in the leftmost panel for the minute hand, and click in new pixels for the minute hand in the desired position. Before closing the window, choose Get Resource Info from the Resource menu, and rename the cursor with an incremental number, as in "Watch 2." You must assign the numbers in order for the clock to look like it's spinning under script control.
12. When you've finished all 8 cursors (Figure 54–2), choose Save from the File menu, and close the window for the stack file (if you leave it open, HyperCard won't be able to open it).

Now you must script the action of the cursor. Here is a script you can use to test the animation of the cursor:

```
on mouseUp
   repeat until the mouse is down
      repeat with x = 1 to 8
         wait 5
         set cursor to ("watch" & x)
      end repeat
   end repeat
end mouseUp
```

This script sets the cursor to "watch" plus a number assigned to the variable x each time through the repeat loop. The delay is entered to prevent the hands from spinning too quickly.

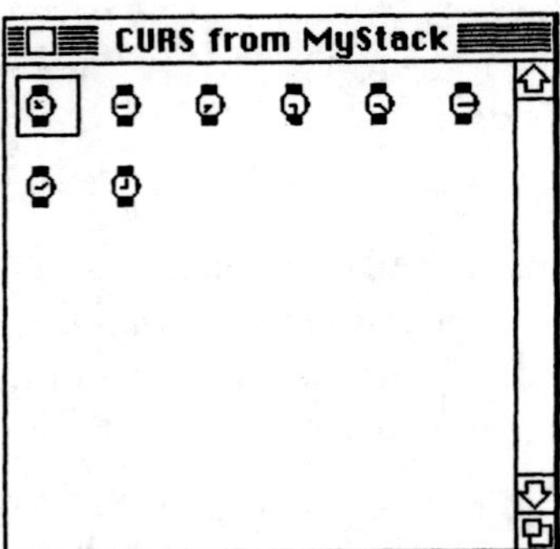

Figure 54–2. A series of eight cursors. When changed in sequence, it looks as though the minute hand sweeps around the dial.

In practice, you want to animate a cursor when a long script is executing, especially when repeat loops are working. One way to handle this is to create a user-defined handler that increments the watch cursor each time you call it from another handler. Because a counter variable must be remembered across different calls to the handler, the counter should be in a global variable (and the variable must be given an initial value of 1, probably in an openStack handler). Here's a script scenario that demonstrates this method:

```
on mouseUp -- a lengthy handler
    repeat with x = 1 to number of bkgnd fields
        advanceCursor -- our handler, below
        -- many statements that act on the fields
    end repeat
end mouseUp

on advanceCursor
    global cursCount
    set cursor to "Watch" && cursCount
    if cursCount = 8
    then put 1 into cursCount
    else add 1 to cursCount
end advanceCursor
```

With the advanceCursor handler in a stack script, you can call it from any other handler in the script. Insert the advanceCursor command inside your repeat loops and sprinkled amid a series of commands in a long handler.

Animating Icons

Virtually the same animation process applies to cursors and icons. For icons, you need to create a series of "frames" that you can call repeatedly. You have a few major advantages working with icons over cursors.

First, icons are bigger: 32 pixels square versus 16 pixels square. That's four times as large. You can get more detail and a larger image in your animation.

Second, unlike cursors, which revert to the Browse tool hand at idle time, icons stay at whatever picture you set it at. You might say that icons are more persistent than cursors.

Third, HyperCard's Icon Editor makes working with a series of icons much easier than working through ResEdit. You can edit an icon or two and immediately try it out on the same stack. In fact, if you design the icons in order, you can even see a preview of how they'll look animated by quickly scrolling through the icons in the Icon Editor.

And fourth, but not least, because icons are attached to buttons, and you can change the location of buttons under script control, you can make your images move around the screen while the images change.

Figure 54–3 shows four icons adapted from the juggler icon that comes with HyperCard. Using the Icon Editor to copy the original to a stack, we cut and pasted elements around to make it look like the juggler is both juggling and dancing (albeit lamely with only one movable leg). In the Icon Editor, we assigned names "Juggler 1," Juggler 2," and so on.

Figure 54–3. Four juggler icons. By changing the icon name in a repeat loop and moving the icon button, it looks as though the juggler is dancing and juggling at the same time.

Then we created a new button whose properties were transparent and did not show the name. After attaching the Juggler 1 icon to the button, we added this handler:

```
on mouseUp
    put 1 into iconCount
    repeat 3 -- total of dances
        repeat with x = 1 to 10
            set icon of me to "Juggle" && iconCount
```

```
            if iconCount = 4
            then put 1 into iconCount
            else add 1 to iconCount
            get loc of me
            add 1 to item 1 of it
            set loc of me to it -- dance right
        end repeat
        repeat with x = 1 to 10
            set icon of me to "Juggle" && iconCount
            if iconCount = 4
            then put 1 into iconCount
            else add 1 to iconCount
            get loc of me
            subtract 1 from item 1 of it
            set loc of me to it -- dance left
        end repeat
    end repeat
end mouseUp
```

This handler sets the juggler into motion both juggling and dancing to the right and left, eventually coming to rest in his original position. Of course, you can modify this to make him move all over the screen if you like. You might even want some music playing as he dances (see below).

Animating Text

No, we're not talking about dancing letters, but rather a technique that gives you flexibility of moving graphical characters around the screen without the 32-pixel limitation of icons—while staying entirely in HyperCard (i.e., not using external commands). The technique was used widely in a publicly distributed demonstration stack for Novell Microsystems, and produced by Emeryville, CA based HyperMedia Group. In this stack, a large butterfly flew across the screen, landing on words and other graphics to draw the viewer's eye to various parts of the message. The butterfly was no mere fixed image moved about the screen. The wings flapped, its body moved—just as it should in animation.

When you start getting into animation of this scale, it's pretty hard to create good looking images unless you are fortunate enough to have artistic talent and training. If, like this author, you have trouble drawing a straight line with the Shift key down (that's a HyperCard painting tools joke), then you had better summon the help of an artist to create the "frames" for this kind of animation.

The technique applies text and font tools in ways we don't normally think of them. It involves creating a new screen font (with a utility such as Fontastic), each character being one of the frames of the object you wish to animate. For example, an animated character at rest might be assigned to the letter "A" in this new graphical font; having the character begin to take a step with the left foot may be letter "B"; and so on. The convenient feature about assigning an art shape to a character in a font is that you can design the character in almost any size. The larger the font size you create, the more detail and smoothness to round edges you can give your character.

As with icon animation, you can not only change the character by putting different letters into the field, but you can also move the location of the field at the same time. And, because you can set the location of an object off the visible area of the card window, you can even make the character appear to run slowly out of the window.

The only points you need to bear in mind when doing text animation are: first to install the font in the system, rather than as a stack resource; and second to use background fields if possible, because they respond slightly faster to HyperTalk commands than card fields.

Dragging Art

A common way of making a fixed shape move around the screen is to script a combination of HyperCard painting tools to select and drag the art. In a typical animated scene, the background picture layer contains all unchanging art—the backdrop. In the card picture layer are one or more distinct shapes. These shapes must not overlap, because the script will be doing the same thing as you do with the Select tool.

To script dragging actions, you'll need to figure out screen coordinates to pass as paramters to such commands as Drag and Click. The Home stack's "xy" utility handler (Chapter 51) helps with this task. Build the script with the Script Editor window open, and switch back and forth between the card window and script as you fill in coordinates (you'll have to start up the xy handler each time you come back to the card window).

In the script below, select a piece of card art, move it to a location, rotate it, and then move it again at a different speed (Figure 54–4):

```
on mouseUp
   lock screen -- so we don't see cursor changes
   choose select tool
   -- surround entire art with Select tool
   drag from 195,120 to 320,160 with commandKey
   set dragSpeed to 40
   unlock screen -- ready to show movement
   -- point 260,140 is roughly the center of the shape
   drag from 260,140 to 300,140 -- motion!
   lock screen -- so we don't see rotate handles
   doMenu "Rotate"
```

```
    -- point 358,160 is lower right handle, which we drag up 20 pixels
    drag from 358,160 to 358,140
    click at 364,170 -- to clear Rotate handles
    -- we now must re-select the object
    drag from 235,120 to 365,175 with commandKey
    set dragSpeed to 100
    unlock screen
    drag from 300,145 to 370,115 -- motion at oblique angle
    choose Browse tool
end mouseUp
```

This script also demonstrates that you have access to every painting menu option in a script that you do by hand. Every click, drag, selection, or effect can be scripted, even though it may take some patience getting the coordinates of precise clicks just right.

Figure 54–4. By selecting an area of a card picture, you may script anything you can do manually, including dragging the shape and rotating it with special effects tools.

When you animate a stack in this way, you usually want the art to revert to its original position so that the next user can experience the same animation. Unlike icon and field animation, whose location you can set by setting their objects' properties, you can't set the location of a piece of art (selected or otherwise). The best way to handle this situation is to lock the stack before any animation, and then unlock the stack when the card closes. Use the CantModify property as the locking device. At the beginning of the animation sequence, enter

```
set cantModify of this stack to true
```

to lock the stack. Then, make sure you have this closeCard handler in the card or background script:

```
on closeCard
    set cantModify of this stack to false
end closeCard
```

With the stack locked, your script can animate the art, but does not save changes. After the card is closed and the art reverts to its original state, it's safe again to unlock the stack if your user needs to enter data that is saved to the stack.

Visual Effects

For beginning animators, it is easy to think of individual cards in a HyperCard stack as being frames in a movie. To achieve apparent motion of shapes on the screen, make each card's art a part of an animation sequence. That's exactly how the Boston Macworld Kiosk stack made it look like the globe was spinning.

Blending the frames in a sequence can be enhanced with the addition of visual effects between cards. Dissolves help smooth out the rough edges between card and art changes. In some instances, the Wipe visual effect makes a moving characters seem to move better, because the wipe direction and resulting effect on a standalone shape helps convey vertical or horizontal motion.

Creating card-by-card animation is the most problematical when it comes to playing the animation on different speed Macintoshes. Because of inherent speed differences in writing information to the screens (sometimes called Screen Input/Output, or Screen I/O for short), animation that runs fine on a Macintosh Quadra may seem painfully slow on a Macintosh Classic. And if you've synchronized sound to one machine's video pace, it will be off on faster and slower machines.

Elaborate HyperTalk and XCMD machinations (there are public domain XCMDs that supply information about the Macintosh model the user is running) might let you adjust the animation to each machine by inserting Wait commands tailored to each Macintosh model, but that's not the way to go on time-sensitive animation. QuickTime animation may be a better solution.

QuickTime™ Animation Overlays

A number of animation programs, such as Macromedia Director, let you save frame sequences into a common format called QuickTime. QuickTime is an Apple system extension that allows faster Macintosh computer models to display animation and video, while also playing sound recorded in the QuickTime movie file. A special QuickTime Tools stack comes with HyperCard 2.2, and provides an excellent introduction to QuickTime and how to embed such elements into your HyperCard stacks.

Creating animation, like any good art, requires talent and experience. Therefore, while many of these tools provide outstanding power in creating and integrating animation, video, and sound into QuickTime movies, they won't turn absolutely everyone into Walt Disney.

Still, the QuickTime XCMDs that are in the QuickTime Tools stack allow a team consisting of an artist and scripter to create some amazing interactive applications. For example, the tools let the scripter trap for user mouse clicks at specific locations in the QuickTime movie window and at specified times within the movie. Knowing where—and when—the user clicks the pointer can let the application branch to a different movie that details the item originally clicked on.

Sound Techniques

HyperCard by itself plays 'snd ' resources, as discussed earlier. What may not be clear is that there are two types of 'snd ' resources, and no easy way to tell them apart. Prior to HyperCard version 2.0, only Type 2 resources could be played through HyperCard; now both types play. The important point is that HyperCard won't play what many long-time Macintosh owners have collected as sound files for use as alternate startup sounds, beeps, and so on. By now, however, many of these sounds have been converted to 'snd ' resources and are available from user groups and bulletin boards.

Creating your own sounds is a lot of fun. Virtually every Macintosh model released in the past few years has come with a built-in microphone, external micorphone, or at least a jack for connecting a microphone. The Sound control panel in System 7 works with these microphones to allow you to record additional sounds into the System file. With a tool such as ResEdit, you may copy those 'snd ' resources from the System file into your stacks.

More flexible is the audio palette that comes as part of the Audio Help stack with HyperCard 2.2. The palette expands (Figure 54–5) to let you record sounds with various compression ratios to keep otherwise large sound resources at reasonable sizes. You may also cut, copy, and paste selections of the recorded waveform for a modicum of sound editing. This palette saves sound resources to the current stack.

More sophisticated software, such as Sound Edit Pro (Macromedia) and AudioShop (Opcode Systems) let you not only record, but edit the sounds and their waveforms prior to moving them into a stack or QuickTime movie sound track. They also afford options of sound compression, which lets more sound be stored on less disk space (at some cost in sound quality). Any sound you copy into HyperCard as a 'snd ' resource can be played with the HyperTalk Play command.

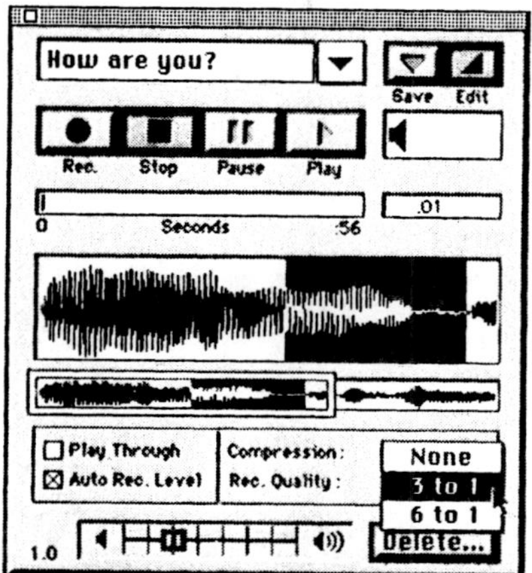

Figure 54–5. The opened audio palette lets you set recording parameters and edit sounds.

If your Macintosh model does not have a microphone, you can add a third-party microphone through the serial port. Macromedia and Articulate Systems produce audio digitizers for Mac models lacking a microphone jack.

Linking Sounds

With sound recording capability of any kind, it is now feasible to use digitized voice to convey information to the user of your HyperCard applications. Rather than having a stack wish you a generic "Have a nice day" when leaving the stack, you could have the stack say the time in a real voice (in contrast to the low quality text-to-speech facilities of an Apple designed software driver called Macintalk II). All it takes is to prerecord a series of sound pieces that are put together when played back. Let's look at how to make a talking clock.

The first task is to use your microphone and sound recording software (even the Sound control panel in System 7) to record the individual sound components, such as each of the numbers of the hours (1 to 12), minutes up to 19 (you already have 1 to 12, so just add zero as "oh" and 13 to 19), the tens of minutes (20, 30, 40, and 50) and the word "o'clock." Assign names to each resource identical to the number recorded. Therefore, the resource that says "twenty" should be named "20." This may seem odd to assign names that are numbers, but there's method to this madness. Also record sounds for the word "o'clock" and the long "oh" sound for a zero.

Once the resources are recorded, named, and transferred to the desired stack, it's time to build the script that converts the system's clock time into speech:

```
on sayTime
    get the time -- e.g., "10:05 AM"
    play char 1 to (offset(":",it)-1) of it -- "10"
    put char (offset(":",it)+1) to (length of word 1 of it) of it into theMins -- "05"
    if char 1 of theMins = "0" then
        if theMins = "00" then play "o'clock"
        else
            play "0" -- "oh"
            play char 2 of theMins -- and the digit
        end if
    else
        play item 1 of doubleDigitVoice(theMins) -- "...ty"
        play item 2 of doubleDigitVoice(theMins) -- and the digit
    end if
end sayTime

function doubleDigitVoice inputValue
    if inputValue < 21
    then return inputValue -- we have 'em all up to 20
    else
        put "10,20,30,40,50,60" into tensList
        if char 2 of inputValue = "0"
        then put empty into ones -- no second digit required
        else put char 2 of inputValue into ones
        return item (char 1 of inputValue) of tensList & "," & ones
    end if
end doubleDigitVoice
```

By naming the resources with the actual numbers they hold, the script can call the resources according to the numbers returned by the Time function. When you place two Play commands in a row, the second command waits for the first sound to finish before it starts playing, but it often preloads the sound while the first is playing (with sufficient memory space). You can use this technique to build many different kinds of voice information that means something to the user.

Video Image Display

Some of the first connections between HyperCard and video were with HyperCard controlling a videodisc player that showed its video output on a separate TV monitor. While this was head and shoulders above previous attempts to blend desktop computers and video sources, it only approached the ideal vision of multimedia: combining computer and video images on the same screen.

QuickTime makes this all possible, and the QuickTime Tools stack gives you the playing power. Capturing video for playback through QuickTime, however, takes a bit more hardware. For Mac models other than the Quadra AV models, it requires a separate video digitizer plug-in card or external box, plus a video camera or other souce (videodisc or video tape player). Most of these hardware add-ons come with enough software bundled to get you started with recording and editing video material, and saving the movies in the QuickTime format. The rest is up to the QuickTime XCMDs in the QuickTime Tools stack that comes with HyperCard 2.2.

Due to the slight degradation that occurs in QuickTime compression, it is best to start with the highest quality video image source as possible. Veteran QuickTime producers prefer the Hi-8 type 8mm video format, unless they have access to commercial-quality ¾-inch camcorders. As you gain more sophistication in producing QuickTime material, you will definitely need to investigate media integration tools that make the job of editing and combining video and sound into movies easier—and more costly. Still, HyperCard can be an extremely easy to program, interactive delivery vehicle for this kind of content.

You should now see how HyperCard and multimedia go hand in hand. The best part is that creative people who never had the technical expertise to bring good design sense of graphics, animation, sound, and video production to desktop computing can now do so. HyperCard makes the computer part much easier than before.

CHAPTER

55

EXPLORING APPLE EVENTS WITH HYPERTALK

HyperCard provides two methods of communicating with other programs. One method (instituted in version 2.1) accesses a System 7 technology called Apple Events via a small set of HyperTalk commands; the other method (introduced with version 2.2) also uses Apple Events, plus an additional technology, called Open Scripting Architecture (OSA). OSA allows knowledgeable users to write scripts in system-level scripting languages, such as AppleScript and Frontier, to communicate with other programs. In this chapter, we focus on the first method: Apple Events with HyperTalk.

What Are Apple Events?

Built into System 7 is an infrastructure that allows programs (including the Finder) to communicate with each other by sending messages that the user doesn't see. The Apple event mechanism is like a railroad system, providing all the tracks, switches, and administration in routing trains (messages) from one program to another. The programs are the ones that load the trains and assign them destinations.

You've already seen a lot within HyperCard about how messages are sent from place to place. A message is always a command, and sometimes it brings some data (parameters) along for the ride. Apple event messages behave the same way. And just like HyperCard, if the recipient doesn't know what to do with a message, the message is ignored. Therefore, for a program to receive and respond to Apple events, it must be Apple event-aware.

The messages that programs send to one another, of course, could vary widely with the program. After all, a spreadsheet program that is fully wired for Apple events would know how to respond to messages about working with rows and columns of numbers, while a word processing program's events would be oriented to working with characters, words, and paragraphs of text.

To help software developers make sense out of the plethora of possible Apple events, the System software group devised the concept of dividing Apple events into logical groups—*suites*. For example, one is called the Required Suite, which contains events that all System 7 savvy applications are supposed to respond to. Here are those events:

Event ID	*Description*
oapp	Open an application as if launched from the Finder
odoc	Open document(s) listed in the accompanying data
pdoc	Open, print, and close document(s) listed in the accompanying data
quit	Quit the application, as if choosing Quit from its File menu

The Event IDs shown above are only a small part of the message that is sent behind the scenes. The full message is a series of complex codes that HyperCard authors normally don't have to worry about. For instance, when running under System 7, HyperCard translates three friendly HyperTalk commands to the complex Apple event syntax without your ever knowing it. The open <application>, open <document> with <application>, and print <document> with <application> are the ways we HyperTalk scripters can access a program's Apple events for those operations. The close command sends other Apple events, depending on whether the parameters refer to an application or a document.

That's about as close as you need to get to the inner workings of Apple events. All of your actual sending and receiving of Apple events are performed in HyperTalk or other high-level scripting languages, such as AppleScript (Chapter 56).

Perhaps the most important concept to grasp at this stage is that Apple events shuffle between programs (before Apple events got their name, the technology was known as program-to-program communication). Access to a document is via its program. Therefore, in this chapter, as we focus on using HyperTalk to send Apple events to other copies of HyperCard on a network, Apple events flow between the copy of HyperCard on your Mac and the copy of HyperCard on another Mac. The specific instructions contained in those events (the data part of an event) and how they are responded to at the other end are determined by the HyperTalk scripts you write in stacks.

System Software Setup

Before programs can talk to each other on a network, several pieces of the System 7 file sharing software need to be setup correctly. This assumes, of course, that the Macs are cabled properly. All connections are via the Printer port. Cabling is the same as that used for multiple Macintoshes sharing a networked printer. LocalTalk or PhoneNet cabling is required.

But once the cabling is done, it's time to turn on all the system software pieces. Here is a summary of what needs attention:

Task	*Where*
Turn on AppleTalk	Chooser
Assign Your User Name	Sharing Setup control panel
Assign Macintosh Name	Sharing Setup control panel
Start Program Linking	Sharing Setup control panel
Allow Guest User Linking	Users & Groups control panel/<Guest>
Engage HyperCard Program Linking	HyperCard's Finder Get Info dialog

Once these settings are made, you can leave them. Should you wish to disallow open access to your programs via Apple events, you can turn off Program Linking in the Sharing Setup control panel. You may also single out individuals on your network whom you will allow access, while prohibiting access to others: establish custom users in the Users & Groups control panel, while disabling Program Linking in <Guest>.

HyperTalk Apple Events Overview

Scripting stacks for Apple events entails only a couple of steps, using a handful of commands and other HyperTalk constructions. Before one copy of HyperCard may send a message to another copy, the sender must first know the address of the recipient HyperCard program on the network. A stack may send Apple events, respond to Apple events, or do both. In the last case, you can create the same stack that goes on every participant's Macintosh to take care of transactions in both directions. Later in this chapter, we demonstrate such a stack in the form of a networked In-Out Board for an office. We'll now examine these component processes in detail.

Addresses

For any message you drop into a mailbox (electronic or snail), the recipient must be labeled by address so the mail system knows where to deliver the message. Apple event messages are no different. An event must be know where it's going. That destination is called an address. Remember that the destination is a program (which may then do something with the message in an open document). That program may reside on someone else's Macintosh on a network; and the network may be divided into more than one zone. Those three elements—zone, Macintosh, and program—are the component parts of an Apple event address.

In HyperTalk, the address format consists of those three elements separated by colons in the form:

```
<zone>:<Macintosh>:<program>
```

The program name is exactly the name of the program as it is shown in the Finder of the addressee's Macintosh. Therefore, if your copy of HyperCard is labeled "HyperCard" on your Mac, but the addressee has named the program "HyperCard 2.2" on the other machine, the latter form must be used in the destination address.

A Macintosh name is the name assigned to the machine in the Sharing Setup control panel (the third field of the Network Identity section). This name is independent from the HyperCard user name. When setting up a Macintosh network, it is a good idea to name the Macintoshes in such a way that other participants on the network would be able to recognize each destination Mac by its name (perhaps assigning some of the user's name to the Macintosh name).

Zone names apply only if your network is divided into multiple zones. If either or both of the zone and Macintosh elements are the same as your own Macintosh, then an asterisk can stand in for the same element as your system. For example, if your Mac and Mary's Mac are in the same zone (or there aren't any zones), the address of HyperCard on Mary's Mac would be:

```
*:Mary's Mac:HyperCard
```

You can find the address of your HyperCard program at anytime with the address global property. Try it yourself, by typing the following command into the Message Box:

```
answer the address
```

You'll see the valid address of your HyperCard copy. Notice that except for the zone name, a Macintosh's address doesn't change even if the Mac is connected to another place on the network. The address is different from a physical pathname to a file on a disk. Apple event addresses do not care about volume names or how deeply nested the target application may be, because the system software registers all applications capable of receiving Apple events when they start up.

Getting Someone Else's Address

To send a message to another copy of HyperCard, your script must obtain (or have stored away) the address of that HyperCard. A script can't get this information from scratch by itself: a human user must become part of the process. This happens in the form of a program linking dialog box (Figure 55–1), which is displayed by the answer program command:

```
answer program <prompt>
```

The dialog presents two columns of information (or three if your network consists of multiple zones). On the left are all Macintoshes on the network (or selected zone) that are open for program linking (in their Sharing Setup control panels). As you select any Macintosh, the list on the right side of the dialog contains the names of all currently running processes on that Macintosh. Notice that for a program to be listed here, it must already be running on the destination Mac. This is a critical point that must be factored into whatever application you design with Apple events in mind. You cannot launch an application on someone else's Macintosh (either via HyperTalk or AppleScript) to send it messages. The user at the recipient end must have the program running for you.

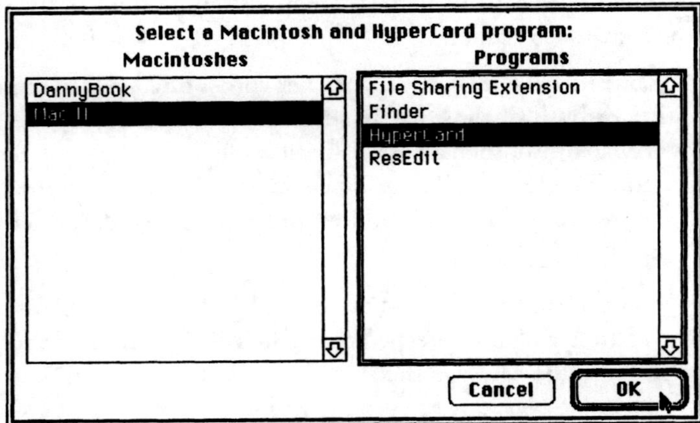

Figure 55–1. The Answer Program dialog lets your script obtain the address of a target program on another Macintosh.

To use this command properly, you must supply a prompt, which appears at the top of the program linking dialog box. Generally, you will provide instructions for the user to select the desired Macintosh and (for linking to HyperCard) HyperCard application, as in:

```
answer program "Select a Macintosh and HyperCard program:"
```

A largely undocumented feature of this command is an extra parameter, which restricts the listing of programs to only versions of HyperCard:

```
answer program <prompt> of type "WILDep01"
```

By showing only whatever copy(ies) of HyperCard is opened on any machine (and preselecting it), the program linking dialog reduces the user's chore to selecting only the desired Macintosh (and zone).

This command returns any errors (including canceling the dialog) into the Result. But if the user completes the selection, the address is placed into It. Because your script will be needing this address for other commands, it is best to then place that value into a local variable:

```
on mouseUp
    answer program "Choose a recipient:" of type "WILDep01"
    if the result is not empty then
        answer "Program Linking not available."
        exit mouseUp
    else put it into targetAddress
    -- continue processing --
end mouseUp
```

HyperTalk includes a function, the programs, which reveals all System 7-savvy processes that are running on the current Macintosh—the same items you see in the Program Linking dialog box for your own Mac. It cannot, however, determine the running programs on any other machine on the network.

What Kind of Messages to Send

When communicating between copies of HyperCard, the most common messages sent are names of handlers in the recipient stack. In other words, you script actions in the recipient stack that execute when called by another copy of HyperCard. These handlers may be the same ones that the stack's primary users also executes—there don't necessarily have to be separate sets of handlers.

Messages may also be any HyperTalk command. And this brings up an important issue about security.

For the Security-Conscious

The power that program linking and Apple events provide in HyperCard is also potentially dangerous if a scripter wishes to be malicious. While no one else on a network can start your copy of HyperCard, if your copy is running, an unfettered scripter has the ability to open any stack and issue any menu command that you can from within HyperTalk, including such things as deleting cards and stacks. The remote scripter won't see your stack on his or her screen, but it is possible to extract data from your stacks without your knowledge.

The most reliable way to guard against this potential intrusion into a Macintosh is to turn off Program Linking in the Sharing Setup control panel. With that item turned off, your programs will not show up in other users' Program Linking dialog box. As you'll also see, below, it is possible to trap for Apple events that come your way, and prevent them from executing. This includes the ability to allow some Apple events to pass while inhibiting others.

For many installations, the work group is a collegial one, and the need for password and Apple event security is small or nonexistent. Still, large corporations or departments working on sensitive material within HyperCard must be aware of the possible breaches of security and how to avoid them.

Sending a Message

A special variation of HyperTalk's Send command is a primary vehicle for transmitting a message to another copy of HyperCard. The syntax is quite simple:

```
send <message> to program <program address> [without reply]
```

The <message> parameter is the command to be obeyed by the receiving program. <Program address> is the address of the destination copy of HyperCard, usually as derived from the Program Linking dialog box (above). We'll cover the reply business in a moment.

How you compose the <message> parameter is very important, especially if the command includes parameters. Let's take a simple example of sending a message to another HyperCard to go to the Practice stack. For this first example, we'll show a complete mouseUp handler, which includes activity to get the address of the target application if it hasn't been stored in a global variable. Later examples will focus on the Send command line(s).

```
on mouseUp
    global targetAddress
    if targetAddress is empty then
        answer program "Choose a recipient:" of type "WILDep01"
        if the result is not empty then
            answer the result
            exit mouseUp
        else put it into targetAddress
    end if
    send "go Practice" to program targetAddress
    if the result is not empty then answer the result
end mouseUp
```

Here we've taken a simple command, go "Practice", and sent it as a single string to the other program. Because HyperCard goes a long way to make good out of bad, the receiving copy of HyperCard takes apart that command and tries to turn whatever is in the message into a valid command—making "Practice" into a stack name parameter of the Go command. This works fine.

Things get a little trickier when you start adding parameters:

```
send "go Practice in a new window" to...
```

returns a result of "No such stack" because HyperCard tries to evaluate everything after the Go command as part of the name of the stack. There are two ways to help this command do what we want. One is to give HyperCard more information:

```
send "go stack Practice in a new window" to...
```

While this variation does the job, it's not as reliable as the preferred way, which is to compose the message so it evaluates as close to the way you'd do it in a script. In a HyperTalk script, the command would be:

```
go "Practice" in a new window
```

The quotes around the name of the stack tell HyperCard exactly where the stack parameter begins and ends, and where any other parameters start. To replicate this in a HyperTalk expression requires the Quote constant:

```
send "go" && quote & "Practice" & quote && "in a new window" to...
```

To help you assemble complex messages like this, it may be better to do so into a local variable, and then send the variable as the message:

```
put  "go" && quote & "Practice" & quote && "in a new window" into theMsg
send theMsg to program targetAddress
```

By using the debugging tools, you can stop execution prior to sending the message and look into the value of the variable in the Variable Watcher, and make sure it looks like a valid HyperTalk command. You may also assemble multiple-line commands so that a series of messages is sent with a single Send command. Be sure to insert a return between commands so that they are on separate lines as they would be in a script.

Waiting for a Reply

When HyperCard sends an Apple event to another program, the Apple event mechanism inside the system software does more than just send the message with wild abandon. Unless instructed otherwise, the sending program waits for the recipient program to acknowledge the message. In the case of HyperCard, this also means that if the message triggers a custom handler in the stack, the acknowledgment isn't sent back until the handler finishes. No additional scripting is required for this acknowledgment—Apple event innards take care of this automatically.

This acknowledgment doesn't start its way back until the message is received and executed at the recipient end. Therefore, if you send a message that displays an alert dialog, as in

```
send "answer Hello" to program targetAddress
```

the reply does not start on its way back to the sending program until the recipient clicks the Answer dialog's OK button.

In the meantime, the sending program is in limbo, waiting patiently for that reply to come. The user on the sending side sees the watch cursor, and no further script execution takes place in the sender's stack. After one minute, the Apple event finally times out, and control returns to the sending user or script.

By the same token, the wait until the handler finishes gives the recipient an opportunity to load the contents of reply data, if desired. For example, the sender may send a message that includes a brief text note for the recipient. At the receiving end, the stack contains a script that displays that note as the prompt part of an Ask dialog box, which also provides a field for a response. The script that displays the dialog also captures the response and loads it into a reply, which is sent back with the Reply keyword. Here are some script examples:

```
on mouseUp -- on sender's side
   answer program "Choose a recipient:" of type "WILDep01"
   if the result is not empty then
      answer the result
      exit mouseUp
   else put it into targetAddress
```

```
        end if
        ask "Enter your outgoing note:"
        send "passNote" && quote & it & quote to program targetAddress
        if the result is not empty
        then answer the result -- the reply
    end mouseUp
```

This script presents the sender with a dialog in which to enter an outgoing note. The contents are passed as an argument to the passNote command, which is sent to the target program. The target stack has the following handler in it to receive the message:

```
    on passNote theNote -- on recipient's side
        ask theNote -- shows incoming note with space for answer
        if it is not empty
        then reply it -- send response back to sender
    end passNote
```

When a handler sends back a reply, the original Send command gets that reply in the form of data within the Result. The generic way of handling the Result, as shown in the mouseUp handler, above, displays both responses from the recipient or any Apple event error messages that come back in case the Send command couldn't be fulfilled.

Result Errors

Due to the wide realm of possibilities that can get in the way of sending an Apple event, it is good practice to check the contents of the Result after each Send command, as shown in an earlier script. Any failure of the command shows up as the Result. Here are some possible errors that could come back in the Result:

```
Not handled by target program
Got error <number> when sending Apple event
<Apple event error message>
<HyperTalk error message>
Timeout
Cancel
```

Any value in the Result indicates that either the transmission failed in some fashion or the recipient has supplied a response.

Blowing Past Replies

For a straight command, there may be no possible reply coming from the recipient. It may also be of no consequence to your script that the target application did not receive the message. If either is the case, then you should append the without reply parameter to the command. When you do this, HyperCard sends the message, and doesn't bother waiting for a reply to find its way back to your stack. In fact, if you send multiple messages to another HyperCard without replies, they queue up in the recipient Mac. For example:

```
repeat 3
   send "answer Hello" to program targetAddress without reply
end repeat
```

This fragment sends three commands in succession, and faster than the user on the recipient machine could dismiss the dialogs. But as that user dismisses the dialog from the first event, the second dialog appears, and so on until no more messages are pending. In the meantime, because the sender didn't wait for replies, that script is merrily executing statements further down the handler.

More Two-way Information

Not all Apple events are commands. You may also use Apple events to obtain information from a stack running on another copy of HyperCard (on your machine or another machine on the network). The HyperTalk command that accomplishes this from the sender side is the Request command, whose syntax is as follows:

```
request <expression> from program <program address>
```

Again, the syntax is simple, and a lot of the rules are the same as for the Send command. The <expression> parameter, however, must be something that the target application can evaluate. That may be things like:

```
contents of fields
properties of objects
HyperTalk functions
user-defined functions
```

Here are examples of these varieties:

```
request "bg fld 1" from program targetAddress
request "name of this stack" from program targetAddress
request "the date" from program targetAddress
request "fileName(long name of this stack)" from program targetAddress
```

What may be difficult to grasp at first about these commands is that the evaluation of the request is performed on the recipient's copy of HyperCard. In other words, when the first example requests the contents of field 1, it means field 1 of the stack that is open on the recipient HyperCard program. There is no connection to fields in the sender's stack. The same goes for properties and HyperTalk functions: the evaluation of the request is being performed only on the recipient's copy of HyperCard: the name of the stack in the target program and the date from the recipient's Mac.

As for user-defined function requests, they must be met by functions in the target stack. It's as if the message were typed into the Message Box of the recipient's HyperCard, with the message going to the current card (and then up the hierarchy). But unlike normal user-defined functions, those designed to receive Apple events require the Reply keyword to return data back to the sender (instead of the Return keyword). Other than that, the function is identical in its construction. For example, below is a complete mouseUp handler that summons a function that runs in a stack on another Mac's HyperCard. The function extracts the folder path to the version of HyperCard running the sending stack:

```
on mouseUp
    global targetAddress
    if targetAddress is empty then
        answer program "Choose a recipient:" of type "WILDep01"
            if the result is not empty then
            answer the result
            exit mouseUp
        else put it into targetAddress
    end if
    put "pathToHC(" & quote & long name of HyperCard & quote & ")" into myMsg
    request myMsg from program targetAddress
    if the result is not empty
    then answer the result
    else put it
end mouseUp
```

Again, we must use the quote constants to assemble the arguments to the function being sent. On the recipient end is the following function:

```
function pathToHC thePath
    set itemDelimiter to colon
    delete last item of thePath
    set itemDelimiter to comma
    reply thePath & colon
end pathToHC
```

Trapping Apple Events

Beyond the command and function handlers that receive Apple event commands from other copies of HyperCard, a stack may also receive events coming from other programs. By and large, OSA scripting (e.g., AppleScript) is a better vehicle for this kind of communication, but we'll present the remaining handful of HyperTalk items that you're free to use instead.

Each time HyperCard receives an Apple event (including the kind from the Send and Request commands in other copies of HyperCard), HyperCard turns the event into a system message, called appleEvent. This message is sent to the current card before the contents of the Apple event, and contains a number of parameters about the event. The formal syntax for the incoming message is:

```
appleEvent <class>,<id>,<sender>
```

The first two parameters are four-character identifiers of the event class (things like aevt and misc) and the event message (e.g., oapp, pdoc, etc.). These identifiers are part of the comparatively complex Apple event syntax that HyperCard and AppleScript shield us from. A complete description of these is available in the *Inside Macintosh* volume that covers Apple events.

The third parameter is the address of the program that sent the event. This is the same kind of address we use in HyperTalk to send messages.

You can trap for this message just like any HyperCard system message. In fact, an appleEvent handler in your Home stack can offer a modicum of protection against nefarious folks on the network from doing damage to your HyperCard stacks. The following handler alerts you to any Apple event sent by any user from any program on the network:

```
on appleEvent class,id,sender
   answer "Do you wish to process an Apple Event from" && ¬
   sender & "?" with "Yes" or "No"
   if it is "Yes" then pass appleEvent
end appleEvent
```

This handler does nothing more than extract the address of the sending program (which would include the user's Macintosh to help you identify the source machine). If you say it's OK, then the event is passed to HyperCard, where the data part of the Apple event is interpreted and carried out (perhaps calling a command or function handler in your stack).

Extracting Apple Event Data

Notice that any data that accompanies the message is not part of this system message. You can, however, find out what the data part is by including a Request command inside the appleEvent handler. If the sender was another copy of HyperCard, the data part consists of the command or function (plus any parameters) that were part of the Send or Request commands on the sender's script. You can use this information, if you like, to let desired AppleEvents pass without the alert in the previous script. Here's one way to do this:

```
on appleEvent class,id,sender
    request appleEvent data
    if it contains "sendNote"
    then pass appleEvent
    else
        answer "Do you wish to process an unexpected Apple Event from" && ¬
        sender & "?" with "Yes" or "No"
        if it is "Yes" then pass appleEvent
    end if
end appleEvent
```

This script lets the sendNote command (see earlier script) pass unscathed, while flagging all other messages. The key part of this construction is the request appleEvent data command, which places the data part of the pending Apple event into It. More advanced versions of this handler could log all Apple events that are sent to your HyperCard (perhaps saved to a text file).

Replying to Other Programs

One final HyperTalk syntax point is how to respond to Apple events that may arrive from programs other than HyperCard. We saw earlier that the Reply command lets you return any kind of text data back to the sending copy of HyperCard. But not all Apple event-aware programs expect data back in that way. They do expect, however, the possibility of error messages. Thus, the command,

```
reply error <expression>
```

can be used to send responses to all Apple event-aware programs, including HyperCard. To demonstrate, here's a simple variation of an earlier appleEvent message handler that allows the sendNote HyperTalk command to pass but responds forcefully to any other message:

```
on appleEvent class,id,sender
    request appleEvent data
    if it contains "sendNote"
    then pass appleEvent
    else reply error "Get lost!"
end appleEvent
```

Applying Apple Events

Our discussion here focuses strictly on HyperCard-to-HyperCard Apple events, because OSA scripting (next chapter) is a better solution for directing other applications from HyperCard. But within HyperCard, Apple events lend themselves to applications that require a modicum of multi-user functionality. This doesn't mean that Apple events suddenly makes

HyperCard multi-user. But by carefully thinking through applications, you can create solutions that offer shared data and communications between HyperCard users on a network.

The key to designing a system is understanding the limitations. First and foremost is that for HyperCard stacks on two machines to speak to each other, both machines must have HyperCard running and those stacks open. Therefore, the kinds of solutions that work best in this environment are those in which multiple people are actively working with each other on the network and/or when one copy of HyperCard and the central stack run on a Mac designated as the centralized file server at all times.

One-on-One

An excellent example of multiple people connected to each other's HyperCard programs is a shareware game called *HyperBattleShip!*, which was created as both a technology exercise and demonstration by the HyperCard team that built Apple events into HyperCard (for version 2.1). The program is available on many HyperCard-oriented bulletin board and user group libraries.

In this game, both players have a copy of the stack running on their machines. The object of the game is the same as the legendary *BattleShip* game: locate the other player's hidden ships within a grid by firing a torpedo at a square. Each player first establishes the locations of his or her five ships (of varying length) by dragging the ships from the palette. Then players take turns clicking in their opponent's grid, one torpedo at a time. When your shot hits an opponent's ship, you both hear great digitized sound effects of the explosion, and the torpedo sender has an indication on the grid where there was a hit. When a ship goes down, the gurgling sound is satisfying for the sinker, and disappointing to the sunken.

A great deal of communication transfers between Macintoshes in this application, and a close examination of the scripts reveals many outstanding techniques to make a one-on-one application work smoothly.

Multi-user Server

Another shareware stack is an In-Out Board application (Figure 55–2). The purpose of this application is to let people in a networked office find out if others on the network are available without having to pick up the phone and hope the voice mail message has some details about when that person may be back.

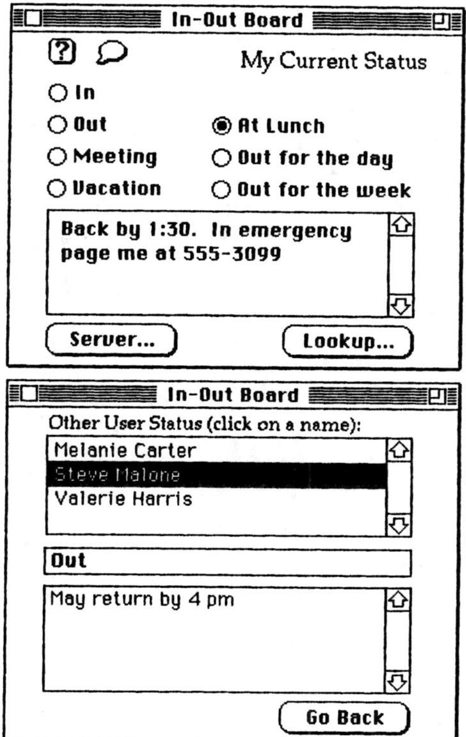

Figure 55–2. An In-Out Board stack that uses Apple events to store and read data from a centralized copy of the stack.

To set up this environment, each user has a copy of the stack, and one must be on a Mac that can run HyperCard plus the stack at all times. One scenario places this stack at the receptionist's Macintosh, or perhaps elsewhere in the lobby where visitors can check for availability of the staff.

The stack uses the HyperCard user name (set in the Home stack preferences) to identify an individual making a change to his or her status. In this version, a series of radio buttons provides a number of pre-written possibilities, plus the option of adding any extra text. As each change is made to a radio button or the text field, that information is sent to the stack acting as the server, where it stores information from every participant.

Clicking the Lookup button leads to the second screen, which reads a list of all people who participate in the In-Out Board (this information is also in the server stack). Clicking on any name sends a request to the server to dig out the details of the user's last status. That information is displayed in the fields on the card.

This application could be enhanced so that the server also stores addresses of all participants. With that information, the server stack could send out updated information to all participants so that anyone looking at a detail screen for a given individual could receive a real-time update.

From here we go to even more power interapplication communication: OSA scripting with AppleScript.

CHAPTER

56

OPEN SCRIPTING (APPLESCRIPT) AND HYPERCARD

A major addition to HyperCard with version 2.2 is HyperCard's ability to play a complete role in the realm of Apple's Open Scripting Architecture (OSA). While perhaps more has been said about one part of OSA—the AppleScript language—than the underlying technology, it's important to understand how all these pieces, including HyperCard, fit into the picture.

What Is Open Scripting?

In its search for a system-level scripting language to link diverse applications together, Apple broadened its view about the problem. Rather than force-feed a single language on the universe, it shaped a foundation upon which multiple languages could be used to accomplish the goal of putting the power of Apple events into the hands of users. The result was a scripting architecture that works entirely in the background as we users and scripters use friendly tools to automate tasks and link up documents from various applications.

In concert with the OSA technology, Apple also developed a scripting language that uses OSA as its transport mechanism. That language is called AppleScript. UserTalk, another scripting language developed for the Frontier technology of UserLand Software, Inc., pre-dates OSA and AppleScript, but its version 2.1 is fully capable of using the OSA wires that are gradually being built into the Macintosh operating system. The point of the OSA technology was to provide the foundation upon which scripting languages could be developed. Some may be friendlier than others; some may be more powerful than others in the way they work with tricky programs, such as the Finder.

HyperCard 2.2's task, therefore, was to be as open to scripting as Open Scripting is. It may be easy to hang your hat on the AppleScript language in this respect, but be aware that HyperCard 2.2, by fully supporting OSA, is equally at home with Frontier, QuicKeys 3.0, and any other OSA-compliant language that should come along in the future.

Our Focus on AppleScript

In this chapter, we elect AppleScript as our language of choice. We believe it is more accessible to those scripters who have worked with HyperTalk but have done little other kinds of programming. AppleScript also comes bundled with HyperCard 2.2, so you can begin experimenting with it right away. Like HyperTalk, AppleScript reads like natural language (in a variety of native languages around the world). Once you become comfortable with

AppleScript, you can then evaluate other languages to see if they supply capabilities you feel may be lacking in AppleScript.

This chapter will only introduce you to what AppleScript looks like and the way you can incorporate AppleScript scripts into HyperCard stacks. To learn AppleScript from the ground up, read *The Complete AppleScript Handbook* (published by Random House Electronic Publishing). To take full advantage of AppleScript's powers (with or without HyperCard) you should become familiar with the information in that publication.

The Object Model

Perhaps the most important aspect of Open Scripting Architecture is the concept of the Object Model. As a HyperCard author, you already have a lot of experience with this idea, because you are accustomed to working with objects in HyperCard: buttons, fields, cards, and so on. Those objects all have properties that define their behavior and appearance. Some objects, especially fields and buttons, have data in them as well.

When a program, such as HyperCard, is said to support the Object Model, it means that the program's designers have written the innards so that the items a user works with—including data—can be defined as distinct objects. Moreover, each object must have a name of some kind to distinguish it from all other objects. In HyperCard, for example, field objects are distinguished from each other by ID (and potentially by part number and name). In other words, background field ID 2 of background 1 of stack "Fred" gives that particular field a location in the cosmos that cannot be confused with any other field.

Good implementations of the Object Model go further, specifying that any piece of data that is subject to manipulation via script can also be identified within the cosmos. For example, in a word processing document, a particular word can be named according to its place within the document (e.g., word 246, or word 23 of paragraph 3). Therefore, everything in the Object Model is an object with a name of some kind.

Scripting, much like HyperTalk scripting, consists of one or more commands that act on a program's objects. The object may be: a program, when the command is to create a blank document; a document window, when the command is to resize the window; an insertion point between two characters, when the command is to insert some text; or a cell in a spreadsheet, when the command is to capture the formatted data from that cell for inclusion into another document.

Where Is AppleScript?

Since the Object Model for any given program is defined by the program's designers, we have an interesting situation with regard to the vocabulary of AppleScript. The language that is built into the AppleScript system extension is tiny—just a handful of very basic commands for getting and setting data or properties and a few more to get programs going. The bulk of the vocabulary comes from the applications you wish to script. In many instances, there are similarities among programs for common processes (partially as a result of Apple event suites), but each program can have its own commands and ways of referring to objects. This is one reason why AppleScript is more difficult to learn for some users than a self-contained vocabulary, such as HyperTalk.

The vocabulary is contained in a resource (of type "aete") in the program. Most script editors, such as the AppleScript Script Editor (part of the AppleScript Run-time software), include an option that lets you view this "dictionary" of terms for each program you intend to script. Figure 56–1 shows a portion of one program's scripting dictionary. The dictionary shows (and partially explains) commands (standard font) and object references (italic) within groupings of Apple event suites. Unfortunately, few applications do a sufficient job of explaining the finer points of using these commands and object references (names) within the dictionaries. Studying extra documentation and lots of experimentation are often needed to understand the dictionary fully.

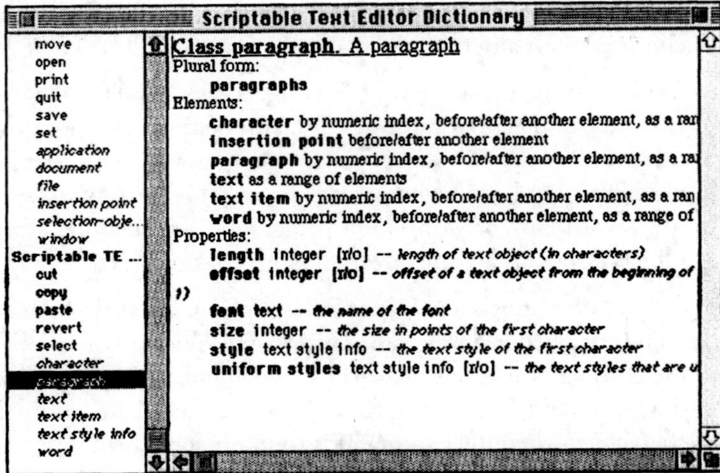

Figure 56–1. A program's scripting dictionary.

Scriptable, Attachable, Recordable

The level of support for Open Scripting is characterized by three possible attributes in a program. The most common is the idea of being *scriptable*. This means that a script (written in a script editor or saved as a double-clickable application) can access information and control the application remotely. HyperCard is scriptable.

A second ability is to allow script writers to write and save scripts within the application. This makes the program *attachable*, meaning that scripts can be attached to the program, documents, or objects in the documents. Such scripts would be triggered by menu commands or user action on the objects. HyperCard is attachable—one of the first, actually. An OSA script can be attached to any HyperCard object that normally holds a HyperTalk script. Thus, scripts can be triggered by system messages (e.g., opening a card or stack), menu choices (in HyperCard custom menus), or other user actions (e.g., clicking a button or entering data into a field).

Some OSA-compatible programs are also *recordable*. The underlying system architecture for scripting lets recordable applications send copies of their actions to a script editor to build scripts for users as they walk through a process manually. HyperCard 2.2 is not recordable, so users of your stacks won't be able to record processes they'd like automated while using your stacks.

Anatomy of an AppleScript Script

Writing scripts in Apple's Script Editor (Figure 56–2) provides an experience that is quite different from writing scripts in HyperTalk. Whereas in HyperTalk, an object's script may consist of several handlers, each one being compiled only when it is first executed in a session, an AppleScript script doesn't necessarily consist of handlers. The script is compiled into machine code *en masse* before it is saved to the disk file. A Run button (or starting the script from the Finder if it is saved as a standalone script) is what triggers the script.

Commands in the script may operate on their own (using AppleScript as the object to which the commands are sent) or they may be directed to a specific application. The latter happens inside a Tell statement, as in:

```
tell application "Scriptable Text Editor"
    -- statements for the Editor
end tell
```

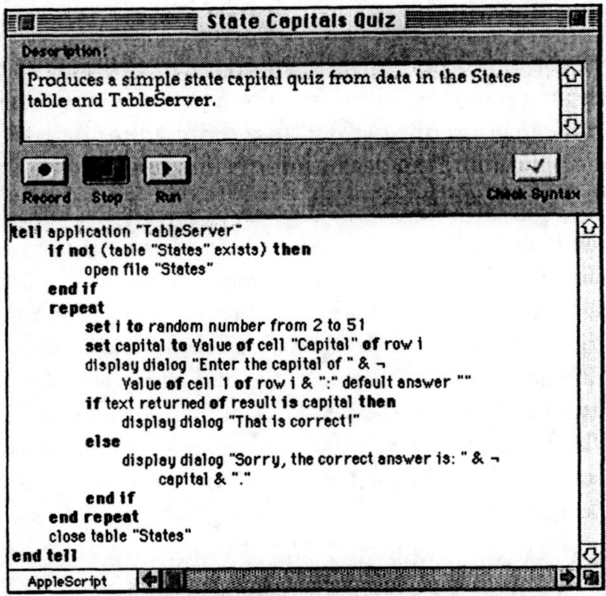

Figure 56–2. A typical script in the AppleScript Script Editor window.

A single script may have any number of these Tell statements in it. The statements may be consecutive:

```
tell application "A"
    -- statements for "A"
end tell

tell application "B"
    -- statements for "B"
end tell
```

or they may be nested if the execution flow requires:

```
tell application "A"
    -- statements for "A"
    tell application "B"
        -- statements for "B"
    end tell
    -- more statements for "A"
end tell
```

Someone writing a script in the Script Editor to summon the powers of HyperCard would create a Tell statement directed at HyperCard. The commands inside that Tell statement would be the commands that are available in HyperCard's dictionary. Conversely, if you write an AppleScript script in HyperCard, you would direct commands to other programs via these Tell statements, using the commands available in those programs.

Open Scripts in HyperCard

At the top of every HyperCard object's script editor window is a popup menu (Figure 56–3). This is where you assign the scripting language for the particular object (you can also set the object's scriptingLanguage property via a script). It is important to realize that the language you select for an object is the one that must be used for all script lines for that object. While you cannot mix HyperTalk and AppleScript in the same object's script, you can still use AppleScript to perform most of what HyperTalk lets you do (see below).

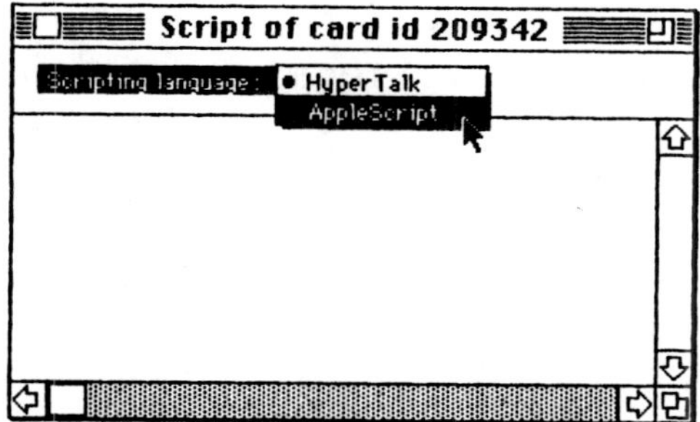

Figure 56–3. The Scripting Language popup menu in HyperCard script windows.

Unlike Script Editor scripts, however, there are no Run buttons to trigger AppleScript scripts in HyperCard objects. The same system messages that trigger HyperTalk scripts are the ones that trigger AppleScript scripts inside objects. Therefore, you will have the appearance of message handlers in object scripts, regardless of the language.

The selected scripting language, however, makes all the difference in the world as to how the script you write is treated with respect to compilation and syntax checking.

Compilation Differences

HyperTalk scripts are not compiled until they are executed. At that, only each handler is compiled when needed. The compiled version is stored in memory only, and is discarded when HyperCard quits or the memory is needed for other purposes. At no time is the compiled version saved to disk.

When you select a language other than HyperTalk as the object's scripting language, however, the compilation scene changes radically. Before the script can be closed and saved, it goes through an open scripting compilation. This is precisely the same compilation that scripts go through in the AppleScript Script Editor—the object's entire script is compiled at once, not handler-by-handler, and is saved to disk in compiled form. If there are any syntax problems anywhere, the script does not compile. You may close the script window, but unless the script compiles successfully, HyperCard ignores all handlers in the object's script (in fact, system messages for which there are handlers in that object, pass right over that object as if there were no handlers there).

Checking Syntax

With an Open Scripting language selected in the popup menu, an additional menu item is available in the Script menu. Check Syntax (Figure 56–4) lets you ask the system to run the script through the compiler. This function is only part of Open Scripting, and is not available for HyperTalk.

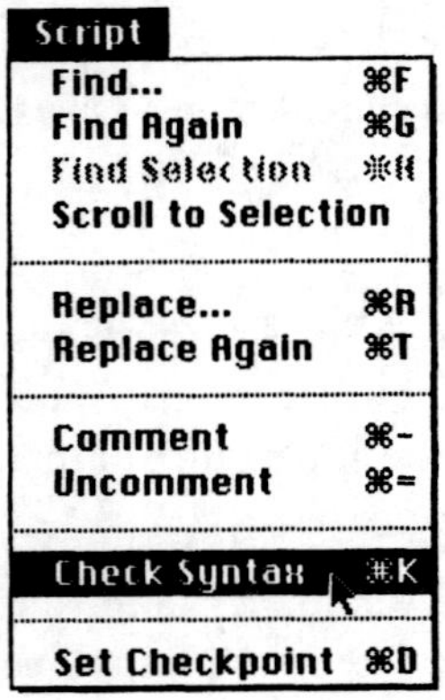

Figure 56–4. Check Syntax compiles an AppleScript script.

On the flip side of the coin, you don't have the facilities of HyperTalk's debugging tools when the scriptingLanguage is AppleScript. As of this writing, AppleScript does not yet have debugging support built into the architecture, so you'll need to employ other methods of checking intermediate values of variables and other debugging techniques (described in *The Complete AppleScript Handbook*).

Mixing Script Languages

While you cannot use multiple scripting languages within an object's script, you can use HyperCard's message hierarchy to "connect" scripts written in different languages. For example, a button script may be written in HyperTalk. One of its commands may require the execution of an AppleScript handler located in another object's script. By calling the command as a normal HyperTalk command, the button script triggers the AppleScript script, which, in turn, could even return some data or other values to the button script.

To make cross-language scripting work correctly, however, requires familiarity with the differences between the ways the two languages handle commands, parameters, and returned values. Figure 56–5 shows a small stack that contains a salesperson's customer data. Only the top fields are filled out on every card. The salesperson can use HyperCard's searching facility to jump around the stack. Also on each customer's card are fields for current receivables data. This data is stored not in the stack, but in a tab-delimited file generated daily by the Accounts Payable department (Figure 56–6). When you want to see the payables situation for a given customer, simply click on the Past Due button.

The script of the Past Due button is as follows:

```
on mouseUp
    set cursor to watch
    put field "Company" into customer
    put "Payables Aging.txt" into theTable
    fetchAging theTable,customer -- custom handler in bkgnd
    put the result into pastDueData
    put 0 into pastDueTotal
    repeat with x = 1 to 4
        put value of item x of pastDueData into fld ("Past Due" && x)
        add value of item x of pastDueData to pastDueTotal
    end repeat
    if pastDueTotal > 10000 then
        beep
        answer "This customer should be put on credit hold."
    end if
end mouseUp
```

The handler extracts the company name from the card, and passes it along with the name of the payable file as arguments to a command called fetchAging. That script is an AppleScript script located in the background:

```
on fetchAging(theTable, customer)
    tell application "TableServer"
        copy {0, 0, 0, 0} to returnValue
        if not (table theTable exists) then
```

```
            open file (theTable)
        end if
        repeat with x from 1 to 4
            copy Value of cell (x + 2) of row customer ¬
                of table theTable to item x of returnValue
        end repeat
        close table theTable saving no
        set AppleScript's text item delimiters to ","
        return returnValue as text
    end tell
end fetchAging
```

Notice a couple important points. First, even though we want the fetch-Aging call in the button handler to return a value, we don't put the call into a HyperTalk function format. This is because AppleScript has only command handlers, which may or may not return values). When such Apple-Script handlers return data, the data can be extracted back in the Hyper-Talk handler from the Result.

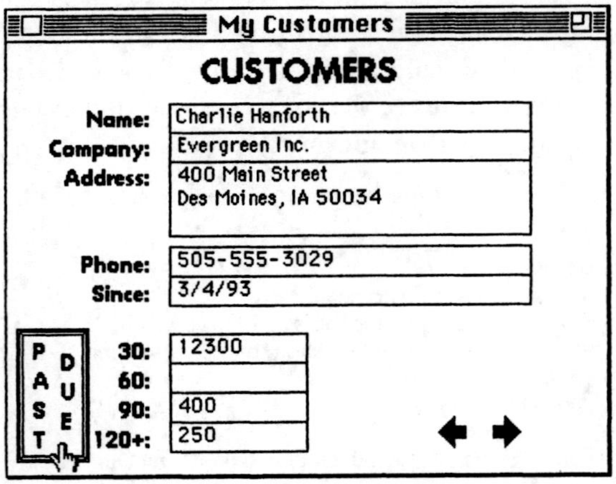

Figure 56–5. A salesperson's customer stack.

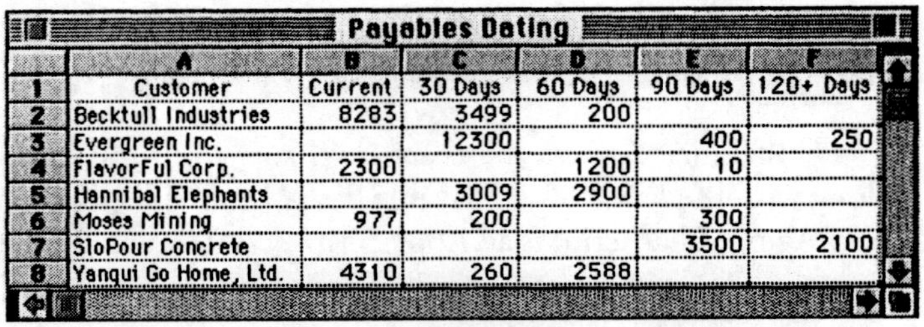

Payables Dating

	A	B	C	D	E	F
1	Customer	Current	30 Days	60 Days	90 Days	120+ Days
2	Becktull Industries	8283	3499	200		
3	Evergreen Inc.		12300		400	250
4	FlavorFul Corp.	2300		1200	10	
5	Hannibal Elephants		3009	2900		
6	Moses Mining	977	200		300	
7	SloPour Concrete				3500	2100
8	Yanqui Go Home, Ltd.	4310	260	2588		

Figure 56–6. The Payables file in its Excel format prior to export as a tab-delimited file.

The second most important point is that the form of parameter passing is different in HyperTalk and AppleScript. The HyperTalk call places the parameters one space away from the command, with no parentheses; the AppleScript handler requires that the parameters appear in parentheses.

To extract the data from the tab-delimited file, the script above uses TableServer (by Change Labs, included with *The Complete AppleScript Handbook*), a window-less scriptable application that simplifies access to tabular data. The job of the fetchAging handler is to extract data from columns 3 through 7 of the row containing the customer's data. Each cell's data is placed into a comma-delimited item within an AppleScript list (a list is contained within curly brackets).

If we returned the curly-bracketed list to HyperTalk, the returned value would be in the AppleScript format. Since HyperTalk can't deal with that data structure directly (except as a string that happens to include curly brackets), we preprocess the returned value on the AppleScript end. The AppleScript handler returns the value as a comma-delimited string, which is just right for our needs back in HyperTalk. The rest of the HyperTalk mouseUp handler parcels out the returned data into the Past Due fields, and alerts the user when the amount exceeds $10,000.

Scriptable Applications

The kind of scripting magic performed with AppleScript or other Open Scripting language is confined to applications that have implemented the Object Model. This can sometimes get confusing when you look into potential software packages for your scripting activities. A program that merely responds to Apple events is not necessarily compatible with Open Scripting systems, such as AppleScript. Even a program that claims to be "scriptable by Apple events" is not necessarily open to AppleScript. As of this writing, there is no consensus on how products should identify their ability to work with AppleScript.

Even if there were, however, you should be cautious when a product claims it is "AppleScript compatible" or even "OSA compatible." The reason is that the amount of support for external scripting varies widely among products making such claims. For example, PageMaker 5.0 grants AppleScript access via its aete resource. But you soon discover that the product does not truly support the Object Model. At most, you can trigger scripts written in PageMaker's own scripting language. This contrasts with a QuarkXPress 3.2, which supports the Object Model almost to the extreme, having created a scripting dictionary that lets external scripters do virtually everything they might want to do with a page layout program. For now, there is no simple way to guard against what we call pseudo-scriptable applications from making misleading claims. The best advice is to try the software with a full-fledge script editor that lets you examine the program's dictionary. If you see lots of commands and object defined, then the product probably supports the Object Model (although some programs merely give you access to menu command equivalents via scripting). In Chapter 66, we'll show you a stack that converses with the Object Model of FileMaker Pro to allow multiple HyperCard users on a network to access information from a multi-user database file.

Scripting HyperCard

HyperCard has implemented the Object Model, which allows scripts written in other programs, such as the Script Editor, to work with data and objects within HyperCard. Stacks that you save as standalone applications have the same aete resource as HyperCard, so your applications are automatically scriptable by other programs. If you are familiar with HyperTalk programming, then accessing HyperCard from AppleScript is remarkably easy. You'll find that many familiar commands and object identifiers work within AppleScript just as they do within HyperTalk.

There are some differences, however, most of which reflect potential conflicts of the HyperTalk and Open Scripting command names. Also, because the scripts are in the AppleScript environment, its rules about getting and setting data apply, not HyperTalk's rules. Let's look at some of the differences you'll encounter when scripting HyperCard from, say, the AppleScript Script Editor.

Getting and Setting Data

Missing from the AppleScript vocabulary is HyperTalk's ubiquitous Put command. To move data into and out of containers in AppleScript, use the Set or Copy commands, as in

```
copy "Norman Bates" to field 1
set field 1 to "Norman Bates"
```

The same goes for moving data from a field to a variable:

```
copy field "Name" to theName
set theName to field "Name"
```

For some scripters of both languages, this difference is the most difficult one to get used to.

Be Specific

You can get by with some constructions in HyperTalk that won't fly in AppleScript. For example, in HyperTalk, the following construction works without flaw:

```
set name of this stack to "My Test Stack"
```

AppleScript, however, doesn't know what "this stack" means. In place of "this," you may use "current," because HyperCard has defined several properties to provide appropriate substitutes (current card, current background, current stack, current tool). But you can also supply a more complete identifier for the intended object, as in

```
set name of stack "Test" to "My Test Stack"
```

The more specific you are with object identifiers, the better your chances of the AppleScript scripts working, even under unexpected situations.

Watch Your Optional Parameters

Some words in HyperTalk commands are optional, such as the "to" in go to stack <stackName>. AppleScript isn't quite as lenient: it chokes on the "to" in a statement. Typically, AppleScript prefers the terse version of commands and arguments. Look at HyperCard's scripting dictionary for the details of any command that is giving you trouble. For example, a HyperTalk Dial command looks like this:

```
dial "555-9090" with modem "ATDT"
```

In AppleScript, however, the dictionary entry (Figure 56–7) doesn't say anything about the "with" word. In fact, the AppleScript version of the above command is:

```
dial "555-9090" modem "ATDT"
```

Subtle differences are scattered around the dictionary, but most are straightforward differences.

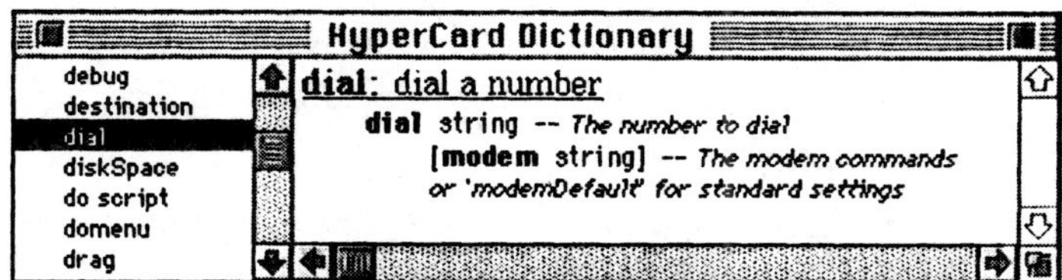

Figure 56–7. HyperCard's OSA scripting dictionary entry for the Dial command.

Arguments to Commands and XCMDs

As mentioned earlier in this chapter, AppleScript's format for command parameters differs from HyperTalk's. AppleScript actually has two different methods of passing and receiving parameters, but from HyperTalk you use only the positional parameter method, which comes closest to HyperTalk's own method.

For one-parameter commands, there is no difference. For example, the following command works in both HyperTalk and AppleScript:

```
beep 2
```

But when you must pass more than one parameter to a command or XCMD, put the parameters in a comma-delimited series inside parentheses (unless the dictionary says otherwise, as noted below). The Picture command is an excellent example. The HyperTalk command to display the Navigator palette's picture resource in a default window style is:

```
picture "Navigator",resource
```

AppleScript's version, however, places those parameters in parentheses:

```
picture("Navigator","resource")
```

Notice, too, that both parameters, as literals, must be quoted strings. Failure to put quotes around "resource," for example, yields an AppleScript run-time error, because AppleScript sees any unquoted word as either an AppleScript reserved word, command, or variable (which would not evaluate to anything in this instance).

Parameters as AppleScript Lists

Some commands in their AppleScript versions must be passed multiple parameters in the form of AppleScript lists. The Max function is an example. In HyperTalk, the following is the proper form:

```
max(10,20,30)
```

The OSA dictionary, however, requests that the parameters be passed as a list. AppleScript lists are comma-delimited series of any string or numeric data inside curly braces. Thus, the AppleScript equivalent is

```
max {10, 20, 30}
```

HyperTalk commands that allow multiple parameters that are separated by the word "or" must be adapted for AppleScript such that the parameters are placed in a list.

AppleScript Data to HyperTalk

A number of AppleScript's data structures don't have good analogs in HyperTalk. Therefore, when data in the form of lists and records, to take a couple popular examples, comes back into a HyperTalk handler, HyperCard tends to leave much of the AppleScript structure intact. For example, we saw in our earlier language mixing stack, above, that some preprocessing of a returned AppleScript list made the remaining HyperTalk work on that data easier, otherwise our HyperTalk script would be faced with parsing items out of curly-bracketed data. All that would have been required was to delete the first and last characters of the returned data, but we decided instead to massage the data before it came back.

AppleScript records, too, come back very much like they are in AppleScript. For example if a HyperTalk button handler calls an AppleScript card handler, here's what we could expect:

```
on mouseUp -- HyperTalk
    put fetchRecord() into myRecord
end mouseUp

on fetchRecord() -- AppleScript
    return {name: "Frank", rank: "General", serialNumber: 10 * 2}
end fetchRecord
```

The value of myRecord in the HyperTalk handler after these scripts execute would be:

```
{name: "Frank", rank: "General", serialNumber: 20}
```

Where you do the parsing or processing of the data depends partly on which of the sides of the transaction you want to be modular and reusable. The more processing you do for a specific data structure (on either end), the more specific the handler becomes to the given task.

Global Variables

It may be important for a script under remote AppleScript control to have some global variables predefined from data in other sources also under AppleScript control. You can get and set HyperTalk global variables from within an AppleScript script.

The behavior is partially like the way you can work with global variables in HyperCard's Message Box. There, a simple statement such as,

```
put "Yo!" into greeting
```

both initializes the global and sets its value to the string. In AppleScript, you can do both jobs at once with a slight modification to the syntax to reflect AppleScript's environment:

```
copy "Yo!" to variable "greeting"
```

Aside from the obvious use of Copy instead of the HyperTalk Put, notice that the global is preceded by the keyword "variable" and that the global variable name is in quotes. If it were not in quotes, AppleScript would see that word as being an undefined AppleScript variable.

To read the value of a global, use the reverse construction:

```
copy variable "greeting" to temp
```

This command places the value of the HyperTalk global into an AppleScript local variable, temp.

Sound

To make AppleScript command a HyperCard stack to produce any sound —from the Play or Dial commands—HyperCard must be the active application. Use AppleScript's Activate command to bring HyperCard to the front:

```
tell application "HyperCard"
    activate
    play "flute" notes "c d e"
    repeat until (sound) is "done"
    end repeat
end tell
```

In this example, we added an AppleScript repeat loop that waits for the Sound function to return "done." If more of the script executed while within HyperCard, you wouldn't need the repeat loop, but if execution activates another program after playing the sound, it's best to let the sound finish.

Creating New Objects

While you always have the option of sending doMenu commands from AppleScript to HyperCard to accomplish anything you can from menus, HyperCard also defines a Make command (in line with other applications) to let you create various objects. The steps involved are no different than doing it from a HyperTalk script. For example, here is an AppleScript script that creates a new background button:

```
tell application "HyperCard"
    set editBkgnd to true
    make new button
    set editBkgnd to false
    choose tool 1
end tell
```

About the only partially unusual element of this script is that from AppleScript, you choose tools by number, which is one of the options of HyperTalk as well.

Opportunities Galore!

Given the depth of HyperCard's numerous objects, properties, commands, and functions, its Open Scripting implementation is a cornucopia of possibilities for being controlled by external scripts. More than likely, however, you will use HyperCard as the controller—turning HyperCard into a master control panel for work and information flow applications built around the power of other well-designed programs. HyperCard can become an ready user interface builder for scripts that perform mighty tasks. As more productivity applications adopt the OSA Object Model, there's no telling what great solutions will come from the minds of HyperCard developers.

CHAPTER

57

CREATING DOUBLE-CLICKABLE APPLICATIONS

HyperCard 2.2 includes facilities for turning a stack into a standalone, double-clickable application. The process takes only a few seconds, yet it combines all the art, code, and data of your HyperCard stack with everything HyperCard needs to do its job. There are advantages and disadvantages to making standalones from HyperCard, which is what we'll be checking out in this chapter.

How To...

You don't actually convert your stack into an application, but rather create a standalone copy of your original stack. This is preferred, because once you create a standalone, you can no longer modify it as an author. Only its data in fields can be changed by the user.

Before you can perform any of these translations, you must be sure a system extension, called StackToApp, is installed in your System Folder (System 6) or your Extensions Folder (System 7). Because it is an INIT type extension, you need to restart your Macintosh after copying it to its resting place. If you followed the Installer program, the extension is probably safely where it should be.

To access the translation, choose Save a Copy from the File menu. In the resulting dialog (Figure 57–1) is a popup menu at the bottom. The default value is to create a copy of the stack as another HyperCard stack. But if you choose Application from this menu, you come to yet another dialog. We'll look at that more closely in a later section, but often you can bypass the choices there to run a quick test of your stack as a standalone.

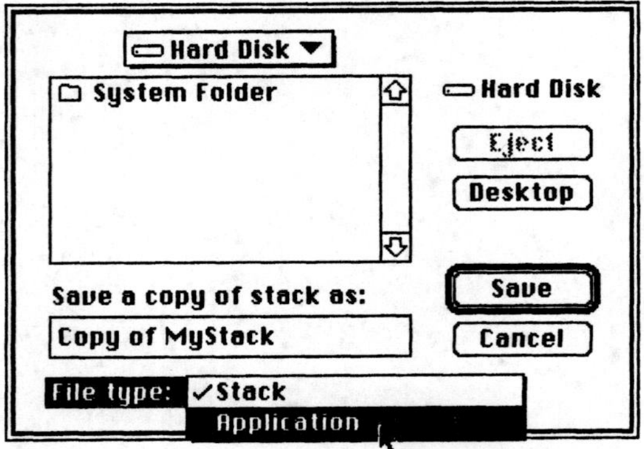

Figure 57–1. The Save A Copy dialog offers a choice for saving a copy as an application.

The original stack stays open afterwards, but on your hard disk is an icon for the application. You could take this file to any Macintosh running System 6.0.5 or later, whether it had any vestige of HyperCard or not, and it would open to the familiar stack you had created. On a Mac running System 7 (and any other required extensions, such as Apple Event Manager and AppleScript), the stack would perform all the HyperCard 2.2 functions you scripted into it.

Application Size

Stuffing the full functionality of HyperCard into the application file with your stack comes at considerable expense in the file size department. Expect overhead on the order of 750K for the privilege. A knowledgable programmer and resource guru might be able to shave some from that total with ResEdit, but for no substantial gain.

For some means of distribution, such as shareware uploads to bulletin board services and user group disks, the size becomes almost prohibitive. Even file compression, such as StuffIt or DiskDoubler, only works that overhead down to the vicinity of 500K. But if you are designing a standalone kiosk kind of stack, or doing custom consulting work, the size of the file won't make much difference, since it eliminates the need for the equally capacious HyperCard and Home stack.

Commercial distribution is a 50-50 proposition. For one, chances are your product ships on multiple disks of compressed files, so there may be room for the overhead in one stack (not all stacks would be turned into standalones). The good news, however, is that distribution of a standalone is royalty-free for the HyperCard stuff that gets imbedded into your stack. That's far better than having to license a HyperCard Player from Apple.

Stack Conversion Considerations

When you translate a stack to a standalone program, you should be sensitive to how the user of your application will perceive the application. For example, unless you do something special with the menus, your application will appear with the Apple menu, plus five HyperCard menus: File, Edit, Go, Font, and Style. These are the same menus that appear in HyperCard at user level two, with some further items disabled. The Apple menu's first item is named "About HyperCard..." just like being in HyperCard.

The problem you should consider is that the user of your stack shouldn't have to know anything about HyperCard or the fact that your application was created with HyperCard. In fact, this knowledge—and many of the HyperCard menu items—will probably confuse the HyperCard-challenged user. As you can see, menus become one of the most essential user interface areas to address when designing a stack that will ultimately be given life as a stand alone-application.

Some suggestions (implemented in the sample stack of Chapter 61) include:

1. Rename the first Apple menu item to read "About" and the name of your application. Then be sure you have a doMenu handler to trap for that, and display some kind of dialog box that reveals the product name, version, and author/publisher. You can use something as simple as the Answer dialog in HyperCard, or use the Picture command to show a fancy color picture window with the relevant data in the PICT.

2. Study each menu and menu item, to make sure it applies directly to an action in your program. Modify any and all menus if necessary to reduce the menu selections to only those that apply to your program. If it means eliminating a menu, such as the Go menu, then do so. This is your program, and its menus should be entirely yours.

3. Include a Quit command in the File menu that performs the same action as the Quit HyperCard menu choice in HyperCard's File menu.

4. Be consistent with the user interface guidelines by maintaining a File and Edit menu. If your stacks have editable fields, be sure the Cut, Copy, and Paste menu items are available.

Bear in mind that the HyperCard that is embedded into standalones is set to userLevel 2. If any of your HyperTalk commands require higher user levels (painting, creating buttons or fields, modifying scripts), then your code must set the userLevel property to the desired level. Otherwise, the user will get error messages that an operation cannot be performed.

Other points to watch for are Home buttons that so frequently appear in HyperCard stacks. Once your stack is a standalone, there is no Home stack, unless the user has HyperCard installed on that machine. A command to go to Home would open that user's Home stack, running off the virtual HyperCard that is stored in your stack. This could get very confusing to the user.

One final task after you've created an application is to verify that the memory partition for your standalone is large enough for any XCMDs or color you may have added to the stack. HyperCard sets the partition to its original 750K minimum/1000K preferred size.

The Application Creation Dialog

Much of what you can edit in the application creation dialog (Figure 57–2) has to do with version control. All items except the Creator and Doc Type fields control information that goes into the vers resource in your application. Of all these items, only one, the long version string, will be readily visible to you or a user. All other items can be further viewed or edited in ResEdit or similar resource editor.

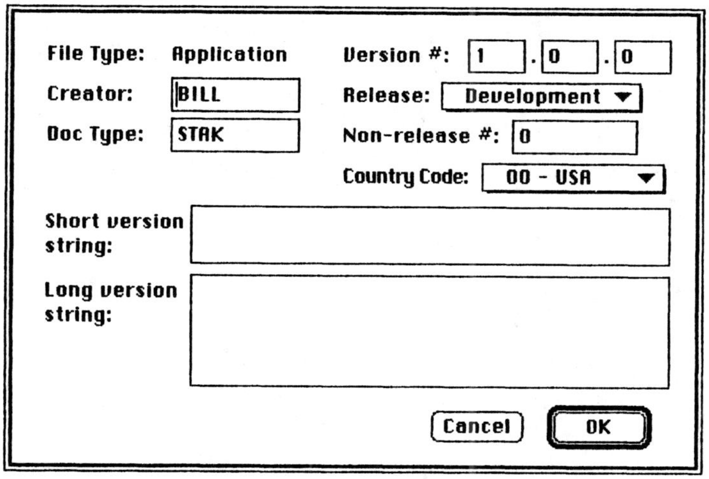

File Type: Application
Version #: 1 . 0 . 0
Creator: BILL
Release: Development
Doc Type: STAK
Non-release #: 0
Country Code: 00 - USA
Short version string:
Long version string:
Cancel
OK

Figure 57–2. The application creation dialog.

Data in the vers resource is used by professional programmers to help them maintain control over the status of each "build" of a software program. As you work on a program, it becomes increasingly important to know which build is which. Therefore, if a tester finds a bug in one build, you know which generation of code to look into. Unfortunately, none of this version information filters back into the stack you copy to the application, so it is up to you to manage the HyperCard stack side of version control.

Version

The template here supplies three fields intended primarily for numbers. It follows a numbering system used very often in Apple's own system software releases. The leftmost number is the primary generation number. Each increment of this digit usually means a significant upgrade to the product, such as going from version 6.0.5 to 7.0.0 of the Macintosh System. Changes to the middle digit usually conveys feature enhancements and other improvements to a product. Such was the case when Apple upgraded System 7 to version 7.1. System 7.1 is the same basic feature set of System 7.0 plus support for WorldScript and improved Font management (among other improvements). The last digit is usually reserved to indicate minor bug fixes to a particular version. Commercial software producers rarely charge for upgrades of this kind, because they either affect just a small percentage of users or fix an egregious bug that should have been caught in testing.

Release

The popup menu for the Release category offers four possibilities. While programmers' views of what constitutes each of these stages varies, our take is as follows:

- Development means that the program design is not yet set, and the programmers may even be working on proof-of-concept ideas at that stage.
- Alpha is usually a stage in at which time the software is released to a limited number of testers who know the product very well and can critically evaluate the changes and enhancements. Feature and user interface changes may likely come from the release of the alpha version.
- In an ideal world, a Beta release is feature-complete. It is now that copies may be distributed to a wider audience of customers for beta-testing. The purpose of this release is to locate and report bugs to the programmers.
- Although a Final release sounds final, it isn't always. Some software providers produce what they call a "final candidate," which is the programmers' best shot at squashing as many bugs as time allows. A copy of this candidate is sent through final testing to make sure all bugs that were supposed to be fixed have been. When this version is signed off, it goes to the disk duplicator.

Non-release

While the version number is an indicator of the goal of a particular round of programming, the non-release number is an indicator of which version of development, alpha, beta, and final candidate the application represents. Common practice is to use a letter and one or more numbers to identify the generation of the build. The letter is d, a, b, or f, depending on the release type. For example, a12 means the twelfth build of the alpha release.

Country Code

In the Country Code popup are the names of the more than 50 versions for which Apple has localized versions of its system software. When the release is for a localized version, make the appropriate choice.

Short Version String

Into this field should go a composite of the data from the other items. For example, if you are working toward version 1.1.0, and have reached the seventh beta build, the string might be:

```
v. 1.1b7
```

Some programmers use the ß symbol for beta and the ∂ symbol for development in this string and the next.

Long Version String

Only the long version string appears in the Get Info dialog box for an application (Figure 57–3). It's a good idea to include a copyright notice here, as well as any other important data, such as:

```
v. 1.1ß7. ©1993 BigSoft Corp. All rights reserved.
```

Unfortunately, not as much can appear in the Get Info dialog as you may want to enter into the template field. It's a good idea to check the results prior to actually releasing the product. If you need to change anything, you'll have to do it in ResEdit, because this dialog cannot be brought back once you create the application.

File Type and Application Icon

Because the resulting program you generate from this exercise is an application, HyperCard automatically generates the file with the application (APPL) file type. This will make it appear as an application in text listings in the Finder (instead of its listing as a HyperCard document when it was a stack).

MyStack as an App Info

MyStack as an App

Kind: application program
Size: 740K on disk (757,133 bytes used)

Where: Hard Disk:

Created: Tue, Oct 26, 1993, 12:35 PM
Modified: Tue, Oct 26, 1993, 12:35 PM
Version: v. 1.1B7. ©1994 LargeCo Software

Comments:

Memory Requirements
Suggested size: 1000 K
Minimum size: 750 K
Locked
Preferred size: 1000 K

Figure 57–3. An application's Get Info dialog shows the long version string.

The generic application icon is assigned to the program when viewed in the Finder (Figure 57–4). The safest, but unfortunately not the surest, way to assign a custom icon to your stack is create a 32-pixel square chunk of art (you can use the ICN# editor in ResEdit for this job), copy it to the Clipboard, open the program's Get Info dialog box, click the generic icon, and choose Paste from the Edit menu. This places the art in a specially-numbered icon resource that System 7 checks before displaying a generic icon (Figure 57–5). That's the rub, however. This special icon stuff works only in System 7, so System 6 users of your stack will see the generic icon.

Figure 57–4. The generic application icon.

With the help of ResEdit (or similar), you can work some magic to assign a custom icon to your application. But to do that safely requires some explanation, and no little effort on your part.

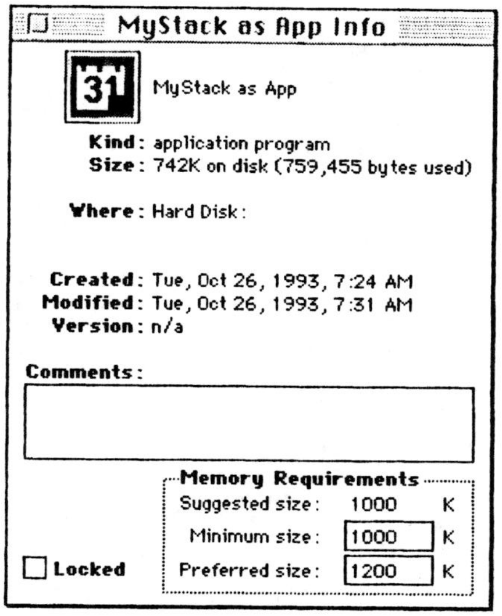

Figure 57–5. Pasting art into the icon space of a file's Get Info box causes the art to supercede the file's normal icon in System 7.

Creators and Doc Types

Hidden from our view all these years is the Finder's powers of knowing which icon belongs to which files, and which documents belong to which programs. The mechanism for that revolves around two sets of four-character identifiers. One, called the Creator (sometimes still called the Signature), identifies the program that generates document files or has companion files associated with it. Related documents are given a unique identifier, called the Doc Type. For example, HyperCard's creator is called WILD (all uppercase in this case-sensitive business), and its stack files are of the doc type STAK. When the Finder goes to display an icon for a stack file, it works its way through the Desktop mechanism to locate the file's creator. The creator has as one of its resources a special icon for its documents. In HyperCard's case, it's the little stack of cards.

The Doc Type also comes into play when trying to open files from the application. While in HyperCard, if you choose Open Stack, the open file dialog displays only HyperCard stacks (of the doc type STAK) and folders (which might contain further files). This doc type information is the same you use in the Answer File HyperTalk command to limit the types of files that appear in the file dialog.

Stack Application Creator and Doc Type

The default values for the creator and doc type of a stack application are "BILL" and "STAK," respectively. The creator is different from HyperCard's but the doc type is the same. This means that when a user chooses Open Stack from the File menu (if that item is in your stack's menu), then other HyperCard stacks will appear in the open file dialog. Since you can open other non-application HyperCard stacks from a stack application, this is a preferred default value.

If you must have a custom icon and wish to have a unique creator and doc type (for ancillary stacks in a multi-stack application), then you need to exercise some care. First of all, there is no way of knowing what other applications in the world have what creator and doc type identifiers. Should you assign either that is also shared by another application on a user's hard disk, there could be considerable problems with opening that program's documents or your ancillary stacks from the Finder.

To prevent the problem, you will need to register a creator and doc type with Apple's Developer Support Center, which maintains a database of this information. The procedure is to contact the Developer Support Center (telephone in Cupertino, CA is (408) 974-4897) and request an application for a creator and document type. When you submit the application, the group compares your request against the existing database, and assigns either the one you want (if it isn't already taken) or one as close as they can find.

The Final Steps in ResEdit

Once you have unique identifiers, it's time to go to work in ResEdit to finish the job. Your application's icon must go into ICN# 128. If you have ancillary stacks, whose icons you'd like to be related to the application's icon, then put that icon into ICN# resource 129. Be sure to supply all versions of the ICN# resource for large and small icons, in monochrome, 8-bit, and 4-bit color (plus mask).

Also while in ResEdit, open the BNDL resource of your application, and make sure the creator (Signature) and document type are your special combination. For your ancillary stacks, open each of them in any program that lets you modify their creator and file type (you can do this in ResEdit by opening the file and choosing Get Info For in the File menu).

When all resource editing is complete, restart the Macintosh, and hold down the Command and Option keys to force the system to rebuild the Desktop file. This is essential to get your new application duly registered with your Finder. Now, if you double-click on any of your ancillary, linked stacks, they will open your application instead of HyperCard. Their listings in the Finder will indicate they are a document of your application, not of HyperCard.

We provide this information about signing up for unique creator and document types not to encourage the practice, but rather to give you a taste of what to expect should you create a commercial product, particularly a multi-stack product. Single-stack products can likely get by with the pasted icon in the Finder way of identifying your application in icon views.

CHAPTER

58

THIRD-PARTY AUTHORING TOOLS

As each generation of HyperCard increases the built-in and bundled tools for stack authors, outside developers continue to find holes in the offerings. Sometimes the holes are places where HyperCard can use some improved performance. In other cases, a particular class of features could use a boost in functionality. In this chapter, we present seven third-party tools that virtually any serious HyperCard stack author should know about—some of them should even be permanent members of the the author's programming tool collection. These tools are presented in alphabetical order, and represent the best general purpose authoring tools for HyperCard scripters.

CommsTalk (Full Moon Software)

A common application for HyperCard among communications-conscious authors is designing easy-to-use front ends to other computers. While a number of commercial on-line services, such as CompuServe, offer their own front-end software to disguise an otherwise complicated and cryptic set of commands, even these packages may be more complicated than necessary if the stack needs to communicate with a limited number of services for a special purpose, such as weather or news retrieval.

Front ends also let program designers reduce connection costs by allowing users, in HyperCard, to do as much as possible while not connected to the service, and keep the bytes flowing at full steam while the connection is made. For example, an electronic mail front end could let a user compose new mail in HyperCard fields, and then send them in quick succession after logging onto the system. Conversely, the front end could download all waiting mail into HyperCard cards and disconnect from the system, allowing the user to read the mail offline, or even away from the office on a PowerBook.

CommsTalk consists of a large set of XCMDs that let stack authors script the behind-the-scenes processes necessary to make connections to remote computers and transfer data. Some authors may even use CommsTalk as the foundation for a HyperCard-based bulletin board service for a work group, dedicating one machine and modem to being the host system.

Solutions possibilities multiply when you add HyperCard 2.2's Open Scripting abilities. Using HyperCard as the user interface, CommsTalk and AppleScript make a powerful team.

CommsTalk relies on the Communications Toolbox part of system software. As such, a number of helpful tools are included. Among them are

XModem error correction file transfer (Figure 58–1) and ADSP, which allows Macintoshes to communicate with each other across a local area network. If you have serious communications requirements for your HyperCard stack development (including VT-102 front ends), then CommsTalk should have the HyperTalk-scriptable solution.

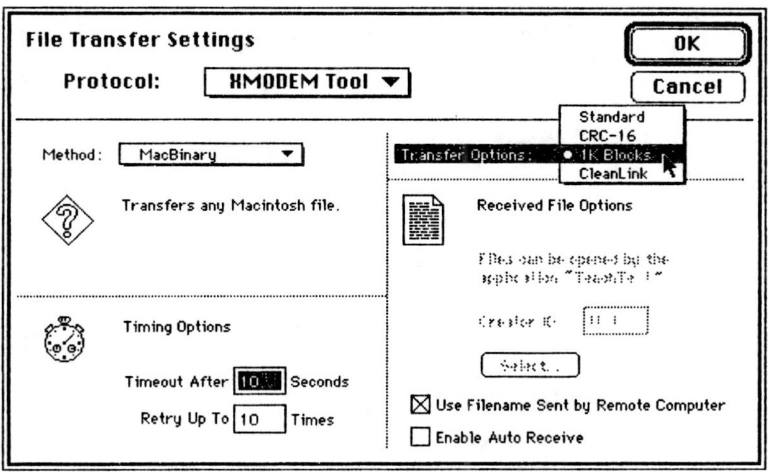

Figure 58–1. XModem file transfer settings available in CommsTalk.

CompileIt! (Heizer Software)

Any HyperTalk scripter who watched a handler operate painfully slowly wishes he or she had the expertise to convert that handler or sluggish parts of it into an external command (XCMD), which tends to run much faster than a HyperTalk script. The price of entry to XCMD writing, however, is usually mastery of languages like Pascal or C, not to mention the Macintosh toolbox—a daunting challenge for the part time scripter.

CompileIt! (Figure 58–2) is an unusual type of compiler, because it allows you to compile HyperTalk scripts into XCMDs and XFCNs. It also provides a way to convert normally exposed HyperTalk code to difficult-to-decipher machine code.

Only certain kinds of scripts lend themselves to effective compilation with CompileIt!. The best ones are those that do not rely on HyperTalk or HyperCard objects in any way. When a compiled script needs to fetch data from a HyperCard field or use one of HyperTalk's constructions (e.g., the Answer command), the compiled XCMD has to make what is known as a *callback* to HyperCard—asking HyperCard to perform the operation. Callbacks take a lot of time compared to operations running solely inside the compiled XCMD. Therefore, use CompileIt! when the XCMD performs internal math or text processing work, especially when the work is of a repetitive nature.

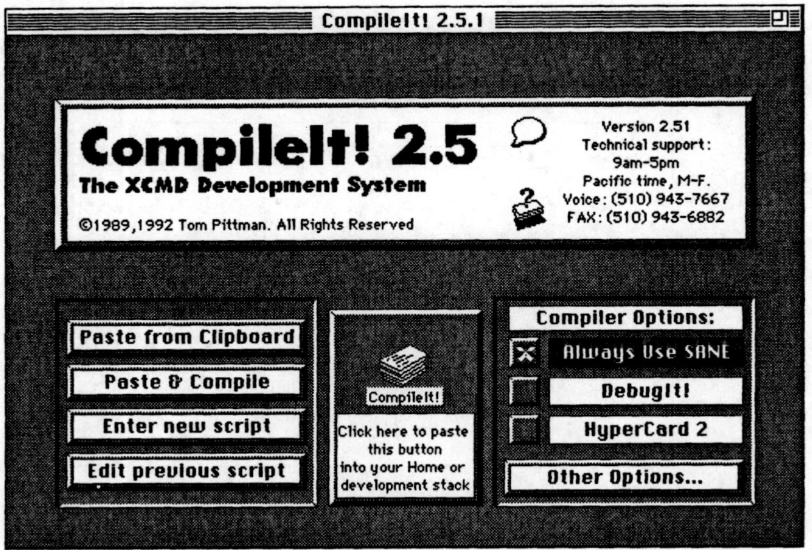

Figure 58–2. CompileIt! from Heizer Software compiles HyperTalk scripts into XCMDs.

Here is an example of a HyperTalk script whose performance was enhanced significantly by compiling it:

```
function returnToTab theText
    put theText into theString
    repeat until last char of theString ≠ return
        delete last char of theString
    end repeat

    repeat until offset(numToChar(13),theString) = 0
        put numToChar(9) into char offset(numToChar(13),theString) of theString
    end repeat
    return theString
end returnToTab
```

This function converts return characters in a text string to tab characters. The source of the data was an external database whose data structure used tab characters in place of carriage returns. Because the text string was passed as an argument to the function, no callbacks to HyperCard were required. The repetitive nature of the handler also improved performance in the compiled version. It ran approximately 20 times faster in the compiled version than in the HyperTalk version.

HyperTalk in HyperCard version 2.x also compiles scripts, so you may wonder why CompileIt! would be of any use. HyperTalk's own compilation takes place the first time you run the script. Even so, a script compiled with CompileIt! can run many times faster than HyperTalk's compiled scripts.

CompileIt! also lets more experienced programmers access the Macintosh ROM Toolbox from within a HyperTalk script—after it's compiled. That's something that even HyperTalk's own compiler doesn't let you do. For many HyperTalk scripters, CompileIt! has offered a gentle way to learn programming with the ROM Toolbox, because you can experiment with single Toolbox calls while accomplishing great things with the resulting XCMDs and letting HyperCard take care of user interface elements. For example, the following script came in handy when we needed to calculate a checksum for text that a stack was sending to another computer (the receiving computer required this calculation as a method of error detection):

```
function chksum sourceText
    put 0 into decValue
    put CharsHandle(sourceText) into myHandle
    repeat with i = 0 to length(sourceText)-1
        add charToNum (myHandle@@.charType[i]) to decValue
    end repeat
    numToHex decValue,6,myString
    put char 5 to 6 of myString into newString
    put char 3 to 4 of myString after newString
    return newString
end chksum
```

The checksum calculation we needed required that the ASCII values of all characters in a string be totaled, next be converted to hexadecimal (base 16) numbers, and then placed in a low-high order for the last two bytes of the hex total. HyperTalk doesn't have commands for decimal-to-hexadecimal conversion, but the ROM Toolbox does (numToHex). In this function, we used another Toolbox ability to work with handles to strings. This is described in the CompileIt! manual, and is beyond the scope of our discussion here, but suffice it to say that performing the repeat through the string to calculate the ASCII value (HyperTalk's charToNum function) ran many dozens of times faster than a straight HyperTalk-style repeat through the string. The bottom line was that we used two Toolbox routines and the rest HyperTalk to accomplish something that HyperTalk couldn't do by itself, without us having to master the entire Toolbox to do it.

CompileIt!'s author, Tom Pittman, also wrote another Heizer utility, called Double-XX, which lets you create standalone, double-clickable applications using CompileIt! XCMDs and a windowing utility, such as WindowScript (below). These applications are much smaller than the standalones that HyperCard 2.2 creates, although you'll need a bit of programming experience to take full advantage of this product. Still, if you get comfortable with CompileIt!, you should check out Double-XX, also available from Heizer Software.

epsiTalk (epsi computer systems, inc.)

Many HyperCard authors have been clamoring for multi-user stacks in HyperCard. While such access and controls are not built into HyperCard, you can attain the goal with epsiTalk, perhaps the best networking tool for HyperCard. The product is a set of XCMDs that lets multiple HyperCard users access the same stack located on a Macintosh somewhere on the network. Each of the clients has a kind of viewer stack, which contains a single card for each background of the server stack. All data is maintained on the server stack, and more than one user can browse or edit the stack at a time. The only restriction—common to multi-user data stores—is record locking (or card locking in HyperCard vernacular). The first user to view data of the server stack has write access to that card; others accessing that card can only view the data that was in the server card, although that view is automatically updated when the first user (who had write access) tabs to another field in the card.

EpsiTalk provides far more than just shared stacks. Its networking tools allow for network-based conferences (Figure 58–3), e-mail, Mac-to-Mac file transfer, and immediate messaging to one or more users on the network (like a text-based intercom). The product is offered in site licenses based on the number of clients. Since any, or more than one, Mac on the network can be the server for any stack (this is a peer-to-peer setup), the client count is the key factor.

Setting up a system based on epsiTalk requires that the shared stacks be running at all times when users may need them. In other words, each "server" Macintosh must have HyperCard running and the shared stacks open for others to access those stacks. In controlled workgroup situations, this is rarely a problem, since the network administrator can dictate which machines are to run what at all times. Still, it could influence the design of your shared HyperCard solution and network hardware setup.

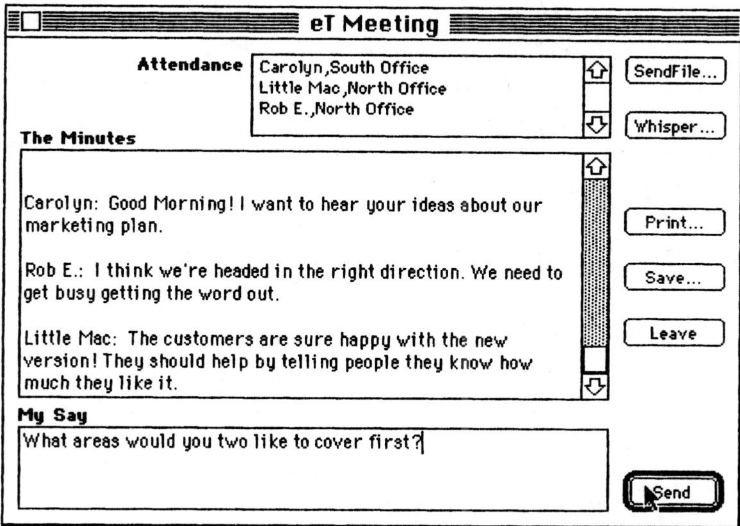

Figure 58–3. The networked conference window of epsiTalk.

HyperHIT Deluxe (Softstream)

Even though HyperCard wasn't designed to be a highly powered database in the traditional sense, that hasn't prevented HyperCard authors from trying to use HyperCard to manage enormous amounts of data or create client-server applications. As such authors have discovered, when the database starts getting into the many thousands of records, searching and sorting performance suffers.

To the rescue have come some HyperCard add-ons that store and manage information in separate data files, rather than using HyperCard as the storage medium. HyperCard becomes, instead, more of a user interface front end to entering or accessing the information stored in the external file. Such files are also indexed, like a traditional database so that searches of tens of thousands of records are significantly faster than HyperCard can achieve.

One of these HyperCard database engines is called HyperHit Deluxe. It consists of a series of XCMD resources that let you build external relational databases and indexes, and also (in the multi-user version) comes with a server application to manage multi-user access. HyperHIT databases can store text, graphics, and sounds, so you could even use HyperHIT as an indexed retrieval system for clip art or sound clips.

HyperHIT is not for novice HyperTalk scripters. A sample e-mail system (Figure 58–4) comes with the multi-user version to help acquaint you to the rather large vocabulary that comprises HyperHit. But if you are trying to manage huge amounts of data with an inviting, graphically oriented HyperCard front end, it will be worth the effort to learn the breadth and depth of the product.

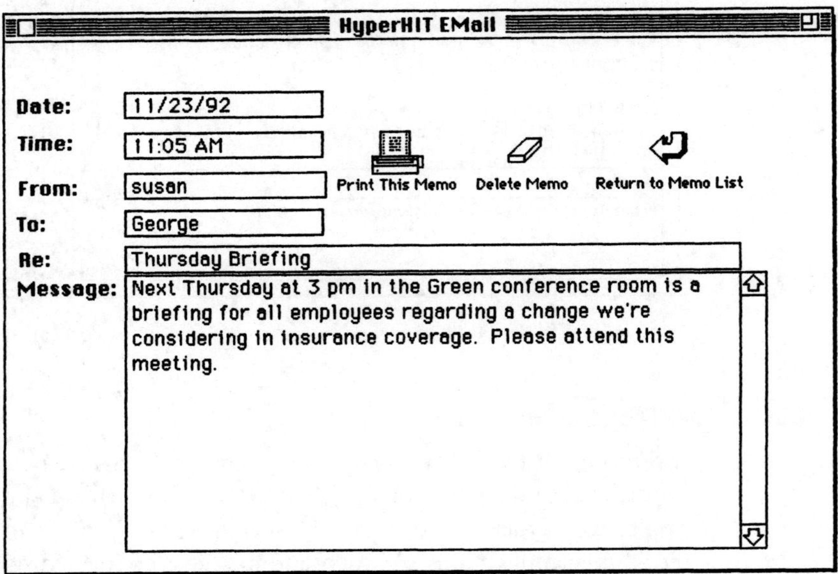

Figure 58–4. A sample e-mail application lets you examine the inner workings of a client-server stack using HyperHIT.

Reports (9-to-5 Software)

HyperCard's own report printing facilities improved with the advent of version 2.0, but it still leaves much to be desired when attempting to produce sophisticated database-style reports. Such reports might extract selected data from a series of cards based on precise selection criteria. The reports may then also produce subtotal and total information of columns of numbers in the report, and even print graphics for letterhead. HyperCard's built-in printing can do no such machinations.

Reports (Figure 58–5) is a combination of XCMD and System Folder files that provides a stack author with a report layout design center. You use part of the program to lay out the elements of your reports—things like where data from specific background fields should go on the page, what font sizes and styles each element should print in, where the subtotal and totals should be, and elements for page headers and footers.

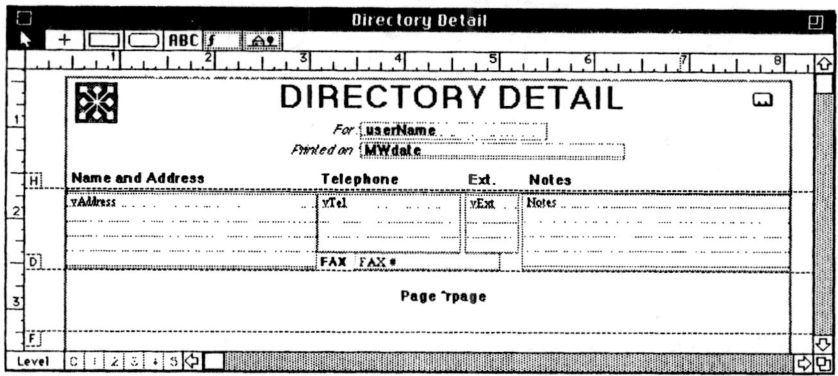

Figure 58–5. Reports provides a full-featured report format layout facility, including the ability to paste graphics for letterhead and the like.

Report formats are saved as external files, usually under 5K in size. Format files may also include HyperTalk handlers that are executed before, during, and after printing of the report. For example, if you wish to accumulate some data from a few different cards for printing into report fields on the page, you would do that with HyperTalk in a BeforeReport handler. An AfterReport handler might fill in a date and time (in a HyperCard field) that an invoice report was printed.

The XCMD needs to go into a stack in the message hierarchy, and acts as an intermediary between HyperCard, the report format file, and the Macintosh Toolbox printing routines. A run-time version of the System folder files (which don't allow report format editing) may also be licensed and included in commercial products. Site licenses are also available for in-house applications.

ResEdit (APDA)

We've made many mentions of this utility in other chapters, but it bears repeating here. If you dabble at all in resources, then ResEdit will pay for itself over and over. Despite the seeming ease of moving resources around with Resource Mover in Power Tools, ResEdit goes much further in this category, because you can freely open the resource forks of all kinds of files, including the System file to extract 'snd ' resources.

More importantly, ResEdit is strong in providing templates for editing many resources, such as cursors, color icons for your stack's Finder icons, and even many resources you don't work with in HyperCard. ResEdit can even be dangerous if you start monkeying around with System, Finder, and application resources, but as long as you work with backups, you end up learning much about the inner workings of the Macintosh and how you might customize certain aspects beyond what tools various control panels provide. We also recommend you buy any third-party book that provides a guide to the abundance of four-character identifiers and the editing templates you'll encounter.

WindowScript (Heizer Software)

Without a doubt, the best dialog-oriented add-on for HyperCard is WindowScript (Figure 58–6), a much improved product over its capable predecessor, Dialoger. WindowScript tops all other dialog-related XCMDs available for a couple reasons. First of all, you design dialogs interactively in the WindowScript stack, turning the job of creating dialogs and their elements into simple point-and-click operations. From a palette of possible dialog item elements, you choose which one you want. The object appears on the dialog making area, and you drag it and resize it as needed. An accompanying palette window displays the possible parameters for that element, which you can edit on-the-fly. Among the types of objects you can program into a dialog box with Dialoger are scrolling lists, editable scrolling fields, popup menus, progress controls, horizontal scroll bars, scrolling lists of icons, and buttons of all varieties.

The other great advantage is that you have complete HyperTalk control over the contents of a dialog and what happens as the user clicks on buttons, selects items in lists and popups, and so on. For example, in the dialog shown in Figure 58–7, the user may enter a number of weeks into the single editable field in the dialog. As the user enters new numbers into the field, a HyperTalk script attached to that dialog dynamically calculates and displays the ending date based on the number of weeks from the starting date. Scripts are stored as part of the dialog specifications in resources, so complex stacks don't have to give up precious script space to dialog handling.

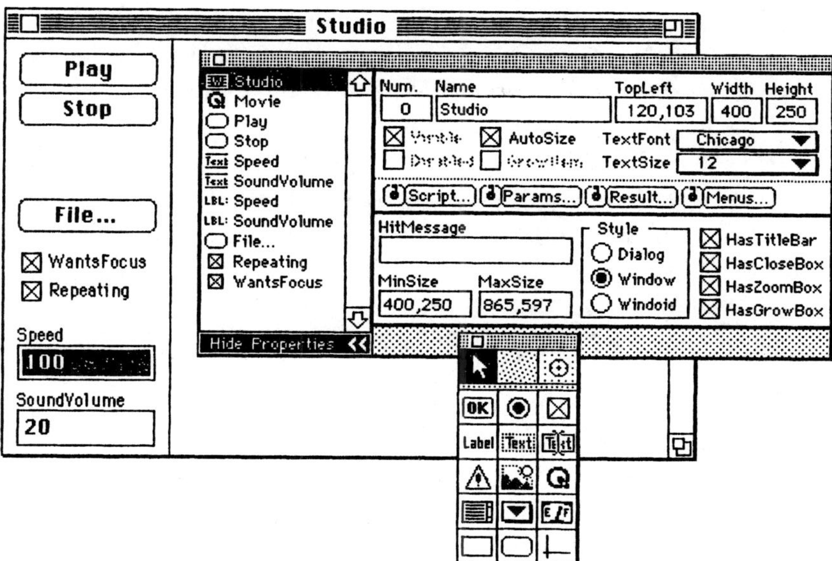

Figure 58–6. WindowScript's interactive dialog builder guides you through various settings for each element.

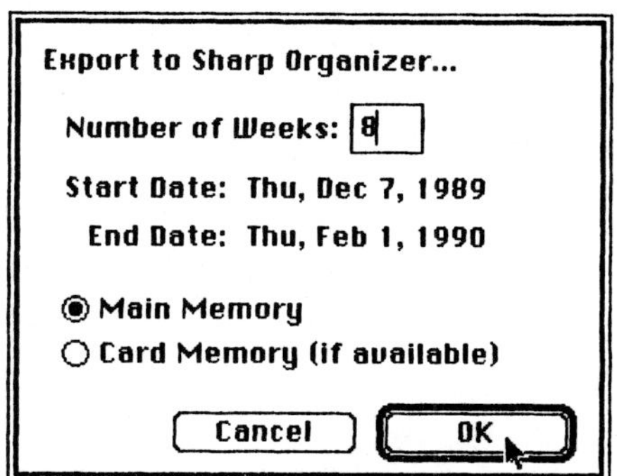

Figure 58–7. In this WindowScript-controlled dialog, as the user enters a new number of weeks, a HyperTalk handler attached to the dialog calculates and displays the end date on the fly.

While HyperCard's Ask and Answer dialogs offer simple dialog control, WindowScript is a significant tool to make HyperCard applications look more like traditional Macintosh applications. As long as you don't over-dialog your stack, WindowScript may well be the tool that adds a high level of design proficiency to your applications ideas.

Now that you know what some of the best authoring tools are, we'll look briefly at what has often been called the Stack Designer's Ten Commandments.

CHAPTER

59

TEN STACK DESIGN ISSUES

HyperCard was a blessing for many macintosh users who had great ideas for applications, but were perhaps not experienced in designing Macintosh software for general consumption. This has led to a lot of stacks that work well for their creators, but are difficult to use if not downright confusing to others for whom the stack was intended.

From examination of hundreds of stacks over the years and experience in the trenches developing stacks for others (some in the form of commercial programs) comes a list of ten issues that every stack author should consider while designing and creating a HyperCard-based application. These ten issues were originally presented in 200 pages of detail (with illustrations) in the *Danny Goodman's HyperCard Developer's Guide* (Bantam Books, now out of print). In this chapter, we present a synopsis of those issues as an introduction to the thought processes for which all authors should prepare themselves.

Issue 1: How HyperCard Literate Is the User?

It may just be human nature, but when we learn a new skill, we often take for granted that other people either already have that skill or can acquire that skill from our enthusiasm about it. Thus, when we become familiar with HyperCard's idiosyncrasies—things like the Home stack's role in the environment, the card-and-stack metaphor, typing Command-period to stop a hopelessly lost script—we begin to assume the user of our stack has comparable knowledge and skill. That, we maintain, is the wrong assumption.

Think back to the very first time you started HyperCard. You probably didn't know what was a button to be clicked on or what was just ornamental art. Now that today's Macintoshes come with nothing more than a HyperCard player, it is unlikely that newcomers would know anything at all about HyperCard. If your stack supplies a special icon button that the user can place in the Home stack for instant access to your stack, don't assume the user knows anything about copying and pasting buttons. Instead, provide a button the user clicks on that does the copying and pasting to the Home stack automatically.

Similarly, because those with the HyperCard Player cannot modify stack objects, you must create front ends to HyperCard's object creation and deletion facilities if those functions are part of your stack's operation. You can guide a user through the process, and have your scripts write new objects' scripts for the user.

You should also be aware that lack of HyperCard literacy (Hyperliteracy) does not mean the user is a Macintosh illiterate. On the contrary, it doesn't take much experience on the Macintosh to know to double click on buttons or retrieve commands from menus. Therefore, be sure your stack behaves predictably when the user double-clicks on your buttons, and that menus are organized clearly. Newly added features of HyperCard 2.2, such as being able to trap for mouse double-clicks and more Macintosh-like button designs, make the job easier to replicate a Macintosh-looking application that a Macintosh-literate user can feel comfortable using.

Issue 2: Designing for all Macintosh Models

Not all Macintoshes are created equal. Some are endowed with performance that goes well beyond mere mortal Macintosh Classics. Some machines are chained to a small internal monitor, while others require external monitors, which are unanimously larger.

These are kinds of issues that face stack designers. Execution speed of a script and screen refresh speed varies widely from Macintosh model to model. Animation sequences on one model may be too fast or slow on other models. The only way you'll know for sure is to test your stack on as many different speed machines as you can get your hands on. With the proliferation of models, this becomes increasingly difficult, but all the more important. Designing on a Macintosh Classic, you cannot begin to imagine what performance you'll get on a Quadra. Conversely, if you design on a very fast machine, perhaps your complex handlers will be unconscionably slow on a Macintosh LC.

Also think about the monitor sizes your potential users will have. It is a disservice to those with built-in 9-inch monitors to design cards that fill a 640 × 480 Macintosh RGB Color monitor. If, on the other hand, you know that your audience will have large monitors, then it may make sense to have full screen cards displaying lots of information and graphics. Experiment, too, with how to handle the space on a 512 × 342 card that is taken up by the menubar on a 9-inch screen. If you design the stack on a large monitor, test it on a 9-inch monitor Mac to make sure the menubar doesn't cover important fields or buttons.

Issue 3: What About the Macintosh User Interface?

HyperCard is a frequent target of Macintosh user interface purists who believe that the regular user interface guidelines published by Apple are the stone tablets all designers should obey. HyperCard allows authors to break a lot of rules—buttons that don't highlight when clicked on and hiding the menubar to name a couple.

For awhile a couple of years ago, the prevailing ideas from the Apple Human Interface group acknowledged HyperCard's potential divergence from the tablets. In so doing, however, the group essentially endorsed a second standard—the HyperCard standard. We disagree strongly with this line of thought. We believe a HyperCard stack author should have the freedom to choose between following the tablets or using new interface elements that may be more appropriate for that application.

With the numerous additions to HyperCard 2.2's features, it is now a comparatively simple task to apply Macintosh user interface elements in a stack design. Standard menus, floating palettes, styled text in fields—these are the stuff of which typical Macintosh applications are made. To follow the guidelines, of course, you'll still have to apply good sense to such things as the content of the File and Edit menus, for instance.

But more importantly, HyperCard is often used to create applications that never existed before. By virtue of HyperCard attracting people with expertise in areas not previously well served by software, some amazing new types of software are being designed, including applications for users who have never seen a Macintosh or computer before. To someone who has never seen a window scroll bar, just the fact that it is a standard Macintosh interface element means nothing. Isn't it better to design an interface to such applications that are so intuitive or self-explanatory that the novice user doesn't need to know the Macintosh "language?"

The bottom line on this issue, therefore, is to choose the interface that makes the most sense for your intended audience. It all comes down to the user's expectations. HyperCard gives you the power to be visually compatible with the rest of the Macintosh software world or to devise an entirely new interface element—perhaps one that will find its way into the mainstream if it catches on with others.

Issue 4: Screen Aesthetics

One of the hazards of putting programming power into so many hands is that many people with good ideas have difficulty expressing those ideas graphically. Given the painting and icon editing tools of HyperCard, it becomes even more imperative that part of a good stack design includes a good graphic design. Here's an 80/20 rule that you should imbed in your designing mind:

> A user will want to use a stack 80% for its information content or information handling ability and 20% for its visual appeal, but the initial perceived value of the stack will be 80% predicated on its visual appeal and 20% on its information abilities.

It is difficult to find artists who have experience designing Macintosh applications screens. This skill is quite different from using the Macintosh as an artistic tool for creation of art to be presented in other media. There is a lot of good art created on the Macintosh, but most of the time it is not appropriate to application design. Make sure that whatever layout and art elements are on your cards contribute to the user interface or information, and don't just embellish it.

Application of color compounds the issue even more. It is easy to go color crazy, assigning bright, conflicting colors to screen elements. It helps, however, to study the work that Apple has done on color. If you notice Apple's own Finder icons, you'll see color selections from the pastel range and various greys. Sparse use of color is also often more effective than broad splashes. Color should be used as an enhancement of the experience, but never detract from the information on the screen.

Issue 5: Stack Structure

Stack structure refers to the way an application is apportioned in stack files, and comes back to a discussion earlier in the book about homogeneous and heterogeneous stacks. This question—how to structure a complex application—is often at the top of the list of concerns stack authors have about an application under construction. Unfortunately, there are no simple rules to follow to answer this question. Still, we can provide some guidelines that might steer you in the right direction.

It is always preferable to put an application into a single stack, if for no other purpose than for easy distribution. A single stack can contain the application and on-line help in different backgrounds. This works particularly well when the application is a focused one—an application that doesn't break up into distinct conceptual modules. In that case, the only limiting factor may be the total size of the stack. If you plan to distribute the application on diskette, you won't want your single, heterogeneous stack to be more than about 775K—it's not quite safe yet to distribute software on 1.4Mb high-density disks, since there are still many users out there with 800K drives.

Working on a single stack has other advantages, too. The Find command, for instance, works across the entire stack for truly global searches. Debugging scripts is easier, especially when there isn't redundant code in multiple stacks that requires updating each time you fix a bug. Compacting your work is also simpler, because a single Compact Stack command compacts the entire application. Finally, it is always easier to subdivide a larger stack into smaller stacks than the other way around. Therefore, it may be best to start development in a single stack, and split it up if you change your mind later.

Designing for multiple stacks makes good sense when the application consists of a number of modules that have related, but distinctly different functionality. This organization, too, has its advantages. Upgrading an application may entail replacing or patching only a single stack file, with comparatively little impact on the data stored in the application. If archiving data from the application is an important function, then the user can archive a single module (replacing it with a blank module for further data accumulation), rather than going through a complex data extraction procedure. Sorting information in a homogeneous stack is obviously much simpler than trying to sort data in a single background of a heterogeneous stack. And finally, the potential for disaster in the form of corrupted or lost stack files, is spread across more files—an entire application won't be blown if a file is lost or damaged.

Other aspects of the structure question include how you organize information in an application that presents lots of it. Should the data and interface be presented hierarchically or in a more hypertextual, non-linear approach? Just because the subject of this book is HyperCard doesn't mean that everything you do with it must be hypertextual. Sometimes a linear, straight line story, with a beginning, middle, and end, is the best method for presenting your information. A reference lookup, however, may be better served with a hierarchical organization—the user follows a path to a specific answer and then bails out. Or you may, in fact, prefer the hypertext approach, giving the user many pathways to related information from any point in the application.

Issue 6: Converting Existing Databases to HyperCard

There are basically two types of databases that authors wish to transfer to HyperCard: field-and-record oriented databases and a series of long text documents (sometimes called textbases). Each one raises questions for the stack designer.

For traditional field-and-record databases, the tendency is to wish to replicate the same field structure in a HyperCard card as in the original database—with each card representing a database record. This is a fine strategy for many applications, but don't feel compelled to duplicate the field structure in HyperCard. Unlike some databases, HyperCard allows multiple-line fields. Moreover, since the HyperTalk language allows extraction of data in chunks of fields (e.g., line 2 of field "Address"), you may combine many database fields into a single HyperCard field if the data looks better and may be used better as a single field for other operations (e.g., printing). Also, because the importation of database data is under script control (see Chapter 49), you can also decide to eliminate old data fields that may have grown irrelevant.

Importing large text bases presents a more substantial design problem. The natural tendency is to dump a huge chunk of text into a scrolling field, probably just as the original document would be seen in a word processing program. The difficulty with this is that forcing the user to scroll through fields is not an engaging way to present information. You would better serve the user by breaking up large text blocks into card-size pieces. Let the user click on arrow buttons to navigate up and back. A visual effect in the transition from card to card makes the navigation much more pleasant than the jerky up and down works of the scroll bar.

Issue 7: Stack Protection

Even though HyperCard offers a number of ways to protect the stack from the casual user, it is usually not a good idea to protect the stack except in very specific circumstances. First of all, protecting stacks against script poachers is a waste of time. Enough software utilities exist in the public domain to unlock protected stacks, making the job trivial for a determined explorer. Second, locking down a stack prevents a knowledgeable HyperCard user from customizing or modifying the stack to suit personal tastes. If you are intent on protecting a script, then you always have the option of compiling it with CompileIt! (Chapter 58) or converting it to an XCMD in another language.

The one situation that calls for locking down a stack is when the stack is running at a free-standing kiosk station for public information purposes. In this case, you'll want to set the cantAbort property to true as well so that once the program starts, it can't be stopped short of turning off the computer (or using a secret keyboard or mouse combination known only to the author). These kinds of applications need to be protected against know-it-alls who will try to stop and interrupt a self-running program to prove they can beat the system.

Issue 8: Engaging the Couch Potato

A good stack design encourages people to use the program and come back to it again and again. It also lures the user past the welcome screen and makes the program's depths irresistible.

Essentially that means turning the stack into an interactive experience. This doesn't have to be restricted to multimedia presentations or even training stacks. Even a database access front end to a mainframe computer can be made inviting with good design. A serious software program that draws users back to it is engaging.

To make stacks engaging is no small feat. You should assume that the potential user has much less interest in what your stack is doing than you do. The design must go to extra lengths to turn a typically passive browser into an interested partner. Successful stacks do this.

Issue 9: Making Stacks Customizable

A significant attraction for HyperCard-based applications is that unlike those hard-coded in other languages, stacks are modifiable by anyone who knows a bit about HyperCard and HyperTalk and has the full HyperCard developer package. If your application lends itself to being modified by the user, then make customization easy.

One important help you can provide is copious comments in your scripts. Document your own custom handlers, especially identifying the nature of parameters passed to them. Leave clues about where handlers are located if a handler in one object calls another in a different object.

Sometimes the stack construction may be very complex, making it difficult for all but expert HyperTalk programmers to figure out the structure and how to modify it. In such cases, you may consider building customization front ends into the application. Don't be surprised if the coding for this kind of front end is as complex or more complex as the program it is customizing. If it's making the job of the user easier, then it's definitely worth it.

Where appropriate, also include a preferences card so that users may establish patterns that take effect every time they use the stack. As with the Home stack, let the preferences card set global properties that your stack can check to present different levels of difficulty or options.

Issue 10: Stackware Is Software

This last item is the most important. Because HyperCard so dramatically lowers the entry barrier to programming, it is easy to believe that you can churn out stacks by the dozen. Stacks: Yes. Good stacks: No.

While more people can get involved with creating Macintosh programs with HyperCard, and the coding aspect comes a lot faster than doing the equivalent application in another language, it still takes the same amount of time and careful thought to design and test a quality HyperCard stack. Apple coined the term *stackware* to include anything produced with HyperCard. Unfortunately, that segregation indicates a different class of software. Nothing could be further from the truth. The development environment may be different, but users' expectations are just as high as applications they find in stores or from other sources. Strive to make your HyperCard applications as good as something *you* would buy. Keep your expectations as high as your potential users, and you'll be on the right track to designing quality HyperCard-based software.

PART V

APPLYING HYPERCARD AND HYPERTALK

CHAPTER 60

INTRODUCTION TO APPLICATIONS

Each of the next six chapters contains detailed specifications for HyperCard applications you can use as they are or adapt for many other purposes. The intent of these examples is to demonstrate HyperTalk techniques and HyperCard design strategies in real working environments.

The applications cover a wide range of complexity, from a simple "brute force" stack (simple to implement, although an experienced HyperTalk hand would be able to accomplish the same stack functions with fewer cards) to stacks whose scripts run a couple of pages of Script Editor printout or use AppleScript to communicate with other programs.

For each stack, we start with an overview of how the stack operates, so that you can appreciate its functions and the interaction among cards, buttons, and fields. Then we let the stack itself do most of the talking. We extracted the object scripts directly from the stack and reproduced them here. When additional comment is necessary, we help explain HyperTalk constructions that may be new to you or that are representative of techniques you should strive for. In all cases, the scripts are examples of HyperTalk programming style and practice as envisioned by the language's creators.

We intentionally did not call on the talents of a screen designer for these stacks. These stacks represent stacks that anyone—including those with less than spectacular painting tool mastery—can recreate. Of course you have some excellent art available to you on the disks that comes with HyperCard 2.2, so feel free to choose other background designs from those stacks.

The only way to become proficient in HyperTalk is to use it on real stacks. Start by recreating the stacks in the following chapters. Then modify them to suit your particular applications. Always be on the lookout for techniques that might apply to the things you want to do with HyperCard.

As you build a HyperCard stack, do it in stages, testing each message handler as you go. When you get alert messages indicating that HyperCard can't do something or doesn't understand a particular construction, click on the alert box's Script button to zoom in on the problem. Make the necessary repair and test the handler again. Keep at it until you've worked out all the kinks. Then move on to the next handler.

Another useful technique when designing your own scripts from scratch is to get the functionality of the script working, even if the code is not especially elegant or compact. Once the handler is doing what it should, go back to it and look for ways of making it more efficient and simpler, or perhaps for ways that it can be shared by other objects when placed at a higher level. You'll see some examples in the next chapters in which there are no button scripts in a stack (at least for the main action buttons). The handlers that perform the action are in the background or stack object, taking their cues from the name of the button clicked by the user (*the target*, in HyperTalk functions parlance). One script ends up performing the tasks of a dozen.

But don't worry if you cannot seem to make your scripts as tightly woven as the examples we show here. The fact that you can make a stack do what you want it to do is a significant accomplishment—and very much in the spirit of HyperCard.

Enjoy!

CHAPTER

61

A CONVERSION CALCULATOR

Many people have need for math conversions between units. Aside from common metric conversions, professionals may need temperature, currency, or other unit conversions, like typesetting points to inches or vice versa.

In this chapter, we present the basis for a calculator that may be customized and extended for whatever unit conversions you need in your work. The sample here deals with linear measure conversions, but the principles apply to any conversion.

Overview

The calculator, equipped with linear unit data, is shown in Figure 61–1. This stack is simplicity itself, consisting of a minimum of fields and buttons. As you'll also see, the scripts are miniscule.

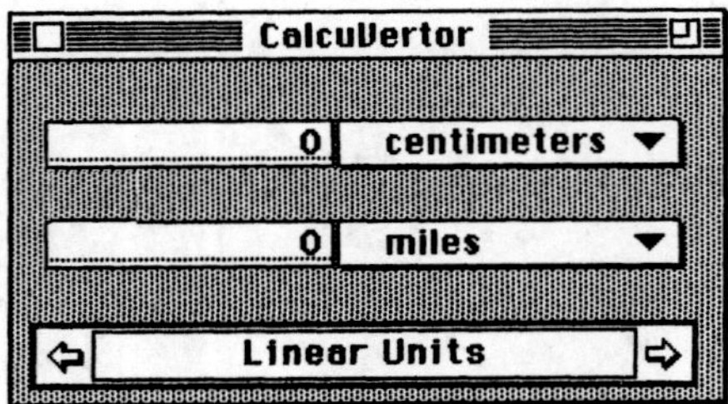

Figure 61–1. The CalcuVertor.

To use the calculator, a user enters a starting value into the top left field. After selecting the units for the before and after calculations (Figure 61–2), the stack does the rest. A change of the units in either popup button or entry of a new number into the top left field causes the calculator to compute the solution.

During calculation, the handler that performs the actual computation performs two conversions. The first converts the input number and units to an intermediate unit—the inch, in this case. Next, the handler converts the inch value into the unit appearing in the lower popup menu. All conversion factors are relative to the inch. Therefore, the conversion factor associated with the feet unit is 12; the factor associated with the centimeter is .3937008. In other words, there are 12 inches to the foot and .3937008 inches to the centimeter. If you plan to make other conversion calculator templates, find an intermediate unit for your conversion calculations.

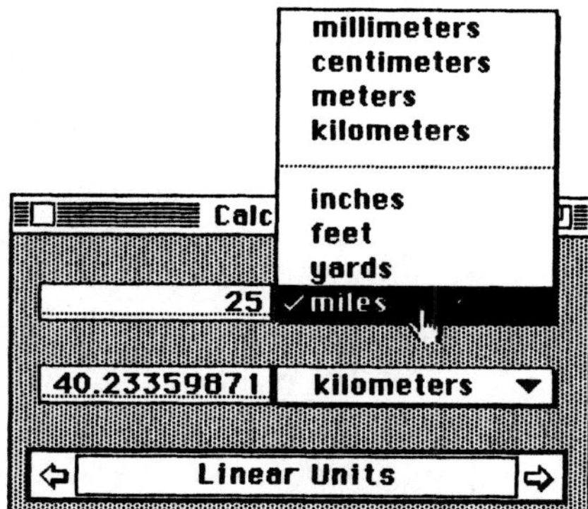

Figure 61–2. Select conversion units from popup buttons.

If there is a mysterious side to this application, it is that the conversion factors are stored in a hidden field. The alignment of the factors is identical to those of the unit listings in the popup menus (Figure 61–3). The calculation is based on the selected items in both popup menus, which reveals the factors necessary for the two conversions.

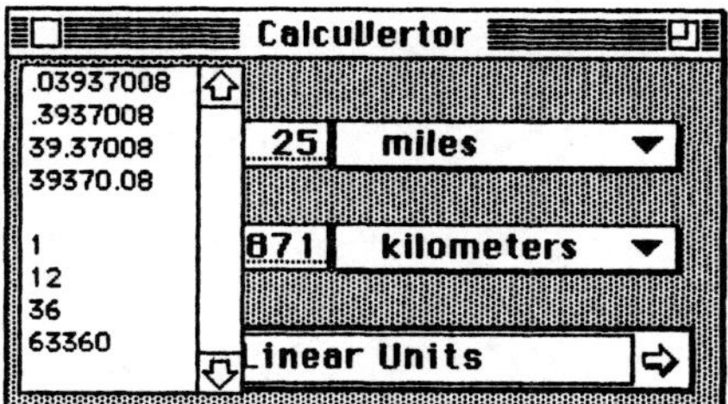

Figure 61–3. A view of the hidden field containing linear unit conversion factors.

Scripts

The vast majority of the action in HyperTalk handlers for this stack occurs in the background script. We begin with the stack-level handlers that would be appropriate for saving this stack as an application. For use as a plain stack, comment out the entire openStack handler.

stack "CalcuVertor"

```
on openStack
    set cursor to watch
    set userLevel to 5
    setupMenus
end openStack
```

```
on setupMenus
    lock screen
    delete menu "Style"
    delete menu "Font"
    delete menu "Go"
    delete menu "Tools"
    get line 1 to 5 of menu "Edit"
    put it into menu "Edit"
    put "Quit" into menu "File" with menuMsg "Quit HyperCard"
    set cmdChar of menuItem 1 of menu "File" to "Q"
    put "About CalcuVertor..." into menuItem 1 of menu "Apple"
end setupMenus

on doMenu what
    if what is "About CalcuVertor..." then
        answer "CalcuVertor.  ©1993 Danny Goodman."
    else if what is "Quit" then
        send "doMenu Quit HyperCard" to HyperCard
    else pass doMenu
end doMenu
```

Comment: We address the user level and menu concerns described in Chapter 57. Here we delete all but the menus we need, plus modify the ones that are left (including preserving HyperCard's top five Edit menu items, which are smart enough to activate when appropriate). We also add an About menu item and dialog.

bkgnd "Calculator"

```
on openCard
    put short name of this card into fld "Template"
    select text of field "Input"
end openCard

on closeField
    if target is not a number
    then put 0 into target
    calculate
end closeField

on calculate
    set numberFormat to "0.########"
    put line (word 2 of selectedLine of cd btn "Input") ¬
    of fld "Conversion Factors" into inputFactor
    put line (word 2 of selectedLine of cd btn "Output") ¬
    of fld "Conversion Factors" into outputFactor
    put inputFactor/outputFactor into scale
    put scale * fld "Input" into fld "Output"
    select text of field "Input"
end calculate
```

Comment: Notice how we use the selectedLine function of each popup button to determine the corresponding line in the hidden Conversion Factors field. Once we have the two factors derived from the field, we calculate the scale to be used as the multiplier for the input data. When the answer is safely in the Output field, we select the text of the Input field so that the user can instantly type another value if desired.

card "Linear Units", button "Input"

```
on mouseUp
   if the selectedText of me is not empty
   then calculate
end mouseUp
```

card "Linear Units", button "Output"

```
on mouseUp
   if the selectedText of me is not empty
   then calculate
end mouseUp
```

Comment: These two handlers are in the popup style buttons. We use card buttons for these popups, because any cards we add require their own set containing names of those units (while the Conversion Factors field will contain card-specific factors). Both button scripts make sure a selection has been made, and then trigger the calculation, which will use whatever the user just selected.

Further Ideas

The most apparent enhancement is adding templates with other kinds of conversions. Just make a new card, enter unit names into the contents of both popup buttons, and enter the conversion factors into the hidden Conversion Factors field. A useful addition might be an item in the Edit menu that copies the answer to the Clipboard for pasting into another document or program.

Another possibility is adding an on-screen version of a numeric keypad. You could then enter numbers into the input field of the calculator by simply clicking on the number buttons in the keypad. But if a user already has a numeric keypad on the keyboard, the on-screen version may actually be slower.

CHAPTER 62

A TIME SHEET

Many professional people must maintain records of time spent with clients or on particular projects. These time sheets are then tabulated for billing purposes. When the professionals are part of a firm, an office manager or controller is usually responsible for distributing and collecting time sheets. By maintaining time sheets in a HyperCard stack, the sheets can be distributed electronically (either on disk or via a local area network), or data may be exported to a text file that the office manager may then combine into a spreadsheet for accounting purposes.

Overview

The Time Sheets stack consists of two backgrounds. While the basic artwork for each background is the same, one background has no fields on it, while the other does.

In the example of the cover card background in Figure 62–1, the artwork for the law firm name, field labels, and hourglass is all in the card graphics layer. The four fields are card fields. Information in this card would be filled out by the person responsible for distributing and tabulating the time sheets for the firm.

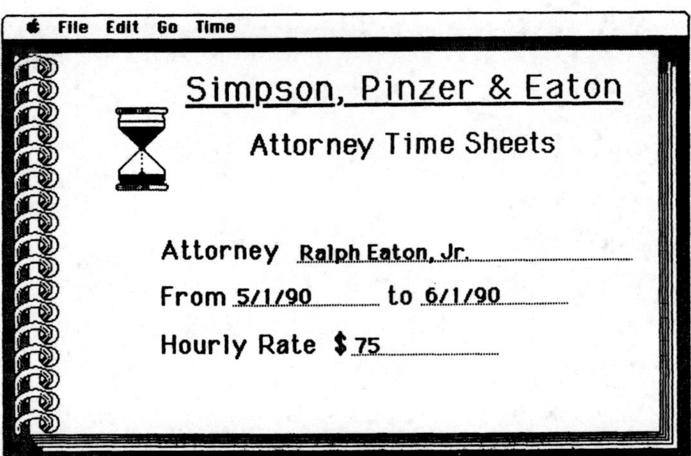

Figure 62–1. Preferences card for the Time Sheet stack. The Hourly Rate field is picked up by the detail cards in the second background.

The cover card shows for a couple of seconds whenever the stack opens. Then the stack moves to the last card in the stack, from which any new card is generated (by the New Card menu command).

Upon creation of a new card, the current date and time are placed in their respective fields (Figure 62–2). The hourly rate is retrieved from the cover card and placed in the appropriate field.

File Edit Go Time

Date: Friday, March 30, 1990

Start Time: 12:42 PM End Time: 2:30 PM

Billing Info: 2.00 hrs @ $75 = $150.00

Client: Will Stevenson

Case Number: B92039

Purpose of Consultation or Service Rendered:
Discussed copyright infringement possibilities in current suit against Templeton, Inc.

Figure 62–2. The Time menu contains all the controls for creating new cards, ending sessions, and exporting the data for accounting purposes.

This stack applies custom menus to their fullest—the application takes complete control of the menubar, eliminating HyperCard menu items that are irrelevant to the application. Menu items are shown in Figure 62–3.

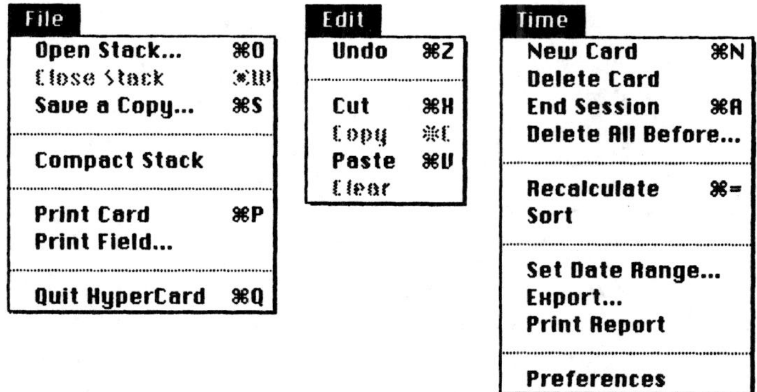

Figure 62–3. The Time Sheet stack menus as modified and created by the setMenus handler. The HyperCard Go menu remains intact.

The total billing amount is calculated after any of three actions: (1) choosing End Session from the Time menu; (2) changing the hourly rate on a card; or (3) adjusting the end time field. The End Session menu item places the current time into the End field and starts computation based on the elapsed time between the start and end times. The script that performs the calculation has been designed in such a way that billing increments are by quarter-hour. Elapsed time display will always be displayed in quarter hour fractions of one hour.

Sorting, as carried out by the handler attached to the Sort menu item, arranges the cards in the stack by client name or date, as the user chooses. A group of menu items lets the user mark a sequence of cards between to dates. Only marked cards are then exported in a tab-delimited text file or printed with a report format setup in HyperCard's print report facility.

Scripts and Properties

Here are the objects and their scripts for the Time Sheet stack.

stack "Time Sheet"

```
on openStack
    go last card
    setMenus
    pass openStack
end openStack

on resumeStack
    go last card
    setMenus
    pass resumeStack
end resumeStack

on closeStack
    reset menubar
    pass closeStack
end closeStack

on suspendStack
    reset menubar
    pass resumeStack
end suspendStack
```

Comment: It's important that a stack clean up after itself whenever a user closes it or suspends it by clicking in another stack window. These handlers reset the menubar each time the user leaves the stack, and restores it upon return. You should do the same for stacks that insert other stacks into the message hierarchy.

```
on setMenus
    set cursor to watch
    lock screen
    reset menubar
    delete menu "Tools"
    delete menu "Objects"
    delete menu "Font"
    delete menu "Style"

    put "Open Stack...,Close Stack,Save a Copy...,-," & ¬
    "Compact Stack,-,Print Card,Print Field...,-," & "Quit HyperCard" into menu "File"
    put "O,W,S,,,,P,,Q" into fileMenuCmds
    repeat with x = 1 to number of items of fileMenuCmds
        set cmdChar of menuItem x of menu "File" to item x of fileMenuCmds
    end repeat

    repeat until number of menuItems of menu "Edit" = 6
        delete last menuItem of menu "Edit"
    end repeat

    create menu "Time"
    put "New Card,Delete Card,End Session," & ¬
    "Delete All Before...,-,Recalculate,Sort,-," & ¬
    "Set Date Range...,Export...,Print Report," & "-,Preferences" into menu "Time"
    put "N,,A,,,=,,,,,,,," into timeMenuCmds
    put ",,endSession,deleteBefore,,recalc,sortEm,," & ¬
    "dateRange,export,printReport,,Prefs" into timeMenuMsgs
    repeat with x = 1 to number of items of timeMenuCmds
        set cmdChar of menuItem x of menu "Time" to item x of timeMenuCmds
        set menuMsg of menuItem x of menu "Time" to item x of timeMenuMsgs
    end repeat
end setMenus
```

Comment: The setMenus handler is a self-contained module that composes the menubar as needed for this stack. It eliminates a number of HyperCard menus not needed for running this stack. It also modifies the File and Edit menus. The Time menu is a new menu added to the end of the menubar. Except for New Card and Delete Card menu items (which end up being passed to HyperCard as-is), menu items in this menu send custom messages in search of custom handlers. These handlers are located in the background script for the Time Sheet cards (below).

One special note is that the Preference menu item takes the user to the Preferences card. As shown in the next script, all items except the last item, are dimmed in the Preferences card, and the item name changes so that the item returns the user to the Time Sheet background.

bkgnd "Cover Card"

card "Preferences"

```
on timeSheets -- from choosing Time Sheets in Time menu
    repeat with x = 1 to 12
        set enabled of menuItem x of menu "Time" to true
    end repeat
    set name of last menuItem of menu "Time" to "Preferences"
    set menuMsg of last menuItem of menu "Time" to "Prefs"
    go to last card of bg "Time Sheets"
end timeSheets
```

bkgnd "Time Sheets"

```
on doMenu whichItem
    if whichItem is "New Card"
    then go to last card of bkgnd "Time Sheets"
    pass doMenu
end doMenu

on newCard
    get the long date
    put it into field "Date"
    convert it to seconds
    put it into line 2 of field "Date"
    put the time into field "Start Time"
    put card field "Rate" of card "Preferences" into field "Hourly"
end newCard
```

Comment: We're using the second line of the Date field to hold the date value in seconds on an unseen line. Having the seconds value available at a moment's notice helps later when marking cards for export and printing as well as deleting all cards before a particular date. The closeField handler for the date field (below) also puts the seconds equivalent into the second line of the field. Also in this handler, we're able to fetch the hourly rate data from the Preferences card without going to that card—something you can do within a single stack, but not across stacks.

```
on endSession -- posts end time & calculates
    if field "End Time" is empty then
        put the time into field "End Time"
        reCalc
    end if
end endSession

--------------------
MENU MESSAGE HANDLERS
------------------

on deleteBefore
    put the date into sampleDate
    convert sampleDate to dateItems
```

```
    put "1" into item 3 of sampleDate -- first of month
    convert sampleDate to short date
    ask "Delete all cards before what date?" with sampleDate
    if it is not empty then
        lock screen
        convert it to seconds
        put it into maxDate
        repeat with x = number of cards of bkgnd "Time Sheets" down to 1
            set cursor to busy
            go to card x of bkgnd "Time Sheets"
            get field "Date"
            convert it to seconds
            if it < maxDate
            then doMenu "Delete Card"
        end repeat
    end if
end deleteBefore
```

Comment: To help the user enter a date in the proper format and to suggest a possible starting date (the first of the current month), we assemble a sample date that is passed as a parameter to the Ask command. In the repeat loop that performs the deletion, note that the cards within the Time Sheets background are counted down from the last card. Batch deletions, in which you use card numbers as counting elements, must be done from the top down so that cards you delete don't upset the card numbering for the rest of cards to be checked.

```
on reCalc
    put field "Start Time" into startTime
    convert startTime to seconds
    put field "End Time" into endTime
    if endTime is empty then
        answer "The end time is missing."
        exit reCalc
    end if
    convert endTime to seconds
    set numberFormat to "0.#########"

    put (endTime - startTime)/(60*15) into quarterHours
    put quarterHours - trunc(quarterHours) into fracQuarter
    put trunc(quarterHours) into quarterCount
    if fracQuarter is not zero then add 1 to quarterCount

    put quarterCount/4 into hours
    set numberFormat to "0.00"
    put quarterCount/4 into field "Total Time"
    put hours * field "Hourly" + 0.0 into field "Total Bill"
end reCalc
```

Comment: The reCalc handler is spaced into three readable groups, each of which performs a distinctly different kind of operation in this handler.

In the first group, the field information is retrieved and placed into variables for manipulation later in the handler. Notice that both times are converted into seconds. The numberFormat property is adjusted to allow for greater precision in calculating time in the following commands.

Group two uses the start and ending time (in seconds) to calculate the number of quarter hours to be counted for billing purposes. Remember that the design calls for a fraction of a quarter hour to be billed as a complete quarter hour. The first line determines the raw number of quarter hours, which may have a fraction as part of it (for example, 5.34 quarter hours). The second line obtains that fractional amount (for example, 5.34 minus trunc(5.34) = 0.34). The whole number of quarter hours goes into the variable quarterCount in line 3 (for example, 5). Then line 4 checks whether the fractional quarter is zero. If it is, the quarter count is not adjusted upward (as in 5 hours and no fractions, which should be billed only as 5 hours). If the fraction is anything but zero, an additional quarter hour is tacked onto the total time to be billed.

In the third group occurs the calculation of the information that goes into the fields. First comes the calculation of the number of hours (with the numberFormat adjusted to two places to the right of the decimal) and then the total billing amount.

```
on sortEm
   push card
   answer "Sort by what?" with "Cancel" or "Client" or "Date"
   if it is "Client"
   then sort by field "Client"
   else if it is "Date"
   then
      sort dateTime by field "Start Time"
      sort dateTime by field "Date"
   end if
   pop card -- still view card we were at
end sortEm
```

Comment: We assume that if the user wants cards sorted by date then the cards should also be sorted by start time so that the entire collection is in chronological order. Therefore, for sorting by date, we first sort by the Start Time field to get the stack stable in starting order; then we sort by the Date field.

```
on dateRange
   ask "Set date range starting with what date?"
   if it is not empty then
      put it into startDate
      convert startDate to seconds
```

```
        ask "Set date range ending with what date?"
        if it is not empty then
            put it into endDate
            convert endDate to seconds
            mark cards where line 2 of field "Date" ≥ ¬
            startDate and line 2 of field "Date" ≤ endDate
        end if
    end if
end dateRange

on export
    if number of marked cards = 0 then
        answer "No data selected for export."
        exit export
    end if
    ask file "Export data to what file?"
    if it is not empty then
        put it into theFile
        open file theFile
        put (cd field "Attorney" of cd "Preferences") & return into headerRecord
        repeat with x = 1 to number of bg fields
            put short name of field x & tab after headerRecord
        end repeat
        put return into last char of headerRecord -- replace tab
        write headerRecord to file theFile
        repeat with x = 1 to number of marked cards
            go to marked card x
            get line 1 of field date
            convert it to short date
            put it & tab into oneRecord
            repeat with y = 2 to number of bg fields
                put field y & tab after oneRecord
            end repeat
            put return into last char of oneRecord
            write oneRecord to file theFile
        end repeat
        close file theFile
    end if
    unmark all cards
end export
```

Comment: This export handler lets the user archive data in a previously selected date range (that date range selection could also be built into this handler to make it one menu operation) to a text file with any valid file name. It also writes the name of the attorney and the names of the fields out as the first record. Each record consists of data items separated by tabs and a return character at the end. Data from the date field is converted to the short date format, which takes up less space in a spreadsheet column.

```
on printReport
    open report printing with template "Time Sheet Summary"
    print marked cards
    close printing
end printReport
```

```
on prefs
    go to card "Preferences"
    repeat with x = 1 to 12
        set enabled of menuItem x of menu "Time" to false
    end repeat
    set name of last menuItem of menu "Time" to "Time Sheets"
    set menuMsg of last menuItem of menu "Time" to "timeSheets"
end prefs
```

Comment: All items in the Time menu except the last are disabled when going to the Preferences card. The last item changes to Time Sheets, with its own menu message.

bkgnd "Time Sheets", button "Done"

```
on mouseUp
    if field "End Time" is empty then
        put the time into field "End Time"
        reCalc
    end if
end mouseUp
```

bkgnd "Time Sheets", button "Prev"

```
on mouseUp
    go to prev card of this bkgnd
end mouseUp
```

bkgnd "Time Sheets", button "Next"

```
on mouseUp
    go to next card of this bkgnd
end mouseUp
```

bkgnd "Time Sheets", field "Date"

```
on closeField
    convert me to long date
    get me
    convert it to seconds
    put it into line 2 of me
end closeField
```

bkgnd "Time Sheets", field "End Time"

```
on closeField
    reCalc
end closeField
```

bkgnd "Time Sheets", field "Hourly"

```
on closeField
    reCalc
end closeField
```

Further Ideas

You can make the Time Sheet form behave even more like a relational database, if you like, by linking it to a stack containing client names and other data. By typing in the client's number, the Time Sheet stack could reach into the Client stack and fetch information like client name, address, and quoted hourly rate.

For a self-employed person, data from these cards could be consolidated into invoice data in another background or stack. This could become the start of a billing system for clients.

CHAPTER

63

A TELEPHONE LOGBOOK

Many executives and self-employed professionals need to record their outgoing telephone calls—the date and time, the person called, the phone number called, the content of the call, and to what account or project the time and phone call charges should be billed. What we'll show you here is the beginning of what could become an elaborate system. It ties directly into the Addresses stack supplied with HyperCard.

Overview

Whenever you are in the Addresses stack (Figure 63–1) and dial a call, a modified dial button script not only dials the number as it always did but also goes to a different stack of telephone logbook pages (Figure 63–2) and generates a new card. When a new card is made, four items in the card are automatically filled in for you: the current date, the time, the name of the person appearing in the Addresses stack card you just dialed, and the phone number just dialed.

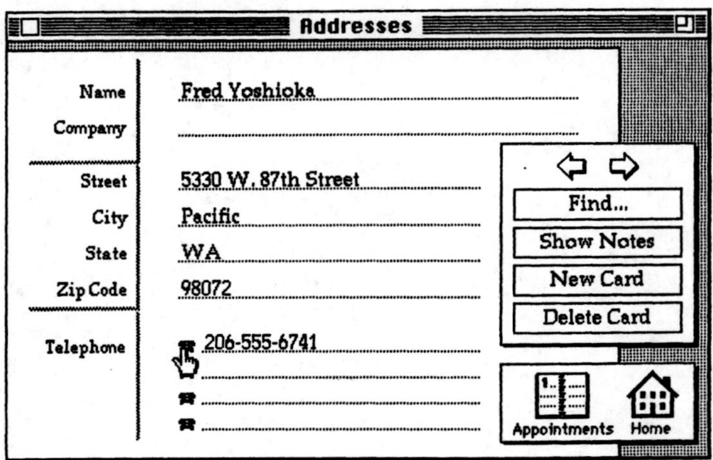

Figure 63–1. We modify the script connected to the Dial buttons to generate a log of each dialed call.

You may also generate a new card while in the Telephone Log stack by choosing New Card from the Edit menu. When you do this, the date and time are placed into the card. Because the card doesn't know whom you're calling, you'll have to type in the name and phone number.

At any time while you are in the Log stack, you may check the person's Addresses stack card by clicking on the rolo icon button in the upper right.

That button's script goes to the Addresses stack and performs a search on the name from the Log card. If no match is found, you are given the choice to make a new Addresses stack card for this person or not. If you choose yes, a new Addresses card is made, placing the person's name in the Name spot and the phone number into the Phone Number field on the Addresses card.

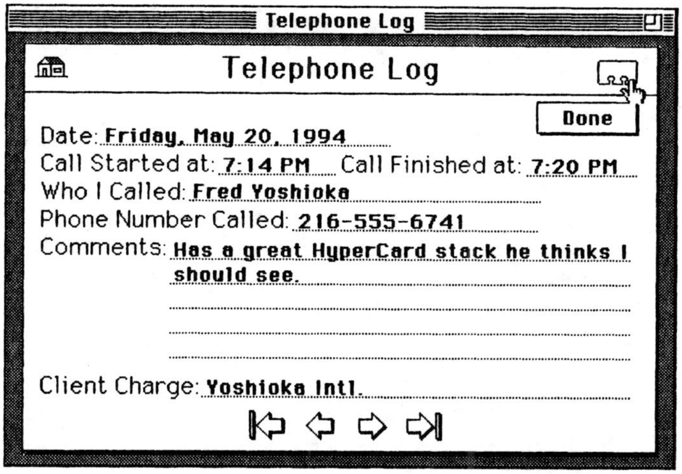

Figure 63–2. A record of each call goes into the Telephone Log card. Many of the fields are automatically filled in by the script.

When you are finished with a call, you may click the Done button near the field labeled Call Finished at. This action places the current time into the adjacent field. If there is already an ending time in that field, a click of that button won't accidentally overwrite the time.

In practice, a professional person would perform a Message Box Find command on a project or client name when it comes time for billing. Also, if you are looking at a telephone bill and don't recognize a number, search for that number to find the outgoing phone call that generated the call.

Scripts

We start with the dial button script in the Addresses stack, as revised for use with the Log stack. No other changes were made to the button or the rest of the Addresses stack. From there we move onto the scripts and properties of the Log stack. Refer to Figure 63–2 to get your bearings when we describe fields and buttons.

stack "Addresses"

background "Body"

```
on dialNo whichLine
    -- add the following lines to the end of this handler --
    put field "Name" into personCalled
    put line whichLine of field "Telephone" into numberCalled
    lock screen
    go stack "Telephone Log"
    makeNewCard -- handler in Log stack
    unlock screen
    put personCalled into field "Person"
    put numberCalled into field "Number"
    select field "Comments" -- ready to type
end dialNo
```

Comment: After dialing the number, this handler places the name and number into their respective variables (personCalled and numberCalled). Then we go to the last card of the Telephone Log stack to keep the new card in chronological order. When the new card is created, the Telephone Log stack's own newCard handler performs some things (you'll see in a moment). Then the name and number are posted to the new log page. Unlocking the screen is optional, because it automatically reverts to false at idle time, but the user will see the name and number being placed into the fields.

stack "Telephone Log"

bkgnd "Log Sheet"

```
on makeNewCard
    go to last card of bkgnd "Log Sheet" -- keep in chrono order
    doMenu "New Card"
end makeNewCard

on newCard -- time and date stamp triggered by makeNewCard
    put the long date into field "Date"
    put the time into field "Start"
end newCard

on openStack
    hide msg
end openStack

on openCard
    hide msg -- in case you use Message Box to Find...
end openCard
```

bkgnd "Log Sheet", button "First"

```
on mouseUp
    visual effect scroll right
    go to first card
end mouseUp
```

bkgnd "Log Sheet", button "Prev"

```
on mouseUp
    visual effect scroll right
    go to prev card
end mouseUp
```

bkgnd "Log Sheet", button "Next"

```
on mouseUp
    visual effect scroll left
    go to next card
end mouseUp
```

bkgnd "Log Sheet", button "Last"

```
on mouseUp
    visual effect scroll left
    go to last card
end mouseUp
```

bkgnd "Log Sheet", button "To Home"

```
on mouseUp
    visual effect iris close
    go home
end mouseUp
```

bkgnd "Log Sheet", button "To Addresses"

```
on mouseUp
    put field "Person" into personCalled
    put field "Number" into numberCalled
    get long id of this card
    put it into saveCard -- in case we need to come back
    set lockScreen to true
    go to stack "Addresses"
    send "find whole personCalled" to HyperCard
    if the result is empty then -- only if no card found
        answer "No card found. Add one?" with "Yes" or "No" or "Cancel"
        if it is "Cancel" then go to saveCard
            -- glad we saved it
        else if it is "Yes" then
            go to last card
            doMenu "New Card" -- new Address card
```

```
            put personCalled into field "Name"
            put numberCalled into field "Telephone"
        end if
    end if
end mouseUp
```

Comment: This handler must send the Find command to HyperCard to bypass the Find handler already in the Addresses stack. If we let that handler take care of the Find command, this handler wouldn't know if the search was successful nor would it know when to add a new card.

bkgnd "Log Sheet", button "Done"

```
on mouseUp
    if field "End" is empty
    then put the time into field "End"
end mouseUp
```

Further Ideas

As you use this stack, you'll find many things you can add that will make its application more carefree. For instance, you'll quickly discover that you leave frequent notes in the Comments field about getting a busy signal or no answer. You might want to add buttons that automatically place those notes into the Comments field with the click of the mouse button.

Another button you can add is one that redials the number in the current card. The handler for this will generate a new card and carry over the name and number items into the new card's fields. You can always add buttons that link to other stacks you need while on the phone, like your appointment book.

If you have other stacks that dial phone numbers, consider modifying those dial scripts to come to the Telephone Log stack and make a new card. Eventually, you can build a highly integrated empire of telephone-related stacks.

CHAPTER 64

A CORPORATE DIRECTORY

When a company starts spreading its people across several buildings and shifts people around offices regularly, it becomes important that both employees and guests find their way to offices quickly. The corporate directory stack is an application that can be recreated simply, and without too much artistry.

Overview

The stack environment shown here consists of one stack with four backgrounds plus a second stack for notes about individual people. This organization allows the corporate data to be maintained on a file server or updated and distributed on disk frequently to people throughout the company. The separate stack with notes contains information you might save about someone listed in the shared stack. Notes won't be overwritten or erased when you copy a newly distributed corporate directory to your disk.

The first background contains an index to all the people listed in the directory (Figure 64–1). A user selects a name, and then clicks on one of the action buttons at the bottom. Notice that although we haven't done anything involving lots of original art, the use of a display font (Tekton Bold) and some horizontal bars have made an otherwise dull screen into something that looks decent. It's amazing how a swath of black in the background picture can make a card design something special.

Figure 64–1. The first card of the stack, with an index of names.

The next background of the main stack consists of a Staff Directory card (Figure 64–2), which contains information about each person employed by the company. Items in the card are filled in as individual text fields. Notice how we've maintained the same button arrangement at the bottom of the screen, and carried the bars over from the first card. When users arrive at this card, they'll know where to look for the action buttons. The arrow buttons take you to the previous and next cards in the stack. We'll get to the Print and Note buttons in a moment. The Dial button is linked to the Extension field. In that button's script is also a second possibility. In case the extension is actually an outside phone number (that is, is longer than four digits), the button dials a 9 and the number in the field (presuming the stack is being used on a corporate phone system).

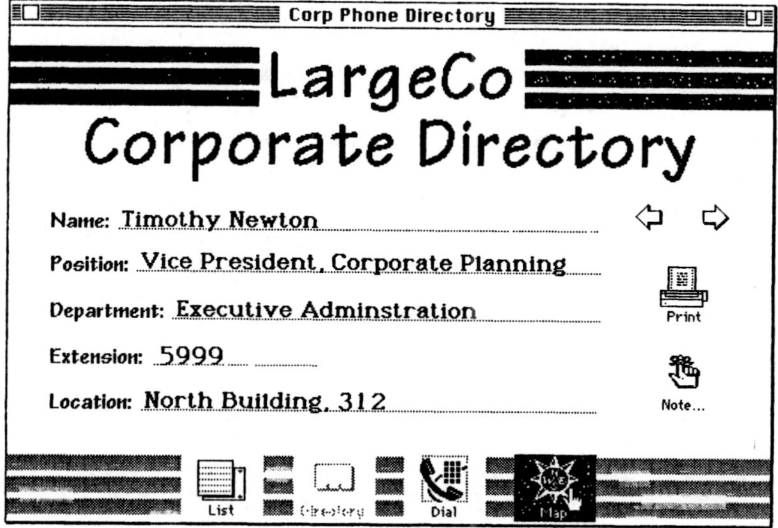

Figure 64–2. The actual directory cards containing staff information.

The Map button links the Directory card to cards in the next background. In this third, Overview Map, background are a few cards containing maps of the entire corporate grounds (Figure 64–3). When you arrive at a card, the building graphic and its label flash three times to show the browser which building the person is located in. Therefore, there are only as many cards in this background as there are buildings to highlight. Each card's name is the name of the building, so the handler in the Map button (on the Directory card) goes to the card whose name is the first item of the Location field in the Directory card.

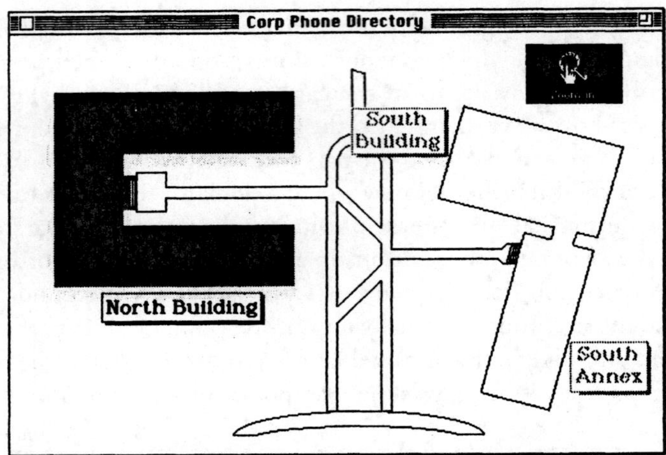

Figure 64–3. An overview map shows which building the person is in.

In the campus map background is a button called Zoom In. This button takes the second item of the Directory card's location field, the office number, and searches for that number in a text field in the final background (Figure 64–4). In this Detail background is a floor plan of one wing of one building. Each card has a card field with the number of a different office, and that office's cubicle is filled with a pattern. Note that the pattern and the field are in the card layer, while the rest of what you see is in the background layer.

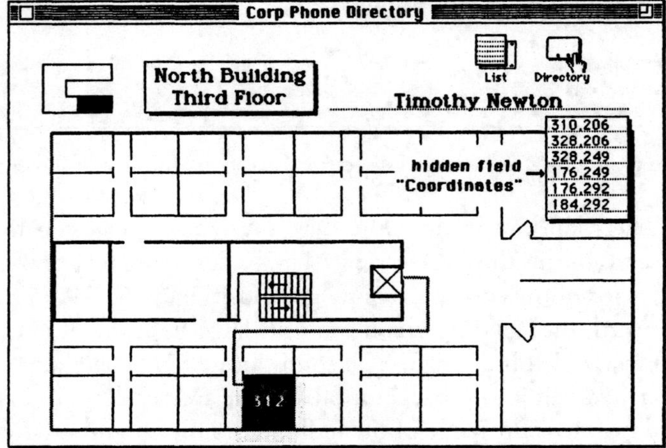

Figure 64–4. A detail map shows the path to the person's office.

When you zoom into this card, the stack draws the route from the elevator to the office three times, erasing it in between each draw but leaving the path there after the animation. The person's name from the Directory card also goes into the field at the upper right. Three buttons offer you additional navigation from here. When you click on the small representation of the building at the upper left, you go back one card, to the campus map. The List button takes you to the first card. And when you click on the Directory button at the upper right, you go back to the Directory card from which you started. Notice that the Zoom In and Directory buttons in the maps are located in the same spot on the screen. That way the browser does not have to shift the mouse around the screen to follow the most common navigation path.

Back on the Directory card, the Print button performs an Open Printing with Dialog command, which lets the user set how many pictures should be printed per page. Then the button's handler performs the electronic equivalent of clicking on the Map and Zoom In buttons, grabbing a snapshot of each of the three cards along the way for printing. A visitor to the company, for example, may want a printout as a roadmap to the person he's seeing.

The Note button opens a second, smaller window to the Directory Notes stack (Figure 64–5). Upon opening the stack, it also looks for a match for the person's name. If none is found, then the browser is prompted to create a new note card for the person.

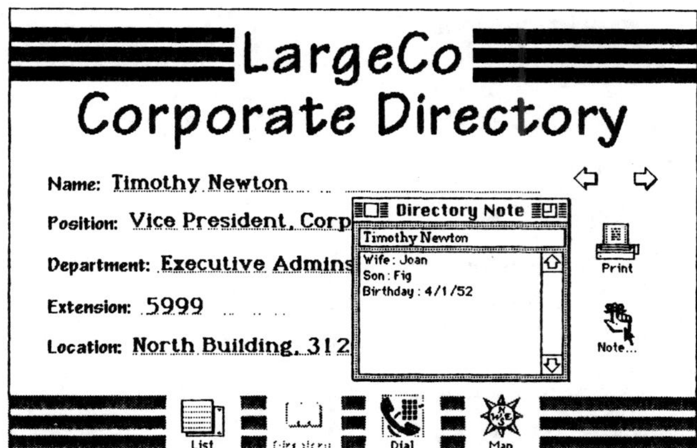

Figure 64–5. The Directory Notes stack is a separate stack and window, which stays on the user's hard disk, even when the main directory stack may be updated with a new copy.

Scripts

What follows are the scripts for each of the objects in the Corporate Directory stack.

Stack "Corporate Directory"

```
on openStack
    -- hide menubar for 9" screens
    if item 2 of the screenRect = 342
    then hide menubar
end openStack

on closeStack
    show menubar -- in case it was hidden
end closeStack
```

bkgnd "Welcome"

```
-- handler used by person who maintains stack,
-- it builds the list in the field from the
-- names of all people in the "Directory" background,
-- sorted by last name.  Names in list are in same
-- order as Directory cards.
on update
    push card
    lock screen
    go to bg "Directory"
    sort this bg by last word of field "Name"
    pop card
    unlock screen
    repeat with x = 1 to number of cards of bg "Directory"
        set cursor to busy
        put field "Name" of card x of bg "Directory" into line x of nameList
    end repeat
    put nameList into fld "Name List"
end update
```

bkgnd "Welcome", field "Name List"

```
on mouseDoubleClick
    send mouseUp to bg btn "Directory"
end mouseDoubleClick
```

Comment: We anticipate that some users will double-click on a name to view that person's directory entry. While there aren't instructions to that effect, it's an extra usability bonus for experienced Mac users.

bkgnd "Welcome", button "Directory"

```
on mouseUp
    visual effect iris open
    if the selectedLine of fld "Name List" is not empty
    then go to card (word 2 of the selectedLine of fld "Name List") of bg "Directory"
end mouseUp
```

bkgnd "Welcome", button "Dial"

```
on mouseUp
    lock screen
    send mouseUp to bg btn "Directory"
    send mouseup to bg btn "Dial"
    unlock screen with visual effect iris open
end mouseUp
```

bkgnd "Welcome", button "Map"

```
on mouseUp
    lock screen
    send mouseUp to bg btn "Directory"
    send mouseup to bg btn "Map"
    unlock screen with visual effect iris open
end mouseUp
```

bkgnd "Welcome", button "Map"

(no script; button disabled for this bkgnd)

bkgnd "Directory"

(no script)

bkgnd "Directory", button "Prev"

```
on mouseUp -- keeps browsing within Directory cards
    visual effect wipe right
    go to prev card of this background
end mouseUp
```

bkgnd "Directory", button "Next"

```
on mouseUp
    visual effect wipe left
    go to next card of this background
end mouseUp
```

bkgnd "Directory", button "Print"

```
on mouseUp
    lock messages
    open printing with dialog
    print this card
    send mouseUp to bkgnd button "See Map"
    print this card
    send mouseUp to bkgnd button "Zoom In"
    print this card
    close printing
    send mouseUp to button "ReturnToDirectory"
end mouseUp
```

Comment: By sending mouseUp to each of the buttons mentioned in the script, the handler is doing the same as the user clicking the buttons. We lock messages to prevent delays for animation we don't need to see. Going to each card, the handler then puts the printed version of the card into the printing queue. At Close Printing, the queue is flushed out, and the last page of printing is sent to the printer.

bkgnd "Directory", button "Note..."

```
on mouseUp
    put field "Name" into searchString
    lock screen
    go to stack "Directory Notes" in a new window
    find whole searchString in field "Name"
    if the result is not empty then
        answer "No note found.  Create a new one?" with "Cancel" or "OK"
        if it is "OK" then
            go to last card
            doMenu "New Card"
            put searchString into field "Name"
        else doMenu "Close Stack"
    end if
end mouseUp
```

Comment: By designing the Notes stack in a small window, it makes sense to display the stack in a separate window along with the directory card. It appears to be a pop up window. Notice, too, that creating a new card is no more trouble than clicking OK in a dialog, with the script entering the name into the field.

bkgnd "Directory", button "List"

```
on mouseUp
    visual effect iris close
    go first card
end mouseUp
```

bkgnd "Directory", button "Directory"

(no script, button disabled in this bkgnd)

bkgnd "Directory", button "Dial"

```
on mouseUp
    put "Now Dialing " & field "Name" & "..." into msg
    if length of field "Extension" ≤ 4
    then dial field "Extension"
    else dial "9" & field "Extension"
end mouseUp
```

bkgnd "Directory", button "Map"

```
on mouseUp
    global name,location
    push card
    put field "Name" into name
    put field "Location" into location
    visual effect iris open
    go to card item 1 of location
    repeat 3
        hide cd picture
        show cd picture
    end repeat
end mouseUp
```

bkgnd "Overview Map"

```
on mouseUp
    -- clicking on the card brings you back to Directory
    pop card
end mouseUp
```

bkgnd "Overview Map", button "Zoom In"

```
on mouseUp
    global location
    push this card -- pushed atop Directory card
    visual effect iris open
    find item 2 of location -- contains office number
end mouseUp
```

bkgnd "Detail"

```
on openCard
    global name
    put name into field "Name"
    showPath 3 -- animation
end openCard

on showPath howMany
    set cantAbort of this stack to true -- aborting would leave
            -- user in painting tool
    choose line tool -- to draw
    set lineSize to 2 -- thick line
    put field "Coordinates" into coordinates -- hidden field
    repeat howMany -- outer loop
        -- supply a way to get out gracefully by
        -- holding down the mouse button
        if the mouse is down then exit repeat
        set pattern to 1 -- white
        set dragSpeed to 0 -- fastest possible
        repeat with x = 1 to number of lines of coordinates - 1
            drag from line x of coordinates ¬
            to line x+1 of coordinates with optionKey -- draw
```

```
            end repeat
            set pattern to 22 -- grey
            set dragSpeed to 100 -- slow enough to see pathway
            repeat with x = 1 to number of lines of coordinates - 1
                drag from line x of coordinates to line x+1 of coordinates with optionKey
            end repeat
        end repeat
        set cantAbort of this stack to false
        choose browse tool
    end showPath
```

Comment: ShowPath is a custom handler that draws the route from the elevator to the office in question. Data points for the drag commands are stored in a normally hidden field (visible in Figure 64–4). These coordinates are loaded into a local variable for quick reading during the repeats. Each pass of the outer loop erases the existing path drawing (white pattern) and draws it slowly in grey. The browser is inhibited from aborting the drawing, because it would leave him in a painting tool, which a non-HyperCard literate user wouldn't know what to do with. We do, however, let the user hold down the mouse button so that the drawing doesn't have to repeat three times. The CantAbort property is reset to false when the drawing is finished.

bkgnd "Detail", button "Directory"

```
on mouseUp
    pop card into it            -- nothing happens to display
    pop card                    -- now pop Directory card
end mouseUp
```

bkgnd "Detail", button "Return"

```
on mouseUp
    pop card -- go back to Overview Map card
end mouseUp
```

bkgnd "Detail", button "List"

```
on mouseUp
    visual effect iris close
    go first card
end mouseUp
```

Further Ideas

There are many ways to streamline this stack. First, in locating the detail floorplan for a particular office, you could do away with the Office field and assign office numbers (plus some non-numeric character) as card names. If the card name is preceded with a word, like "cubicle," the script can still use the location global variable to help track that card. Before doing the Go command, precede item 2 of the location variable with the word "cubicle." Then go to that card name. Going to a card name is inherently faster than finding a text string.

Scanned photographs of each individual would also improve the information quotient of the Directory background cards. Additional personnel information, such as hire date, might also be added, provided the information can be made public.

One more point. Because only the data in the Directory background is likely to change often, it might be better to break up this environment into two stacks, one with the actual directory, one with all the maps. Maintenance on individual hard disks or file servers would be much simpler. In such a structure, be sure that any Go commands pointing to cards in the other stack have the stack name as a parameter to the command.

CHAPTER

65

A NEW AND IMPROVED TO DO LIST

In this chapter, we'll enhance the to do list stack first shown in Chapter 19. If you make the changes as indicated in this chapter, you'll have a To Do stack with a card for every day of the year. It's also a smart To Do List, because it automatically carries over unfinished items from the previous day. As a bonus, we throw in a script that makes cards for as many days as you like.

Overview

To make the changes to the old stack, start with a new stack cloned from the original one. When you're finished with the modifications in this chapter, the stack will look like the card shown in Figure 65–1. Start with the old stack by choosing New Stack from the File menu to copy the background from the earlier stack. Make sure you select the Copy Current Background button in the standard file dialog. Next delete the day letter buttons at the top. Following the field and button exposures of Figures 65-2 and 65–3 (and their captions), add fields and buttons to the background. You can re-use the M and W icon button art from before, but you'll need to create a D icon, in the same manner detailed in Chapter 19. Don't worry about the highlighting of the D, W, or M buttons. The scripts will take card of that.

A new feature added to this version is the ability to check off each item in a line. A narrow locked text field is placed to the left of each items column. When you click on the field at a particular line, a script places a check mark on that line of the narrow check-off field. For one field to handle the entire column requires a little math to measure the coordinates of a mouse click, but it's not too difficult to understand.

The only tricky part of this stack is a hidden field called Progress. It is a background field, whose content signifies whether today's To Do card has carried over unfinished items from the last day's card you worked with. An openCard handler in the background compares the current date with the date in the card's date field. If the card is for today, then the handler checks to see if the Progress field is empty. If it is, then it's time to perform the carry over procedure.

To create a hidden field, create it as a normal field. Most hidden fields don't have to be of any particular size or font, but since this field actually appears while unfinished items are carried over, it should be a style and font that stands out on the card, as shown in Figure 65–4.

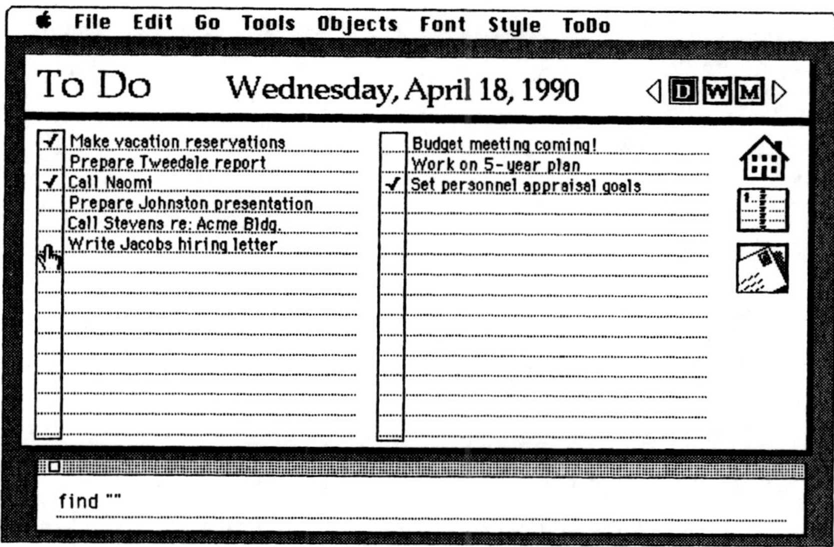

Figure 65–1. The new and improved To do list. With the help of HyperTalk scripts, the stack comes alive with automatic carryover of unfinished items, and a card for each day of the year, complete with multiple choices for navigation intervals.

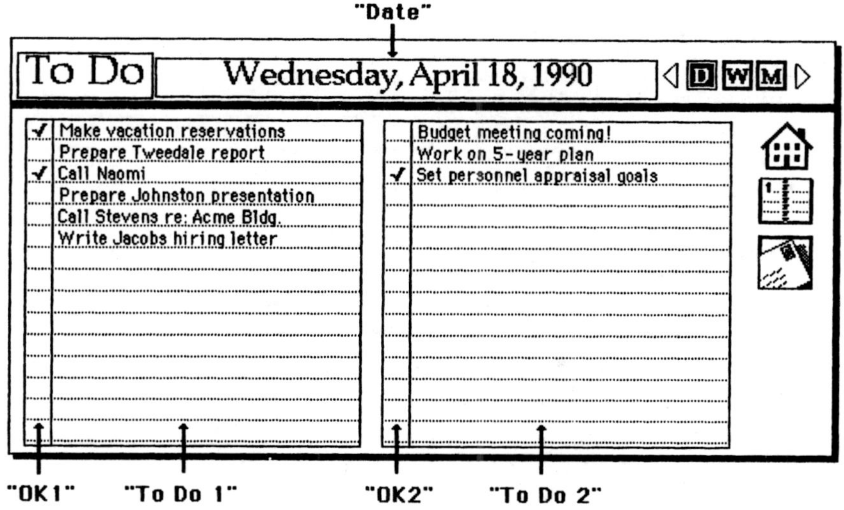

Figure 65–2. Fields referred to in the scripts. The "OK" fields are rectangle style with bold face text. Other than that, they have the same font properties as the "To Do" fields.

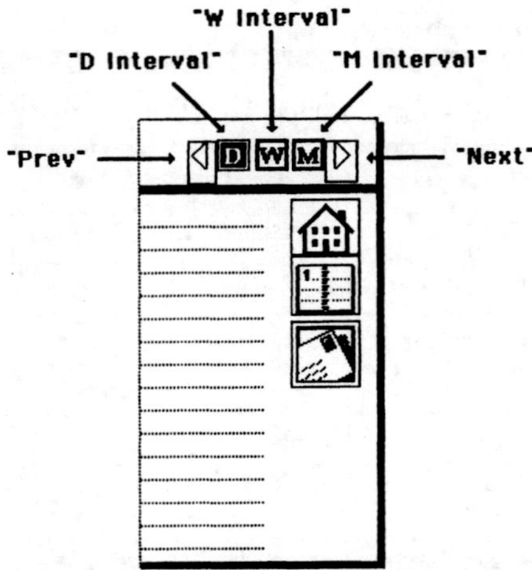

Figure 65–3. Navigation background buttons mentioned in script listings. The left and right arrows are icons that come with HyperCard. The irregular button size is due to icon placement in the resources. D, W, and M buttons are icons, like the daily buttons of the Chapter 19 To Do List stack.

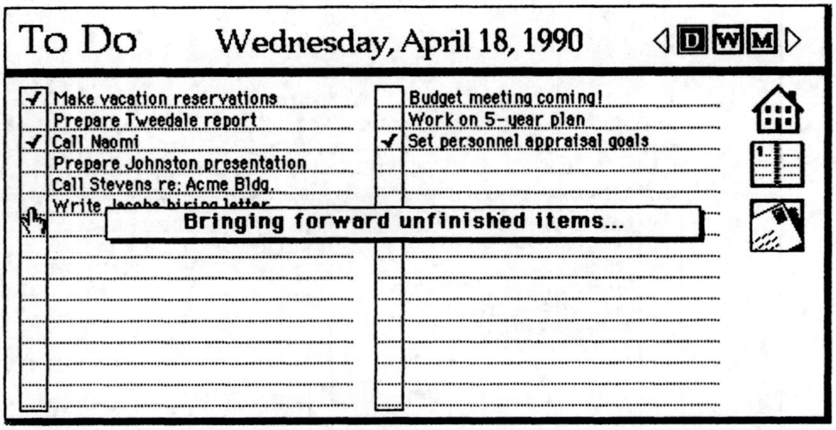

Figure 65–4. When carrying over unfinished items, the normally hidden "Progress" field lets the user know what's happening.

A separate menu for this stack offers three choices (Figure 65–5). The first choice, named Today, simply takes you to today's card, no matter where in the stack you might be. The second choice, Delete All Before, lets you delete a batch of old cards. When you choose this menu item, a dialog box prompts you to enter a date before which all cards should be deleted.

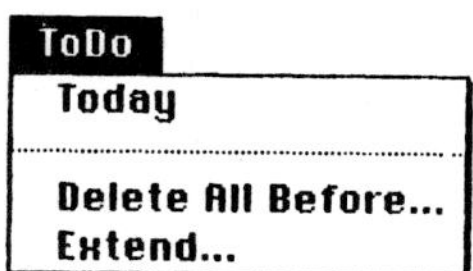

Figure 65–5. The extra menu is added in the setMenus handler, and removed upon closing or suspending the stack.

The last choice in the To Do menu, Extend, builds the stack's cards for you. If the stack is empty, then it builds cards from today's date to whatever end date you specify. After that, this menu command looks to see how far you've built the stack before, and begins adding cards after that date to whatever end date you like. As the script creates and dates each card, you see the action.

Once the stack is filled out with dated cards, the stack automatically goes to the current day's To Do card whenever you open the stack.

Pay special attention to the handlers in the To Do background script. All script action for this stack (other than menu-related action) is contained in the background script. That means that even all the button activity on a card is handled by the background script. This is starting to get a bit advanced, but you should see how it is done. The result is a remarkably compact application.

Scripts

In the stack script is the openStack handler, which sets an important global property and the menus. All menu message handlers and the closeStack handler (which deletes the To Do menu) are also in the stack script. The handlers in this application are more lengthy than other applications in this book, because they are meant to demonstrate a complete application that you could give to someone else. That means we've had to build in many error checking elements to make sure a user who didn't know much about HyperCard wouldn't be left in some mode that only an experienced HyperCard user would know how to escape from.

stack "My To Do List 2.0"

```
on openStack
    global interval
    setMenu
    put word 1 of short name of the selectedButton of bg family 1 into interval
    today
    pass openStack
end openStack
```

```
on resumeStack
    setMenu
end resumeStack

on closeStack
    deleteMenu
end closeStack

on suspendStack
    deleteMenu
end suspendStack

on setMenu
    create menu "ToDo"
    put "Today,-,Delete All Before...,Extend..." ¬
    into menu "ToDo" with menuMsgs "today,,deleteB4,extend"
end setMenu

on deleteMenu
    if there is a menu "ToDo"
    then delete menu "ToDo"
end deleteMenu
```

Comment: We add the menu items to a new menu, called ToDo (menu titles are best portrayed in the menubar as single words, even if the words must be contrived, like this one). Each menu item (other than the dividing line) has a menu message attached to it. Corresponding handlers are contained in the stack script (although they could be in the background script if you like—keeping stack-related items in the stack script make sense, however).

The Interval global variable is used in a background handler (skip) to determine which of the three navigation interval buttons, Day, Week, or Month, is highlighted. Upon opening the stack, we set the global by checking which of the three buttons is the selected button. Since we had assigned all three buttons to background family 1, this is a simple task with the selectedButton property. The interval value is extracted from the name of the highlighted button. Being associated with the same family, these buttons have their highlighting taken care of, as if they were radio buttons.

```
on today -- go to today's card
    find whole the long date
    if the result is not empty then
        answer "Cannot find today. Would you like to extend" &&¬
        "the stack?" with "No" or "Yes"
        if it is "Yes" then extend
    end if
end today
```

Comment: We use Find Whole here so that when the search is successful, the entire date is encircled by the rectangle. If we had used plain Find, only the first word of the date would be so highlighted upon a successful search. Notice here that we build some error checking to see whether the search was successful. If not, we assume the user may want to extend the stack. If they do, then script execution goes to the extend handler, below.

```
on deleteB4 -- delete cards before a certain date
    put the date into refDate
    convert refDate to dateItems
    put 1 into item 3 of refDate -- suggest 1st of current month
    convert refDate to short date
    ask "Delete all cards before what date?" with refDate
    set cursor to watch
    if it is not empty then
        put it into maxDate
        convert maxDate to seconds
        push card
        go to first card of bkgnd "To Do"
        repeat
            set cursor to busy
            if the mouse is down then exit repeat -- bail out
            get field "Date"
            convert it to seconds
            if it < maxDate then
                if number of cards of this bkgnd > 1
                then doMenu "Delete Card"
                else
                    repeat with x = 2 to number of bkgnd fields
                        put empty into field x
                    end repeat
                    exit repeat
                end if
            else exit repeat
        end repeat
        pop card into cardTest
        if cardTest contains "My To Do List 2.0" then go cardTest
        doMenu "Compact Stack"
    end if
end deleteB4
```

Comment: We begin by calculating a possible date before which the user would like to delete all cards. Our assumption is that the most likely date is the first day of the current month. Therefore, by substituting a value in the dateItems version of the date, we convert to a short date format of the first day of the current month. That date, in the local variable called refDate, is supplied as a possible date in the Ask dialog box. By being in the short date format, we also demonstrate a valid date format for the user.

Provided that the user has supplied some date (It is not empty), the response is assigned to the date before which all cards are to be deleted (maxDate). That value is in seconds to make for easy comparison against dates converted from each card's Date field. Then, starting with the first card of the background, the handler fetches the Date field, converts the value to seconds, and compares it against maxDate. If it's less than maxDate, then the card should be eliminated. As long as there are more than one card in the background, then it's a simple matter of deleting the card. Otherwise, we need to clear the fields, except for the shared background field (field number 1) which contains the "To Do" title. Therefore, a simple repeat loop puts empty into all fields except field 1.

Prior to going to the first card of the background, the handler pushed the current card. Since we'll probably want to go back to that card automatically once the old cards are deleted, we can usually pop the card. But, if the original card was one that was deleted in the process, that card is no longer pop-able—it was deleted from the queue of pushed cards. Therefore, we first pop whatever card is at the front of the push/pop queue to see whether it is in the current stack by popping the card into a variable and checking the contents of the variable. If the popped card isn't part of the current stack, then the Pop command is ignored, otherwise, we go to that card.

One last bit of cleanup work is to compact the stack. This is a good idea after adding or deleting a large number of objects, like cards.

```
on extend
   put (24*60*60) into oneDay -- number of seconds
   push card -- so we'll come back when finished
   go to last card of bkgnd "To Do"
   get field "Date"
   if it is empty then
      put the date into startDate
      convert startDate to seconds
   else
      put it into startDate
      convert startDate to seconds
      add oneDay to startDate -- start with next date
   end if

   convert startDate to short date
   ask "Extend To Do cards from" && startDate && "to:"
   set cursor to watch
   if it is empty then exit extend
   else
      put it into endDate
      if endDate is not a date
         answer "Sorry, invalid date. Use the date format: " && the short date & "."
         exit extend
      end if
   end if
```

```
        convert endDate to seconds
        convert startDate to seconds
        if endDate < startDate then
            answer "Ending date must be after starting date."
            exit extend
        end if

        put ((endDate - startDate) div oneDay) + 1 into cardCount
        repeat cardCount
            set cursor to busy
            if the mouse is down then exit repeat -- bail out
            if field "Date" is not empty -- dated card exists
            then doMenu "New Card"
            convert startDate to long date
            put startDate into field "Date"
            convert startDate to seconds
            add oneDay to startDate
        end repeat
        pop card -- return where we started
        doMenu "Compact Stack"
        beep -- let you know it's finished
    end extend
```

Comment: This long handler has lots of error checking in it. It starts by calculating the date with which it should start adding cards. If the stack is empty (i.e., the field Date is empty), then it starts by getting today's date from the Macintosh clock. If the stack has previously been built (and has a date in it's Date field), then we add one day to the counter so that the next card it builds is not the same as the last card's date.

Next, we temporarily convert the startDate variable to the short date format so we can make the date value part of the Ask command dialog. If the user enters anything into the dialog, then the handler performs a bit of a test for a valid entry. The test is by means of the Convert command. If the entry is not a valid date, then the Convert command returns a notice to that effect with the Result function afterward. This is not a foolproof system, since the Convert command can be fooled into thinking it has a valid date, when in fact the value is garbage. But without writing a more complex date validation handler or external command (XCMD), this will do for our purposes here. In any case, if the Result function indicates an error, an Answer dialog demonstrates the proper format for date entry with a copy of today's date in the short date format.

Another bit of error checking comes by making sure the specified end date is later than the starting date. To allow anything else would wreak havoc in the repeat loop that follows.

And speaking of repeat loops, we have to figure out how many cards to add to the end of the stack. The formula that evaluates to an integer for the variable cardCount, DIVs the number of seconds between start and end time by the number of seconds in a day. We then add 1 to it to include the last day of the specified range. The repeat loop, itself, cycles through the dates adding a new card (or filling in the first, blank card), converting the date to the long date format for display, converting back to seconds, and adding one day's seconds for the next time around the loop.

Because the process could take awhile for a big build on a slower Macintosh, we've built in a beep to let you know the job is done, along with a stack compaction for safety.

bkgnd "To Do"

```
on openCard
   if field "Date" = the long date and field "Progress" is empty
   then carryOver
end openCard
```

Comment: Every time a card opens, this handler checks to see if it is today's card. If so, and if the hidden Progress field is empty, then it executes the carryOver handler, below.

```
on mouseUp
   global interval -- contains either "D", "W", or "M"
   if "interval" is not in short name of the target
   then pass mouseUp
   put word 1 of short name of the selectedButton ¬
   of bg family 1 into interval -- just the letter
end mouseUp
```

Comment: This handler takes care of all three interval buttons. After reinitializing the global variable, this handler looks for a target name that contains the word *interval.* If the target doesn't contain that word, the mouseUp message is passed up the hierarchy (where it will not find any other handlers). The three buttons that set the D, W, and M interval are labeled *D Interval, W Interval,* and *M Interval,* respectively. The first word of the name (that is, the letter) goes into the global variable, interval. This variable is used in the skip handler.

```
on skip direction -- navigate by day, week, month
   global interval
   if interval is "D" or interval is "W" then
      get number of this card
      if interval is "D"
      then add direction to it
      else add direction*7 to it
```

```
            go card it
        else
            get field "Date"
            convert it to dateItems
            put (item 2 of it + direction) mod 13 into item 2 of it
            if item 2 of it = 0 then
                put (13 + direction) mod 13 into item 2 of it
                add direction to item 1 of it
            end if
            convert it to long date
            find (word 2 to 4 of it)
        end if
        if the result is not empty and direction is 1 then extend
    end skip
```

Comment: This handler performs the skipping back and ahead through the cards, depending on which interval you have selected. The direction parameter, passed by the left and right arrow buttons, is either -1 (back) or 1 (forward). When the interval variable is D, the direction is added to the number of the current card, and the handler issues a Go command to that card number; when interval is W, the direction times 7 (days in a week) is added to the current card number, and the Go command sends you to the previous or next week, depending on the direction.

Because the number of days in a month varies, you cannot simply add or subtract 30 days to the card and go there. You must invoke help from the date arithmetic facilities of HyperTalk. Starting with the date in the current card (it can work with the date parts in line 2 of the Date field), all necessary conversions are made, including accounting for the changeovers between years (when item 2 of dateItems is zero). Converting the new date back to the long date format, the handler then applies the Find command to locate the card matching words 2 to 4 of the long date.

In either the Go or Find methods, if the Result function returns any indication of failure, then the handler branches to the Extend handler to offer building of additional cards.

```
on checkOff colNum
    put ((the clickV - top of the target) div textHeight of the target) + 1 into lineNum
    if line lineNum of bkgnd field ("To Do" && colNum) is not empty then
        if line lineNum of bkgnd field ("OK" & colNum) is empty then
            put "√" into line lineNum of bkgnd field ("OK" & colNum)
        else
            put empty into line lineNum of background field ("OK" & colNum)
        end if
    end if
end checkOff
```

Comment: Clicking on the locked fields to the left of each itemized listing causes one of two messages to be sent, CheckOff 1 or CheckOff 2, depending on which column the user clicks. This handler takes care of those messages.

The first full line calculates the line number that should get the check mark. It starts with the vertical coordinate of the click location, and subtracts the top coordinate of the field, netting the actual number of pixels down the top of the field that the user clicked. Next that value is DIV'ed by the textHeight property of the field. We add 1 to make sure that the first line is not zero, as the previous calculations would lead us to believe. By specifying the various properties of the field in the formula, rather than hard-coding the actual pixel measurements on the screen, we have generalized this calculation for use in other instances or when this field is adjusted in location or font specifications later. The same code will work without modification.

When you click on the first line of the locked field, a 1 is put into the lineNum variable. Before worrying about checking or unchecking the line, the handler first makes sure that there is something in the To Do field for that line and column. If we didn't make this test, then the user could check and uncheck empty lines of the To Do fields, which wouldn't make much sense. If the clicked line of the locked field is empty, the handler places the checkmark (the character you get by pressing Option-V) on that line. If the line is not empty (meaning a check mark is already there), the mark is removed.

```
on carryOver
    set lockMessages to true
    set cursor to busy
    put "Bringing forward unfinished items..." into field "Progress"
    show field "Progress"
    lock screen
    repeat until number of this card = 1
        set cursor to busy
        go prev card
        if field "Progress" is not empty
        then exit repeat
    end repeat

    put empty into carry1 -- temporary holder for col. 1 data
    put empty into carry2 -- temporary holder for col. 2 data
    put "To Do 1" into toDo1 -- one word field name equivalent
    put "To Do 2" into toDo2 -- one word field name equivalent
    repeat until field "Date" is the long date
        repeat with x = 1 to 2 -- columns 1 and 2
            repeat with y = 1 to number of lines of field ("To Do" && x)
                set cursor to busy
```

```
                if line y of field ("OK" & x) is empty ¬
                and line y of field ("To Do" && x) is not empty
                then
                    do "put line y of field toDo" & x & "& return after carry" & x
                end if
            end repeat
        end repeat
        go to next card
    end repeat

    put carry1 after field "To Do 1"
    put carry2 after field "To Do 2"
    hide field "Progress"
end carryOver
```

Comment: The carryOver handler must look back from today's card and find the last time data was carried over. This will be the nearest card whose Progress field has the indication from the previous carry over. Then the handler must sweep up all the unchecked items in every card from that day to the current day, and display those items in their respective lists in fields To Do 1 and To Do 2.

The handler starts by setting lockMessages to true. This halts all open- and close-object handlers that might impede progress as we dash backward in time and then forward. To show the user something is in fact happening, the Progress field gets some informative text and is displayed. We'll leave this text here as the marker for the next carryOver handler execution to check. We also lock the screen so the user doesn't see all the card flipping we do in the rest of the handler (it also goes faster when not refreshing the screen).

The first repeat loop works backward until it finds something in the Progress field. This is the card from which to start the carrying over process. Thus, we set local variables carry1 and carry2 to empty, and place the full field names of the two columns of data into single local variable names. We do the latter to aid us in executing a HyperTalk statement with the Do keyword.

The main repeat construction here is a series of three nested repeat loops. The outer loop counts us through the cards from the starting point to today's card. Inside that loop is a counter that makes sure we perform the extraction of data on both the left and right column fields. For each line of each To Do field, we check to make sure that the locked OK field for that column (either "OK1" or "OK2") is empty (i.e., has no checkmark in it) and that the line of the To Do field is not empty (i.e., contains some to do item). If so, then we add the line from the To Do field plus a return character to the local variable carry1 or carry2, whichever one is appropriate for the To Do field being examined. We must use a Do keyword to carry this out in a repeat loop when we use the value of the repeat loop counter (x) as an indexed value for the local variable (carry & x).

As we move from card to card, the carry1 and carry2 variables accumulate the text of unfinished items. Since we finally reach today's card (as the exit point of the outer repeat loop of the big repeat construction), we put the contents of those variables after fields To Do 1 and To Do 2 (we use "after" in case other items are already in those fields). Finally, we hide the Progress field, with its contents intact. This card will then be the starting point for the next time items need to be carried over.

bkgnd "To Do", field "OK1"—left side locked field to check off finished items

```
on mouseUp
    checkOff 1
end mouseUp
```

bkgnd "To Do", field "OK2"—right side locked field to check off finished items

```
on mouseUp
    checkOff 2
end mouseUp
```

bkgnd "To Do", button "Next"—right facing arrow

```
on mouseUp
    skip 1
end mouseUp
```

bkgnd "To Do", button "Prev"—left facing arrow

```
on mouseUp
    skip -1
end mouseUp
```

Further Ideas

If you plan to keep a To Do file open for more than a couple of years, you may wish to add a Y button to the card and a yearly interval routine to the script. Another handler could sort the items in the lists according to a priority number you assign to each item.

Also, don't forget the powers of printing reports supplied in HyperCard. You may wish to specify one or more report formats to take your To Do lists with you when you leave your Macintosh.

CHAPTER

66

MULTI-USER DATABASE ACCESS

The application in this chapter joins HyperCard 2.2 with FileMaker Pro via AppleScript. It is meant not as an example of a finished stack, but as a workshop for those interested in controlling programs such as FileMaker via AppleScript. It demonstrates a number of techniques used to extract data from a multi-user database file (the FileMaker Pro file), keep a multi-user database and displayed HyperCard record in synch, select records from a database file, and enter a new record into a database file.

The Scenario

We start first with the database. Figure 66–1 shows the field layout of the database—a straightforward name-and-address database consisting of a layout with eight fields. Importantly, it was setup within FileMaker to be a Multi-User file by choosing Multi-User from the File menu within FileMaker Pro. While there is one copy of the file on the network, others may access the file through their own copy of FileMaker Pro.

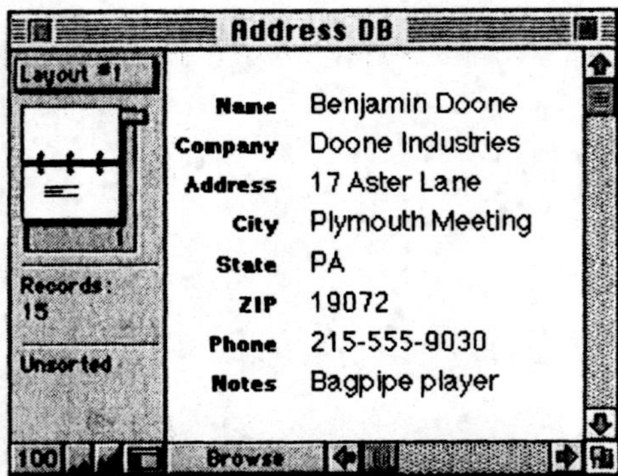

Figure 66–1. The FileMaker Pro side of this solution.

In this example, the HyperCard stack mimics the entire field layout of the FileMaker Pro database (Figure 66–2). In practice, it is more likely that such a stack would display only a subset of fields from the database file; or it may show additional data from either another file or from a document in yet a different application also running at the same time.

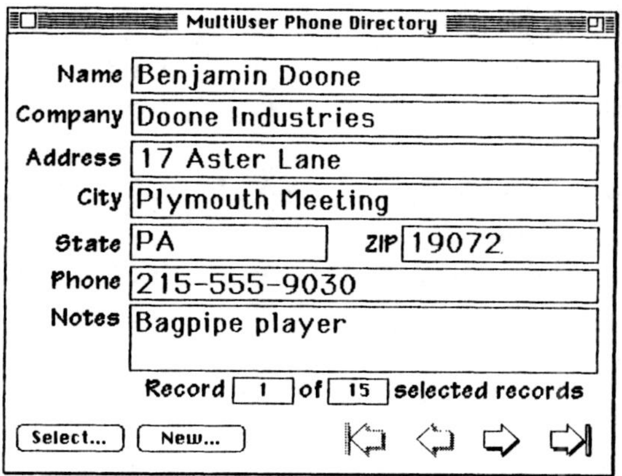

Figure 66–2. The HyperCard client stack.

Stack Structure

Because all the data is stored in the FileMaker file, and not HyperCard, this stack consists of only three cards:

- Data viewer and editor (Figure 66–2)
- New record creator (Figure 66–3)
- Record selector

Most of the action takes place in the first card, where records are browsed and edited. Buttons on this card lead to each of the other two for their special purposes. All cards have the same field layout, with field names and numbers mapping identically to those in the FileMaker database file.

HyperCard-FileMaker Interaction

The stack communicates quite a bit with FileMaker and this database file. Let's look at the various actions that trigger this communication.

First, when the stack opens, it opens the database file if it isn't already open (although things run more smoothly if FileMaker is already opened to the file when the stack opens). The stack then reads the first record from the database, and inserts that data into the data viewing card. It also fills in some other data, such as the total number of records, and hidden data that the stack uses later.

As the user clicks on one of the navigation buttons, the stack reads the appropriate record (first, previous, next, or last) from the database file, and inserts that data into the cards fields. The record number and the hidden fields are updated accordingly.

Making a change to any field triggers a closeField message which writes the updated information from that field to the database file. At the same time, an idle handler compares the data in the viewer card against the corresponding record in the database file. If there are any discrepancies because a record has been updated by another user on the network, the new data is placed into the viewer card.

To add a new record, the user navigates to the appropriate card (Figure 66–3), where the fields may be filled in. When the record is complete, a click of the Add New button inserts the new record into the FileMaker database.

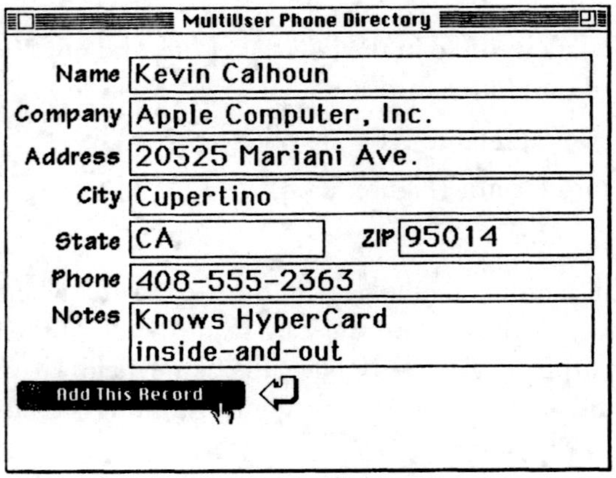

Figure 66–3. The New Record card.

The Selection card was designed to mimic the operation of a FileMaker database file. It presents the same fields as the data file. The user enters into one field the information it wants FileMaker to use in its selection of a subset of records. A click of the Select button sends the appropriate commands to FileMaker to single out only those records that meet the criterion. Alternatively, the user may have FileMaker select all records in the data file.

Upon returning to the viewing card, the number of selected records appears in its appropriate field. In the FileMaker file, this user (among as many as may be accessing the file on the network) has only those selected records available for ready viewing. As it turns out, each user may have a completely different set of selected records at the same time, some of which overlap with other users.

AppleScript and FileMaker Record Locking

FileMaker Pro provides record locking for its multi-user database files. In other words, while one user is updating a record, no other user may modify that record. A message goes out saying that the record cannot be edited at that time.

Things change, however, when the multi-user file is accessed by multiple users via AppleScript. Because a FileMaker field is never officially open to accomplish changes sent via scripting, no one is ever locked out from sending updated information to a record. Literally two users could update separate field data in the same record at the same time. In this HyperCard stack solution, the idle handler keeps checking the contents of the currently viewed record against its copy in the FileMaker database. Thus, immediately after the two people make changes to different fields, the changes are reflected on both users' screens. If both were modifying the same field, the user making the last change wins.

The Scripts

Now we present the scripts for the stack and its objects. Some scripts are in HyperTalk, others in AppleScript.

stack "MultiUser Phone Directory" (Scripting Language: AppleScript)

```
on openStack
    getFirstRecord
    tell application "HyperCard" to copy (seconds) to variable "lastCheck"
    copy 1 to card field "Record Number" of card 1
    enableBtns("Next", "Last")
    disableBtns("Prev", "First")
end openStack
```

Comment: Upon opening the stack, we extract the first record of the database (described next), put a 1 into the Record Number field, initialize a HyperTalk global variable that is used elsewhere as a timer between synchronizing checks, enable the Next and Last arrow buttons, and disable the First and Prev arrow buttons (we're at the first record, so the user shouldn't be able to navigate to anything less than the first record).

```
on getFirstRecord
    tell application "FileMaker Pro"
        if not (Exists Database "Address DB") then
            Open file "Address DB"
            Show every Record
        end if
        get Record 1
        tell me to plugData(result)
        set recordCount to Count Layout 1 class Record
        tell Application "HyperCard" to copy recordCount ¬
            to card field "Layout Total" of card 1
    end tell
end getFirstRecord
```

Comment: This handler, called by the openStack handler, makes sure that FileMaker and the database file are open. It also starts the session by telling FileMaker that this user wants to have all records selected. Next, it gets the data from the first record and passes it to another handler (described next), which is the generic one used throughout this stack to distribute data from the database into the HyperCard fields. To fill out the final field of the card, which says how many selected records are available to the user, the script gets the total number of records in the database's first layout (there is only one layout in this database), and then directs HyperCard to put that value into the Layout Total field. Alternatively, we could have ended the FileMaker tell statement one line sooner, and merely copied the recordCount data to the field—the default object would have been HyperCard, so we wouldn't have had to tell it specifically.

```
on plugData(theData)
    copy AppleScript's Item Delimiters to oldDelims
    set AppleScript's Item Delimiters to tab
    repeat with i from 1 to count of text items of theData
        copy text item i of theData to field i of card 1
    end repeat
    copy theData to field "Raw Data" of card 1
    set AppleScript's Item Delimiters to oldDelims
end plugData
```

Comment: Statements in this handler are all directed to HyperCard by default, except for the calls to AppleScript to massage its Item Delimiters property. The data passed in from the database is in the form of a tab-delimited record, so we need to extract each item and copy it into the corresponding field in the card. We use an indexed repeat loop for the task. If you wanted only some of the fields to go into the card, it would require a slightly more detailed working to get those items into the desired fields—perhaps copying a numbered text item of data into a named field. Before restoring AppleScript's Item Delimiters property, we also store a raw copy of the incoming data into a hidden field. We'll use this later for comparison against the current FileMaker record to see if there have been any changes since the last time we checked (five seconds earlier).

```
on updateIndexCount(indexCount)
    copy indexCount to card field "Record Number" of card 1
end updateIndexCount
```

Comment: This handler is shared by the four arrow button scripts. Those buttons (described below) obtain some other record from the database, after which they pass the number of the current record to this handler for input into the displayed Record Number field.

```
on disableBtns(btn1, btn2)
    tell application "HyperCard"
        set enabled of card button btn1 to false
        set enabled of card button btn2 to false
    end tell
end disableBtns

on enableBtns(btn1, btn2)
    tell application "HyperCard"
        set enabled of card button btn1 to true
        set enabled of card button btn2 to true
    end tell
end enableBtns
```

Comment: A couple user interface-oriented handlers serve as general-purpose button enablers and disablers. Other scripts within this stack monitor whether the current record is the first or last record. If it is the first record, for example, then the script calls the disableBtns handler, passing the names of the First and Prev buttons for disabling. The user won't be able to click on those buttons.

```
on writeField(newData, fieldName, recordNumber)
    tell application "FileMaker Pro"
        Set Data of Cell fieldName of Record (recordNumber as integer) to newData
    end tell
end writeField
```

Comment: Sending new data to FileMaker is a job for AppleScript, yet the closeField handler that triggers the action is in the HyperTalk-based card script (below). The closeField handler calls this writeField handler in this AppleScript-based stack script, passing all requisite parameters of the new field data, name of the destination field, and the record number. Examine the closeField handler, below, to see how the parameters are sent in HyperTalk format, but received here in AppleScript format (in parentheses).

```
on checkForUpdate
    if (selectedField of application "HyperCard") = "" then
        copy card field "Record Number" of card 1 to recNum
        copy field "Raw Data" of card 1 to rawData
        tell application "FileMaker Pro"
            Get Data of Record (recNum as integer)
            copy result to currentData
            if currentData ≠ rawData then
                tell me to plugData(currentData)
            end if
            set recordCount to Count Layout 1 class Record
            tell Application "HyperCard" to copy recordCount ¬
                to card field "Layout Total" of card 1
        end tell
    end if
end checkForUpdate
```

Comment: Whenever the idle handler (in the first card's script) says it's time to compare records, it calls this handler. The first if-then statement tests whether the user is editing a field. In HyperTalk, the selectedField property returns a field identifier whenever a field has a text insertion pointer in it. But when that value is empty, it means that no field is being edited, so it's safe to tie up the Mac for a moment to compare records.

The first tasks entail grabbing some field data, such as the number of the record currently shown in the card, plus the raw data for that record. Then we head over to FileMaker, where the script gets the database record for the same record showing in the HyperCard card. If the two don't match, then we call plugData of our own script (thus the "tell me") to update our card. This is in case some other user has modified information in this record. Finally, we also double-check the total number of records in the database (whether or not the current record changed), and place its value into the visible field showing the total number of records. This is important in case another user has added a record to the database.

card "Browse Record" (Scripting Language: HyperTalk)

```
on closeField
    put target into newData
    put short name of target into fldName
    writeField newData,fldName,card fld "Record Number"
end closeField
```

Comment: Closing a field means the user has made a change to information in one of them. This one handler takes card of the updating task for all fields on the card. It uses the target keyword to extract both the data and the field name. Then it passes those bits of information plus the record number to the writeField AppleScript handler in the stack script. Parameters on this end of the transaction are in HyperTalk format.

```
on idle
    global lastCheck
    if not (the suspended) and the seconds - lastCheck > 5 then
        checkForUpdate
        put the seconds into lastCheck
    else pass idle
end idle
```

Comment: While a user views this card, this idle handler sends the checkForUpdate message to the AppleScript-based handler in the stack script. This happens only every five seconds (the value can be changed, of course) and only when the stack is the active stack in an active HyperCard. Therefore, when not the frontmost stack and application, we don't tie up the Mac processing or network traffic with synchronization calls.

card "Browse Record", button "First" (Scripting Language: AppleScript)

```
on mouseUp
    tell application "HyperCard" to set cursor to watch
    tell application "FileMaker Pro"
        set indexCount to 1
        Get Data Record indexCount
        copy result to theData
    end tell

    tell Application "HyperCard"
        lock screen
        enableBtns("Next", "Last")
        plugData(theData)
        updateIndexCount(indexCount)
        disableBtns("Prev", "First")
        unlock screen
    end tell
end mouseUp
```

Comment: Clicking this button retrieves the first of the selected records in the FileMaker database. HyperCard does the rest, with screen locked for speed and visual integrity. The four inner commands call handlers discussed above.

card "Browse Record", button "Prev" (Scripting Language: AppleScript)

```
on mouseUp
    tell application "HyperCard" to set cursor to "watch"
    copy card field "Record Number" to indexCount
    set indexCount to indexCount - 1

    tell application "FileMaker Pro"
        if Exists Record indexCount then
            Get Data Record indexCount
            copy result to theData
            tell Application "HyperCard"
                lock screen
                enableBtns("Next", "Last")
```

```
                plugData(theData)
                updateIndexCount(indexCount)
                if indexCount = 1 then
                    disableBtns("Prev", "First")
                end if
                unlock screen
            end tell
        end if
    end tell
end mouseUp
```

Comment: A little more action is required to get the previous record. We start with the Record Number field value and decrease it by one. Next we find out if such a record exists in the FileMaker database. If so, then we get the record and perform the rest of the work inside HyperCard. Notice that we nest the HyperCard Tell statement inside the FileMaker one. This is necessary (and perfectly acceptable) because we don't want that stuff to execute unless a FileMaker condition is met.

card "Browse Record", button "Next" (Scripting Language: AppleScript)

```
on mouseUp
    tell application "HyperCard" to set cursor to "watch"
    copy card field "Record Number" to indexCount
    set indexCount to indexCount + 1
    tell application "FileMaker Pro"
        if Exists Record indexCount then
            copy (Count Layout 1 class Record) to totalRecords
            Get Data Record indexCount
            copy result to theData
            tell Application "HyperCard"
                lock screen
                enableBtns("Prev", "First")
                plugData(theData)
                updateIndexCount(indexCount)
                if indexCount = totalRecords then
                    disableBtns("Next", "Last")
                end if
                unlock screen
            end tell
        end if
    end tell
end mouseUp
```

Comment: Just like the "Prev" button, but the record number is incremented by one.

card "Browse Record", button "Last" (Scripting Language: AppleScript)

```
on mouseUp
    tell application "HyperCard" to set cursor to "watch"
    tell application "FileMaker Pro"
        set indexCount to Count Layout 1 class Record
        Get Data Record indexCount
```

```
        copy result to theData
    end tell

    tell application "HyperCard"
        lock screen
        enableBtns("First", "Prev")
        plugData(theData)
        updateIndexCount(indexCount)
        disableBtns("Next", "Last")
        unlock screen
    end tell
end mouseUp
```

Comment: Very much like the "First" button, but it uses the total number of records in the layout as the counter to get to the record.

card "Browse Record", button "Select..." (Scripting Language: HyperTalk)

```
on mouseUp
    go to card "Search"
end mouseUp
```

card "Browse Record", button "New..." (Scripting Language: HyperTalk)

```
on mouseUp
    go to card "New Record"
    select text of bg fld 1 -- put text pointer into first field for user
end mouseUp
```

card "New Record", button "Add This Record" (Scripting Language: AppleScript)

```
on mouseUp
    if field "Name" is "" and field "Company" is "" then
        display dialog "You need at least a Name or Company for a record."
    else
        tell application "HyperCard" to set cursor to "watch"
        copy "" to newData
        repeat with i from 1 to 8
            if newData ≠ "" then
                set newData to newData & tab & field i of card 2
            else
                set newData to field i of card 2
            end if
        end repeat

        tell application "FileMaker Pro"
            Create new Record with data newData
            set recordCount to Count Layout 1 class Record
        end tell
```

```
        copy recordCount to card field "Layout Total" of card 1
        lock screen
        repeat with i from 1 to 8
            copy "" to field i of card 2
        end repeat
    end if
end mouseUp
```

Comment: Although this looks to be a long handler, it isn't very complex. This is the button users click to add a record (entered into the fields) to the FileMaker database. We perform a little bit of error checking as an example —saying that we want the database record to contain either a name or company name. If that condition is met, then we set HyperCard's cursor to the watch and begin pre-processing the data.

Because we'll be appending data to a variable, we initialize the variable with an empty string. Then we go through all eight fields and assemble a tab-delimited record. The only distinction we make among the records is for the first record. Due to AppleScript's string concatenation form (in which you set the variable to the original variable plus some additional text), we append only the data for the first record; for each additional record we append the delimiting tab and the next record. This leaves our complete recording ending in something other than a tab.

With the data assembled, we call upon FileMaker to create a new record. After that, we get a count of the records in the current selection, so we can update the Total Records field in the first card. Finally, we lock the screen and clear all fields of data so we don't accidentally create a duplicate record by clicking the button again.

card "New Record", button "Go Back" (Scripting Language: HyperTalk)

```
on mouseUp
    go to card "Browse Record"
end mouseUp
```

card "New Record", button "Search" (Scripting Language: HyperTalk)

```
on enterKey
    send mouseUp to cd btn "Select"
end enterKey
```

Comment: The lone handler in the Search card's script is the one that traps for the Enter key to trigger the Select button, which is a default style button.

card "Search", button "Select" (Scripting Language: AppleScript)

```
on mouseUp
    set allFields to {"Name", "Company", "Address", ¬
        "City", "State", "ZIP", "Phone", "Notes"}
    set searchFields to {}
    set searchStrings to {}

    repeat with i from 1 to 8
        if field i of card 3 ≠ "" then
            set searchFields to searchFields & (item i of allFields)
            set searchStrings to searchStrings & field i of card 3
        end if
    end repeat

    if searchFields = {} then
        display dialog "No search specifications were entered. Try again."
    else
        tell application "FileMaker Pro"
            Show (every Record where Cell (item 1 of searchFields) ¬
                contains item 1 of searchStrings)
            set matchCount to Count Database 1 class Record
            if matchCount = 0 then
                display dialog "No matches were found."
            else
                tell Application "HyperCard"
                    go card 1
                    openStack
                end tell
            end if
        end tell
    end if
end mouseUp
```

Comment: Users click this button to have FileMaker select a subset of records based on selection criteria typed into a field in the form. The handler begins by initializing some variables. The first, allFields, contains an AppleScript list of names for all fields in the database. We'll use this later to help construct the selection criteria. Two other variables are initialized as empty lists, to which we will be appending items.

A repeat loop cycles through all fields on the Search card, and begins filling in the names of the search fields and the text entered by the user. While this example shows you how to gather and assemble multiple fields of data into these variables, the actual search, below, is performed only on the first field to contain any data.

Before we head off to FileMaker, we make sure there is something to search for. If so, we command FileMaker to show all records meeting our search criteria (based on the first field containing a matching string and its data). FileMaker can then give us the number of selected records. If no records match, then we alert the user so he or she can specify other criteria. Otherwise, we head for the data viewing card and send an openStack message to set us up as if we were coming into the stack from fresh. But since the database file is already open, it won't select every record (in the getFirstRecord handler)—only the selected records are visible.

card "Search", button "Go Back" (Scripting Language: HyperTalk)

```
on mouseUp
    go to card "Browse Record"
end mouseUp
```

card "Search", button "Select All" (Scripting Language: AppleScript)

```
on mouseUp
    tell application "FileMaker Pro"
        Show every Record
        tell Application "HyperCard"
            go card 1
            openStack
        end tell
    end tell
end mouseUp
```

Comment: This simple handler commands FileMaker to select all records in the database file. We then go back to the viewing card and see the first record.

Further Ideas

This example stack only scratches the surface with the kinds of links you can create between a HyperCard stack and documents from a variety of applications. Perhaps the most important point to remember is to keep an open mind about mixing HyperTalk and AppleScript in various objects in a stack. As with developing any application, sketch and dream about the ideal solution first—then figure out how to accomplish it with the tools you have.

A Final Note

If you have worked your way through this book one page at a time, you are to be congratulated for having the desire and perseverance to learn HyperCard inside out. We hope that in the spirit of HyperCard's creator, Bill Atkinson, you will share your experiences with others. Most importantly, we hope HyperCard unlocks your imagination to create new uses for the Macintosh in areas we haven't yet dreamed.

APPENDIX

A

WHAT'S NEW IN HYPERCARD 2.2

Improvements to HyperCard in version 2.2 are broadbased. Some are as subtle as user interface refinements, while others enhance HyperCard's reach across other applications. In this chapter, we highlight the new features of HyperCard 2.2, and point you to discussions elsewhere in the book for the details.

WorldScript Compatibility

With the release of System 7.1, Apple began delivering a technology that makes it possible for program developers (like the HyperCard team) to allow users of multiple languages—especially combinations of Roman and non-Roman languages—to mix the language scripts (i.e., sets of characters) in the same fields. Therefore, a field may contain both Kanji characters and English. HyperCard supports this feature transparently, although it will primarily be users in countries other than the U.S. that will even notice.

Open Scripting Architecture Support (Chapter 56)

Many more times more flexible and powerful than the simple Apple event support introduced with HyperCard version 2.1 (Chapter 55), Open Scripting Architecture (OSA), is another Apple-based technology that facilitates programs working with each other. The vehicle is user scripting, in the form of system-level scripting languages that work with OSA. AppleScript, which comes with HyperCard 2.2, is one of those languages. HyperTalk and AppleScript scripts can coexist in the same stack (although in different objects).

Standalone Stack Builder (Chapter 57)

As simply as saving a copy of a stack, you may turn your HyperCard 2.2 stacks into standalone, double-clickable applications that don't require HyperCard or the HyperCard Player to run. The feature is royalty-free for everyone.

Improved Object Layer Control (Chapters10, 11, 36)

Buttons and fields are also now known by their part numbers within the card and background domains. Therefore, you can specify the precise order of each part within the domain. Under script control, you can also assign an object to a specific layer with a single call, instead of sending up or back through the heap of other layers.

New Button and Field Info Dialogs (Chapters 10, 11)

Both info dialogs for buttons and fields received a major facelift. Previously long lists of radio buttons have been replaced by popup menus. Both display a preview of the object based on the currently selected choices in the dialog.

Standard Buttons (Chapters 11, 36)

Four new button styles let authors create user interfaces that more closely resemble Macintosh applications. The styles include standard rounded rectangle buttons, default rounded rectangle buttons (like highlighted OK buttons in dialogs), oval buttons, and popup buttons to create popup menus.

Buttons As Containers (Chapter 11, 36)

While the popup buttons require the ability to store information for the items to be displayed in the popup, any button may hold text data. This obviates using tricks such as storing data in a button's script.

Disabling Buttons (Chapter 36)

Buttons now contain a property that lets them be disabled either manually via the button's info dialog, or via a script. A disabled button is dimmed on the screen, like any disabled Macintosh button.

Radio Button Families (Chapters 11, 36)

By assigning a group of radio buttons to a family (done easily in the button's info dialog), HyperCard now handles the highlighting and unhighlighting of related buttons. A single function reveals which button of the family is currently selected, eliminating the need for repeat loops to find the highlighted button.

List Fields (Chapter 10, 36)

A new property, autoSelect, lets you turn any field into a list field—one that automatically selects a line clicked by the user. Unlike other scripted schemes for highlighting a clicked line in a field, these highlighted lines are independent of any other field or button highlighting that takes place on a card. A related property allows multiple, contiguous line selections. New functions (which behave more like field properties) let you extract the line number of the selection or the selected text itself.

Deletion Undo

Accidental deletion of buttons or fields may be undone.

Card Sizes (Chapter 6)

Card window sizes include a 640-by-400 size for most PowerBook screens. The 9" monochrome size is now called Classic.

New Visual Effects (Chapters 9, 36)

Four variations of a Push visual effect add to the existing library of effects.

MouseDoubleClick Message (Chapter 22)

HyperCard now sends a mouseDoubleClick message whenever it detects a control-panel-speed double-click on a single object.

Modal Dialogs Now Movable

Virtually every dialog box you use as a HyperCard author is now draggable while it is displayed. Therefore, if necessary, you can move a window to see the card beneath it to help make choices in the dialog.

Report Printing (Chapter 4, 34)

New choices for each report item include up to four side borders for the field and inverted (black-to-white and vice versa) printing within the field. Also, the previously undocumented feature of precision adjustment of report items is now a clearly visible checkbox in the Print Report dialog. Report formats may now be copied by HyperTalk with the Copy command.

RAM Partition (Chapter 1)

A minimum of 800K is now recommended, but 1M is a much more comfortable memory space for basic HyperCard operations.

Balloon Help

Many menu and dialog items have the benefit of Ballon Help in System 7.

Message Box Improvements

Font, size, and style of the Message Box are adjustable through the Font and Style menus. Style changes affect the entire Message Box. Typing Command-A selects all text in the Message Box.

There Is Operator (Chapter 44)

The There Is A operator's scope has increased to be able to look for external windows, card and background pictures, scripting language installation in the System, applications, documents, files, and disk volumes.

Sorting Container Contents by Key (Chapter 29)

You may now specify a key within a sortable container, such as the second item or last word. This goes not only for lines of a container, but items as well.

Convert Command (Chapter 28)

You can let the Convert command perform a modicum of data validation by requesting that the source date or time be in a specific format.

DoMenu with Modifier Keys (Chapter 33)

Scripts may now perform the equivalent action of choosing a menu item while holding down the Command, Shift, or Option keys.

Searching International Characters (Chapter 3, 29)

All Find command variations now allow the inclusion of the International specification. This turns off HyperCard's default behavior of converting non-English characters to their English equivalents (e.g, "ç" is regarded and searched as "c").

More Locking (Chapter 30)

The Lock and Unlock commands accept Recent to adjust that property more directly via command than setting the property.

Reading and Writing Files (Chapter 32)

Both the Read From File and Write To File commands allow parameters specifying a negative offset from the end of the file. Rather than calculate the length of a file and a positive starting point, you can read from or write to a position -n from the end of the file. Also, HyperCard no longer has a 16K limit to reading chunks of data from a file.

Destination Function (Chapter 43)

HyperCard knows the name of the stack to which it is about to navigate. Retrieving the Destination function in a closeCard handler lets you determine whether the user is headed to another stack in your multiple-stack system (and thus you don't have to reset the menubar or stop using stacks).

DiskSpace Function (Chapter 42)

A new function lets you establish the amount of available space on any disk mounted on the Desktop.

Sum Function (Chapter 41)

A single function returns the total of all values in a comma-delimited list of parameters.

Phone Dialing Properties (Chapter 36)

Two new properties, dialingVolume and dialingTime, provide additional control over audio and modem dialing, respectively.

Environment Property (Chapter 36)

A script may now check the Environment property to determine whether the stack is being run in a development version of HyperCard of one of the locked down versions (HyperCard Player or standalone stack).

Menubar Rect (Chapter 36)

The menubar has a new Rect property, which a script may use to determine the space occupied by the menubar (and therefore whether any point may be within that rectangle).

Bug Fixes

The HyperCard team had been assembling a list of bugs reported by users for years prior to the release of version 2.2. This release reflects the greatest effort thus far to eliminate known bugs.

APPENDIX B

SOURCE LIST

Adobe Systems, Inc.
1585 Charleston Rd.
Mountain View, CA 94039-7900

Aldus Corp
411 First Ave. South
Seattle, WA 98104

APDA
20525 Mariani Avenue
MS: 33-G
Cupertino, CA 95014

Articulate Systems
6500 W. Cummings Park
Woburn, MA 01801

Caere Corp.
100 Cooper Court
Los Gatos, CA 95030

Canon USA, Inc.
One Canon Plaza
Lake Success, NY 11042-1113

CE Software, Inc.
1801 Industrial Circle
P.O. Box 65580
West Des Moines, IA 50265

Chang Laboratories, Inc.
10228 N. Stelling Rd.
Cupertino, CA 95014

Claris Corp.
5201 Patrick Henry Dr.
Santa Clara, CA 95052-8168

CompuServe Inc.
5000 Arlington Centre Blvd.
Columbus, OH 43220

DCA
1000 Alderman Dr.
Alpharetta, GA 30201

Electronic Arts
1450 Fashion Island Blvd.
San Mateo, CA 94404

Flash-It
Nobu Toge
P.O. Box 7114
Menlo Park, CA 94026

Full Moon Software, Inc.
P.O. Box 700237
San Jose, CA 95170-0237

Heizer Software, Inc.
1941 Oak Park Blvd.
Pleasant Hill, CA 94523

Macromedia, Inc.
600 Townsend St.
San Francisco, CA 94103

Microsoft Corporation
16011 N.E. 36th Way
Redmond, WA 98073

Nine to Five Software Company, Inc.
3360 Mitchell Lane, Suite 105
Boulder, CO 80301

Opcode Systems, Inc.
3950 Fabian Way
Palo Alto, CA 94303

Random House Electronic Publishing
201 E. 50th Street
New York, NY 10022

Softstream International Inc.
10 Twin Ponds Road
S. Dartmouth, MA 02748

Sophisticated Circuits, Inc.
19017 120th Ave., NE
Suite 106
Bothell, WA 98011

System Technology Corp.
1860 Fern Palm Drive
Edgewater, FL 32141

Userland Software, Inc.
400 Seaport Ct.
Redwood City, CA 94063

The Voyager Company
1351 Pacific Coast Highway
Santa Monica, CA 90401

APPENDIX C

HYPERTALK 2.2 QUICK REFERENCE

Commands and Keywords

add	<numeric expr> to <container>	(520)
answer	<question> [with <reply> [or <reply> [or <reply>]]]	(549)
answer	file <prompt> [of type <file type>]	(588)
answer	program <prompt>	(968)
ask	<question> [with <reply>]	(551)
ask	file <prompt> [with <default>]	(590)
ask	password [clear] <prompt> [with <reply>]	(551)
beep	[<num of beeps>]	(512)
choose	<toolname> tool	(504)
choose	tool <num>	(504)
click	at <point> [with <mod. key1>[,<key2> [,<key3>]]]	(506)
close	[<document> in|with] <application>	(488)
close	file <file name>	(586)
close	printing	(622)
convert	<date expr> [from <date format> [and <date format>]] ¬ to <date format>	(525)
create	<menu expr>	(605)
create	stack <stack expr> [with <bkgnd expr>] [in [a] ¬ new window]	(581)
debug	checkpoint	(640)
delete	<chunk expr> of <container>	(496)
delete	[<menuItemExpr> of | from] <menuExpr>	(605)
dial	<phone num> [with [modem] <modem commands>]	(500)
disable	[<menuItemExpr> of] <menuExpr>	(616)
divide	<container> by <numeric expr>	(524)
do	<HyperTalk statements>	(636)
doMenu	<menu item> [,<menu name>] [without dialog] ¬ [with <mod. key1> [,<key2>]]	(602)
drag	from <point> to <point> [with <mod. key1> ¬ [,<key2> [,<key3>]]]	(507)
edit	script of <object expr>	(577)
enable	[<menuItemExpr> of] <menuExpr>	(616)
exit	<handler> | repeat | to HyperCard	(630)
export	paint to file <file name>	(599)
find	[international] <string> [in <field expr>] ¬ [of marked cards]	(530)
find	[international] char[acter]s <string> [in <field expr>] ¬ [of marked cards]	(530)

<table>
<tr><td>find</td><td>[international] string <string> [in <field expr>] ¬
[of marked cards]</td><td>(530)</td></tr>
<tr><td>find</td><td>[international] whole <string> [in <field expr>] ¬
[of marked cards]</td><td>(530)</td></tr>
<tr><td>find</td><td>[international] word <string> [in <field expr>] ¬
[of marked cards]</td><td>(530)</td></tr>
<tr><td>flash</td><td>[<num of flashes>]</td><td>(549)</td></tr>
<tr><td>get</td><td><expr></td><td>(496)</td></tr>
<tr><td>get</td><td>[the] <property> [of <object>]</td><td>(572)</td></tr>
<tr><td>global</td><td><variableName 1> [, <variableName 2> , ¬
<variableName 3>,...]</td><td>(575)</td></tr>
<tr><td>go</td><td>[to] <card, bkgnd, or stack expr> [without dialog]</td><td>(480)</td></tr>
<tr><td>go</td><td>[to] <next | prev[ious] | first | last | any> marked card</td><td>(540)</td></tr>
<tr><td>go</td><td>[to] <stack expr> [in [a] new window] ¬
[without dialog]</td><td>(480)</td></tr>
<tr><td>go</td><td>[to] marked card <num></td><td>(540)</td></tr>
<tr><td>help</td><td></td><td>(485)</td></tr>
<tr><td>hide</td><td>card | background picture</td><td>(569)</td></tr>
<tr><td>hide</td><td>menubar | <window name> | <button or field ¬
expr> | titlebar</td><td>(564)</td></tr>
<tr><td>hide</td><td>picture of <card expr> | <background expr></td><td>(569)</td></tr>
<tr><td>hide</td><td>groups</td><td>(571)</td></tr>
<tr><td>import</td><td>paint from file <file name></td><td>(599)</td></tr>
<tr><td>lock</td><td>error dialogs</td><td>(632)</td></tr>
<tr><td>lock</td><td>messages</td><td>(632)</td></tr>
<tr><td>lock</td><td>recent</td><td>(489)</td></tr>
<tr><td>lock</td><td>screen</td><td>(553)</td></tr>
<tr><td>mark</td><td><card expr></td><td>(540)</td></tr>
<tr><td>mark</td><td>cards where <boolean expr></td><td>(540)</td></tr>
<tr><td>mark</td><td>cards by finding <string> [in <field expr>]</td><td>(540)</td></tr>
<tr><td>mark</td><td>all cards</td><td>(540)</td></tr>
<tr><td>multiply</td><td><container> by <numeric expr></td><td>(523)</td></tr>
<tr><td>open</td><td>[<document> with] <application></td><td>(485)</td></tr>
<tr><td>open</td><td>file <file name></td><td>(586)</td></tr>
<tr><td>open</td><td>printing [with dialog]</td><td>(622)</td></tr>
<tr><td>open</td><td>report printing [with template <name> | with dialog]</td><td>(624)</td></tr>
<tr><td>palette</td><td><PLTE resource name> [,<point>]</td><td>(555)</td></tr>
<tr><td>pass</td><td><message></td><td>(632)</td></tr>
<tr><td>picture</td><td><name>,<type>,<windowStyle>,<visible>, ¬
<bitDepth>,<floating></td><td>(556)</td></tr>
</table>

play <snd rsrc name> [tempo <speed>] [<notes>] ¬
[#|b] [octave] [length] (513)
play stop (513)
pop card [into | before | after <container>] (483)
print <expr> (620)
print <field expr> (620)
print <file name> with <application> (598)
print all | <num> cards | this <card> |<card expr> (622)
print card [from <point> to <point>] (622)
print marked cards (540)
push [this | recent] card [of <stack expr>] (483)
push background [of <stack expr>] (483)
push stack (483)
put <expr> <prep.> [<menuItemExpr> of <menuExpr> ¬
[with menuMessages <message name>] (605)
put <expr> [into | after | before <container>] (492)
read from file <file name> [at <position>] for <num> (592)
read from file <file name> [at <position>] until <character> (592)
reply [error] <expr> (972)
request <expr> from program <address> (974)
reset menubar (605)
reset paint (577)
reset printing (622)
return <expr> (807)
save <stack expr> as <stack expr> (583)
select <button expr> | <field expr> | me | target (579)
select [before | after] <chunk expr> of <field expr> (498)
select [before | after] <chunk expr> of Message Box (498)
select [before | after] text of <field expr> (498)
select empty (498)
send <message> to <object expr> (634)
send <message> to program <address> [without reply] (970)
set [the] <property> [of <object>] to <new setting> (572)
show [<num> | all] cards (567)
show marked cards (540)
show menubar|<window>|<btn or fld expr> [at <point>] | ¬
titlebar (567)
show card | background picture (569)
show picture of <card expr> | <background expr> (569)
show groups (571)

<table>
<tr><td>sort</td><td>[[[marked] cards of] <stack expr>] |<bkgnd expr>] ¬
[ascending|descending] [text|numeric|international ¬
datetime] by <expr></td><td>(534)</td></tr>
<tr><td>sort</td><td>[[lines|items] of] <container> [ascending|descending] ¬
[text|numeric|international|datetime] by <expr> of each</td><td>(535)</td></tr>
<tr><td>start</td><td>using <stack expr></td><td>(637)</td></tr>
<tr><td>stop</td><td>using <stack expr></td><td>(637)</td></tr>
<tr><td>subtract</td><td><numeric expr> from <container></td><td>(521)</td></tr>
<tr><td>type</td><td><string expr> [with <mod. key1>[,<key2> [,<key3>]]]</td><td>(508)</td></tr>
<tr><td>unlock</td><td>error dialogs</td><td>(632)</td></tr>
<tr><td>unlock</td><td>messages</td><td>(632)</td></tr>
<tr><td>unlock</td><td>recent</td><td>(489)</td></tr>
<tr><td>unlock</td><td>screen [with <visual effect name> [<speed>] ¬
[to <image>]</td><td>(553)</td></tr>
<tr><td>unmark</td><td><card expr></td><td>(540)</td></tr>
<tr><td>unmark</td><td>cards where <boolean expr></td><td>(540)</td></tr>
<tr><td>unmark</td><td>cards by finding <string> [in <field expr>]</td><td>(540)</td></tr>
<tr><td>unmark</td><td>all cards</td><td>(540)</td></tr>
<tr><td>visual</td><td>[effect] <effect name> [<speed>] [to <image>]</td><td>(546)</td></tr>
<tr><td>wait</td><td>[for] <num> [ticks | seconds]</td><td>(628)</td></tr>
<tr><td>wait</td><td>until <boolean expr></td><td>(628)</td></tr>
<tr><td>wait</td><td>while <boolean expr></td><td>(628)</td></tr>
<tr><td>write</td><td><string expr> to file <file name> [at <position>]</td><td>(595)</td></tr>
</table>

Global Properties

<table>
<tr><td>address</td><td><network address of Mac></td><td>(967)</td></tr>
<tr><td>blindTyping</td><td><true of false></td><td>(643)</td></tr>
<tr><td>cursor</td><td><ID num of name></td><td>(644)</td></tr>
<tr><td>debugger</td><td><debugger name></td><td>(645)</td></tr>
<tr><td>dialingTime</td><td><ticks></td><td>(646)</td></tr>
<tr><td>dialingVolume</td><td><0 through 7></td><td>(646)</td></tr>
<tr><td>dragSpeed</td><td><num></td><td>(647)</td></tr>
<tr><td>editBkgnd</td><td><true or false></td><td>(648)</td></tr>
<tr><td>environment</td><td><development or player></td><td>(648)</td></tr>
<tr><td>id</td><td><application signature></td><td>(649)</td></tr>
<tr><td>itemDelimiter</td><td><character></td><td>(649)</td></tr>
<tr><td>language</td><td><language name></td><td>(650)</td></tr>
<tr><td>lockErrorDialogs</td><td><true or false></td><td>(650)</td></tr>
<tr><td>lockMessages</td><td><true or false></td><td>(652)</td></tr>
</table>

lockRecent <true or false> (653)
lockScreen <true or false> (654)
longWindowTitles <true or false> (655)
messageWatcher <message watcher XCMD name> (656)
name <pathname of current HyperCard> (656)
numberFormat <format string> (657)
powerKeys <true or false> (658)
printMargins <left, top, right, bottm> (659)
printTextAlign <left | center | right> (659)
printTextFont <font name> (659)
printTextHeight <line height point size> (659)
printTextSize <font size> (659)
printTextStyle <plain | bold | italic | underline | outline | shadow> (659)
scriptEditor <editor XCMD name> (660)
scriptTextFont <font name> (660)
scriptTextSize <font size> (660)
stacksInUse <return-delimited list> (661)
suspended <true or false> (661)
textArrows <true or false> (662)
traceDelay <ticks> (662)
userLevel <1 through 5> (663)
userModify <true or false> (664)
variableWatcher <variable watcher XCMD name> (665)

Menu Properties

checkMark <true or false> (666)
cmdChar <character> (667)
commandChar <character> (667)
enabled <true or false> (668)
markChar <character> (666)
menuMessage <message name> (669)
menuMsg <message name> (669)
name <menu or menu item text> (670)
rect <menubar coordinates> (671)
textStyle <style> (672)
visible <true or false> (672)

Window Properties

botRight	<point>	(680)
bottom	<integer>	(679)
bottomRight	<point>	(679)
buttonCount	<integer>	(673)
commands	<return-delimited list>	(673)
dithering	<true or false>	(675)
globalLoc	<point>	(675)
globalRect	<rectangle>	(675)
hBarLoc	<integer>	(676)
height	<integer>	(680)
hideIdle	<true or false>	(677)
hideUnused	<true or false>	(677)
hilitedButton	<integer>	(673)
id	<integer>	(678)
left	<integer>	(679)
loc[ation]	<left>,<right>	(681)
name	<window name>	(678)
nextLine	<expr>	(682)
number	<integer>	(678)
owner	<owning application or XCMD>	(683)
properties	<comma-delimited list>	(673)
rect[angle]	<left>,<top>,<right>,<bottom>	(684)
right	<integer>	(679)
scale	<integer between -5 and 5>	(675)
scroll	<left>,<top>	(685)
top	<integer>	(679)
topLeft	<point>	(679)
vBarLoc	<integer>	(676)
visible	<true or false>	(686)
width	<integer>	(680)
zoom	<in or out>	(675)
zoomed	<true or false>	(686)

Painting Properties

brush	<brush num 1 to 32>	(687)
centered	<true or false>	(688)
filled	<true or false>	(688)

grid <true or false> (689)
lineSize <line thicknesses 1, 2, 3, 4, 6, 8 pixels> (689)
multiple <true or false> (690)
multiSpace <1 to 9> (690)
pattern <pattern num 1 to 40> (690)
polySides <num of polygon sides greater than two> (691)
textAlign <left | center | right> (692)
textFont <font name> (692)
textHeight <leading> (692)
textSize <font size> (692)
textStyle <bold | italic | underline | outline | shadow | condense | ¬
extend | plain> (692)

Stack Properties

cantAbort <true or false> (693)
cantDelete <true or false> (694)
cantModify <true or false> (695)
cantPeek <true or false> (696)
freesize <bytes> (697)
size <bytes> (697)
name <file name> (700)
reportTemplates <list> (703)
script <script text> (704)
scriptingLanguage <language name> (705)

Background Properties

cantDelete <true or false> (694)
id <id num> (698)
name <name text> (700)
number <num in sequence of bkgnds> (701)
script <script text> (704)
scriptingLanguage <language name> (705)
showPict <true or false> (706)

Card Properties

cantDelete <true or false> (694)
id <id num> (698)
marked <true or false> (699)
name <name text> (700)
number <num in sequence of cards> (701)

owner	<bkgnd name or ID>	(701)
rect[angle]	<left>,<top>,<right>,<bottom>	(702)
script	<script text>	(704)
scriptingLanguage	<language name>	(705)
showPict	<true or false>	(706)

Field Properties

autoSelect	<true or false>	(707)
autoTab	<true or false>	(707)
botRight	<point>	(711)
bottom	<integer>	(711)
bottomRight	<point>	(711)
dontSearch	<true or false>	(708)
dontWrap	<true or false>	(709)
fixedLineHeight	<true or false>	(710)
height	<integer>	(711)
id	<id num>	(710)
left	<integer>	(711)
loc[ation]	<left>,<right>	(711)
lockText	<true or false>	(712)
multipleLines	<true or false>	(713)
name	<field name>	(714)
number	<num in sequence of fields in same domain>	(715)
partNumber	<num in sequence of objects in same domain>	(715)
rect[angle]	<left>,<top>,<right>,<bottom>	(716)
right	<integer>	(711)
script	<script text>	(717)
scriptingLanguage	<language name>	(717)
scroll	<pixels>	(718)
sharedText	<true or false> (bkgnd fields only)	(720)
showLines	<true or false>	(712)
style	<transparent | opaque | rectangle | shadow | scrolling>	(721)
textAlign	<left | center | right>	(722)
textFont	<font name>	(722)
textHeight	<leading>	(722)
textSize	<font size>	(722)
textStyle	<bold | italic | underline | outline | shadow | condense | ¬ extend | plain>	(722)
top	<integer>	(711)
topLeft	<point>	(711)

visible <true or false> (723)

wideMargins <true or false> (712)

width <integer> (711)

Button Properties

autoHilite <true or false> (724)

botRight <point> (724)

bottom <integer> (724)

bottomRight <point> (724)

enabled <true or false> (725)

family <family num 0 through 15> (726)

height <integer> (725)

hilite <true or false> (726)

icon <icon num or name> (727)

id <id num> (728)

left <integer> (724)

loc[ation] <left>,<right> (728)

name <button name> (729)

number <num in sequence of buttons in same domain> (730)

partNumber <num in sequence of objects in same domain> (731)

rect[angle] <left>,<top>,<right>,<bottom> (731)

right <integer> (724)

script <script text> (732)

scriptingLanguage <language name> (732)

sharedHilite <true or false> (bkgnd buttons only) (734)

showName <true or false> (724)

style <transparent | opaque | rectangle | shadow | roundRect | ¬
checkBox | radioButton | standard | default | oval | ¬
popup> (735)

textAlign <left | center | right> (735)

textFont <font name> (735)

textHeight <leading> (736)

textSize <font size> (736)

textStyle <bold | italic | underline | outline | shadow | condense | ¬
extend | plain> (736)

titleWidth <pixel count> (736)

top <integer> (724)

topLeft <point> (724)

visible <true or false> (737)

width <integer> (725)

Functions

the abbr date	(746)
the abbrev date	(746)
the abbreviated date	(746)
the charToNum of <character>	(769)
the clickChunk	(762)
the clickH	(758)
the clickLine	(762)
the clickLoc	(758)
the clickText	(762)
the clickV	(758)
the commandKey	(754)
the date	(746)
the destination	(802)
the diskSpace	(794)
the foundChunk	(766)
the foundField	(767)
the foundLine	(767)
the foundText	(766)
the heapSpace	(794)
the length	(760)
the long date	(746)
the long time	(747)
me	(800)
the menus	(791)
the mouse	(756)
the mouseClick	(756)
the mouseH	(752)
the mouseLoc	(752)
the mouseV	(752)
the number of <chunk components> of <expr>	(761)
the number of [card | bkgnd] buttons	(784)
the number of [card | bkgnd] fields	(784)
the number of backgrounds	(784)
the number of cards [of <bkgnd expr>]	(784)
the number of marked cards	(784)
the number of menuItems of <menu expr>	(784)
the number of menus	(784)
the number of windows	(784)
the numToChar of <ASCII value>	(769)

SANE Functions

Operators

Constants

Control Structures

System Messages

appleEvent	(442)
arrowKey	(435)
close	(442)
closeBackground	(429)
closeCard	(429)
closeField	(429)
closePalette	(444)
closePicture	(444)
closeStack	(429)
commandKeyDown	(430)
controlKey	(436)
deleteBackground	(429)
deleteButton	(429)
deleteCard	(429)
deleteField	(429)
deleteStack	(429)
doMenu	(438)
enterInField	(433)
enterKey	(432)
exitField	(430)
functionKey	(436)
help	(442)
idle	(439)
keyDown	(430)
mouseDoubleClick	(427)
mouseDown	(424)
mouseDownInPicture	(443)
mouseEnter	(427)
mouseLeave	(427)
mouseStillDown	(424)
mouseUp	(424)
mouseUpInPicture	(443)
mouseWithin	(427)
moveWindow	(442)
newBackground	(429)
newButton	(429)
newCard	(429)
newField	(429)

INDEX

9 781583 480045